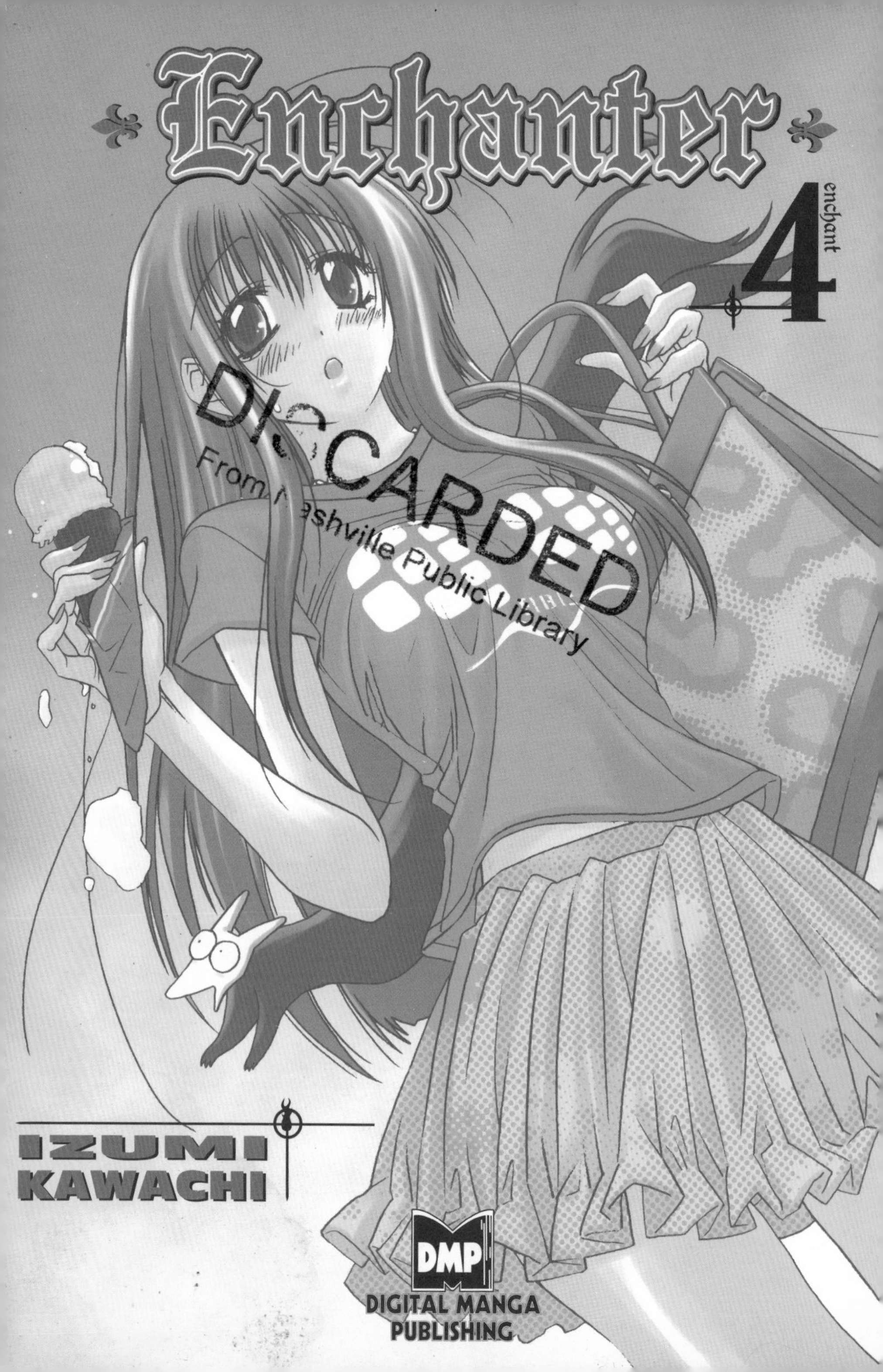
Enchanter
enchant 4
IZUMI KAWACHI
DMP
DIGITAL MANGA PUBLISHING

Enchanter ⊕4

CONTENTS

Translation   Sachiko Sato
Lettering   IHL
Graphic Design   Fred Lui / Wendy Lee
Editing   Stephanie Donnelly
Editor in Chief   Fred Lui
Publisher   Hikaru Sasahara

English Edition Published by
DIGITAL MANGA PUBLISHING
A division of DIGITAL MANGA, Inc.
1487 W 178th Street, Suite 300
Gardena, CA 90248

www.dmpbooks.com

First Edition: May 2007
ISBN-10: 1-56970-863-0
ISBN-13: 978-1-56970-863-7

1 3 5 7 9 10 8 6 4 2

Printed in China

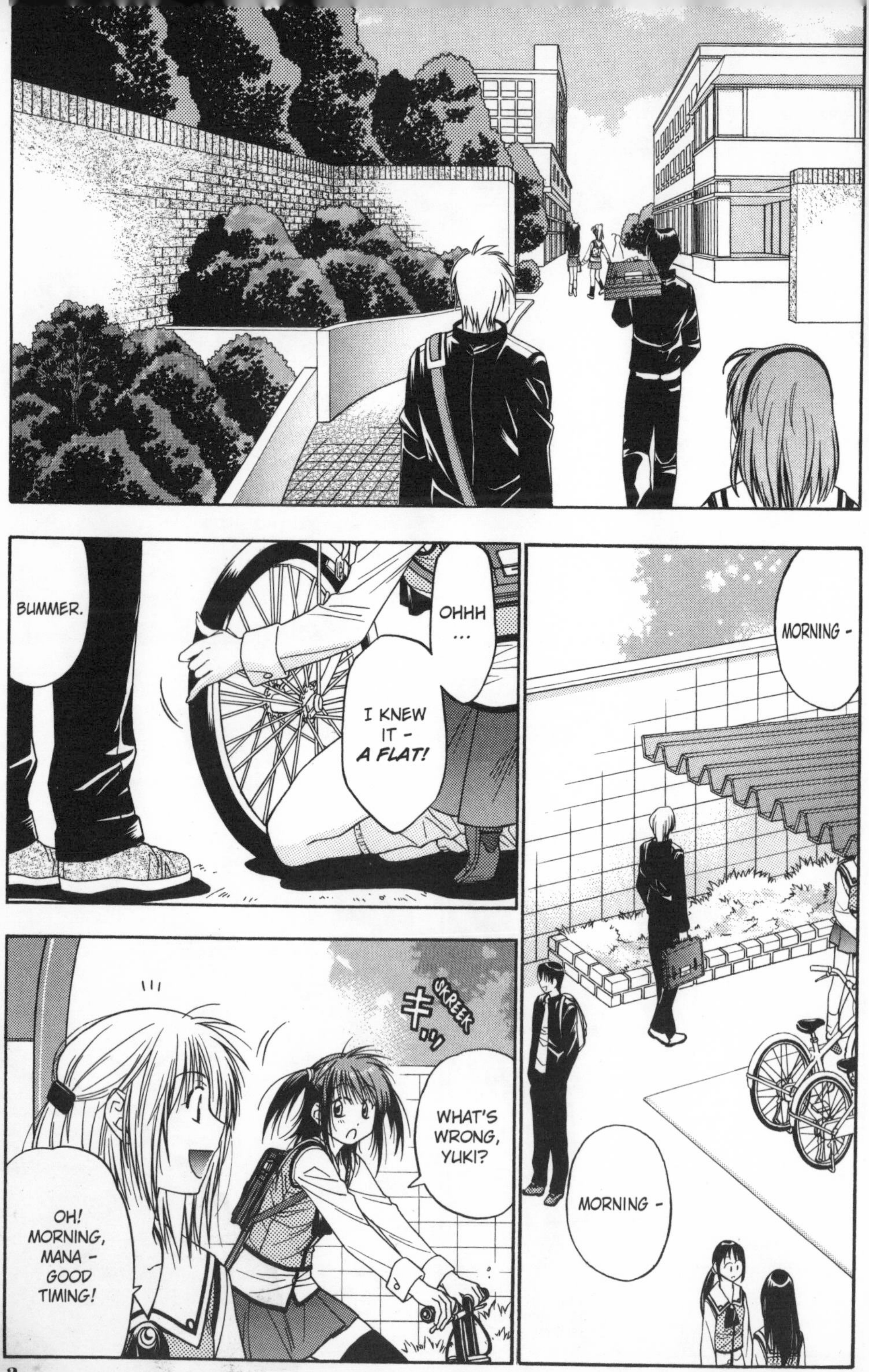
MORNING -
MORNING -
OHHH ...
I KNEW IT - A FLAT!
BUMMER.
SKREEK
WHAT'S WRONG, YUKI?
OH! MORNING, MANA - GOOD TIMING!

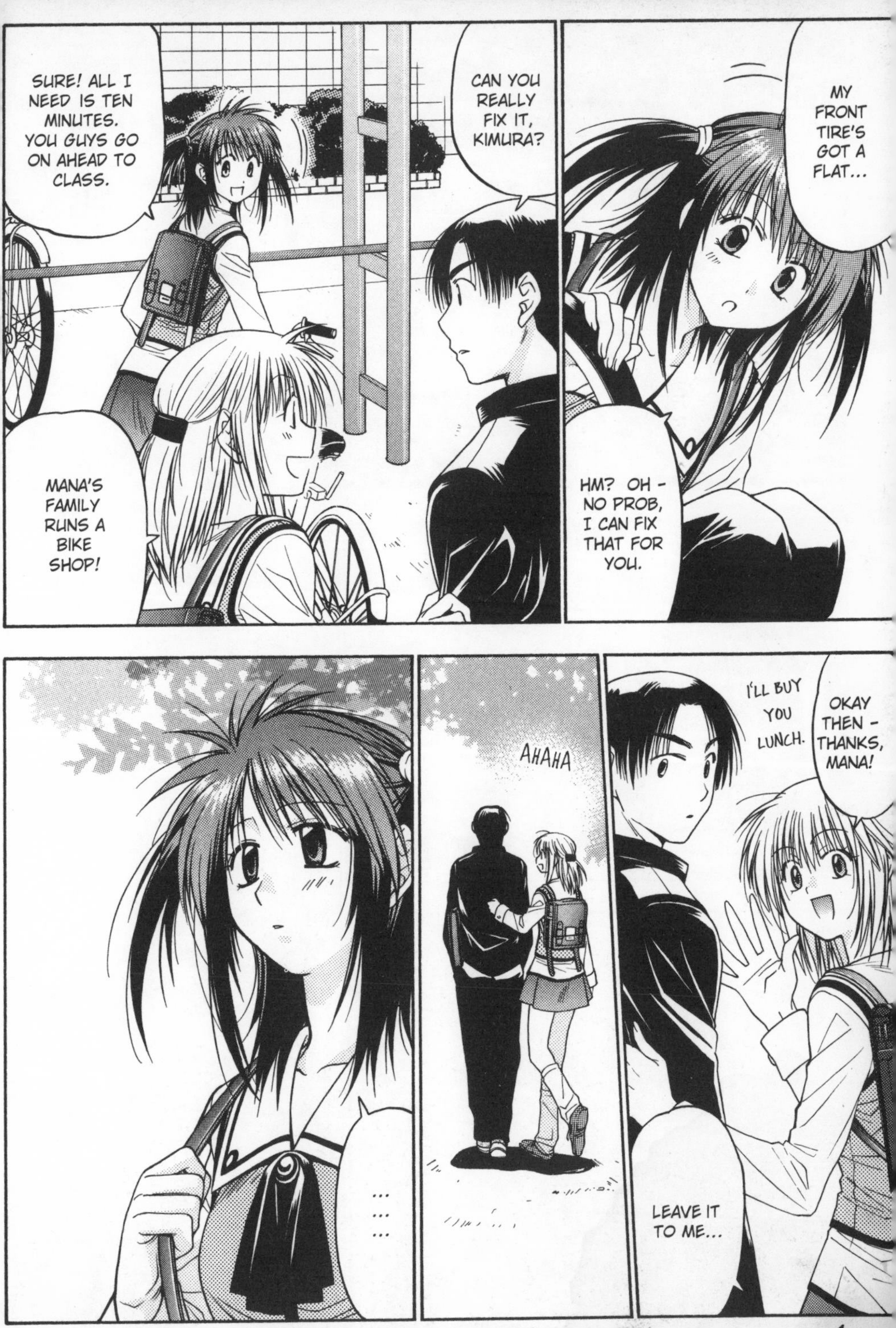
MY FRONT TIRE'S GOT A FLAT...
HM? OH - NO PROB, I CAN FIX THAT FOR YOU.
CAN YOU REALLY FIX IT, KIMURA?
SURE! ALL I NEED IS TEN MINUTES. YOU GUYS GO ON AHEAD TO CLASS.
MANA'S FAMILY RUNS A BIKE SHOP!
OKAY THEN - THANKS, MANA!
I'LL BUY YOU LUNCH.
LEAVE IT TO ME...
AHAHA
... ...

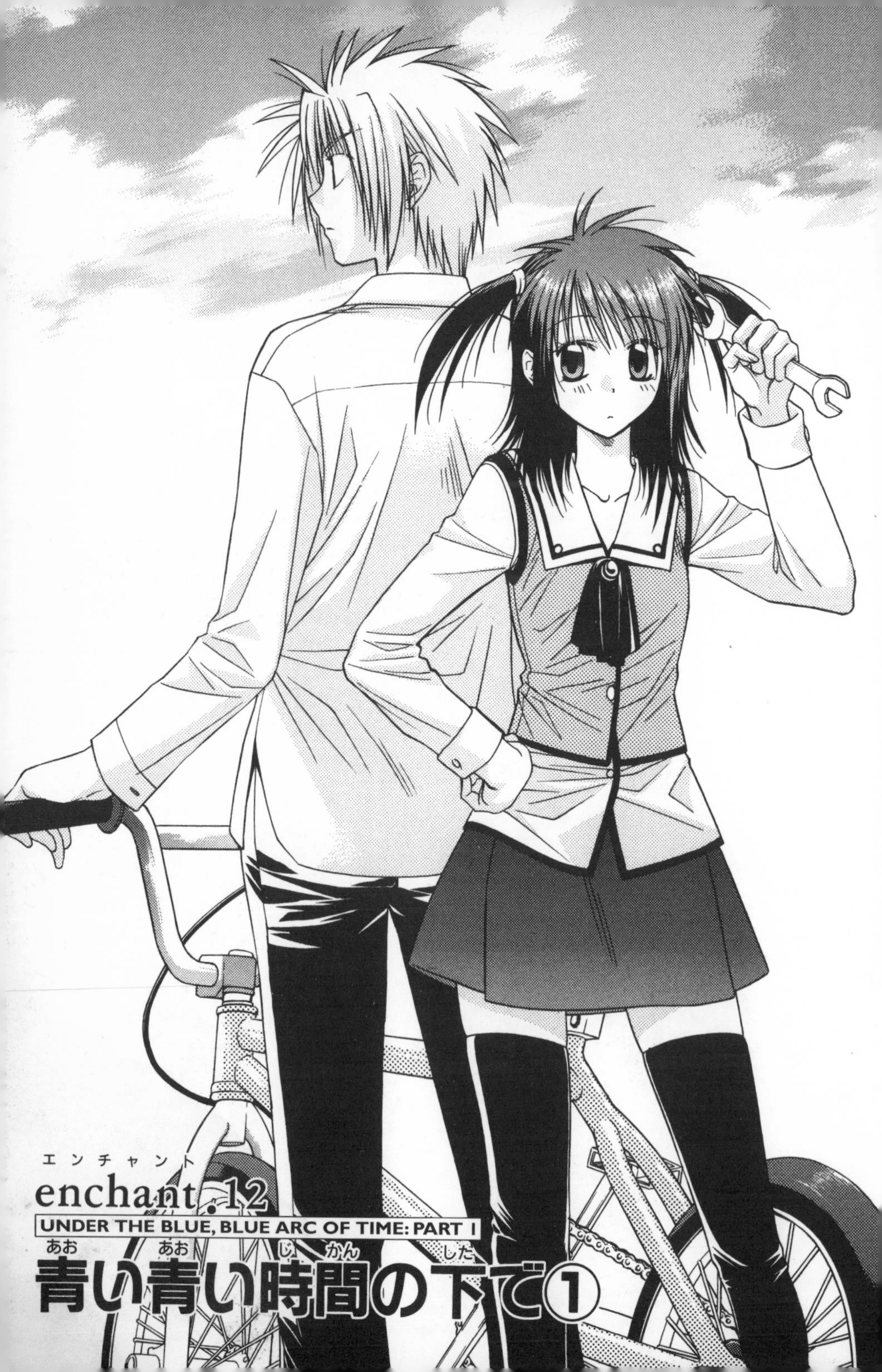
エンチャント
enchant.12
UNDER THE BLUE, BLUE ARC OF TIME: PART 1
青い青い時間の下で①

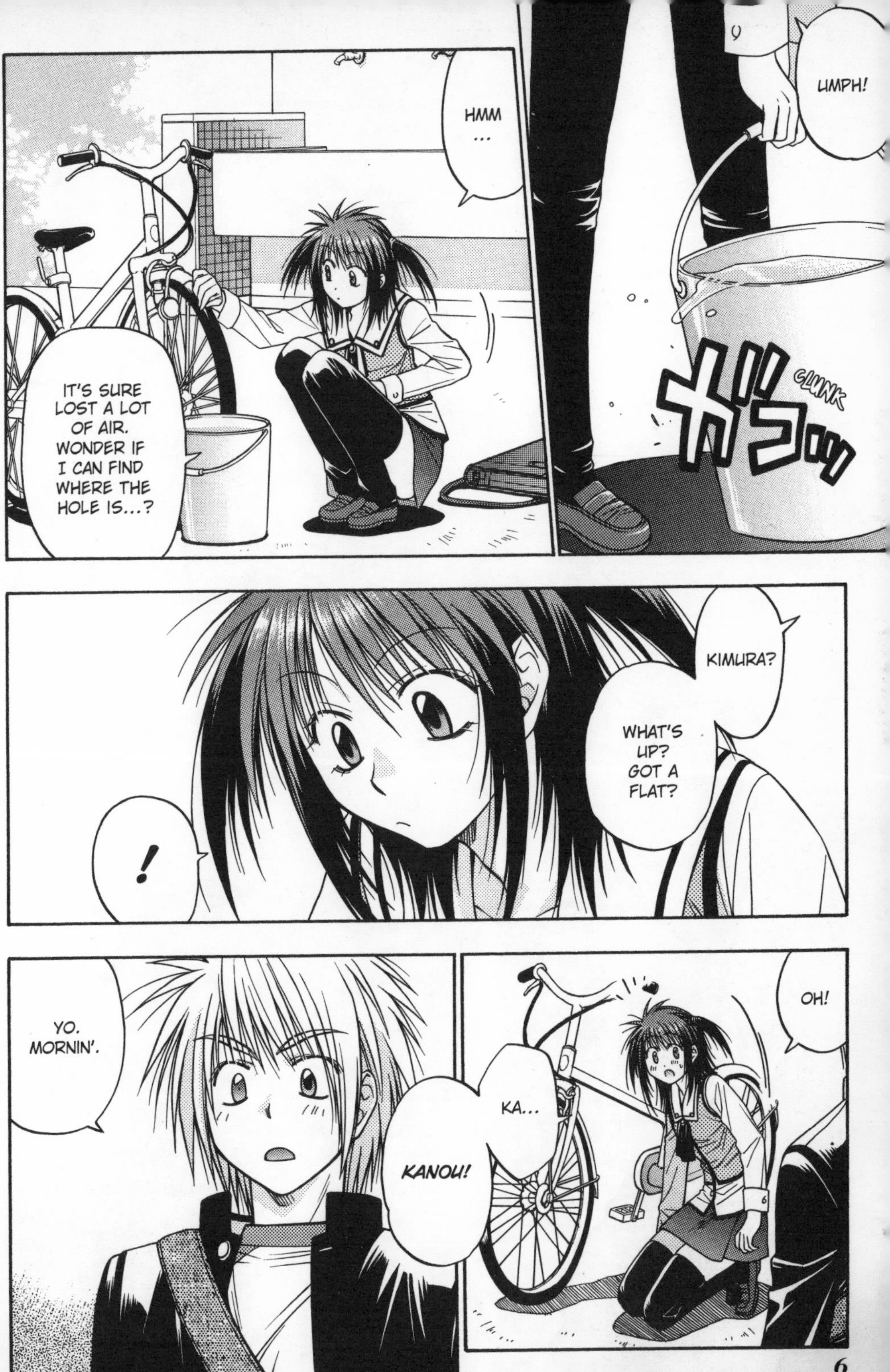
UMPH!
CLUNK
ガコッ
HMM ...
IT'S SURE LOST A LOT OF AIR. WONDER IF I CAN FIND WHERE THE HOLE IS...?
KIMURA?
WHAT'S UP? GOT A FLAT?
!
OH!
KA...
KANOU!
YO. MORNIN'.

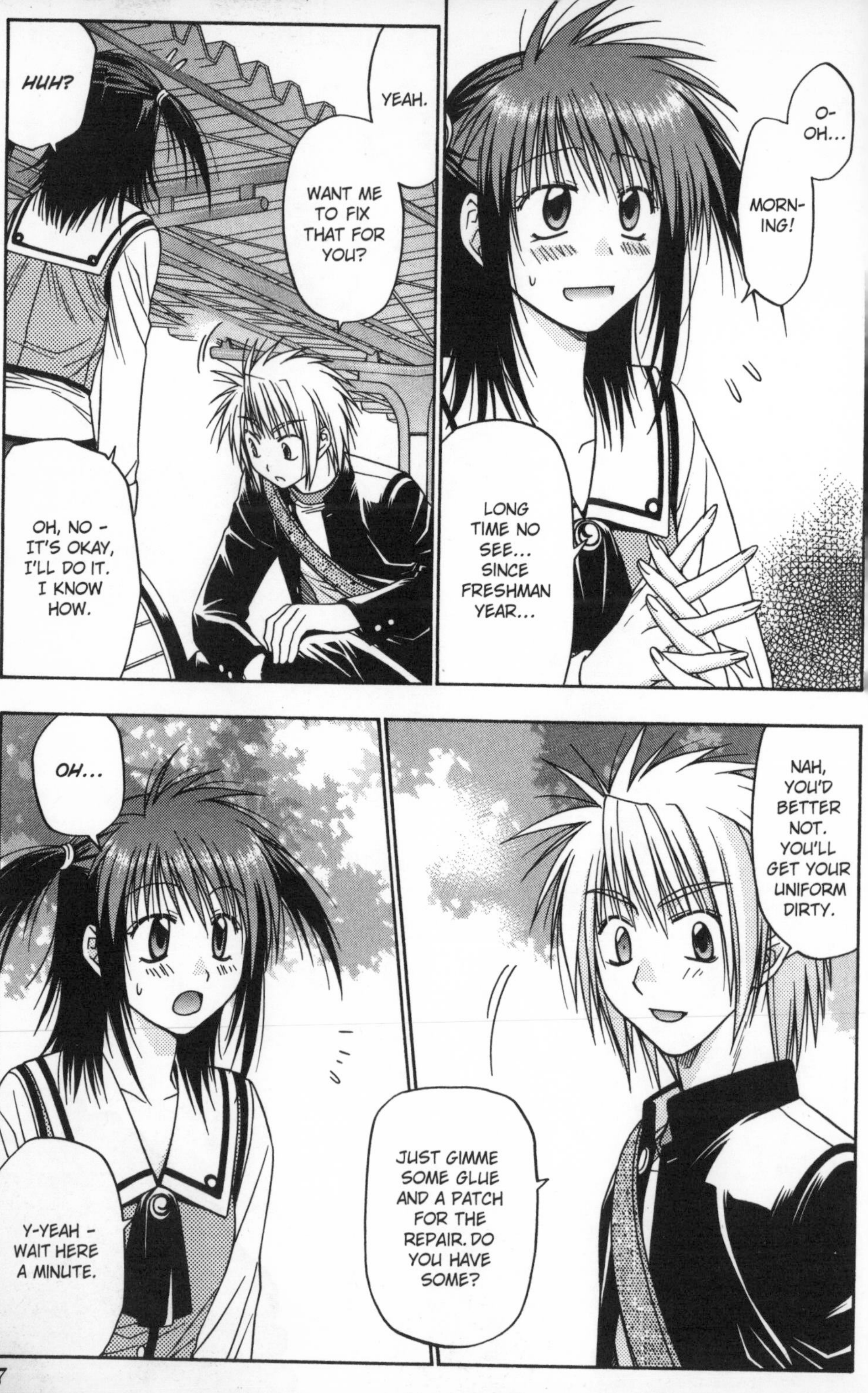
O-OH... MORNING!
LONG TIME NO SEE... SINCE FRESHMAN YEAR...
HUH?
YEAH.
WANT ME TO FIX THAT FOR YOU?
OH, NO - IT'S OKAY, I'LL DO IT. I KNOW HOW.
NAH, YOU'D BETTER NOT. YOU'LL GET YOUR UNIFORM DIRTY.
JUST GIMME SOME GLUE AND A PATCH FOR THE REPAIR. DO YOU HAVE SOME?
OH...
Y-YEAH - WAIT HERE A MINUTE.

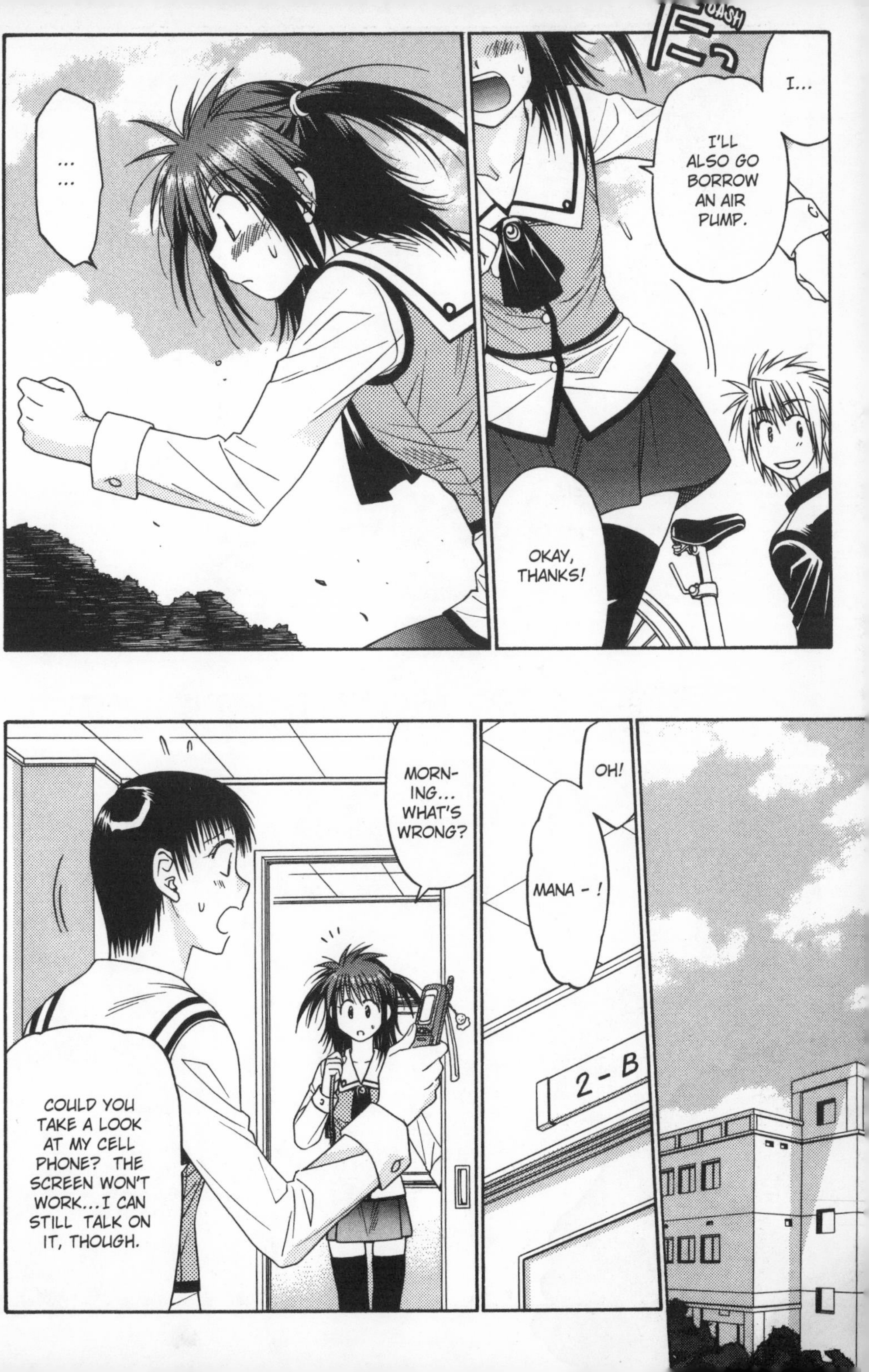
I...
I'LL ALSO GO BORROW AN AIR PUMP.
OKAY, THANKS!
... ...
OH!
MANA - !
MORNING-ING... WHAT'S WRONG?
COULD YOU TAKE A LOOK AT MY CELL PHONE? THE SCREEN WON'T WORK...I CAN STILL TALK ON IT, THOUGH.
2 - B

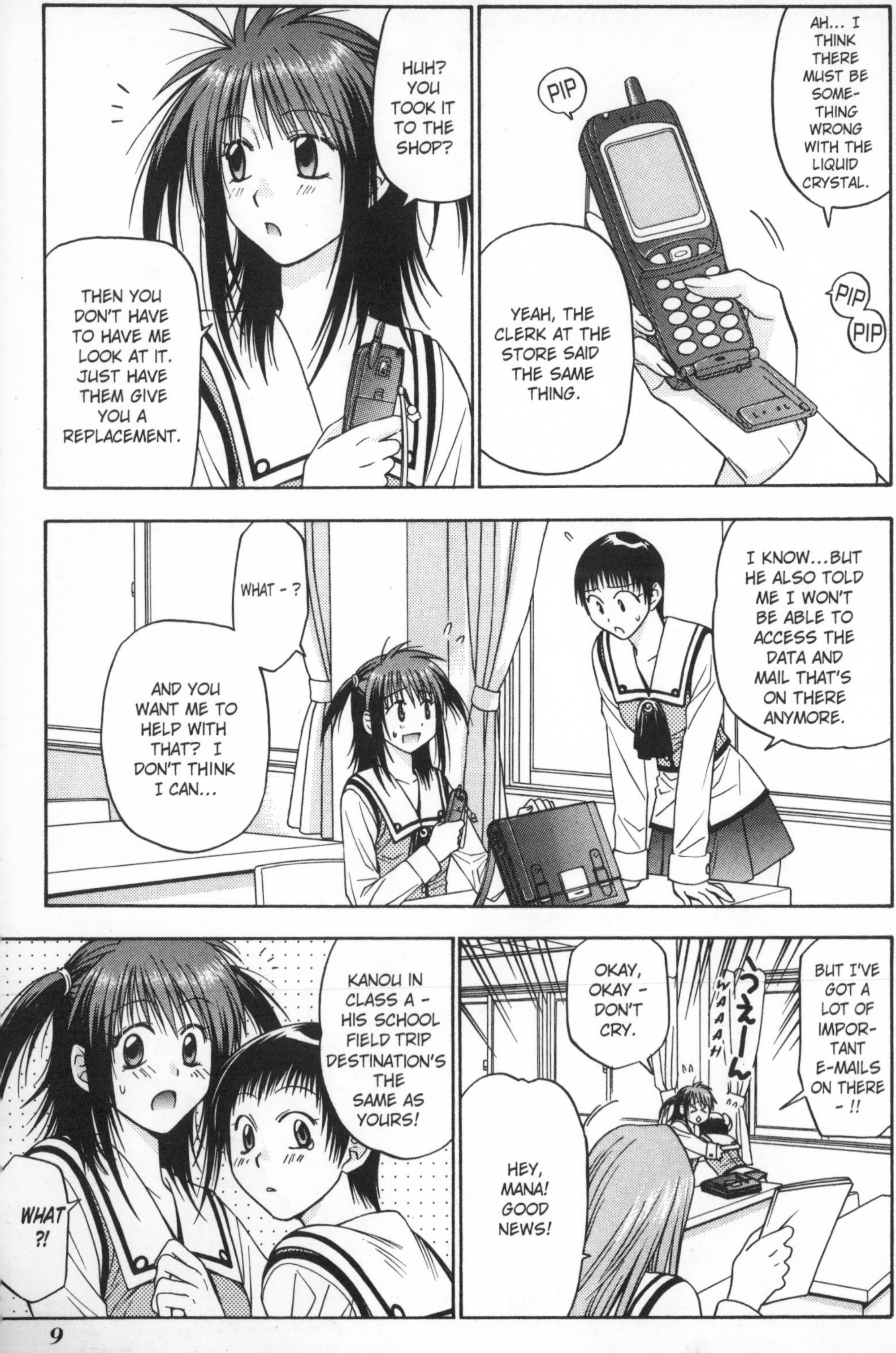
AH... I THINK THERE MUST BE SOME-THING WRONG WITH THE LIQUID CRYSTAL.
PIP
PIP
PIP
YEAH, THE CLERK AT THE STORE SAID THE SAME THING.
HUH? YOU TOOK IT TO THE SHOP?
THEN YOU DON'T HAVE TO HAVE ME LOOK AT IT. JUST HAVE THEM GIVE YOU A REPLACEMENT.
I KNOW...BUT HE ALSO TOLD ME I WON'T BE ABLE TO ACCESS THE DATA AND MAIL THAT'S ON THERE ANYMORE.
WHAT - ?
AND YOU WANT ME TO HELP WITH THAT? I DON'T THINK I CAN...
BUT I'VE GOT A LOT OF IMPOR-TANT E-MAILS ON THERE - !!
うえーん
WAAAH
OKAY, OKAY - DON'T CRY.
HEY, MANA! GOOD NEWS!
KANOU IN CLASS A - HIS SCHOOL FIELD TRIP DESTINATION'S THE SAME AS YOURS!
WHAT ?!

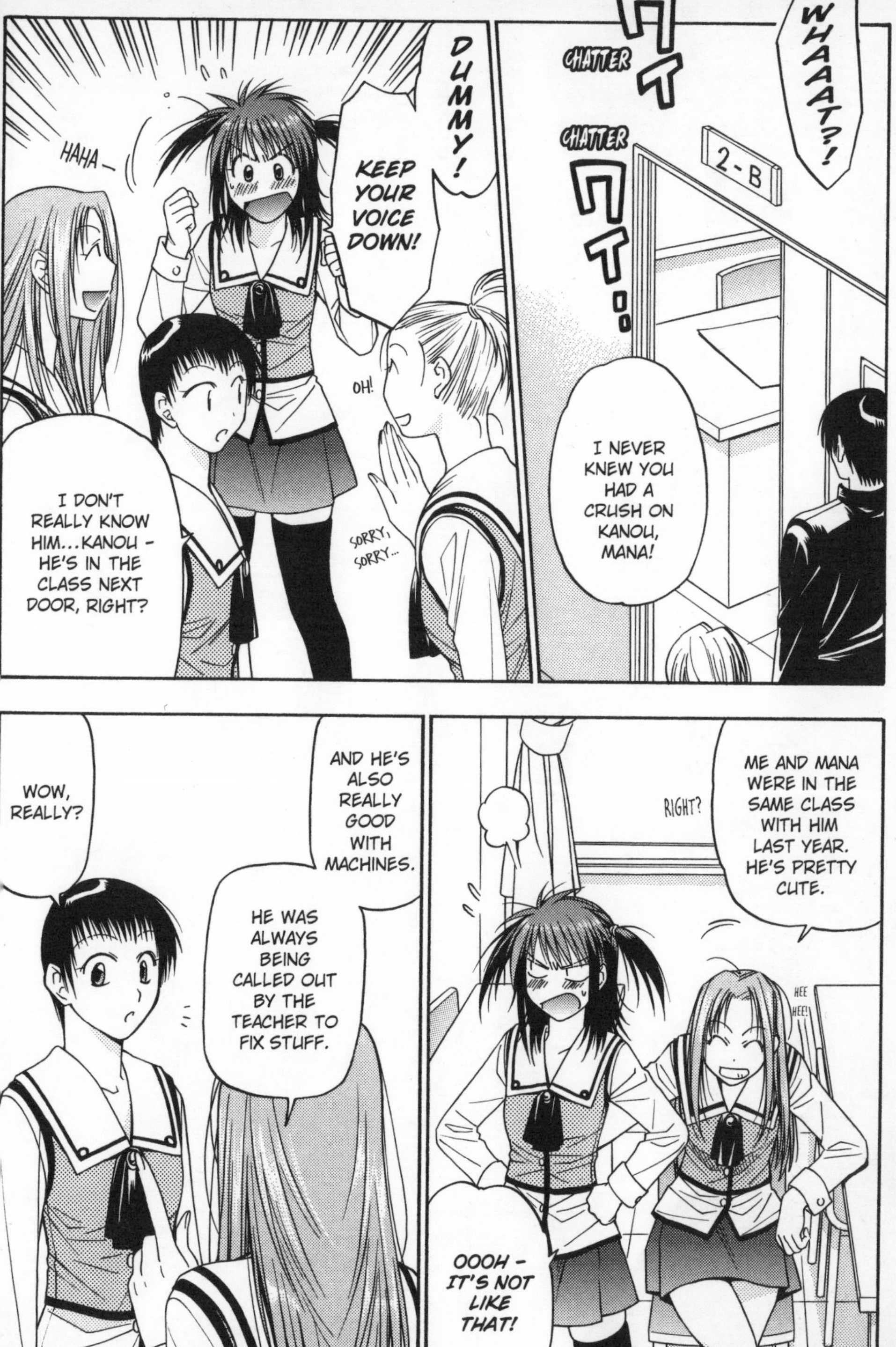
WHAAAAT?!
CHATTER
ワイ
CHATTER
ワイ..
I NEVER KNEW YOU HAD A CRUSH ON KANOU, MANA!
DUMMY! KEEP YOUR VOICE DOWN!
HAHA -
OH!
SORRY, SORRY...
I DON'T REALLY KNOW HIM...KANOU - HE'S IN THE CLASS NEXT DOOR, RIGHT?
ME AND MANA WERE IN THE SAME CLASS WITH HIM LAST YEAR. HE'S PRETTY CUTE.
RIGHT?
HEE HEE!
OOOH - IT'S NOT LIKE THAT!
AND HE'S ALSO REALLY GOOD WITH MACHINES.
WOW, REALLY?
HE WAS ALWAYS BEING CALLED OUT BY THE TEACHER TO FIX STUFF.

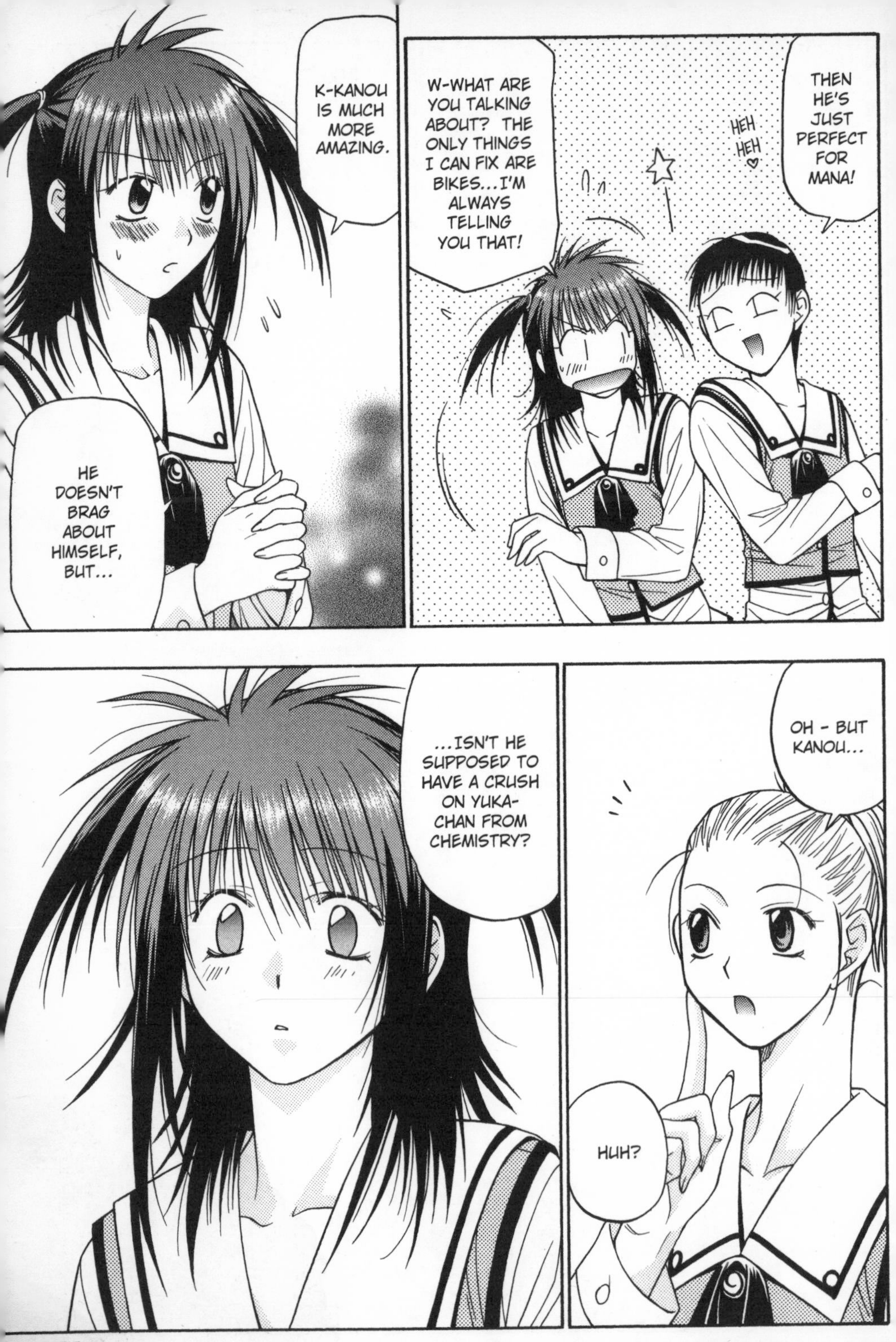
THEN HE'S JUST PERFECT FOR MANA!
HEH HEH ♡
W-WHAT ARE YOU TALKING ABOUT? THE ONLY THINGS I CAN FIX ARE BIKES...I'M ALWAYS TELLING YOU THAT!
K-KANOU IS MUCH MORE AMAZING.
HE DOESN'T BRAG ABOUT HIMSELF, BUT...
OH - BUT KANOU...
HUH?
...ISN'T HE SUPPOSED TO HAVE A CRUSH ON YUKA-CHAN FROM CHEMISTRY?

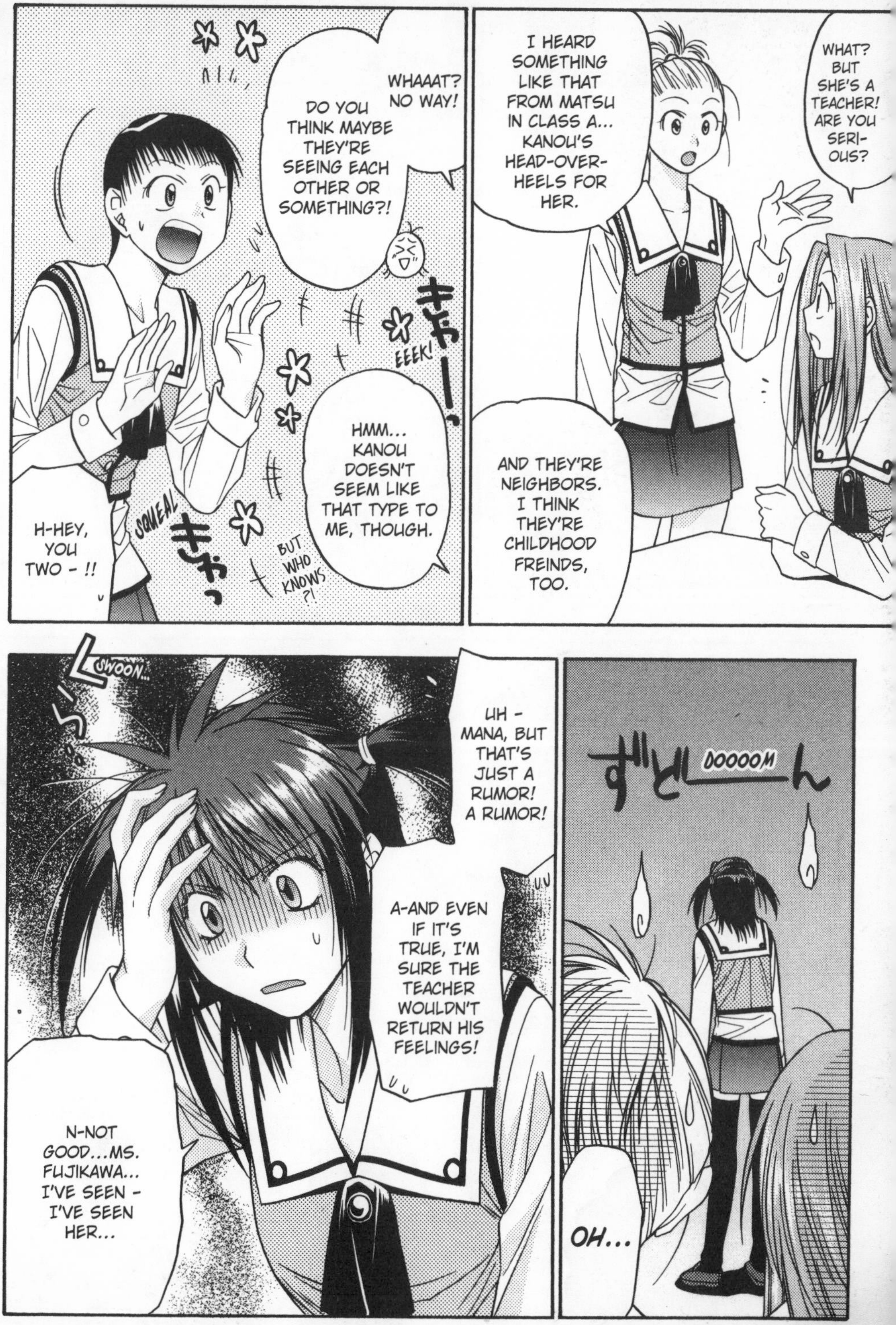
I HEARD SOMETHING LIKE THAT FROM MATSU IN CLASS A... KANOU'S HEAD-OVER-HEELS FOR HER.
WHAT? BUT SHE'S A TEACHER! ARE YOU SERI-OUS?
AND THEY'RE NEIGHBORS. I THINK THEY'RE CHILDHOOD FREINDS, TOO.
WHAAAT? NO WAY!
DO YOU THINK MAYBE THEY'RE SEEING EACH OTHER OR SOMETHING?!
EEEK!
HMM... KANOU DOESN'T SEEM LIKE THAT TYPE TO ME, THOUGH.
BUT WHO KNOWS ?!
SQUEAL
H-HEY, YOU TWO - !!
DOOOOM
OH...
SWOON...
UH - MANA, BUT THAT'S JUST A RUMOR! A RUMOR!
A-AND EVEN IF IT'S TRUE, I'M SURE THE TEACHER WOULDN'T RETURN HIS FEELINGS!
N-NOT GOOD...MS. FUJIKAWA... I'VE SEEN - I'VE SEEN HER...

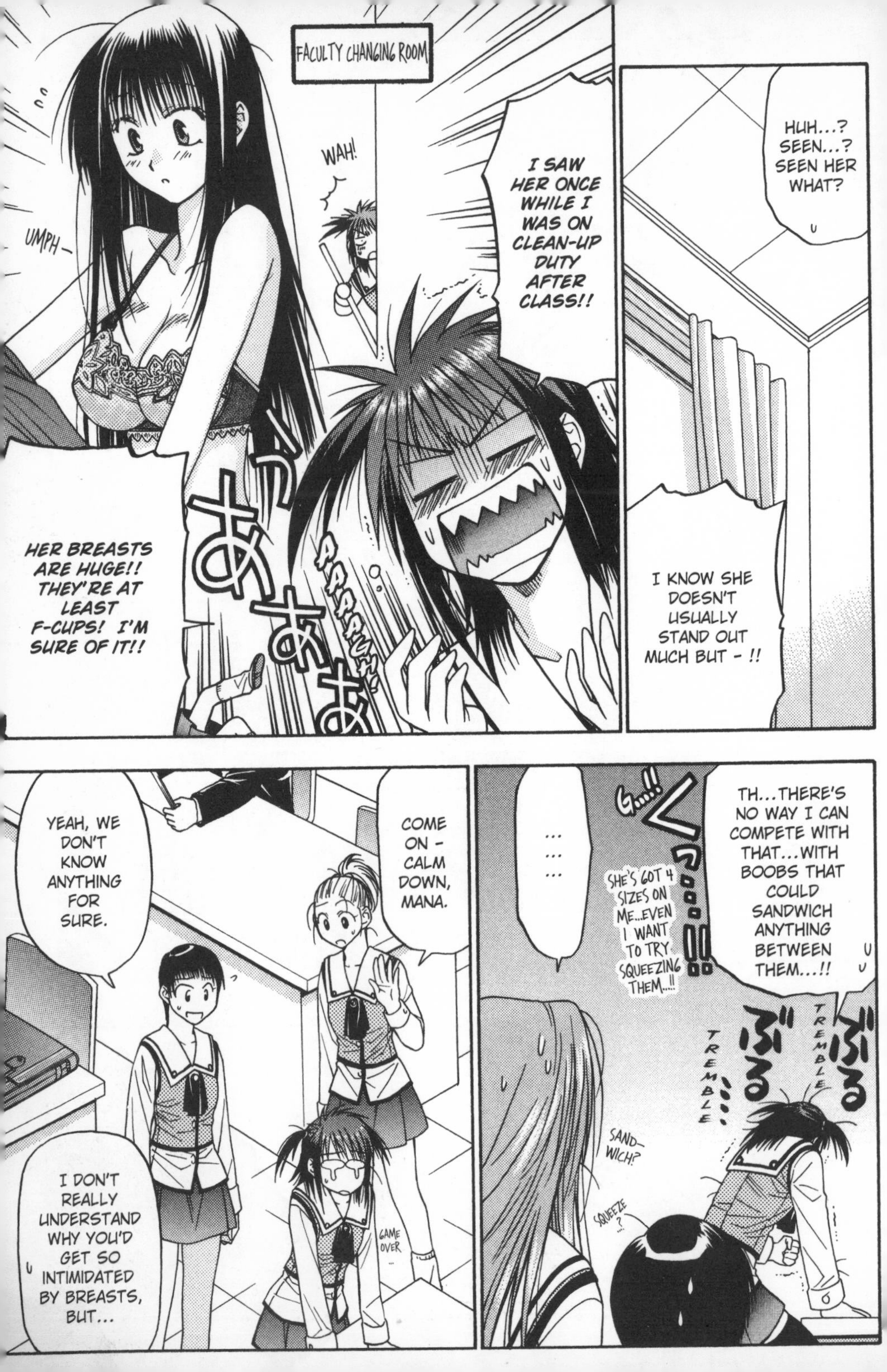
HUH...? SEEN...? SEEN HER WHAT?
I KNOW SHE DOESN'T USUALLY STAND OUT MUCH BUT - !!
FACULTY CHANGING ROOM
I SAW HER ONCE WHILE I WAS ON CLEAN-UP DUTY AFTER CLASS!!
WAH!
UMPH -
HER BREASTS ARE HUGE!! THEY'RE AT LEAST F-CUPS! I'M SURE OF IT!!
PAAAAUGH!
TH...THERE'S NO WAY I CAN COMPETE WITH THAT...WITH BOOBS THAT COULD SANDWICH ANYTHING BETWEEN THEM...!!
G...!!
SHE'S GOT 4 SIZES ON ME...EVEN I WANT TO TRY SQUEEZING THEM...!!
...
...
...
ぶるぶる
TREMBLE TREMBLE
SAND-WICH?
SQUEEZE?
COME ON - CALM DOWN, MANA.
YEAH, WE DON'T KNOW ANYTHING FOR SURE.
GAME OVER ...
I DON'T REALLY UNDERSTAND WHY YOU'D GET SO INTIMIDATED BY BREASTS, BUT...

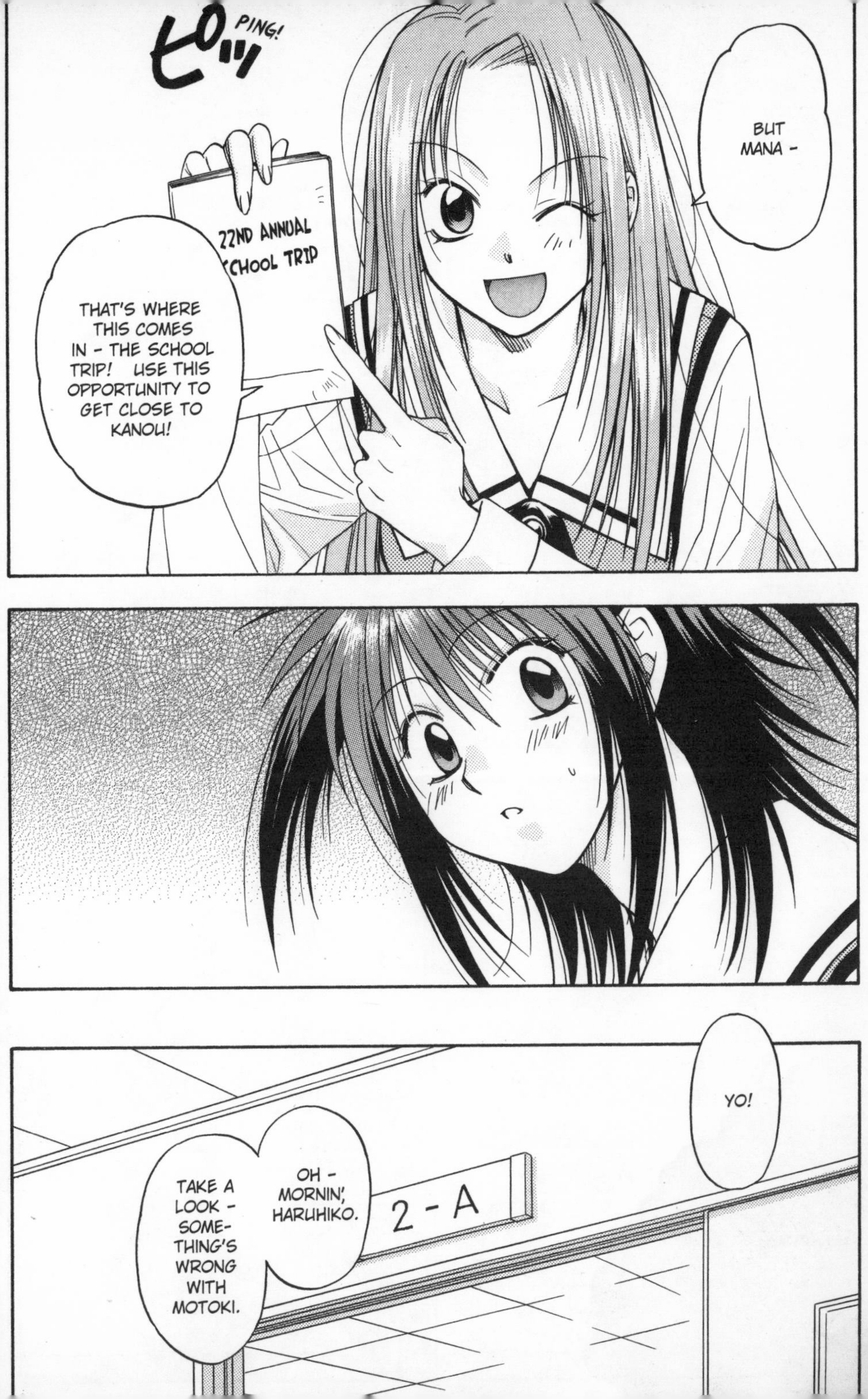
BUT MANA -
PING!
22ND ANNUAL
SCHOOL TRIP
THAT'S WHERE THIS COMES IN - THE SCHOOL TRIP! USE THIS OPPORTUNITY TO GET CLOSE TO KANOU!
YO!
2 - A
OH - MORNIN', HARUHIKO.
TAKE A LOOK - SOME-THING'S WRONG WITH MOTOKI.

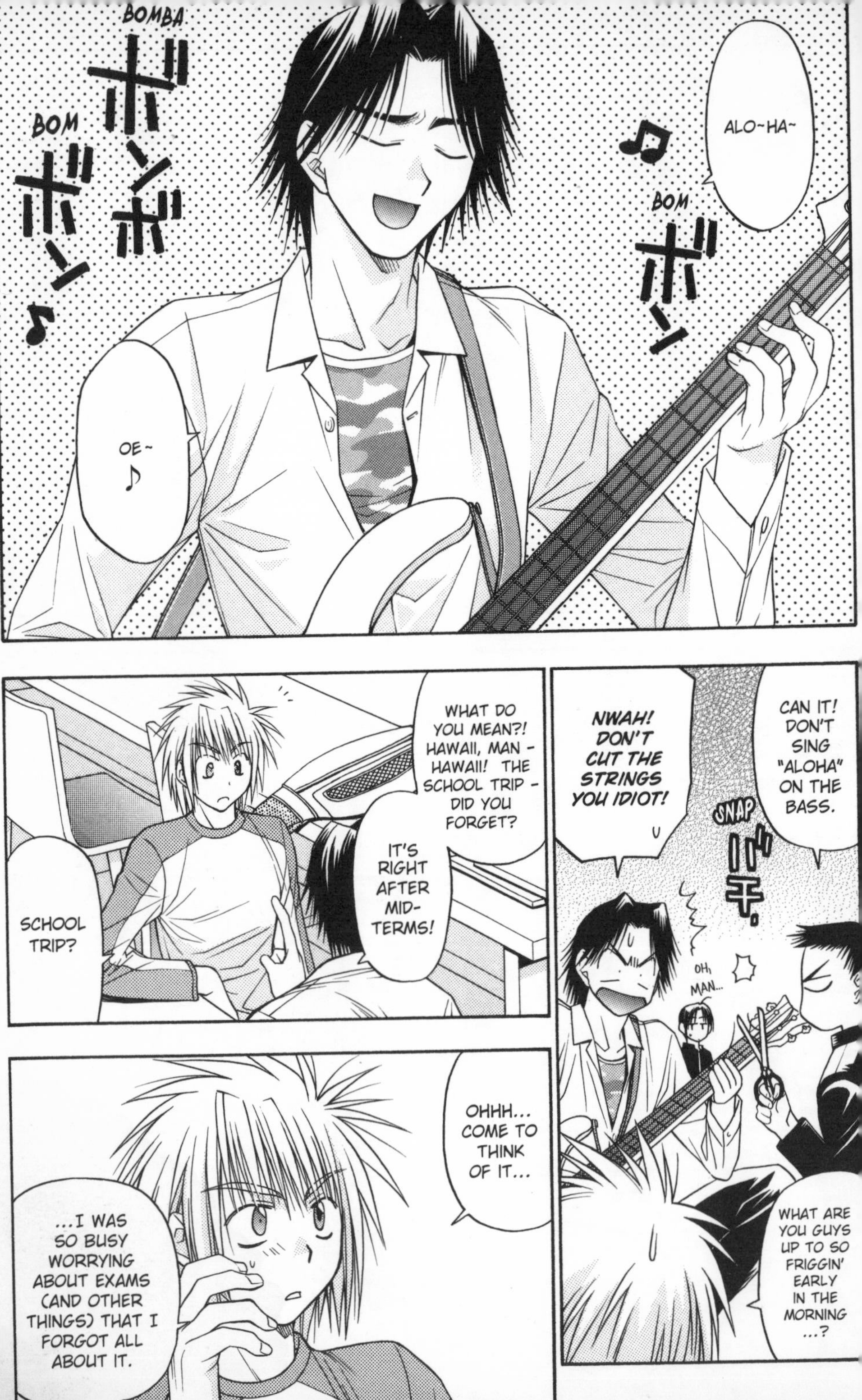
ALO~HA~
BOM
ボン
BOMBA
BOM
OE~ ♪
CAN IT! DON'T SING "ALOHA" ON THE BASS.
NWAH! DON'T CUT THE STRINGS YOU IDIOT!
SNAP
OH, MAN...
WHAT ARE YOU GUYS UP TO SO FRIGGIN' EARLY IN THE MORNING ...?
WHAT DO YOU MEAN?! HAWAII, MAN - HAWAII! THE SCHOOL TRIP - DID YOU FORGET?
IT'S RIGHT AFTER MID-TERMS!
SCHOOL TRIP?
OHHH... COME TO THINK OF IT...
...I WAS SO BUSY WORRYING ABOUT EXAMS (AND OTHER THINGS) THAT I FORGOT ALL ABOUT IT.

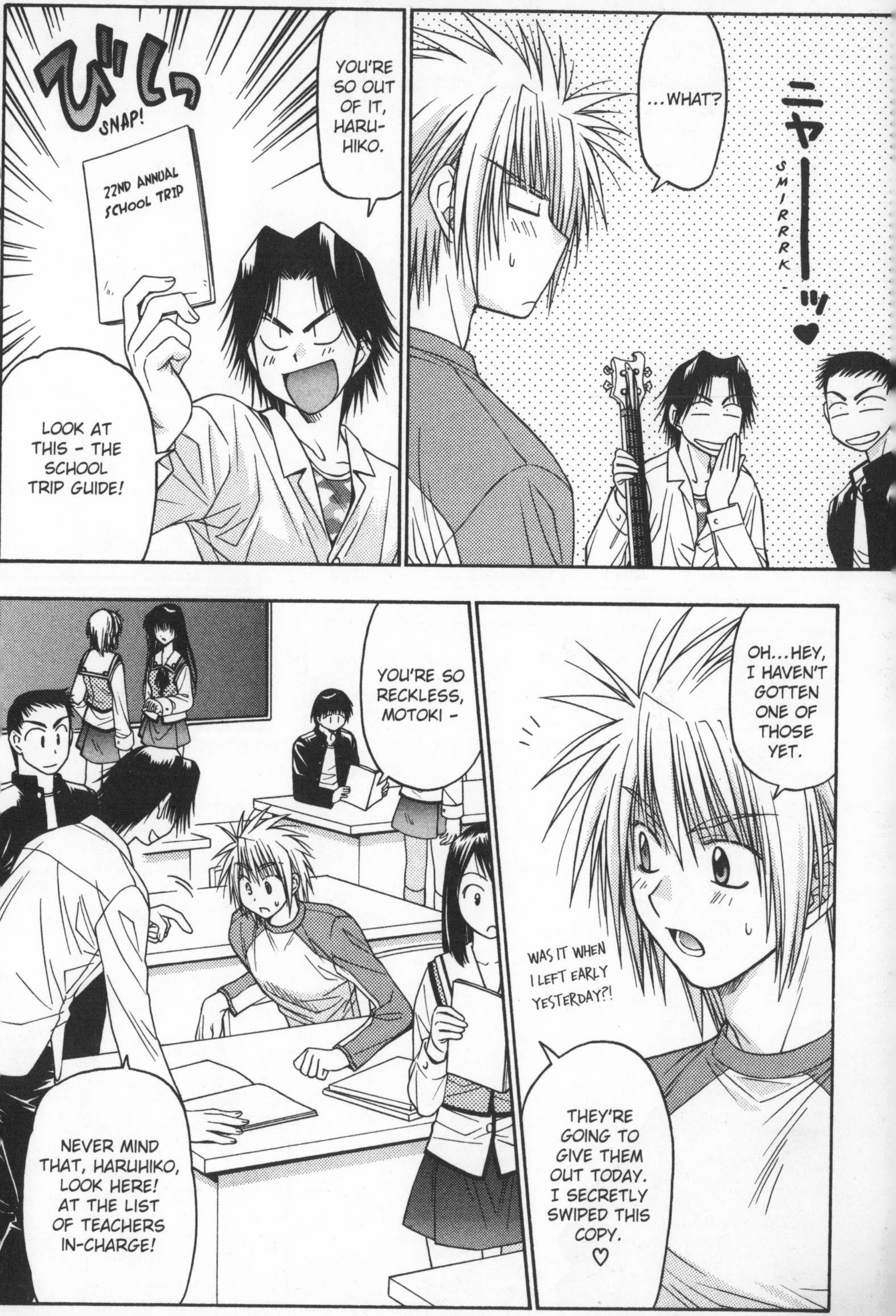
...WHAT?
ニャーーッ♥
SMIRRRK
YOU'RE SO OUT OF IT, HARUHIKO.
びくっ
SNAP!
22ND ANNUAL SCHOOL TRIP
LOOK AT THIS - THE SCHOOL TRIP GUIDE!
OH...HEY, I HAVEN'T GOTTEN ONE OF THOSE YET.
WAS IT WHEN I LEFT EARLY YESTERDAY?!
THEY'RE GOING TO GIVE THEM OUT TODAY. I SECRETLY SWIPED THIS COPY. ♡
YOU'RE SO RECKLESS, MOTOKI -
NEVER MIND THAT, HARUHIKO, LOOK HERE! AT THE LIST OF TEACHERS IN-CHARGE!

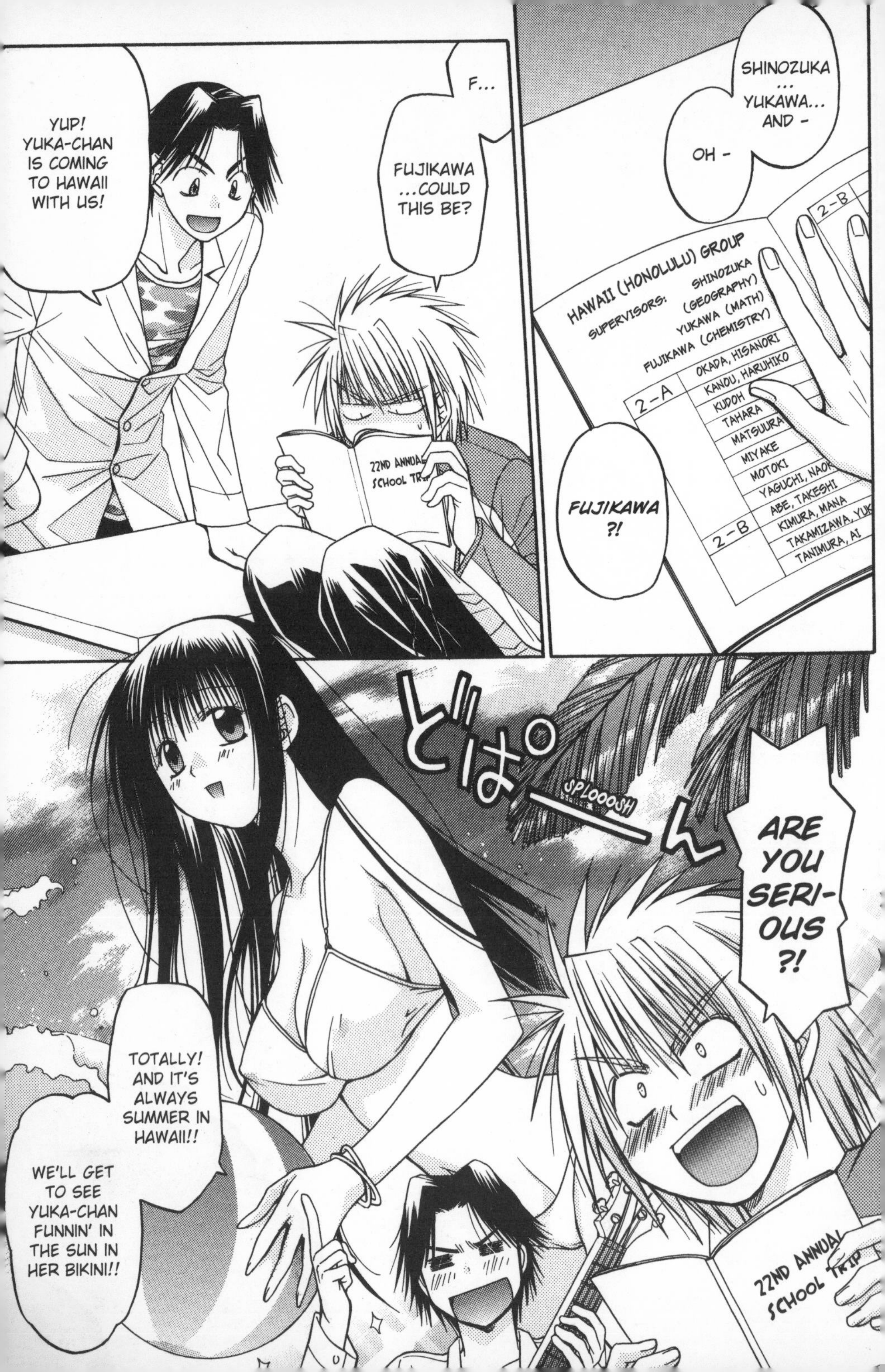
SHINOZUKA ... YUKAWA... AND -
OH -
FUJIKAWA ?!
HAWAII (HONOLULU) GROUP
SUPERVISORS: SHINOZUKA (GEOGRAPHY)
YUKAWA (MATH)
FUJIKAWA (CHEMISTRY)
2-A OKADA, HISANORI
KANOU, HARUHIKO
KUDOH
TAHARA
MATSUURA
MIYAKE
MOTOKI
YAGUCHI, NAOK
2-B ABE, TAKESHI
KIMURA, MANA
TAKAMIZAWA, YUK
TANIMURA, AI
2-B
F...
FUJIKAWA ...COULD THIS BE?
YUP! YUKA-CHAN IS COMING TO HAWAII WITH US!
22ND ANNUAL SCHOOL TRIP
どぱーん
SPLOOOSH
ARE YOU SERI-OUS ?!
TOTALLY! AND IT'S ALWAYS SUMMER IN HAWAII!!
WE'LL GET TO SEE YUKA-CHAN FUNNIN' IN THE SUN IN HER BIKINI!!
22ND ANNUAL SCHOOL TRIP

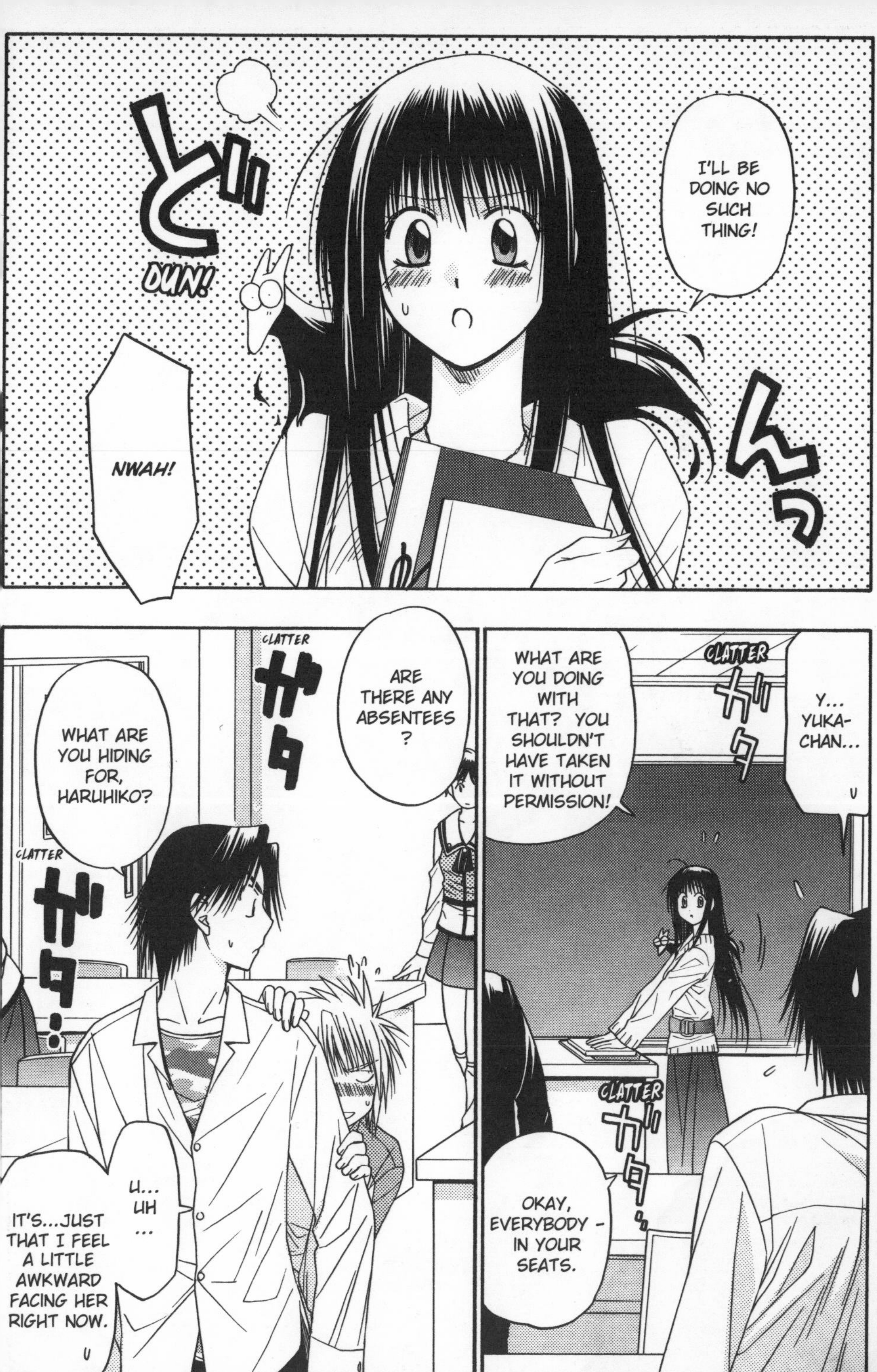
I'LL BE DOING NO SUCH THING!
DUN!
NWAH!
Y... YUKA-CHAN...
CLATTER
WHAT ARE YOU DOING WITH THAT? YOU SHOULDN'T HAVE TAKEN IT WITHOUT PERMISSION!
CLATTER
OKAY, EVERYBODY - IN YOUR SEATS.
ARE THERE ANY ABSENTEES?
CLATTER
WHAT ARE YOU HIDING FOR, HARUHIKO?
CLATTER
U... UH ...
IT'S...JUST THAT I FEEL A LITTLE AWKWARD FACING HER RIGHT NOW.

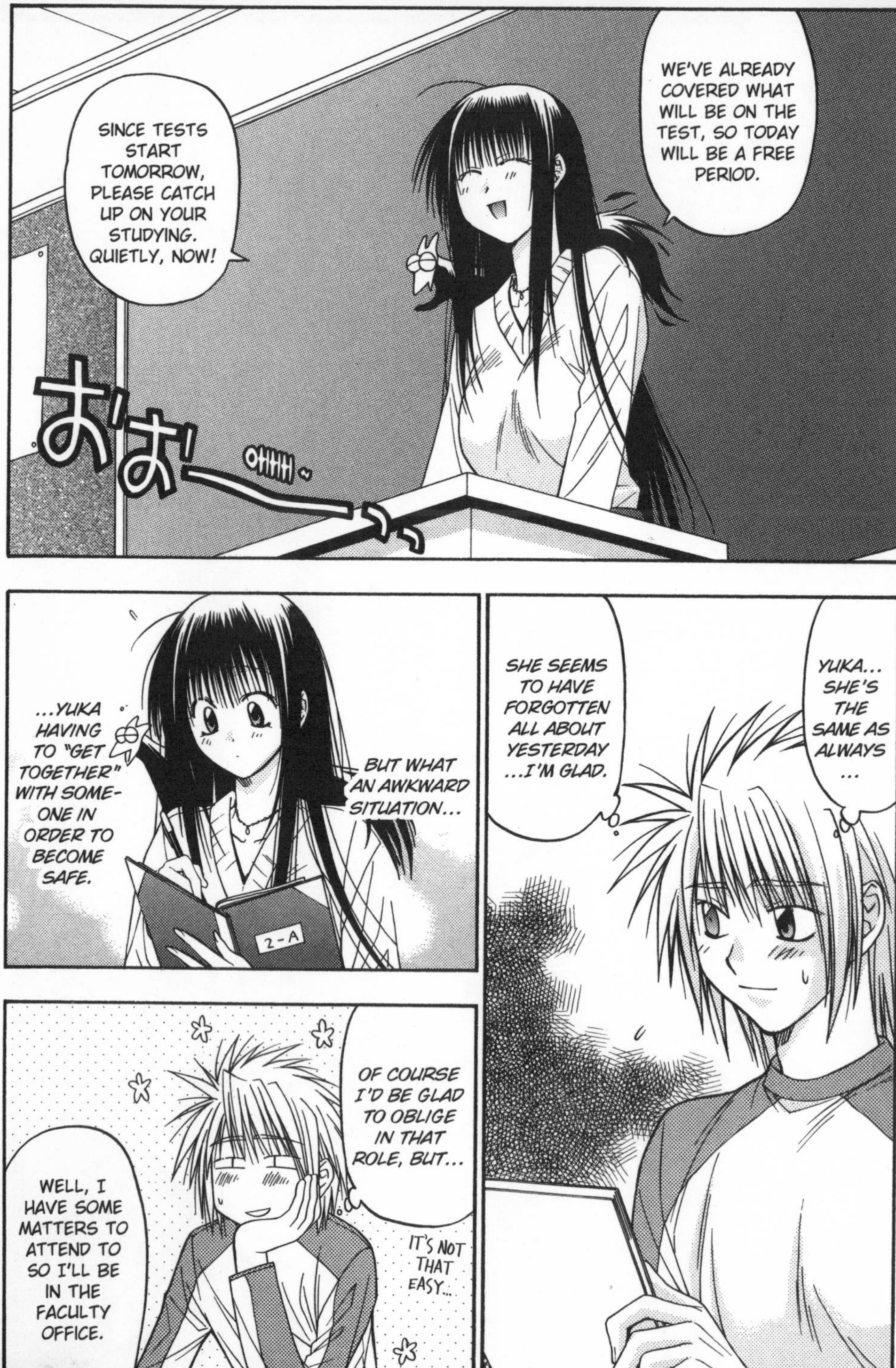
WE'VE ALREADY COVERED WHAT WILL BE ON THE TEST, SO TODAY WILL BE A FREE PERIOD.
SINCE TESTS START TOMORROW, PLEASE CATCH UP ON YOUR STUDYING. QUIETLY, NOW!
おお〜っ
OHHH~
YUKA... SHE'S THE SAME AS ALWAYS...
SHE SEEMS TO HAVE FORGOTTEN ALL ABOUT YESTERDAY ...I'M GLAD.
BUT WHAT AN AWKWARD SITUATION...
...YUKA HAVING TO "GET TOGETHER" WITH SOME-ONE IN ORDER TO BECOME SAFE.
2-A
OF COURSE I'D BE GLAD TO OBLIGE IN THAT ROLE, BUT...
IT'S NOT THAT EASY...
WELL, I HAVE SOME MATTERS TO ATTEND TO SO I'LL BE IN THE FACULTY OFFICE.

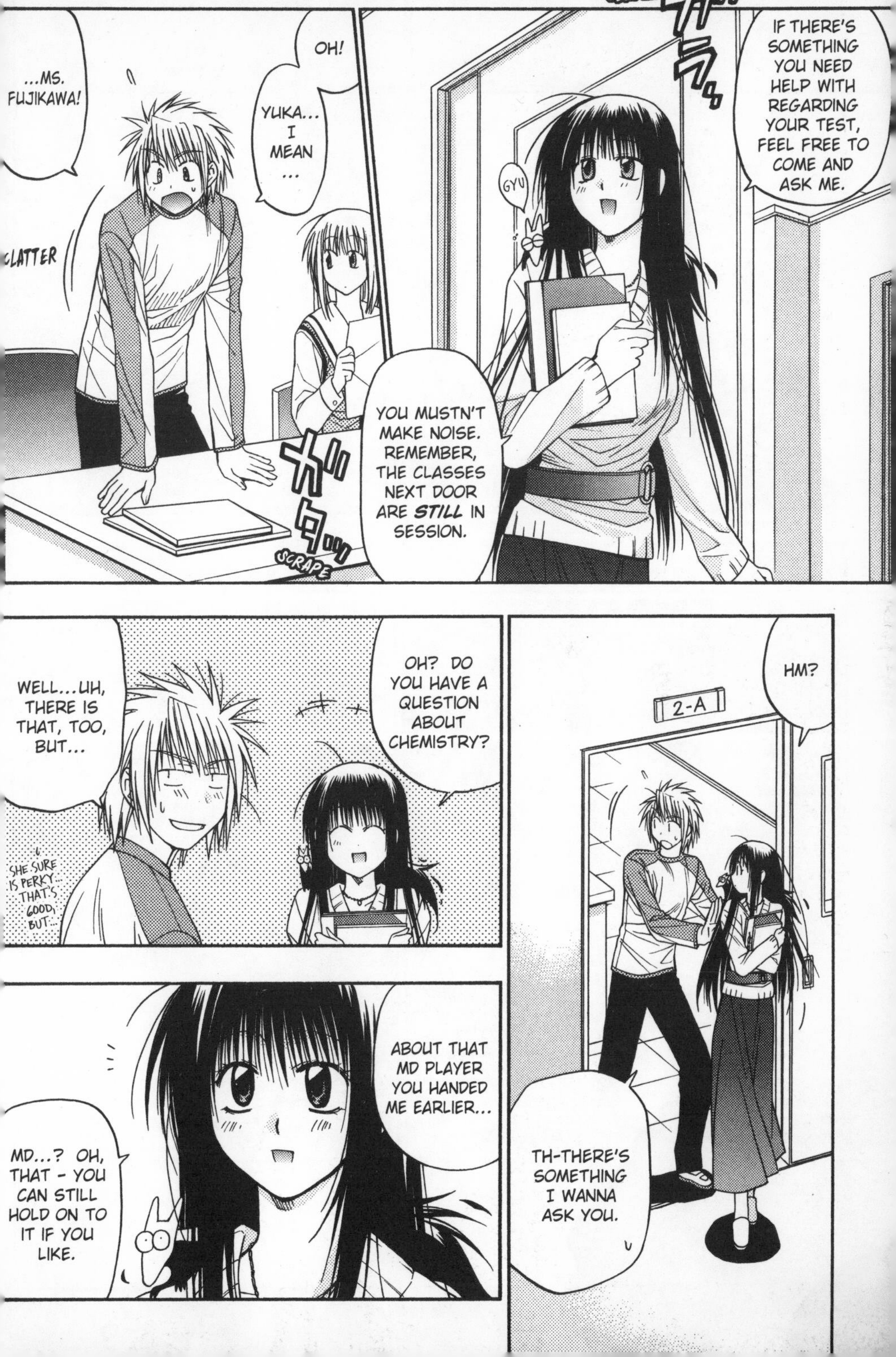
CLAK...
IF THERE'S SOMETHING YOU NEED HELP WITH REGARDING YOUR TEST, FEEL FREE TO COME AND ASK ME.
GYU
YOU MUSTN'T MAKE NOISE. REMEMBER, THE CLASSES NEXT DOOR ARE *STILL* IN SESSION.
OH!
YUKA... I MEAN ...
...MS. FUJIKAWA!
CLATTER
SCRAPE
HM?
2-A
TH-THERE'S SOMETHING I WANNA ASK YOU.
OH? DO YOU HAVE A QUESTION ABOUT CHEMISTRY?
WELL...UH, THERE IS THAT, TOO, BUT...
SHE SURE IS PERKY... THAT'S GOOD, BUT...
ABOUT THAT MD PLAYER YOU HANDED ME EARLIER...
MD...? OH, THAT - YOU CAN STILL HOLD ON TO IT IF YOU LIKE.

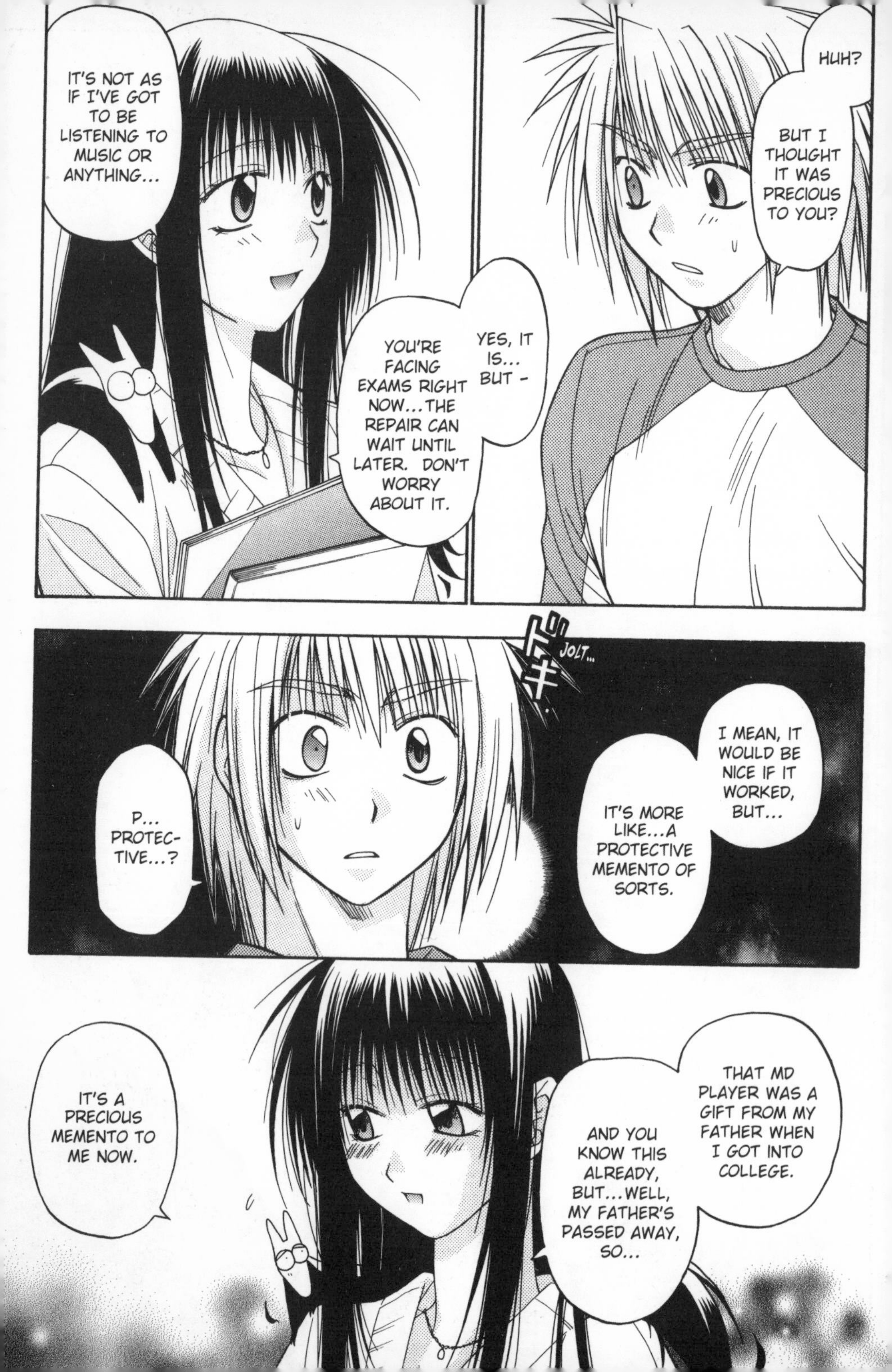
HUH?
BUT I THOUGHT IT WAS PRECIOUS TO YOU?
YES, IT IS... BUT -
YOU'RE FACING EXAMS RIGHT NOW...THE REPAIR CAN WAIT UNTIL LATER. DON'T WORRY ABOUT IT.
IT'S NOT AS IF I'VE GOT TO BE LISTENING TO MUSIC OR ANYTHING...
JOLT...
I MEAN, IT WOULD BE NICE IF IT WORKED, BUT...
IT'S MORE LIKE...A PROTECTIVE MEMENTO OF SORTS.
P... PROTECTIVE...?
THAT MD PLAYER WAS A GIFT FROM MY FATHER WHEN I GOT INTO COLLEGE.
AND YOU KNOW THIS ALREADY, BUT...WELL, MY FATHER'S PASSED AWAY, SO...
IT'S A PRECIOUS MEMENTO TO ME NOW.

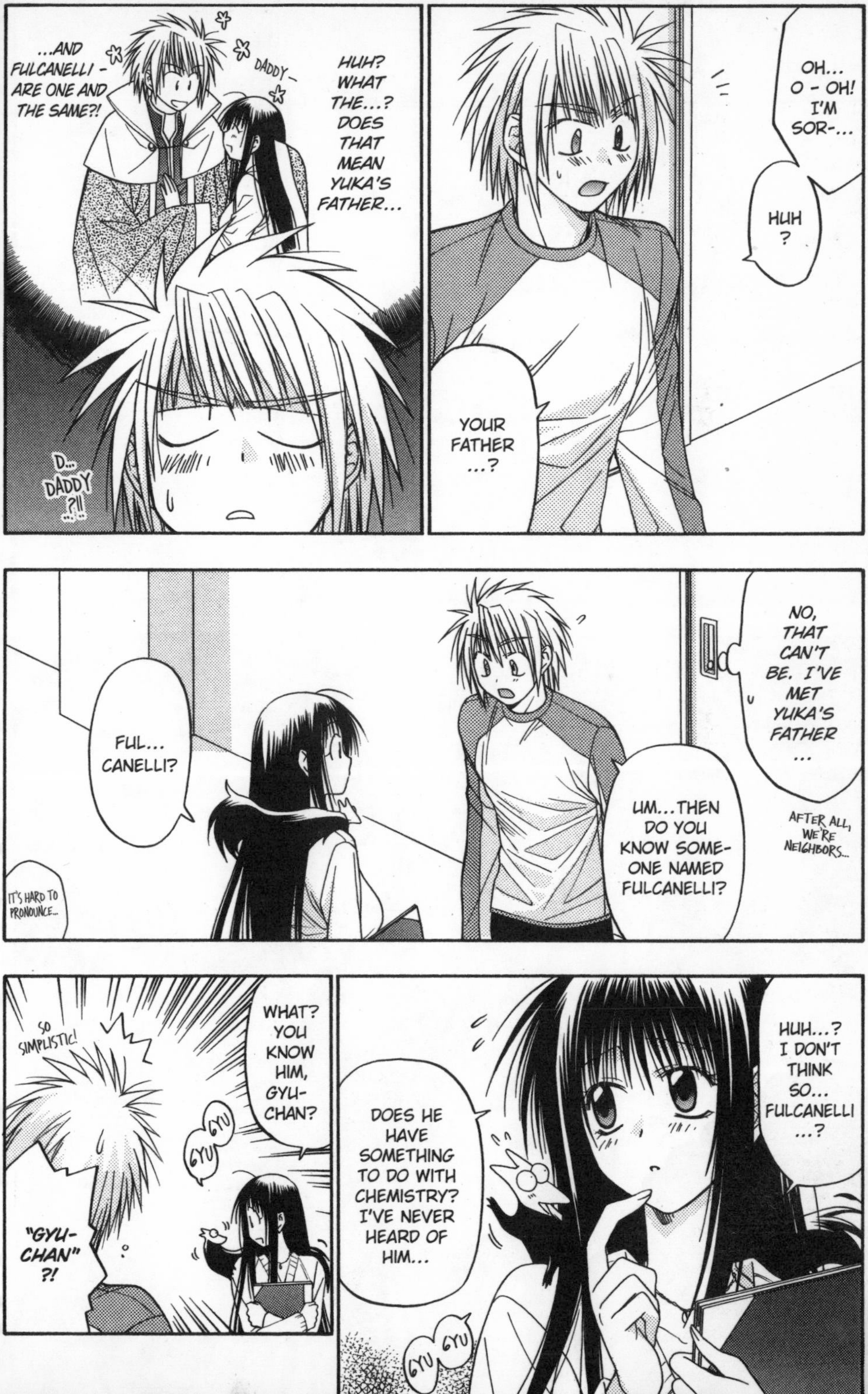
OH... O - OH! I'M SOR-...
HUH ?
YOUR FATHER ...?
HUH? WHAT THE...? DOES THAT MEAN YUKA'S FATHER...
DADDY~
...AND FULCANELLI - ARE ONE AND THE SAME?!
D... DADDY ...?!!
NO, THAT CAN'T BE. I'VE MET YUKA'S FATHER ...
AFTER ALL, WE'RE NEIGHBORS...
UM...THEN DO YOU KNOW SOME-ONE NAMED FULCANELLI?
FUL... CANELLI?
IT'S HARD TO PRONOUNCE...
HUH...? I DON'T THINK SO... FULCANELLI ...?
DOES HE HAVE SOMETHING TO DO WITH CHEMISTRY? I'VE NEVER HEARD OF HIM...
GYU GYU
WHAT? YOU KNOW HIM, GYU-CHAN?
SO SIMPLISTIC!
GYU GYU
"GYU-CHAN" ?!

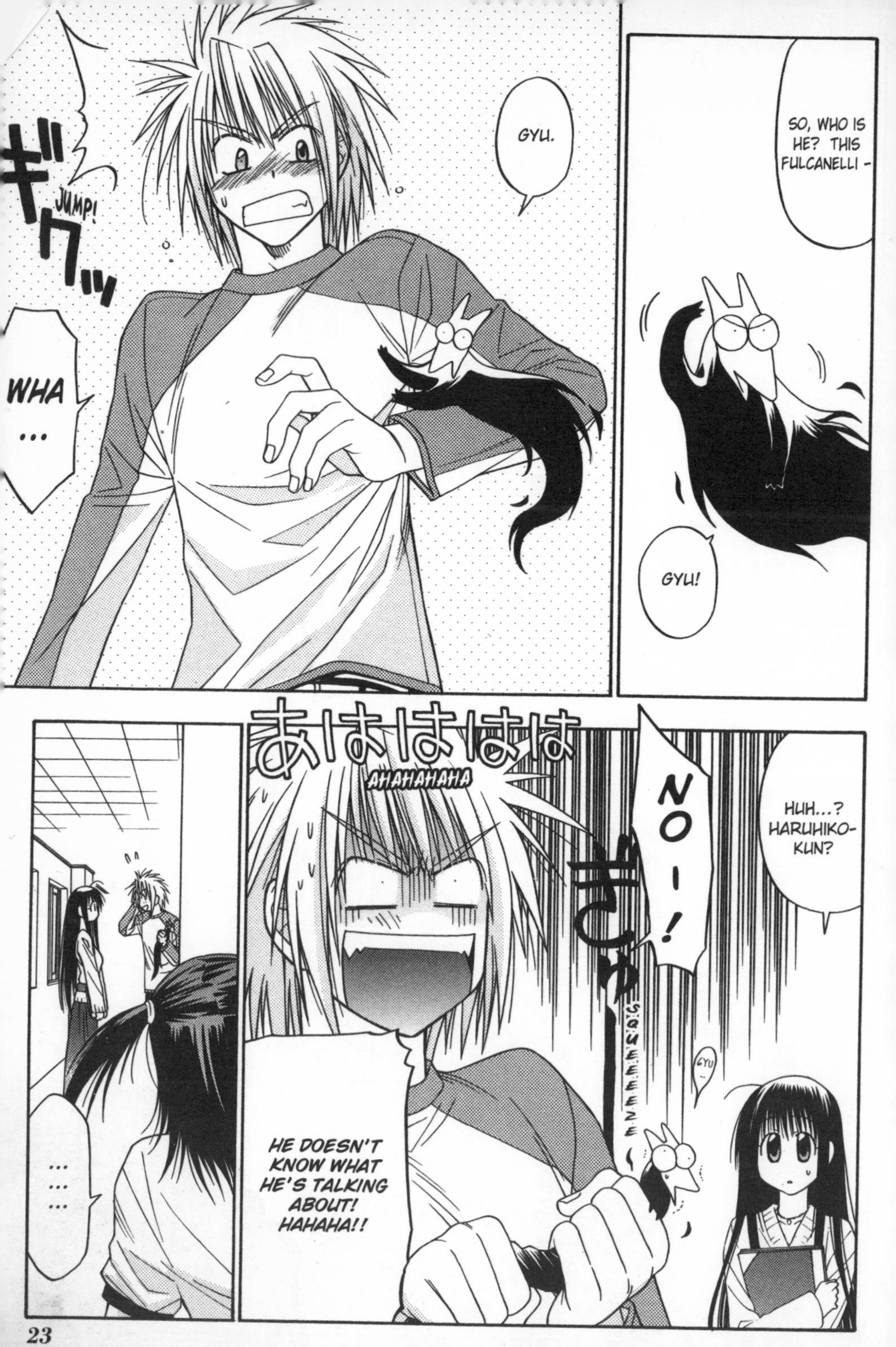
SO, WHO IS HE? THIS FULCANELLI -
GYU!
GYU.
ギクッ
JUMP!
WHA ...
HUH...? HARUHIKO-KUN?
GYU ...
NO-!
ぎゅ
SQUEEEEEZE
あははははは
AHAHAHAHA
HE DOESN'T KNOW WHAT HE'S TALKING ABOUT! HAHAHA!!
... ...

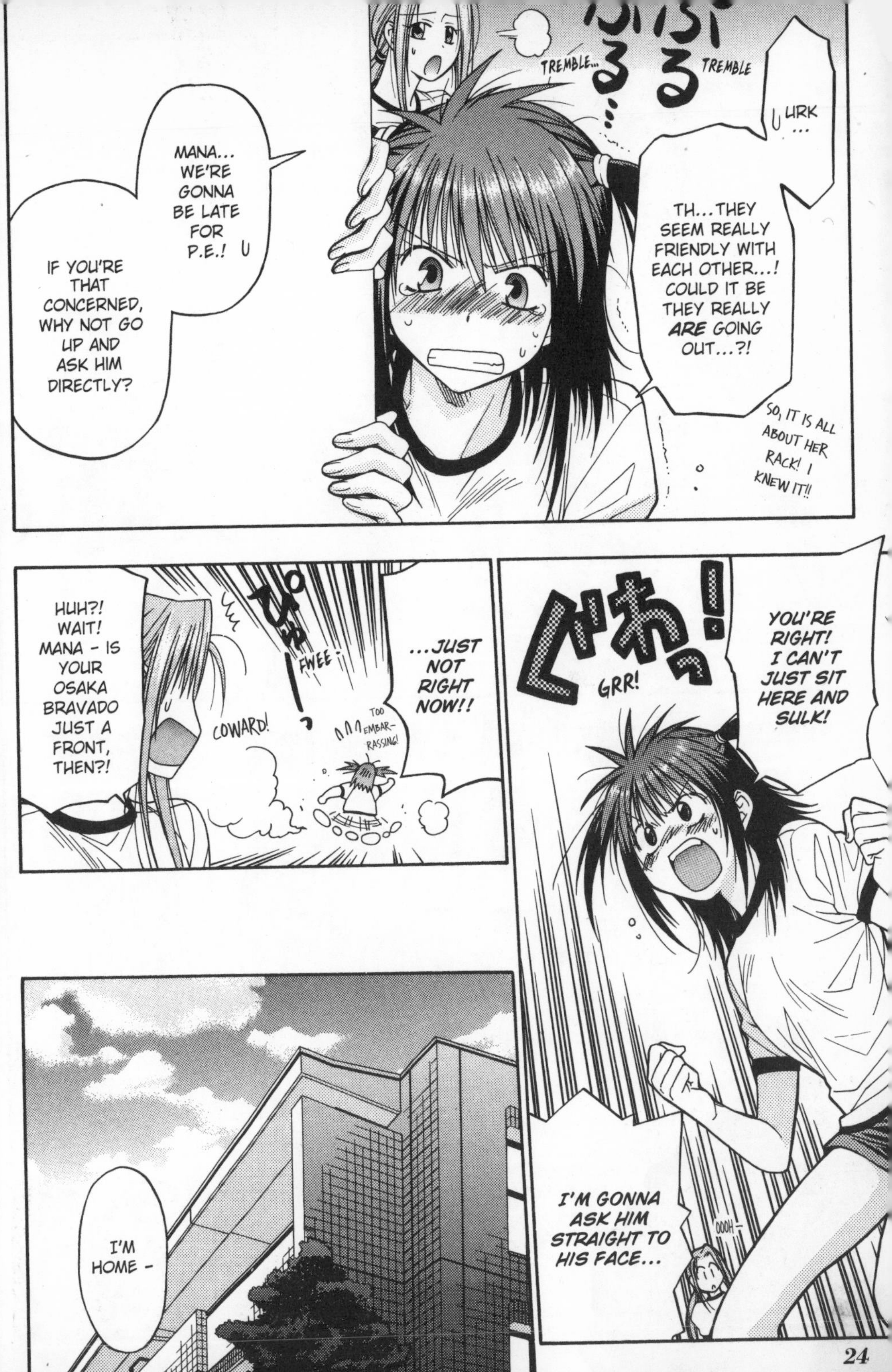
ぷるぷる
TREMBLE... TREMBLE
URK...
TH... THEY SEEM REALLY FRIENDLY WITH EACH OTHER...! COULD IT BE THEY REALLY **ARE** GOING OUT...?!
SO, IT IS ALL ABOUT HER RACK! I KNEW IT!!
MANA... WE'RE GONNA BE LATE FOR P.E.!
IF YOU'RE THAT CONCERNED, WHY NOT GO UP AND ASK HIM DIRECTLY?
ぐあっ!
GRR!
YOU'RE RIGHT! I CAN'T JUST SIT HERE AND SULK!
I'M GONNA ASK HIM STRAIGHT TO HIS FACE...
OOOH-
...JUST NOT RIGHT NOW!!
FWEE
TOO EMBARRASSING!
COWARD!
HUH?! WAIT! MANA - IS YOUR OSAKA BRAVADO JUST A FRONT, THEN?!
I'M HOME -

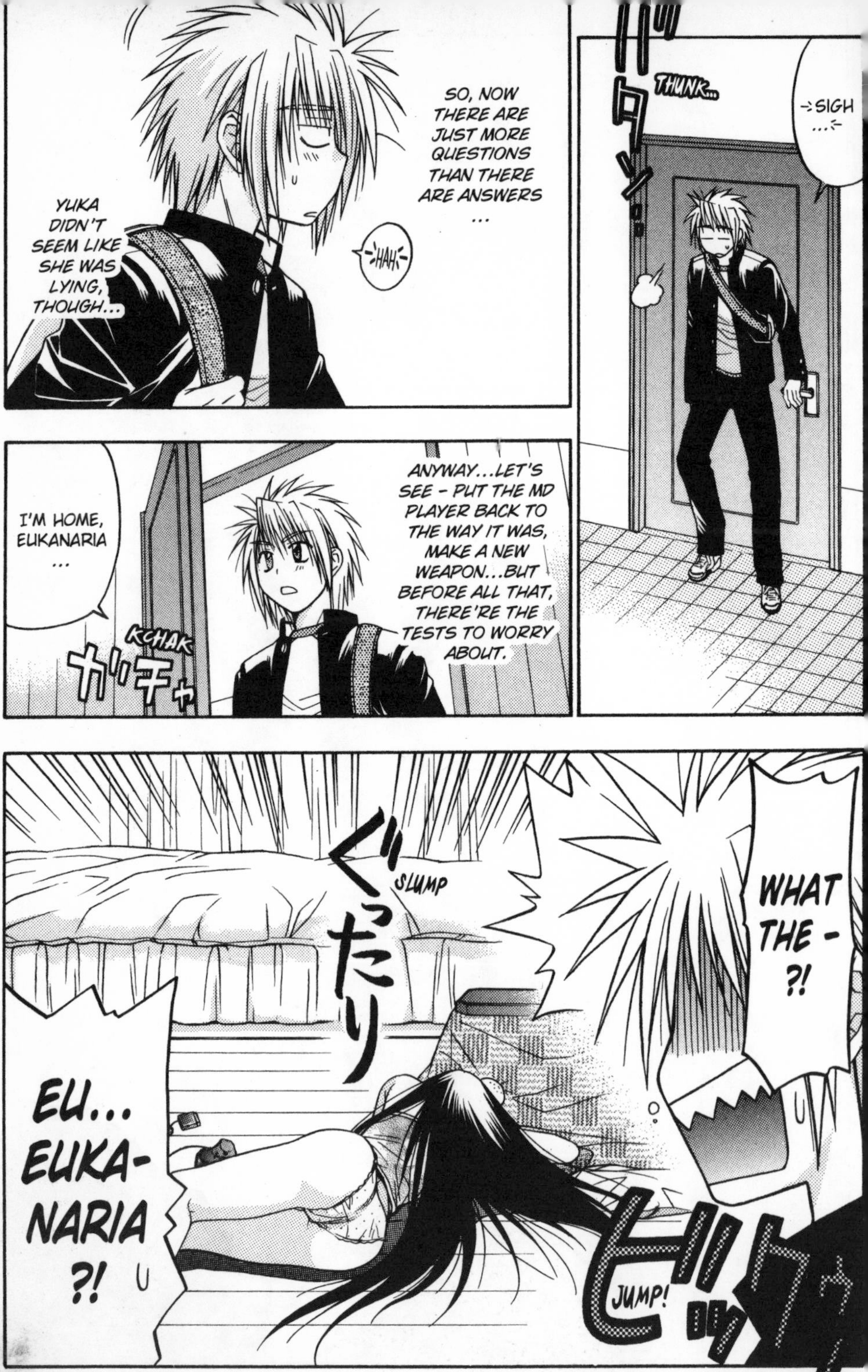
–SIGH …–
バタン
THUNK...
SO, NOW THERE ARE JUST MORE QUESTIONS THAN THERE ARE ANSWERS …
–HAH–
YUKA DIDN'T SEEM LIKE SHE WAS LYING, THOUGH...
ANYWAY...LET'S SEE - PUT THE MD PLAYER BACK TO THE WAY IT WAS, MAKE A NEW WEAPON...BUT BEFORE ALL THAT, THERE'RE THE TESTS TO WORRY ABOUT.
I'M HOME, EUKANARIA …
ガチャ
KCHAK
WHAT THE - ?!
ぐったり
SLUMP
ビクッ
JUMP!
EU... EUKA-NARIA ?!

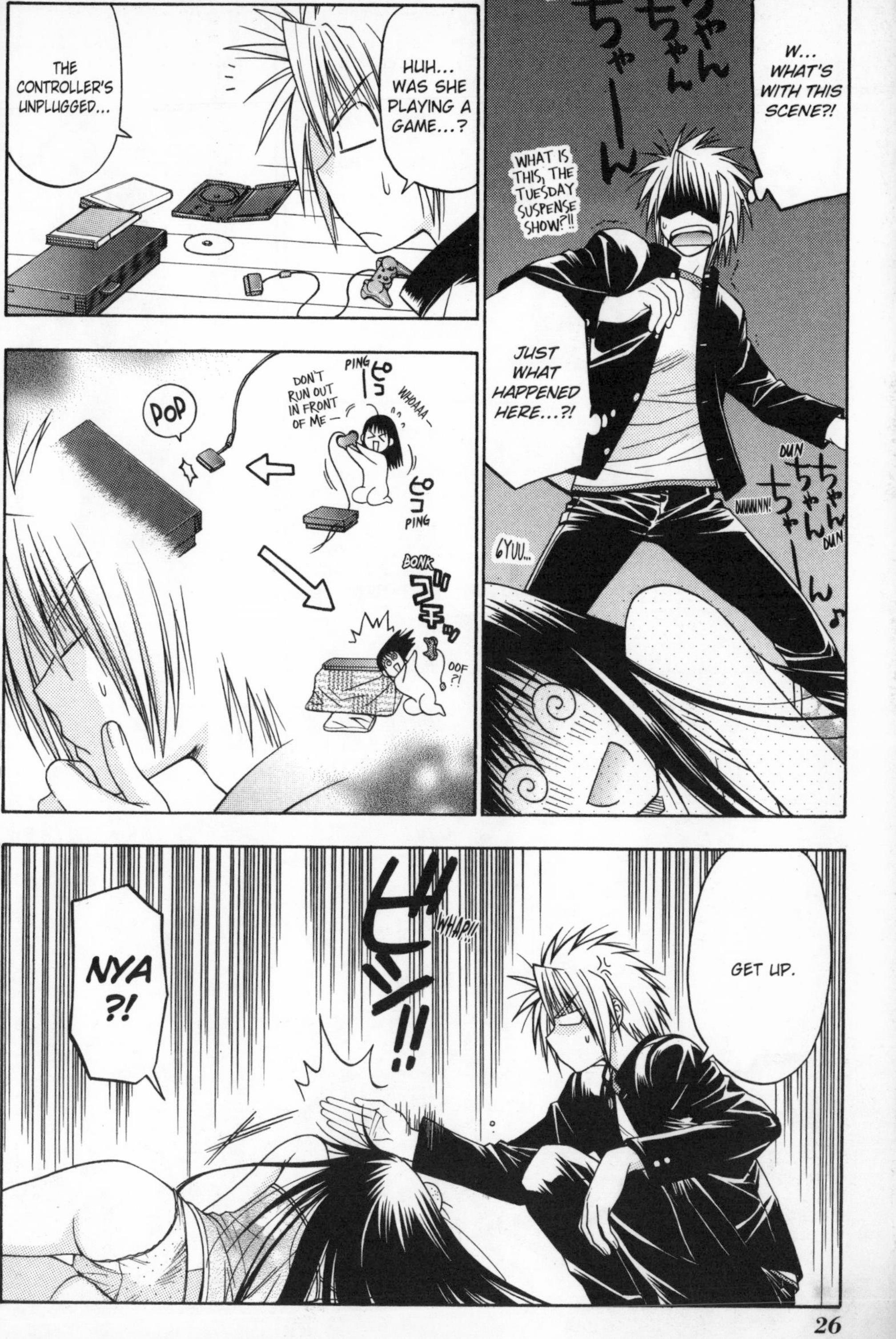
DUUUUNN!
DUN
ちゃんちゃんちゃーん
W... WHAT'S WITH THIS SCENE?!
WHAT IS THIS, THE TUESDAY SUSPENSE SHOW?!!
JUST WHAT HAPPENED HERE...?!
DUN
ちゃんちゃんちゃーん♪
DUUUUNN!
DUN
GYUU...
HUH... WAS SHE PLAYING A GAME...?
THE CONTROLLER'S UNPLUGGED...
PING
ピコ
DON'T RUN OUT IN FRONT OF ME —
WHOAAA —
ピコ
PING
POP
BONK
ゴチッ
OOF ?!
GET UP.
WHAP!!
ビシッ!!
NYA ?!

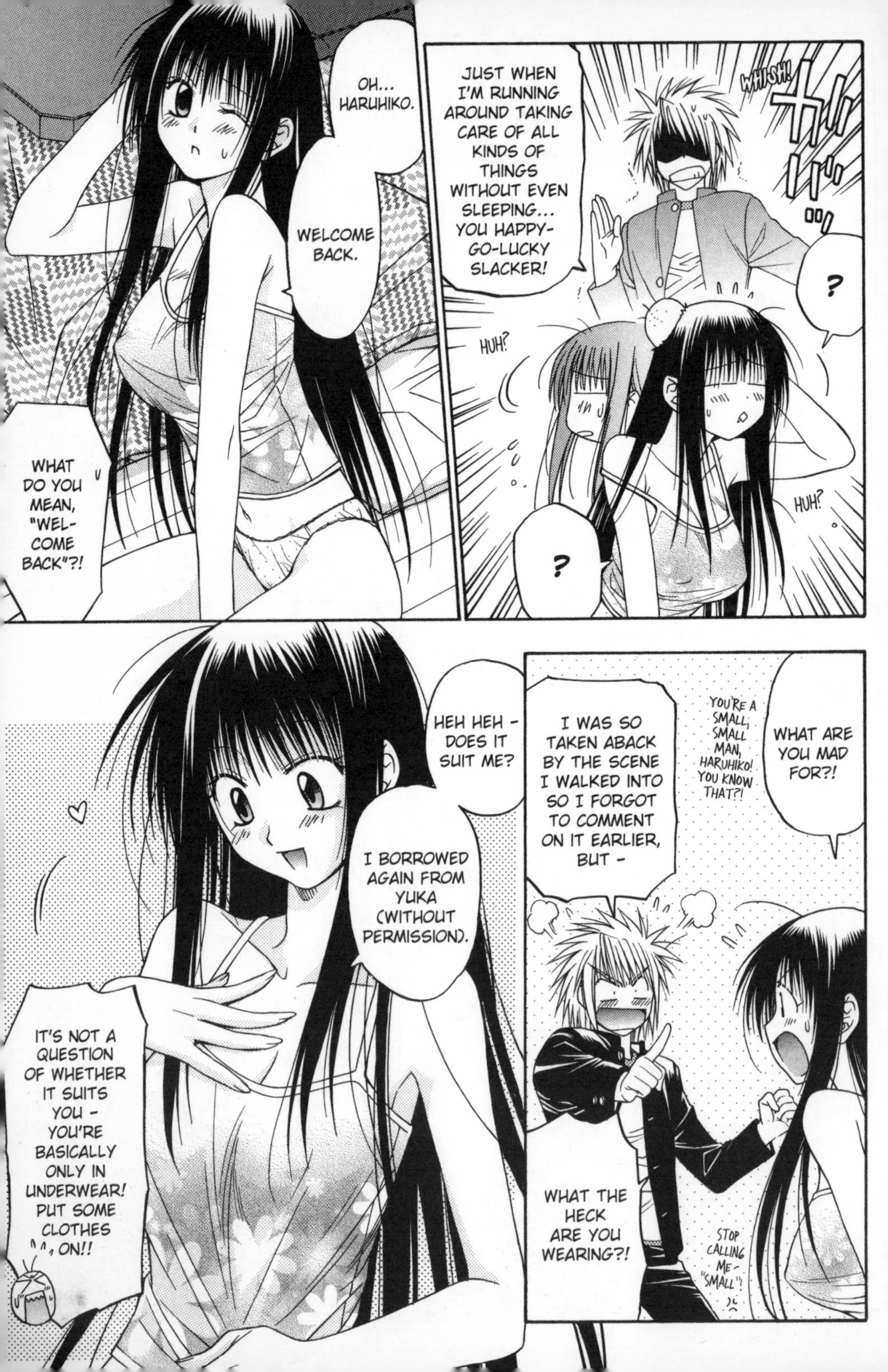
WHISH!
JUST WHEN I'M RUNNING AROUND TAKING CARE OF ALL KINDS OF THINGS WITHOUT EVEN SLEEPING... YOU HAPPY-GO-LUCKY SLACKER!
?
HUH?
HUH?
?
OH... HARUHIKO.
WELCOME BACK.
WHAT DO YOU MEAN, "WEL-COME BACK"?!
WHAT ARE YOU MAD FOR?!
YOU'RE A SMALL, SMALL MAN, HARUHIKO! YOU KNOW THAT?!
I WAS SO TAKEN ABACK BY THE SCENE I WALKED INTO SO I FORGOT TO COMMENT ON IT EARLIER, BUT -
WHAT THE HECK ARE YOU WEARING?!
STOP CALLING ME "SMALL"!
HEH HEH - DOES IT SUIT ME?
I BORROWED AGAIN FROM YUKA (WITHOUT PERMISSION).
IT'S NOT A QUESTION OF WHETHER IT SUITS YOU - YOU'RE BASICALLY ONLY IN UNDERWEAR! PUT SOME CLOTHES ON!!

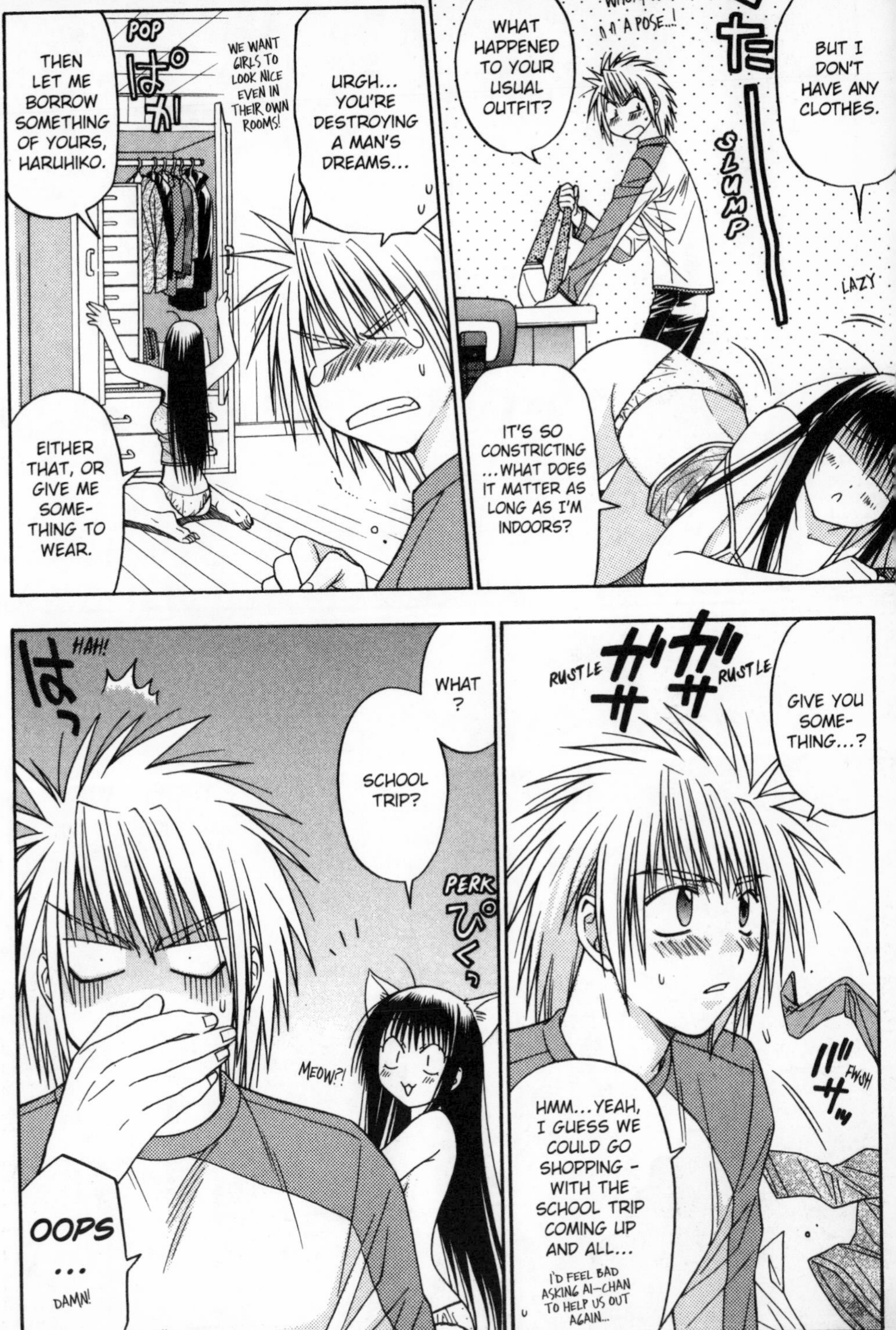
BUT I DON'T HAVE ANY CLOTHES.
SLUMP
LAZY
WHAT HAPPENED TO YOUR USUAL OUTFIT?
WHOA, WHAT A POSE...!
IT'S SO CONSTRICTING ...WHAT DOES IT MATTER AS LONG AS I'M INDOORS?
URGH... YOU'RE DESTROYING A MAN'S DREAMS...
WE WANT GIRLS TO LOOK NICE EVEN IN THEIR OWN ROOMS!
POP
THEN LET ME BORROW SOMETHING OF YOURS, HARUHIKO.
EITHER THAT, OR GIVE ME SOME-THING TO WEAR.
RUSTLE
RUSTLE
GIVE YOU SOME-THING...?
FWSH
HMM... YEAH, I GUESS WE COULD GO SHOPPING - WITH THE SCHOOL TRIP COMING UP AND ALL...
I'D FEEL BAD ASKING AI-CHAN TO HELP US OUT AGAIN...
WHAT?
SCHOOL TRIP?
PERK
HAH!
MEOW?!
OOPS...
DAMN!

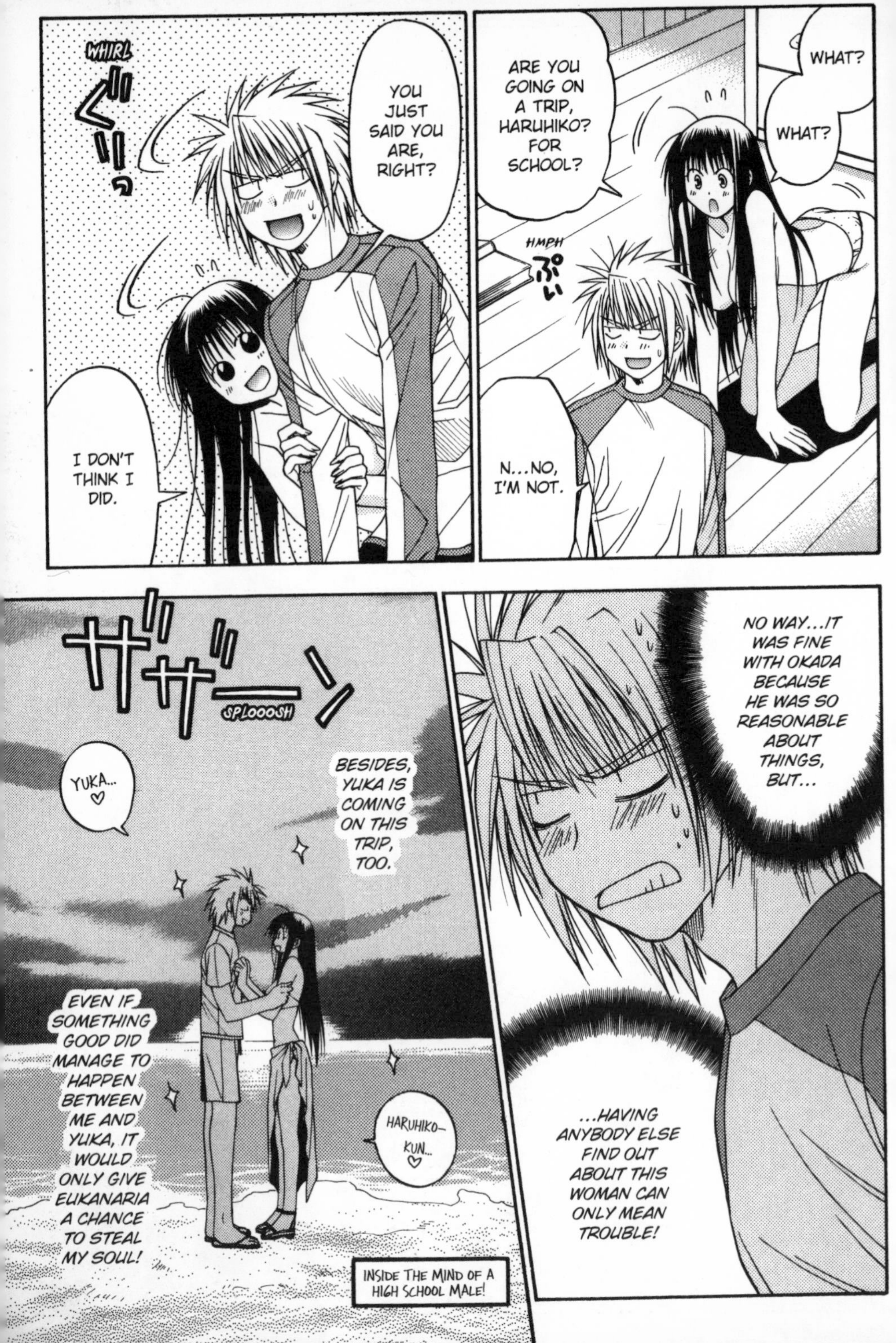
WHAT?
WHAT?
ARE YOU GOING ON A TRIP, HARUHIKO? FOR SCHOOL?
HMPH
ぷい
N...NO, I'M NOT.
WHIRL
YOU JUST SAID YOU ARE, RIGHT?
I DON'T THINK I DID.
NO WAY...IT WAS FINE WITH OKADA BECAUSE HE WAS SO REASONABLE ABOUT THINGS, BUT...
...HAVING ANYBODY ELSE FIND OUT ABOUT THIS WOMAN CAN ONLY MEAN TROUBLE!
SPLOOOSH
YUKA... ♡
BESIDES, YUKA IS COMING ON THIS TRIP, TOO.
HARUHIKO-KUN... ♡
EVEN IF SOMETHING GOOD DID MANAGE TO HAPPEN BETWEEN ME AND YUKA, IT WOULD ONLY GIVE EUKANARIA A CHANCE TO STEAL MY SOUL!
INSIDE THE MIND OF A HIGH SCHOOL MALE!

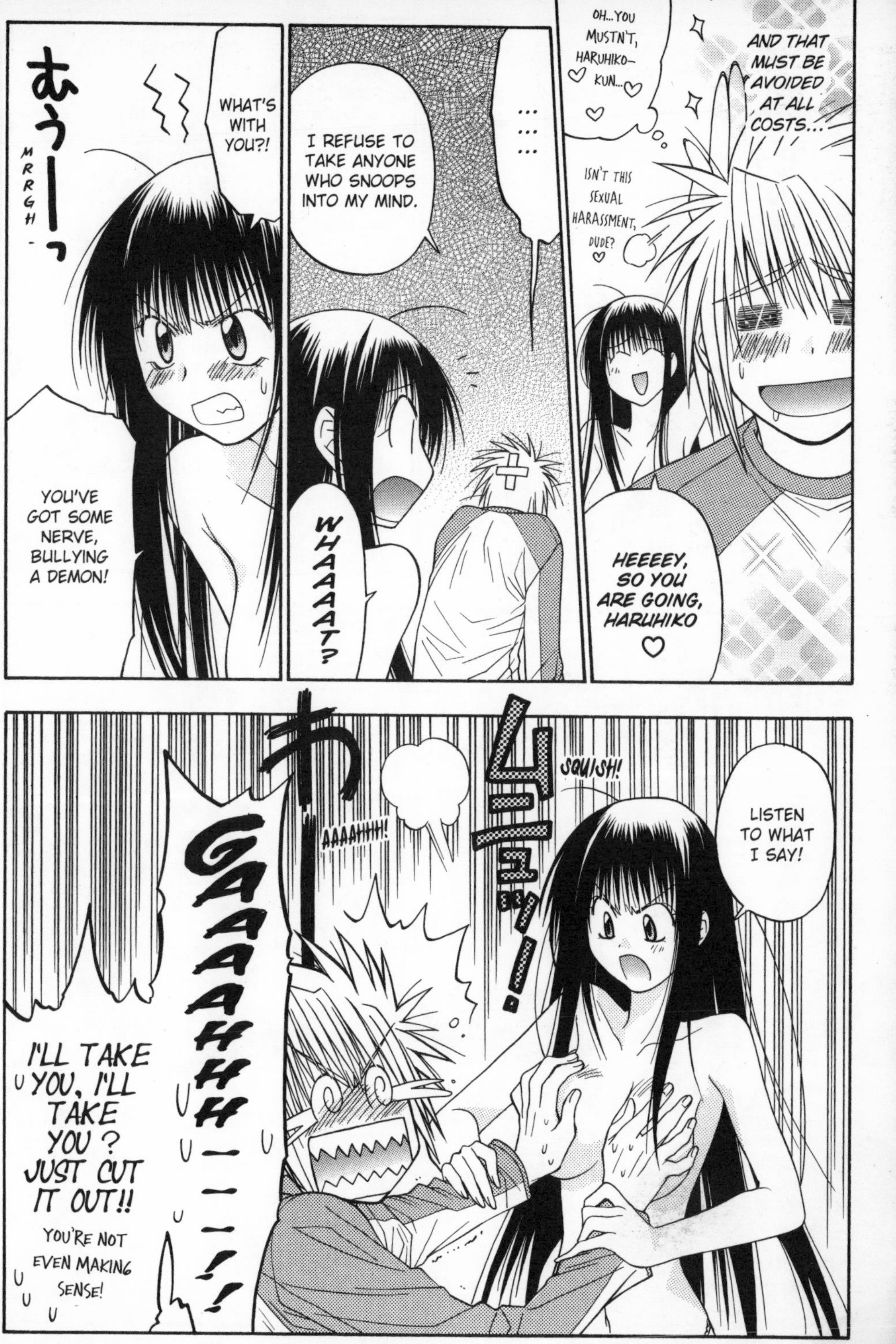
AND THAT MUST BE AVOIDED AT ALL COSTS...
OH...YOU MUSTN'T, HARUHIKO-KUN...♡
ISN'T THIS SEXUAL HARASSMENT, DUDE?
HEEEEY, SO YOU ARE GOING, HARUHIKO ♡
... ...
I REFUSE TO TAKE ANYONE WHO SNOOPS INTO MY MIND.
WHAAAAAT?
WHAT'S WITH YOU?!
むうーっ
MRRGH-
YOU'VE GOT SOME NERVE, BULLYING A DEMON!
LISTEN TO WHAT I SAY!
ムニュッ!!
SQUISH!
わーーー
AAAAHHH!
GAAAAAHHHH------!!
I'LL TAKE YOU, I'LL TAKE YOU? JUST CUT IT OUT!!
YOU'RE NOT EVEN MAKING SENSE!

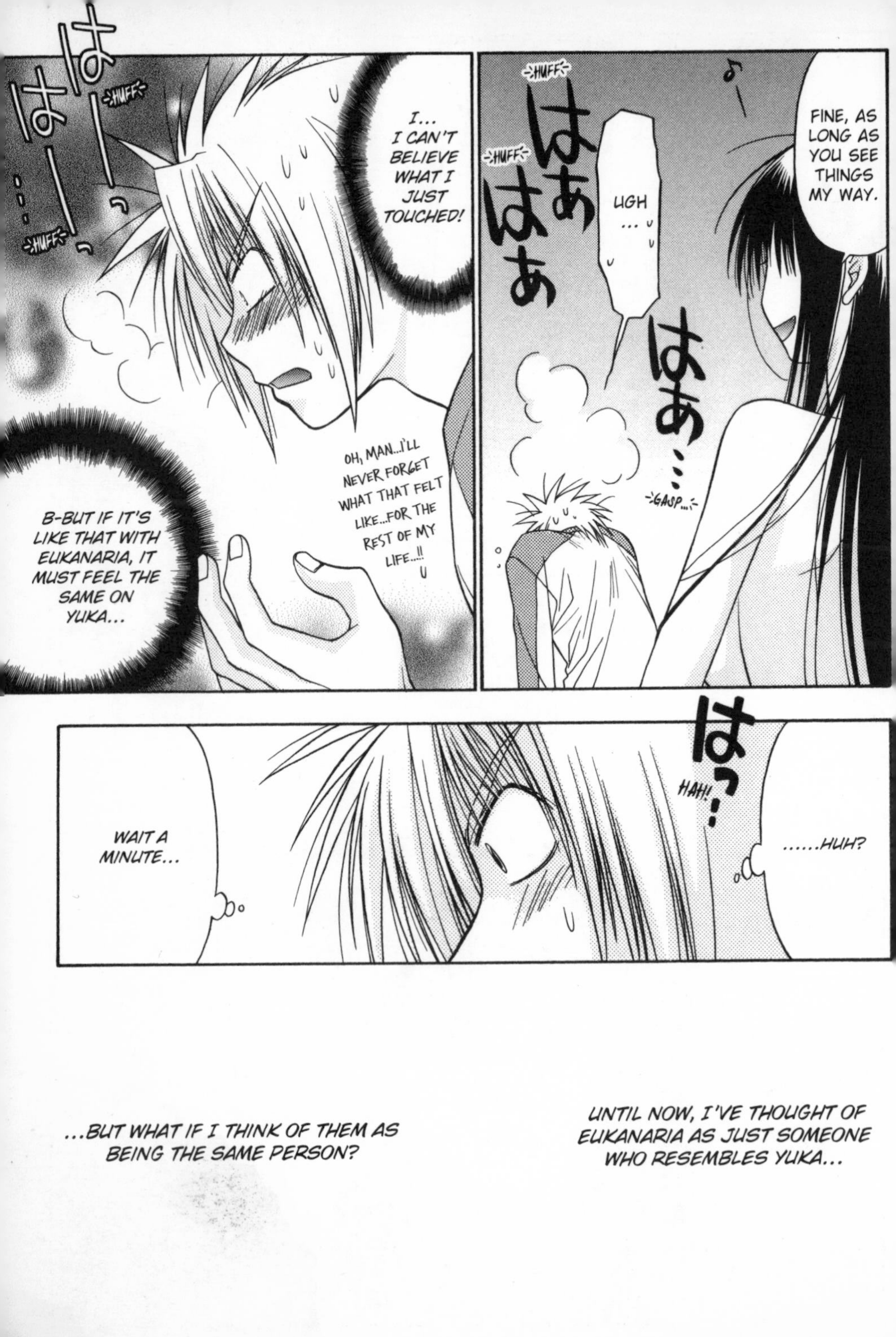
FINE, AS LONG AS YOU SEE THINGS MY WAY.
UGH ...
HUFF
はぁ はぁ
HUFF
はぁ…
GASP...
I... I CAN'T BELIEVE WHAT I JUST TOUCHED!
はー、はー、…
HUFF
HUFF
OH, MAN...I'LL NEVER FORGET WHAT THAT FELT LIKE...FOR THE REST OF MY LIFE...!!
B-BUT IF IT'S LIKE THAT WITH EUKANARIA, IT MUST FEEL THE SAME ON YUKA...
......HUH?
はっ!!
HAH!
WAIT A MINUTE...
UNTIL NOW, I'VE THOUGHT OF EUKANARIA AS JUST SOMEONE WHO RESEMBLES YUKA...
...BUT WHAT IF I THINK OF THEM AS BEING THE SAME PERSON?

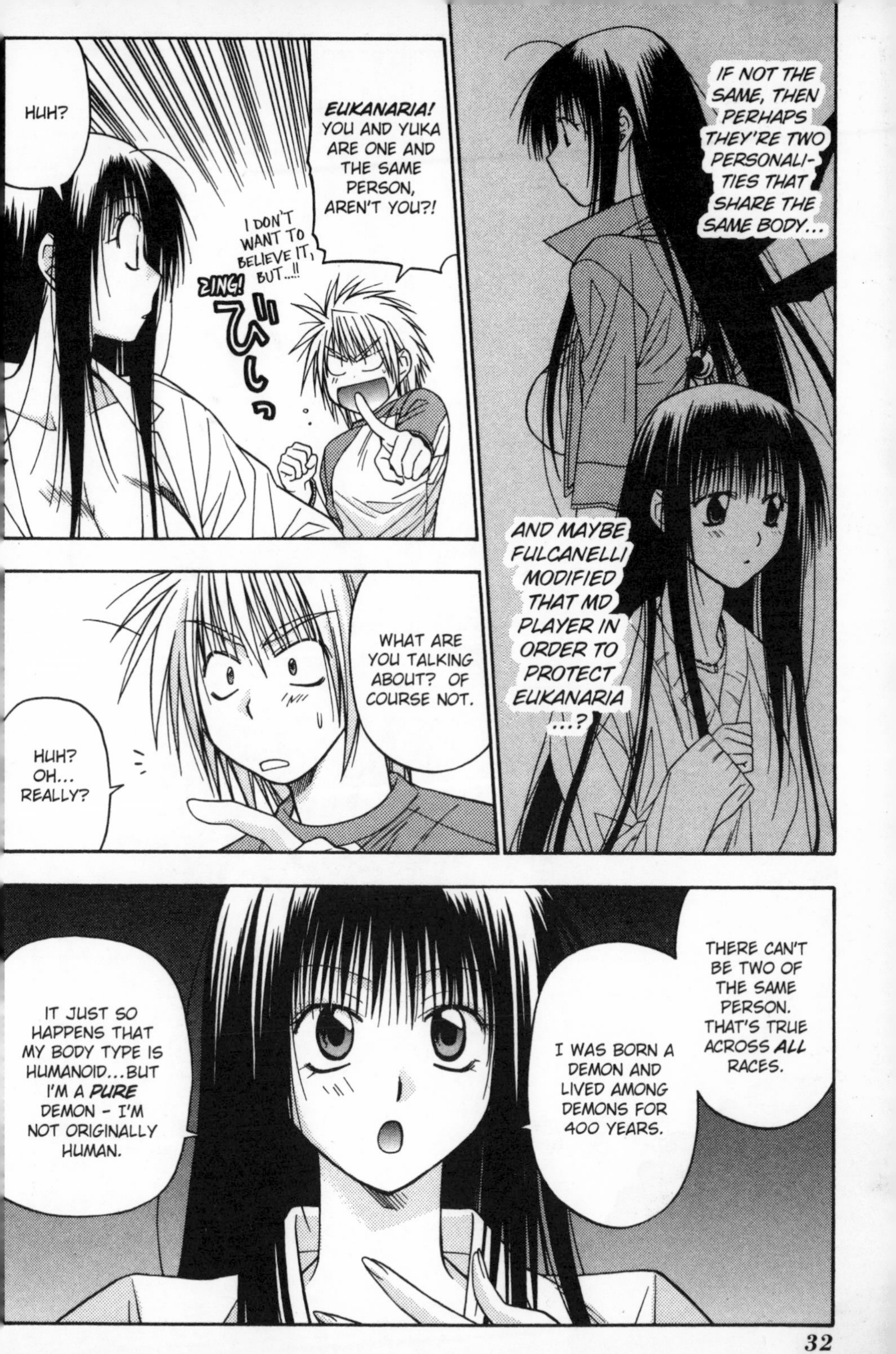
IF NOT THE SAME, THEN PERHAPS THEY'RE TWO PERSONALITIES THAT SHARE THE SAME BODY...
AND MAYBE FULCANELLI MODIFIED THAT MD PLAYER IN ORDER TO PROTECT EUKANARIA ...?
EUKANARIA! YOU AND YUKA ARE ONE AND THE SAME PERSON, AREN'T YOU?!
I DON'T WANT TO BELIEVE IT, BUT...!!
ZING!
びしっ
HUH?
WHAT ARE YOU TALKING ABOUT? OF COURSE NOT.
HUH? OH... REALLY?
THERE CAN'T BE TWO OF THE SAME PERSON. THAT'S TRUE ACROSS ALL RACES.
I WAS BORN A DEMON AND LIVED AMONG DEMONS FOR 400 YEARS.
IT JUST SO HAPPENS THAT MY BODY TYPE IS HUMANOID...BUT I'M A PURE DEMON - I'M NOT ORIGINALLY HUMAN.

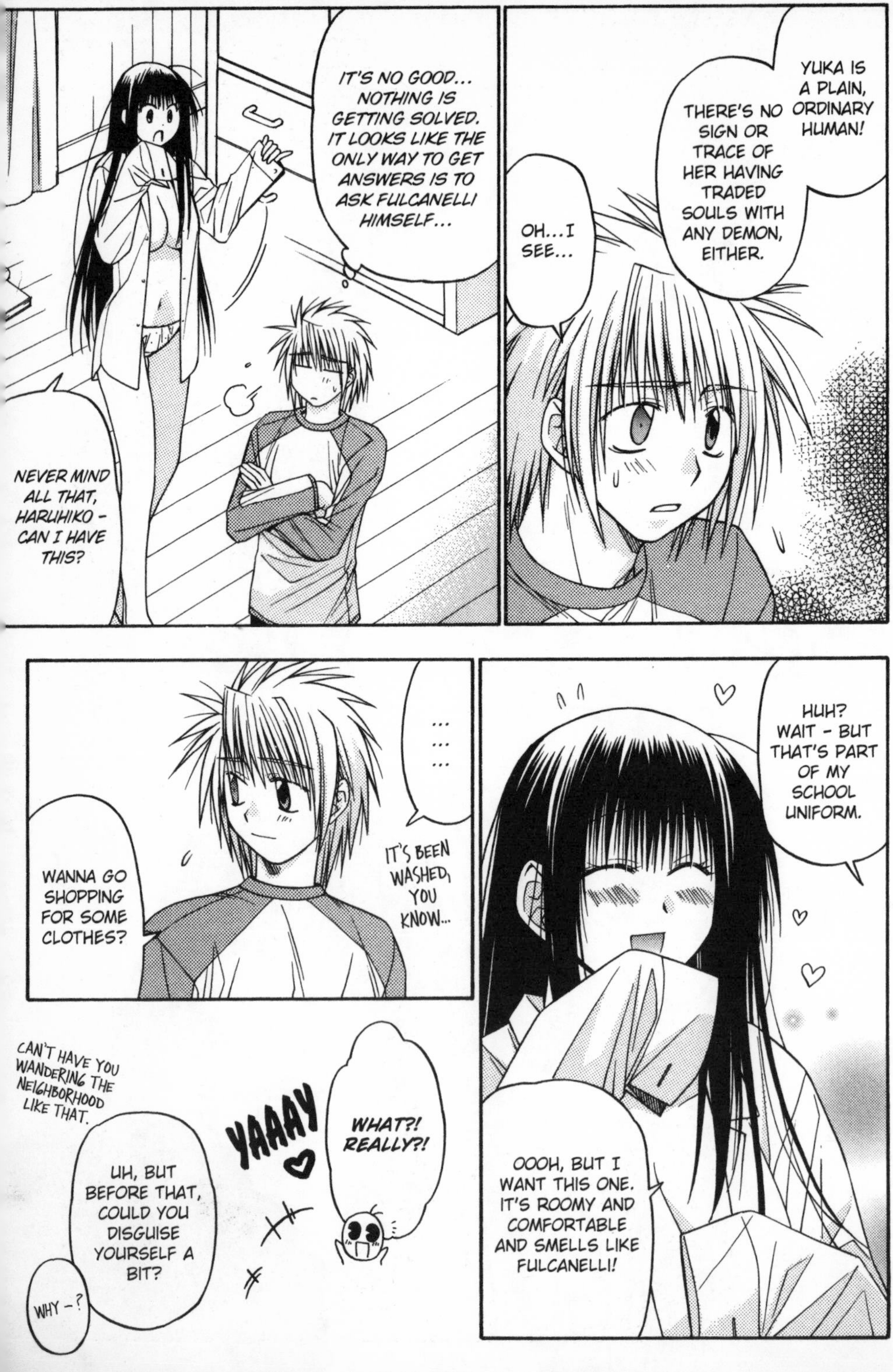
YUKA IS A PLAIN, ORDINARY HUMAN!
THERE'S NO SIGN OR TRACE OF HER HAVING TRADED SOULS WITH ANY DEMON, EITHER.
OH...I SEE...
IT'S NO GOOD... NOTHING IS GETTING SOLVED. IT LOOKS LIKE THE ONLY WAY TO GET ANSWERS IS TO ASK FULCANELLI HIMSELF...
NEVER MIND ALL THAT, HARUHIKO - CAN I HAVE THIS?
HUH? WAIT - BUT THAT'S PART OF MY SCHOOL UNIFORM.
OOOH, BUT I WANT THIS ONE. IT'S ROOMY AND COMFORTABLE AND SMELLS LIKE FULCANELLI!
... ...
IT'S BEEN WASHED, YOU KNOW...
WANNA GO SHOPPING FOR SOME CLOTHES?
WHAT?! REALLY?!
YAAAY
CAN'T HAVE YOU WANDERING THE NEIGHBORHOOD LIKE THAT.
UH, BUT BEFORE THAT, COULD YOU DISGUISE YOURSELF A BIT?
WHY -?

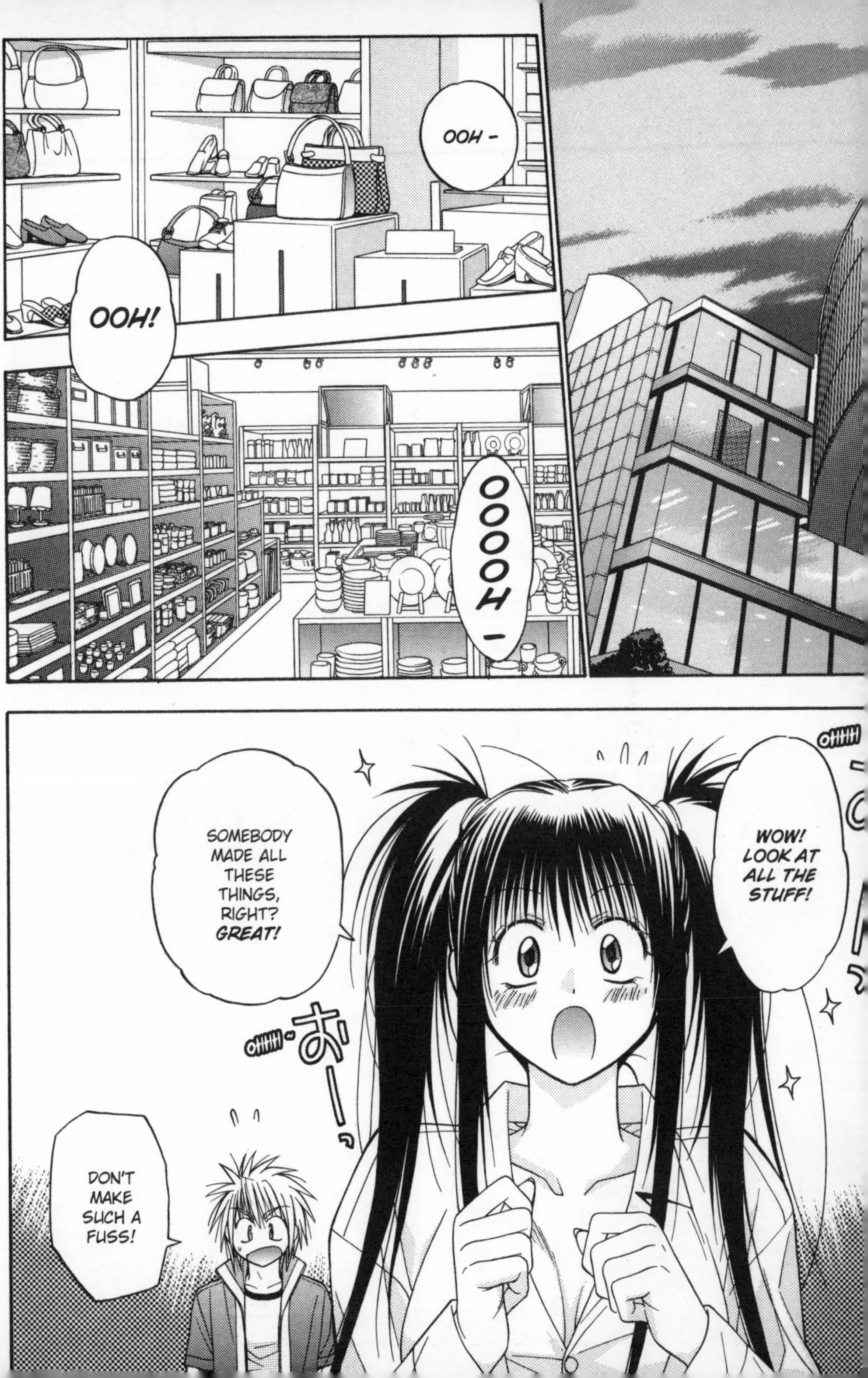
OOH -
OOH!
OOOOH -
WOW! LOOK AT ALL THE STUFF!
SOMEBODY MADE ALL THESE THINGS, RIGHT? GREAT!
DON'T MAKE SUCH A FUSS!

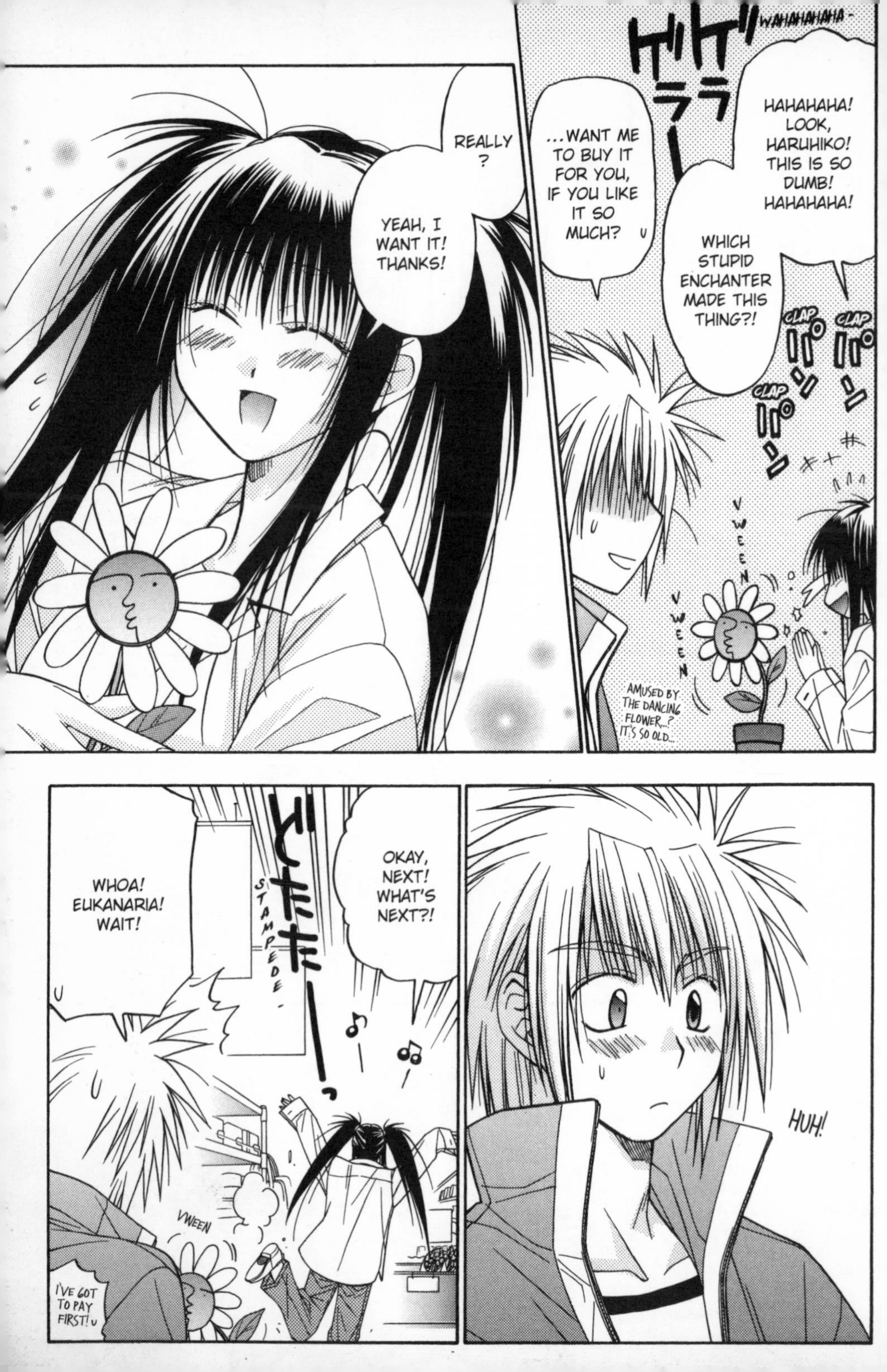
WAHAHAHAHA-
HAHAHAHA! LOOK, HARUHIKO! THIS IS SO DUMB! HAHAHAHA!
WHICH STUPID ENCHANTER MADE THIS THING?!
...WANT ME TO BUY IT FOR YOU, IF YOU LIKE IT SO MUCH?
CLAP
CLAP
CLAP
VWEEN
VWEEN
AMUSED BY THE DANCING FLOWER...? IT'S SO OLD...
REALLY?
YEAH, I WANT IT! THANKS!
HUH!
OKAY, NEXT! WHAT'S NEXT?!
STAMPEDE
WHOA! EUKANARIA! WAIT!
VWEEN
I'VE GOT TO PAY FIRST!

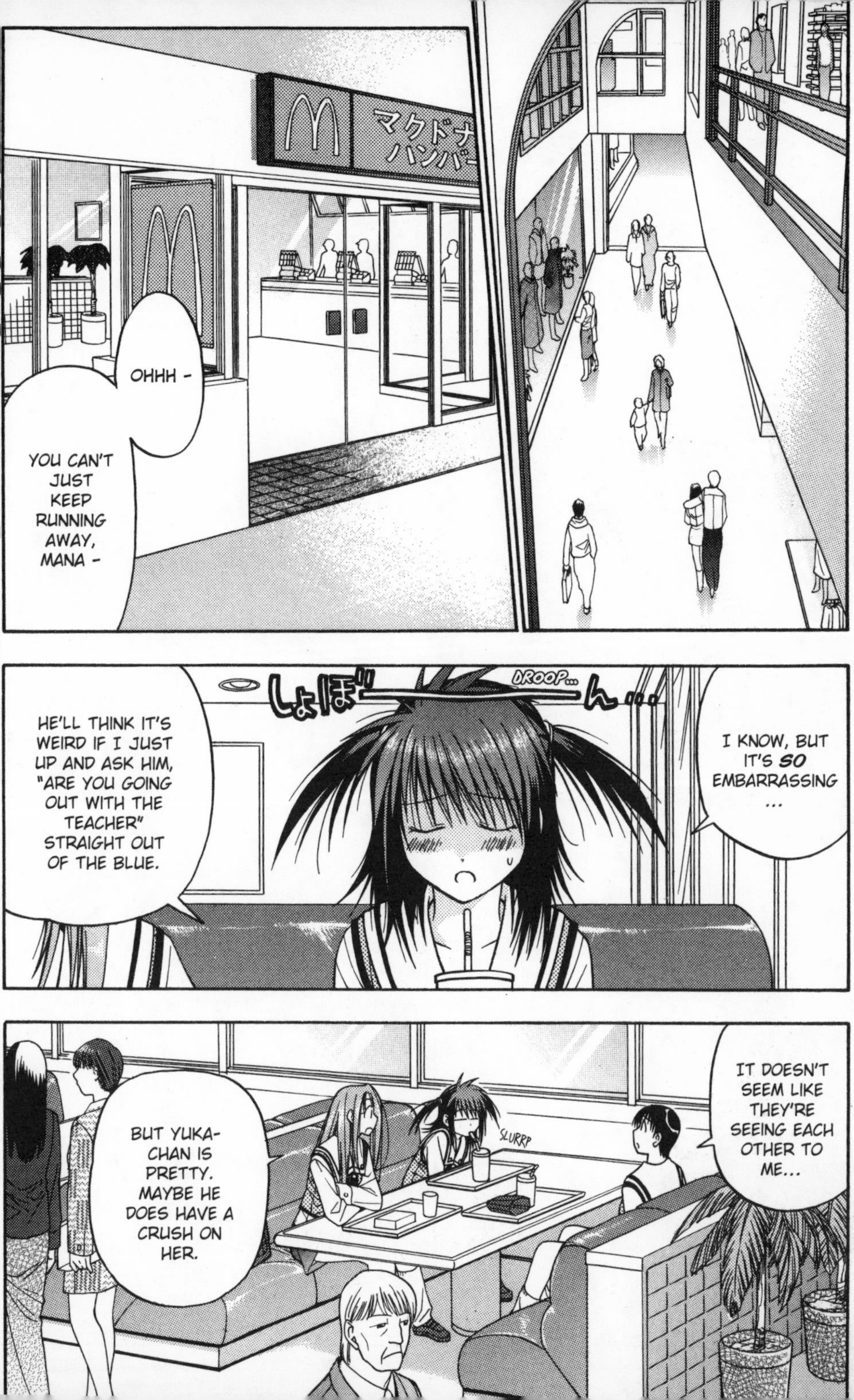
マクドナ
ハンバー
OHHH -
YOU CAN'T JUST KEEP RUNNING AWAY, MANA -
I KNOW, BUT IT'S *SO* EMBARRASSING ...
DROOP...
しょぼーん...
HE'LL THINK IT'S WEIRD IF I JUST UP AND ASK HIM, "ARE YOU GOING OUT WITH THE TEACHER" STRAIGHT OUT OF THE BLUE.
IT DOESN'T SEEM LIKE THEY'RE SEEING EACH OTHER TO ME...
SLURRP
BUT YUKA-CHAN IS PRETTY. MAYBE HE DOES HAVE A CRUSH ON HER.

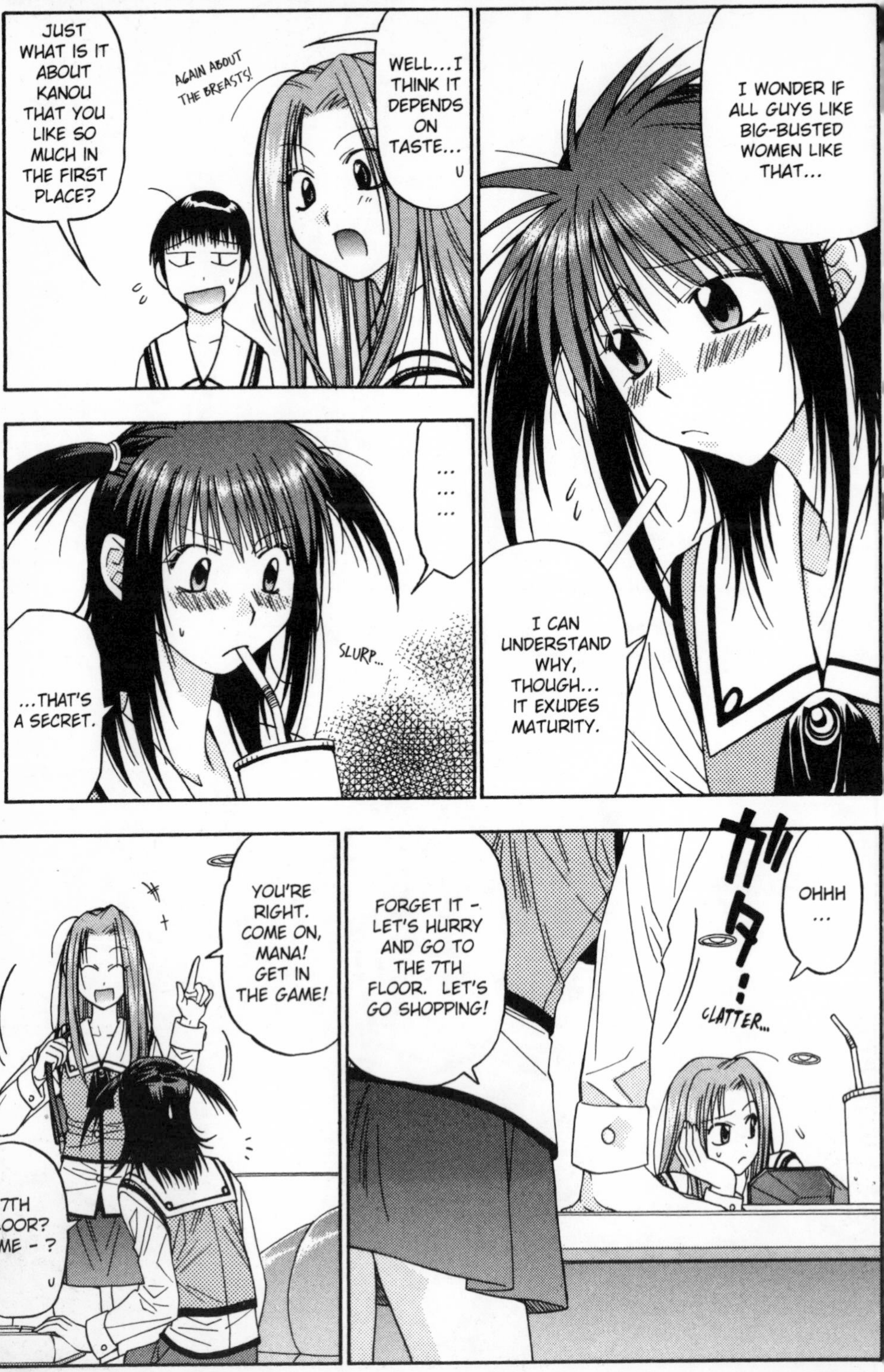
I WONDER IF ALL GUYS LIKE BIG-BUSTED WOMEN LIKE THAT...
I CAN UNDERSTAND WHY, THOUGH... IT EXUDES MATURITY.
WELL...I THINK IT DEPENDS ON TASTE...
AGAIN ABOUT THE BREASTS!
JUST WHAT IS IT ABOUT KANOU THAT YOU LIKE SO MUCH IN THE FIRST PLACE?
... ...
SLURP...
...THAT'S A SECRET.
OHHH ...
ガタ!!
CLATTER...
FORGET IT - LET'S HURRY AND GO TO THE 7TH FLOOR. LET'S GO SHOPPING!
YOU'RE RIGHT. COME ON, MANA! GET IN THE GAME!
7TH FLOOR? GAME - ?

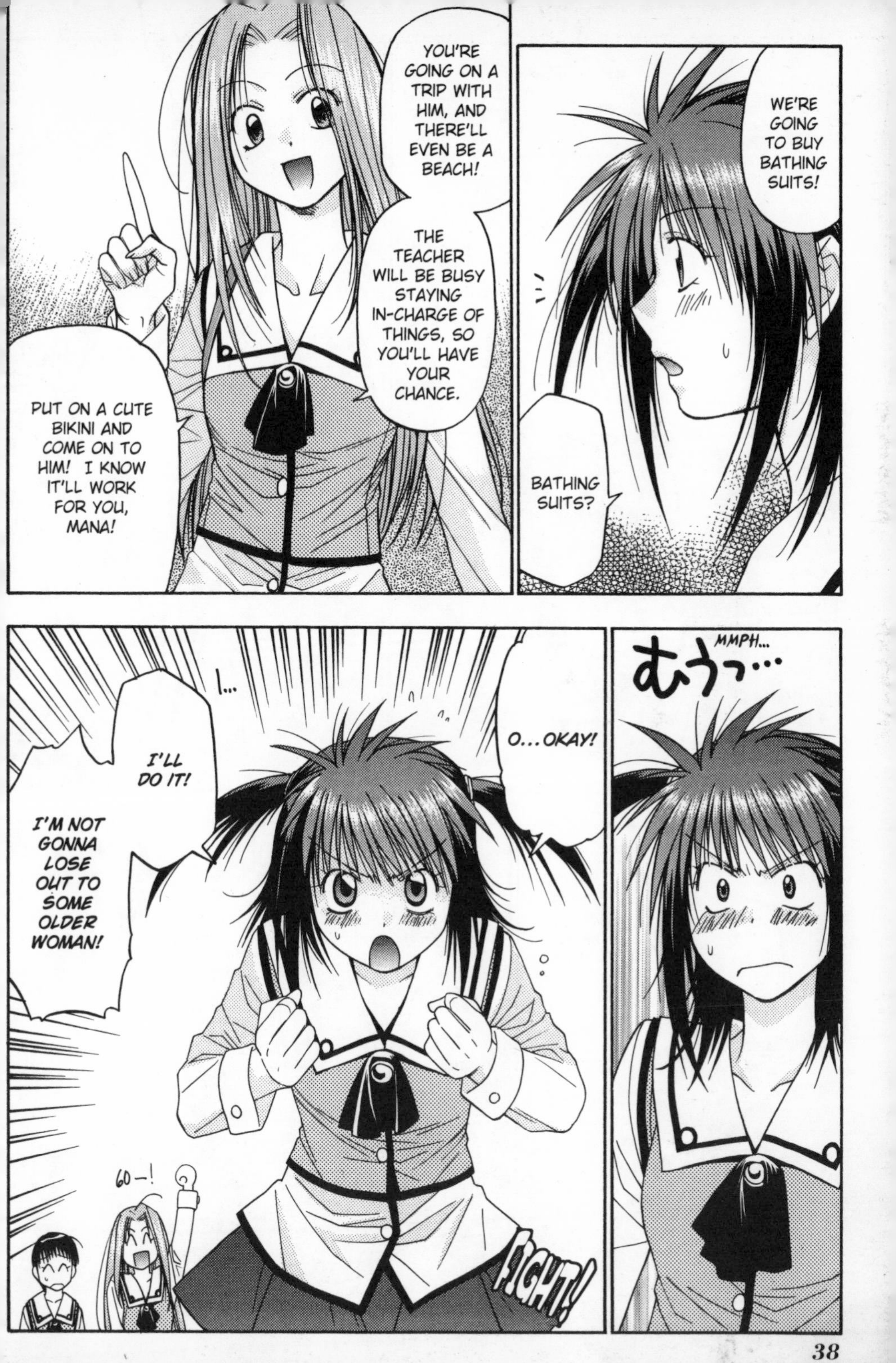
WE'RE GOING TO BUY BATHING SUITS!
BATHING SUITS?
YOU'RE GOING ON A TRIP WITH HIM, AND THERE'LL EVEN BE A BEACH!
THE TEACHER WILL BE BUSY STAYING IN-CHARGE OF THINGS, SO YOU'LL HAVE YOUR CHANCE.
PUT ON A CUTE BIKINI AND COME ON TO HIM! I KNOW IT'LL WORK FOR YOU, MANA!
むぅっ…
MMPH...
O...OKAY!
I...
I'LL DO IT!
I'M NOT GONNA LOSE OUT TO SOME OLDER WOMAN!
GO—!
FIGHT!

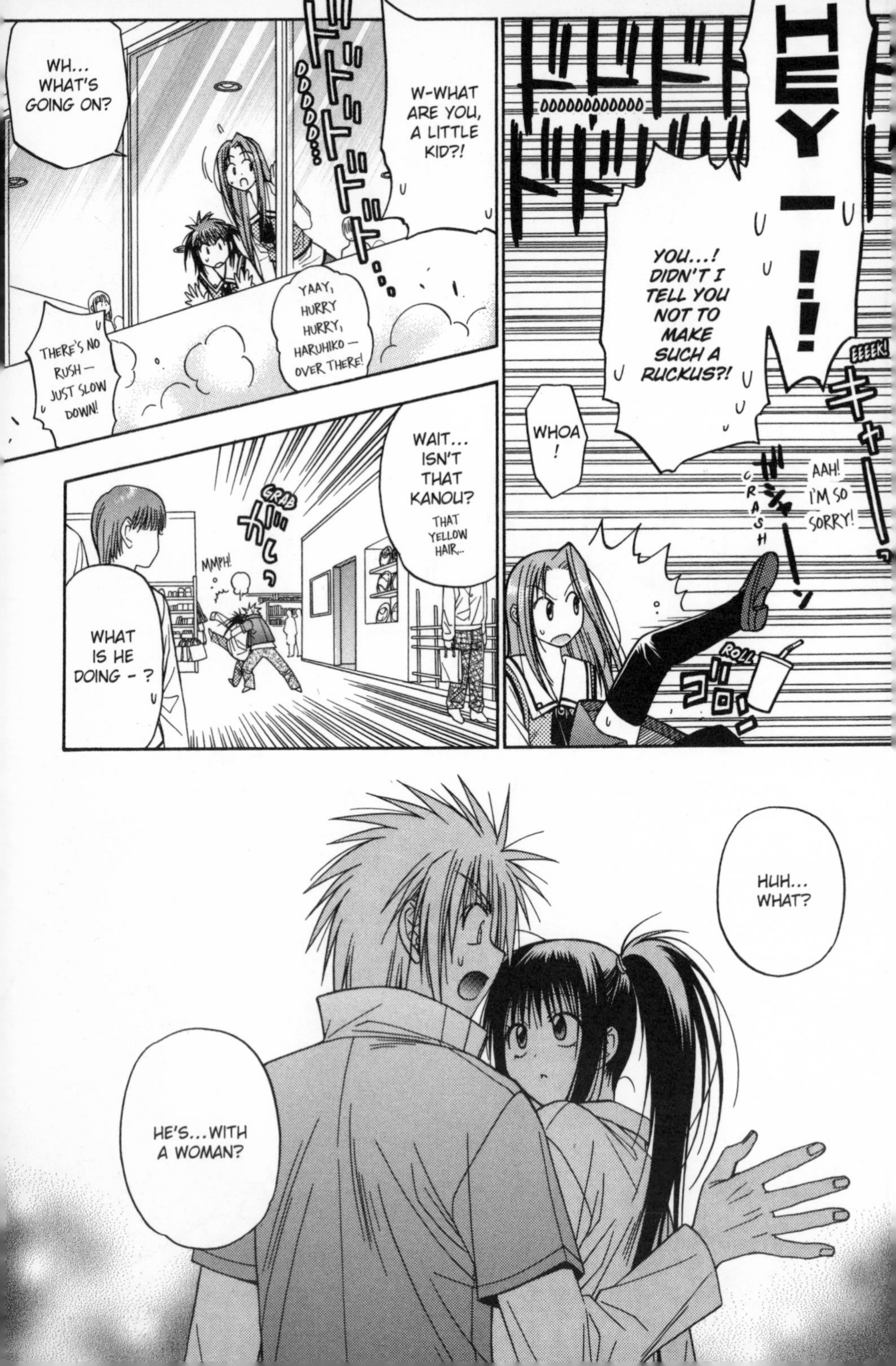
HEY—!!
DDDDDDDDDDDD
YOU...! DIDN'T I TELL YOU NOT TO MAKE SUCH A RUCKUS?!
EEEEK!
WHOA!
AAH! I'M SO SORRY!
CRASH
ROLL
W-WHAT ARE YOU, A LITTLE KID?!
DDDDDD...
WH... WHAT'S GOING ON?
YAAY, HURRY HURRY, HARUHIKO — OVER THERE!
THERE'S NO RUSH — JUST SLOW DOWN!
WAIT... ISN'T THAT KANOU?
THAT YELLOW HAIR...
GRAB
MMPH!
WHAT IS HE DOING - ?
HUH... WHAT?
HE'S...WITH A WOMAN?

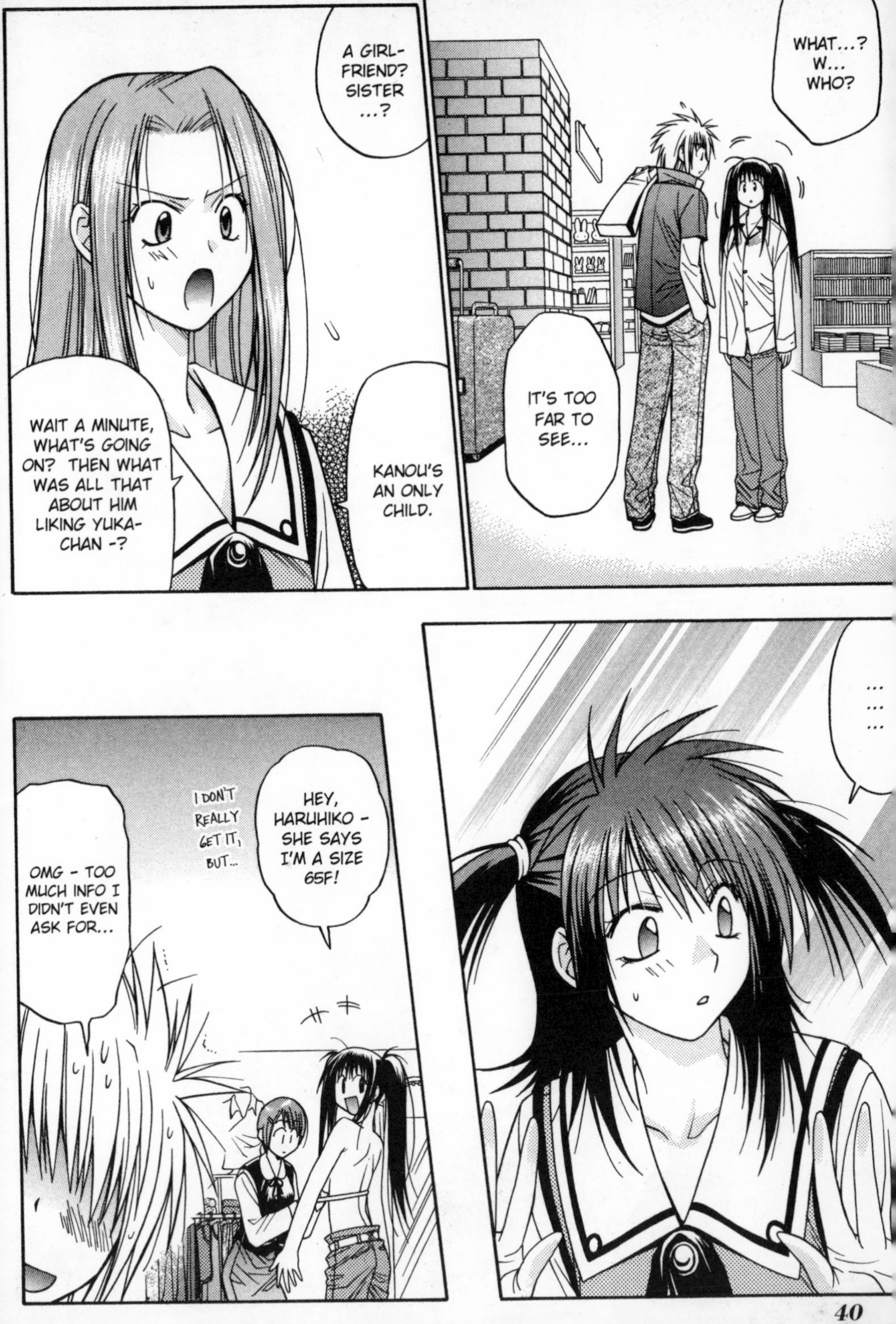
WHAT...? W... WHO?
IT'S TOO FAR TO SEE...
A GIRL-FRIEND? SISTER ...?
KANOU'S AN ONLY CHILD.
WAIT A MINUTE, WHAT'S GOING ON? THEN WHAT WAS ALL THAT ABOUT HIM LIKING YUKA-CHAN -?
... ...
HEY, HARUHIKO - SHE SAYS I'M A SIZE 65F!
I DON'T REALLY GET IT, BUT...
OMG - TOO MUCH INFO I DIDN'T EVEN ASK FOR...

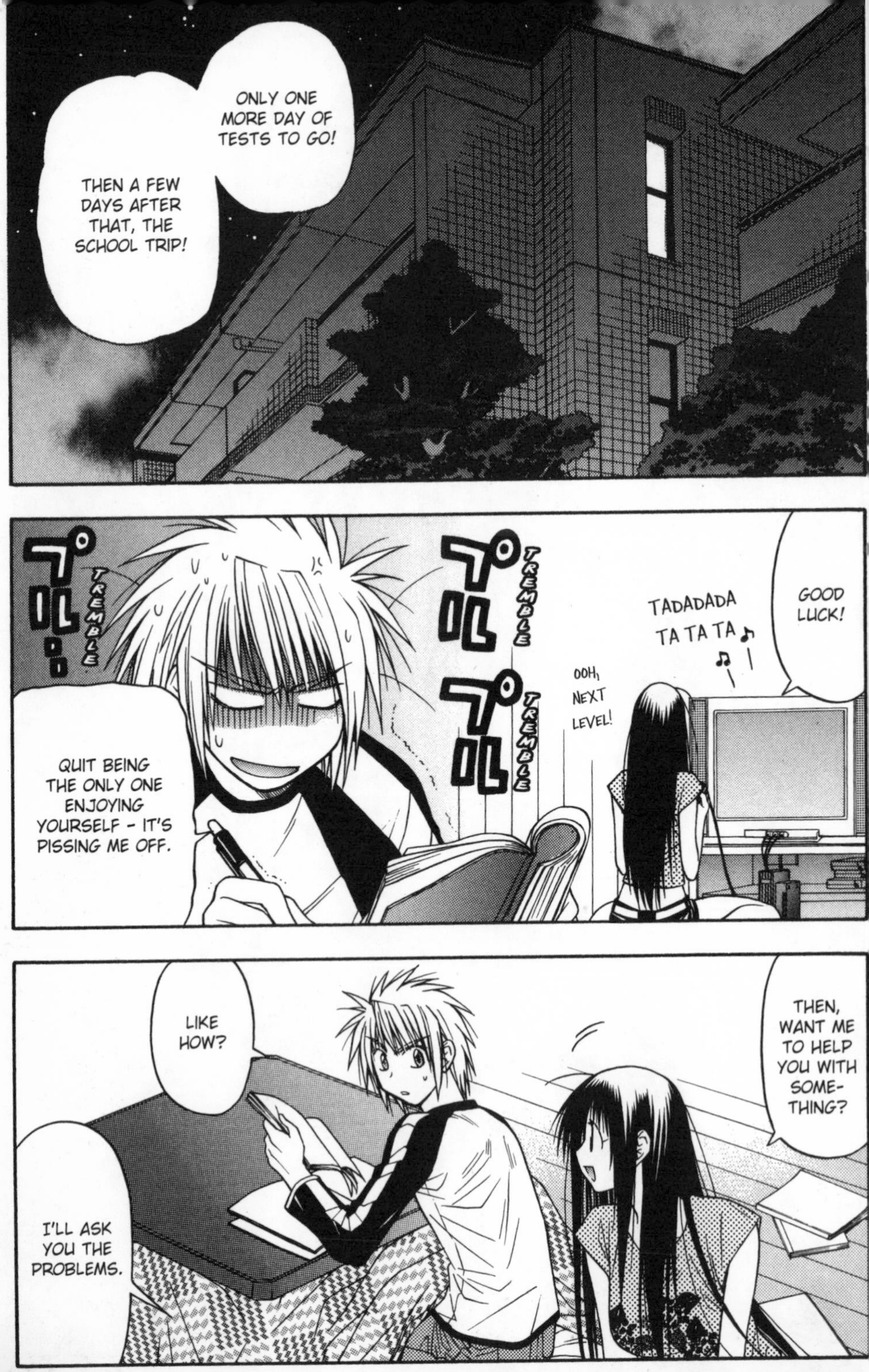
ONLY ONE MORE DAY OF TESTS TO GO!
THEN A FEW DAYS AFTER THAT, THE SCHOOL TRIP!
GOOD LUCK!
TADADADA TA TA TA ♪ ♪
OOH, NEXT LEVEL!
TREMBLE
TREMBLE
TREMBLE
QUIT BEING THE ONLY ONE ENJOYING YOURSELF - IT'S PISSING ME OFF.
THEN, WANT ME TO HELP YOU WITH SOME-THING?
LIKE HOW?
I'LL ASK YOU THE PROBLEMS.

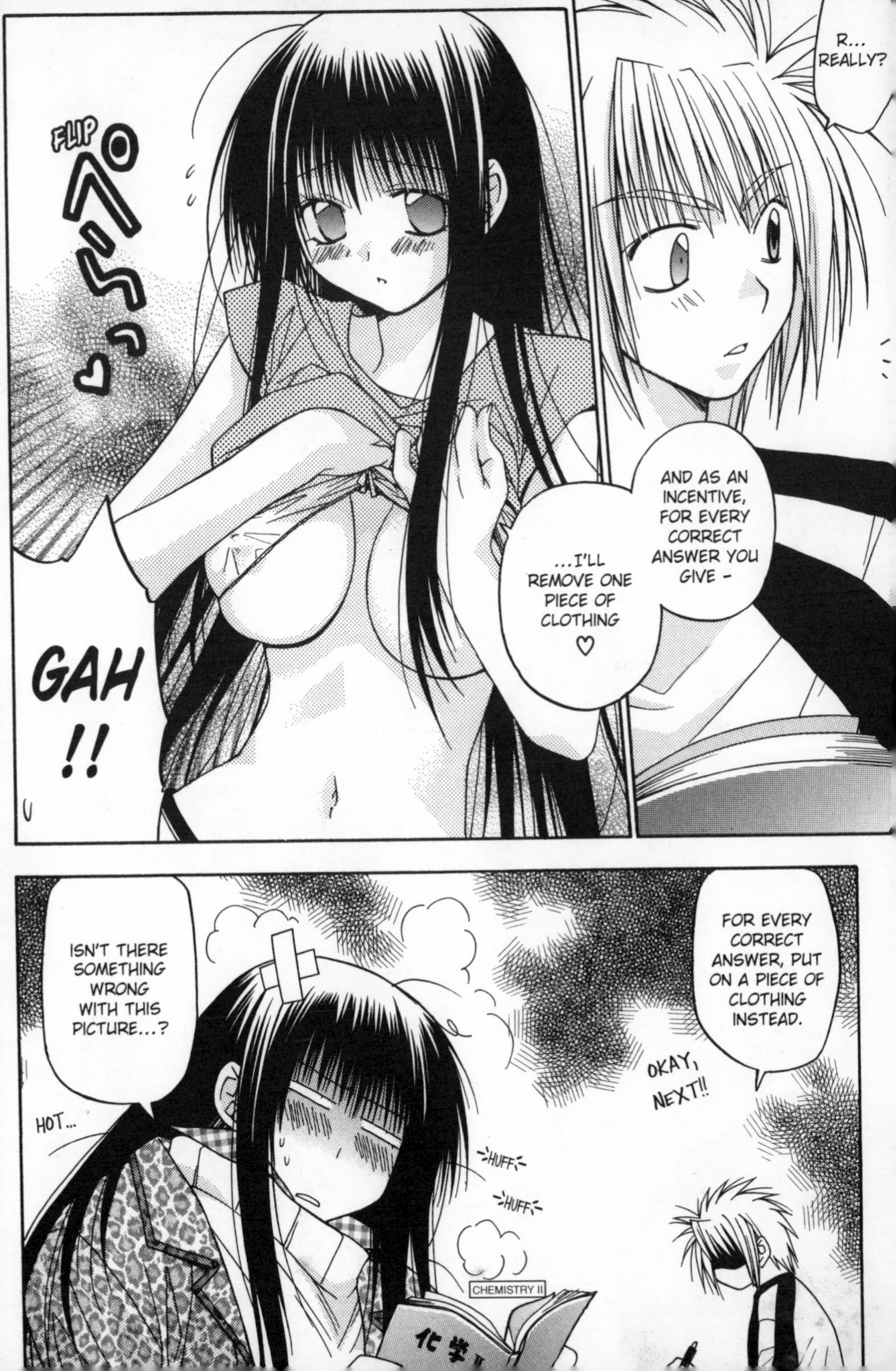
R... REALLY?
AND AS AN INCENTIVE, FOR EVERY CORRECT ANSWER YOU GIVE –
...I'LL REMOVE ONE PIECE OF CLOTHING ♡
FLIP
GAH!!
FOR EVERY CORRECT ANSWER, PUT ON A PIECE OF CLOTHING INSTEAD.
OKAY, NEXT!!
ISN'T THERE SOMETHING WRONG WITH THIS PICTURE...?
HOT...
HUFF
HUFF
CHEMISTRY II

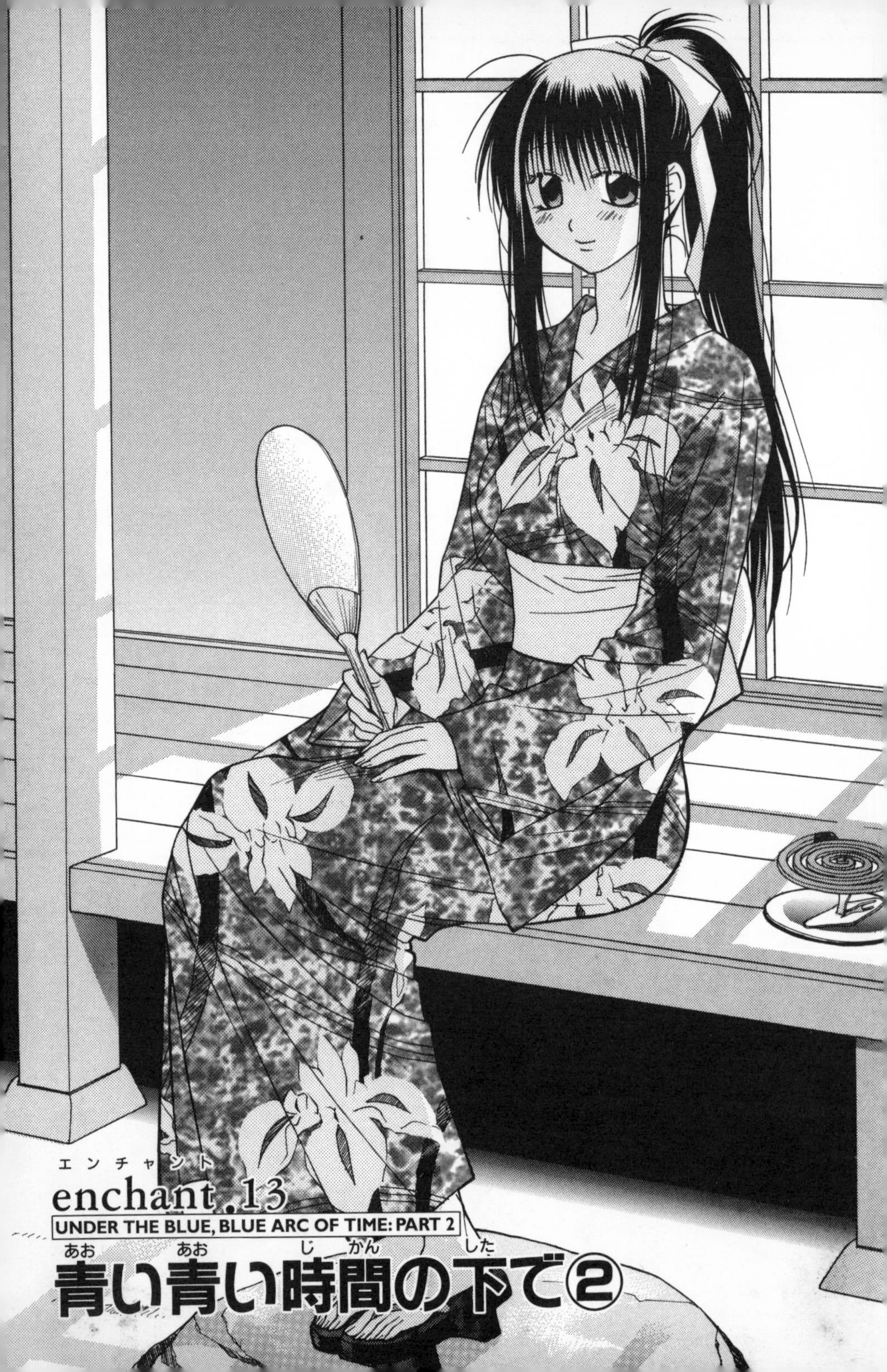
エンチャント
enchant.13
UNDER THE BLUE, BLUE ARC OF TIME: PART 2
あお あお じかん した
青い青い時間の下で②

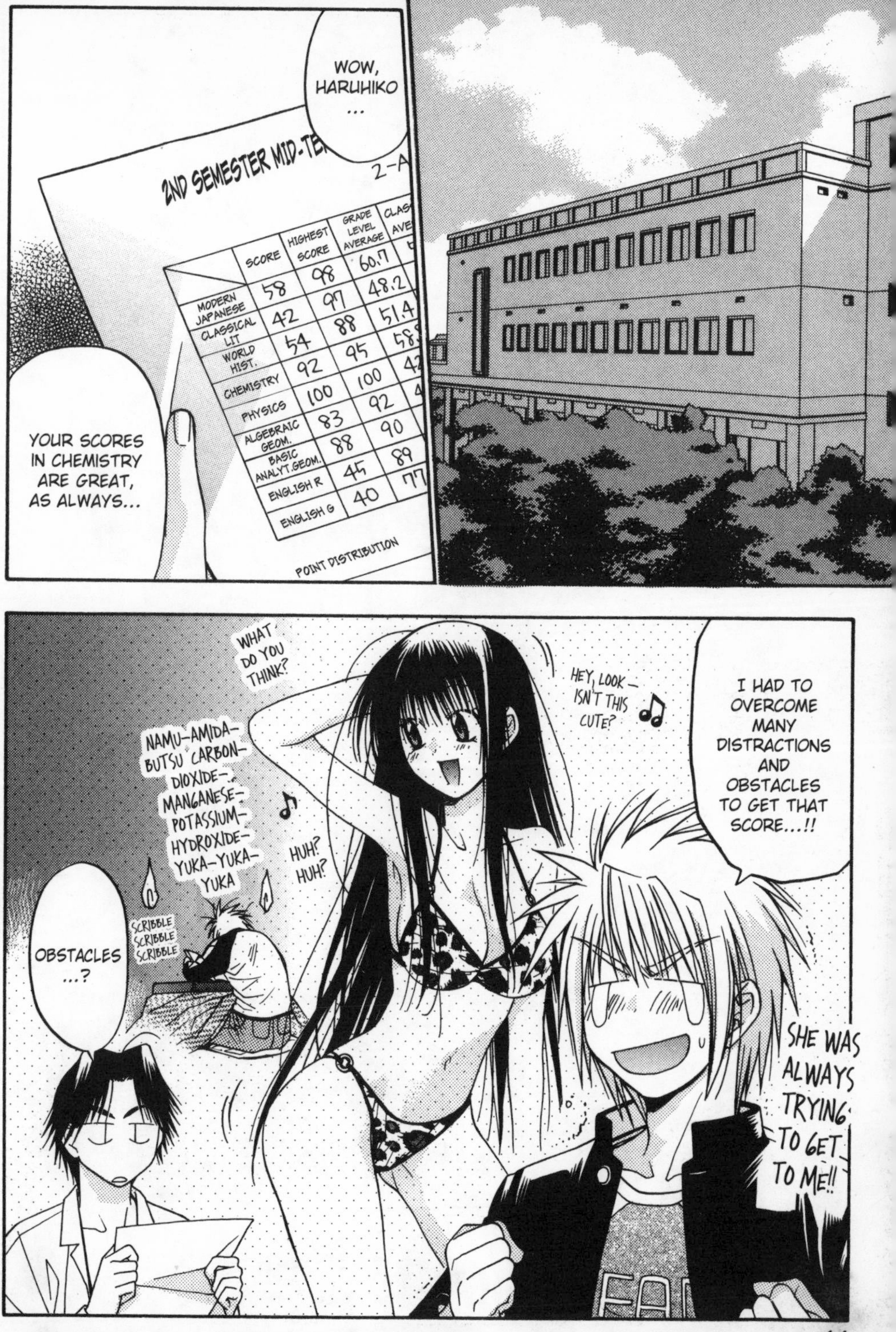
WOW, HARUHIKO ...
2ND SEMESTER MID-TE
2-A
SCORE
HIGHEST SCORE
GRADE LEVEL AVERAGE
MODERN JAPANESE 58 98 60.7
CLASSICAL LIT 42 97 48.2
WORLD HIST. 54 88 51.4
CHEMISTRY 92 95
PHYSICS 100 100
ALGEBRAIC GEOM. 83 92
BASIC ANALYT. GEOM. 88 90
ENGLISH R 45 89
ENGLISH G 40
POINT DISTRIBUTION
YOUR SCORES IN CHEMISTRY ARE GREAT, AS ALWAYS...
I HAD TO OVERCOME MANY DISTRACTIONS AND OBSTACLES TO GET THAT SCORE...!!
SHE WAS ALWAYS TRYING TO GET TO ME!!
HEY, LOOK- ISN'T THIS CUTE?
WHAT DO YOU THINK?
NAMU-AMIDA-BUTSU CARBON-DIOXIDE-MANGANESE-POTASSIUM-HYDROXIDE-YUKA-YUKA-YUKA
HUH? HUH?
SCRIBBLE SCRIBBLE SCRIBBLE
OBSTACLES ...?

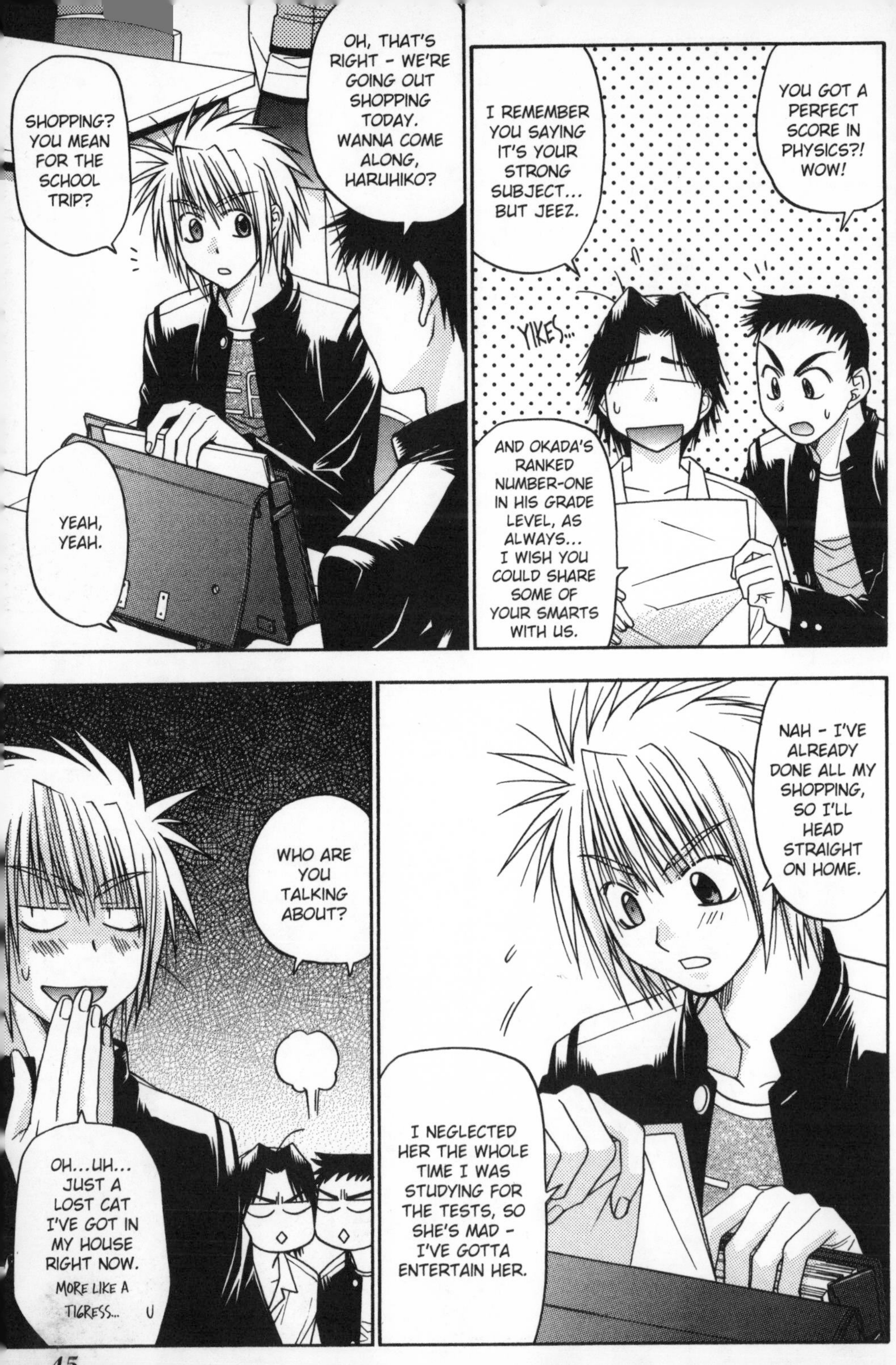
YOU GOT A PERFECT SCORE IN PHYSICS?! WOW!
I REMEMBER YOU SAYING IT'S YOUR STRONG SUBJECT... BUT JEEZ.
YIKES...
AND OKADA'S RANKED NUMBER-ONE IN HIS GRADE LEVEL, AS ALWAYS... I WISH YOU COULD SHARE SOME OF YOUR SMARTS WITH US.
OH, THAT'S RIGHT - WE'RE GOING OUT SHOPPING TODAY. WANNA COME ALONG, HARUHIKO?
SHOPPING? YOU MEAN FOR THE SCHOOL TRIP?
YEAH, YEAH.
NAH - I'VE ALREADY DONE ALL MY SHOPPING, SO I'LL HEAD STRAIGHT ON HOME.
I NEGLECTED HER THE WHOLE TIME I WAS STUDYING FOR THE TESTS, SO SHE'S MAD - I'VE GOTTA ENTERTAIN HER.
WHO ARE YOU TALKING ABOUT?
OH...UH... JUST A LOST CAT I'VE GOT IN MY HOUSE RIGHT NOW.
MORE LIKE A TIGRESS...

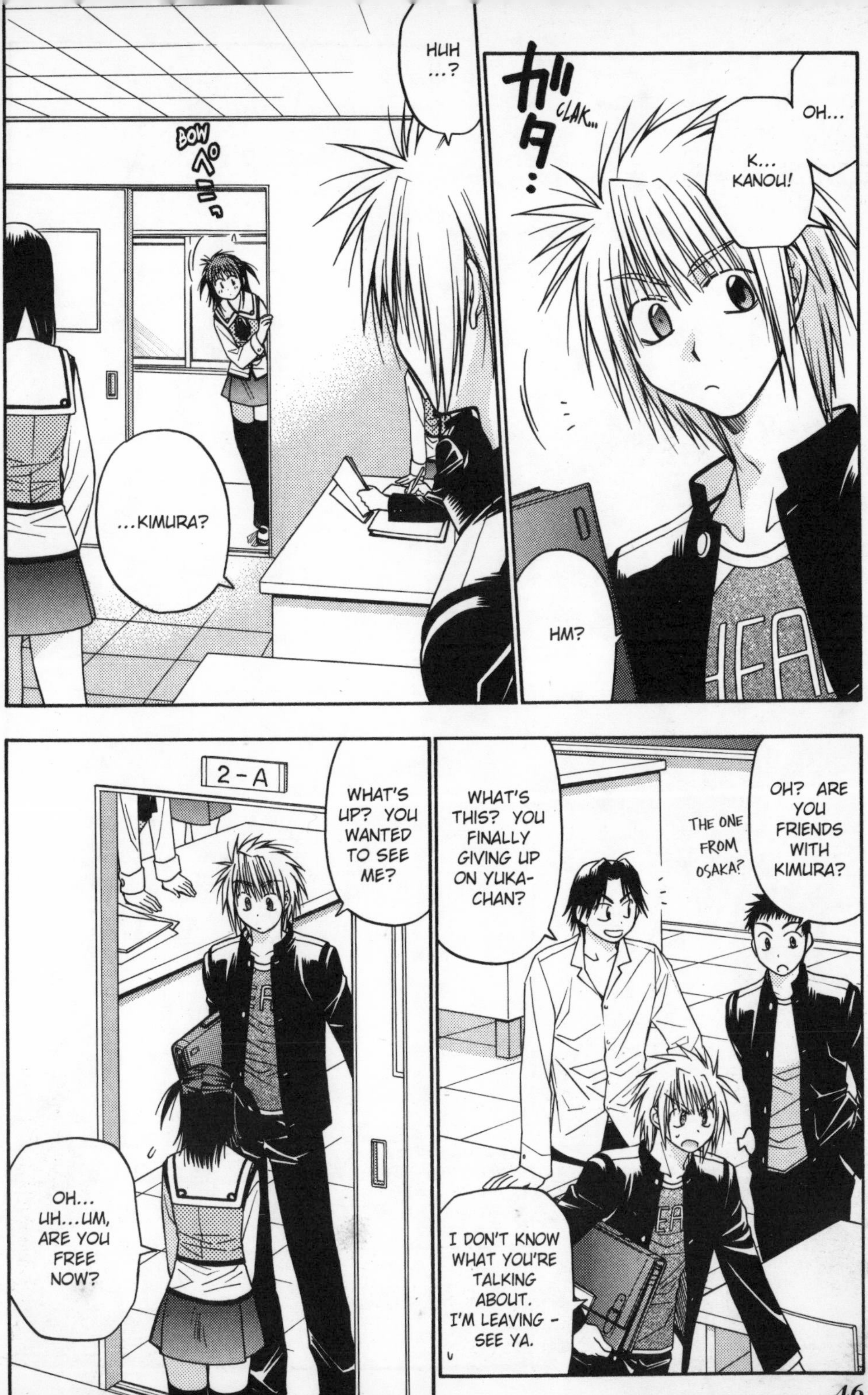
OH...
K... KANOU!
ガタ CLAK...
HM?
HUH ...?
BOW ぺこっ
...KIMURA?
OH? ARE YOU FRIENDS WITH KIMURA?
THE ONE FROM OSAKA?
WHAT'S THIS? YOU FINALLY GIVING UP ON YUKA-CHAN?
I DON'T KNOW WHAT YOU'RE TALKING ABOUT. I'M LEAVING - SEE YA.
2-A
WHAT'S UP? YOU WANTED TO SEE ME?
OH... UH...UM, ARE YOU FREE NOW?

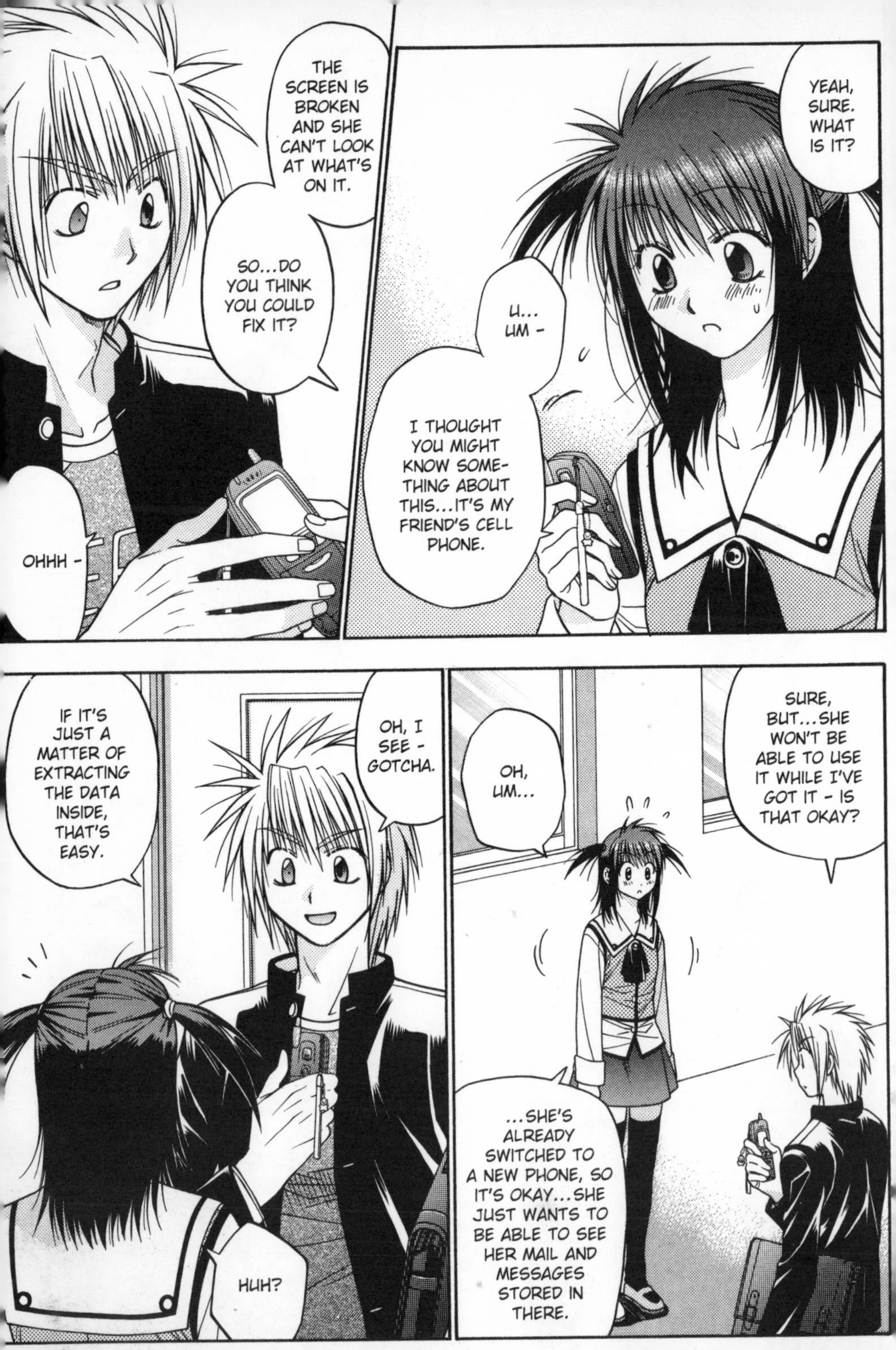
YEAH, SURE. WHAT IS IT?
U... UM -
I THOUGHT YOU MIGHT KNOW SOME-THING ABOUT THIS...IT'S MY FRIEND'S CELL PHONE.
THE SCREEN IS BROKEN AND SHE CAN'T LOOK AT WHAT'S ON IT.
SO...DO YOU THINK YOU COULD FIX IT?
OHHH -
SURE, BUT...SHE WON'T BE ABLE TO USE IT WHILE I'VE GOT IT - IS THAT OKAY?
OH, UM...
...SHE'S ALREADY SWITCHED TO A NEW PHONE, SO IT'S OKAY...SHE JUST WANTS TO BE ABLE TO SEE HER MAIL AND MESSAGES STORED IN THERE.
OH, I SEE - GOTCHA.
IF IT'S JUST A MATTER OF EXTRACTING THE DATA INSIDE, THAT'S EASY.
HUH?

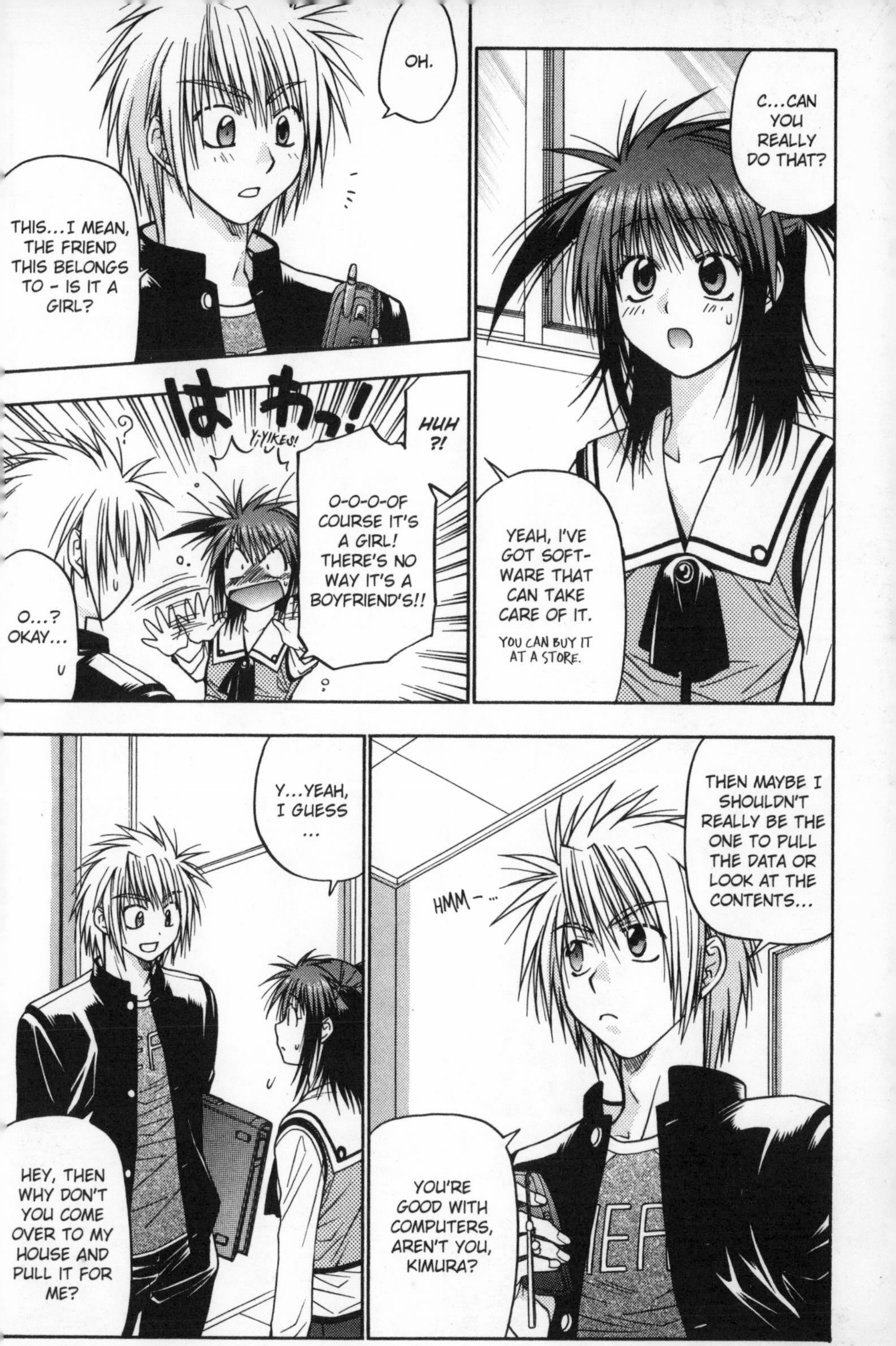
C...CAN YOU REALLY DO THAT?
YEAH, I'VE GOT SOFT-WARE THAT CAN TAKE CARE OF IT.
YOU CAN BUY IT AT A STORE.
OH.
THIS...I MEAN, THE FRIEND THIS BELONGS TO - IS IT A GIRL?
HUH ?!
はわっ!
Y-YIKES!
O-O-O-OF COURSE IT'S A GIRL! THERE'S NO WAY IT'S A BOYFRIEND'S!!
O...? OKAY...
THEN MAYBE I SHOULDN'T REALLY BE THE ONE TO PULL THE DATA OR LOOK AT THE CONTENTS...
HMM-...
YOU'RE GOOD WITH COMPUTERS, AREN'T YOU, KIMURA?
Y...YEAH, I GUESS ...
HEY, THEN WHY DON'T YOU COME OVER TO MY HOUSE AND PULL IT FOR ME?

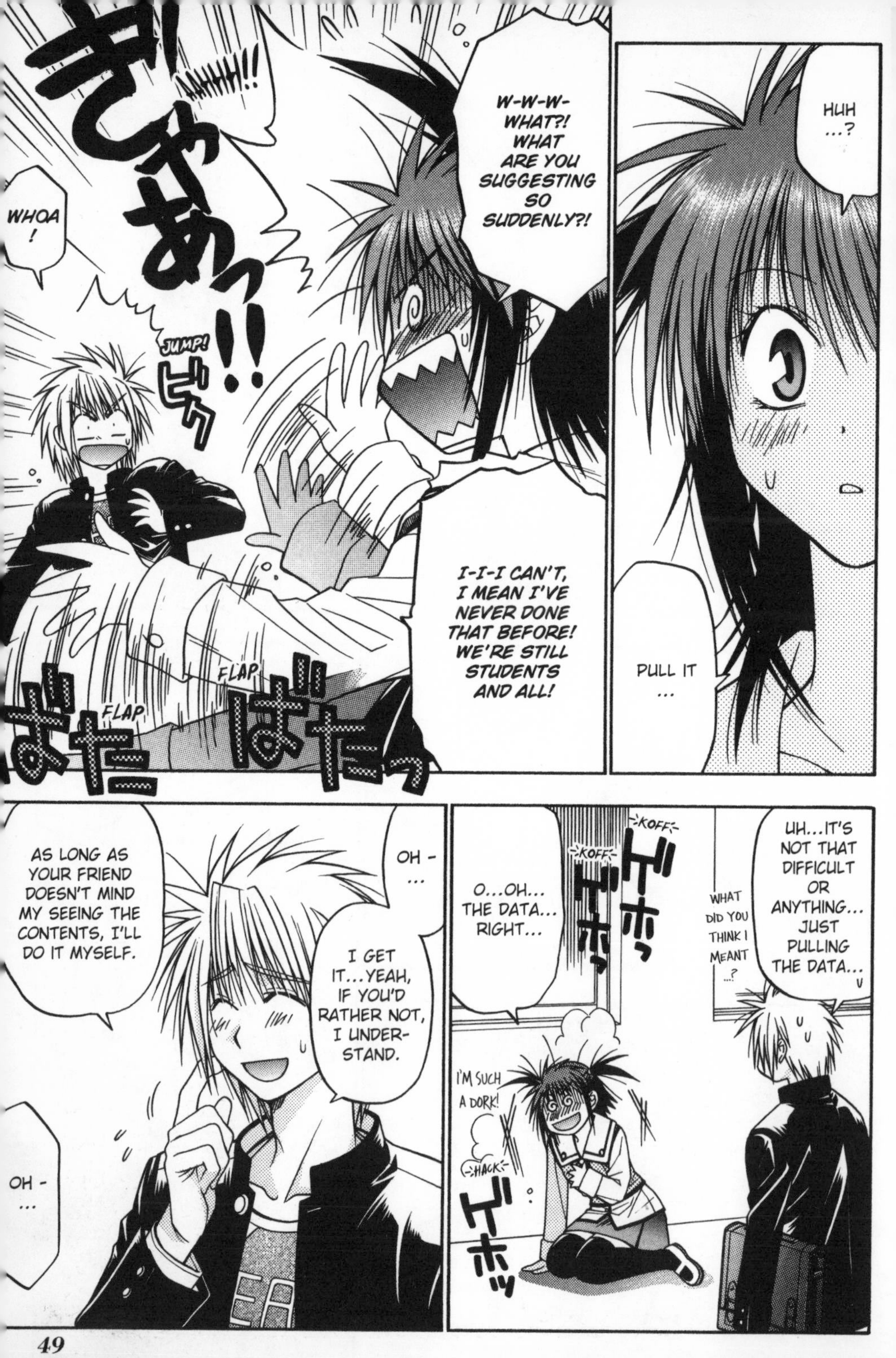

HUH ...?
PULL IT ...
W-W-W-WHAT?! WHAT ARE YOU SUGGESTING SO SUDDENLY?!
I-I-I CAN'T, I MEAN I'VE NEVER DONE THAT BEFORE! WE'RE STILL STUDENTS AND ALL!
きゃあっ!!
AHHHH!!
WHOA!
JUMP!
ビク
FLAP
ばたっ
FLAP
ばたっ
UH...IT'S NOT THAT DIFFICULT OR ANYTHING... JUST PULLING THE DATA...
WHAT DID YOU THINK I MEANT ...?
KOFF
ゲホっ
KOFF
ゲホっ
O...OH... THE DATA... RIGHT...
I'M SUCH A DORK!
HACK
ゲホッ
OH - ...
I GET IT...YEAH, IF YOU'D RATHER NOT, I UNDER-STAND.
AS LONG AS YOUR FRIEND DOESN'T MIND MY SEEING THE CONTENTS, I'LL DO IT MYSELF.
OH - ...

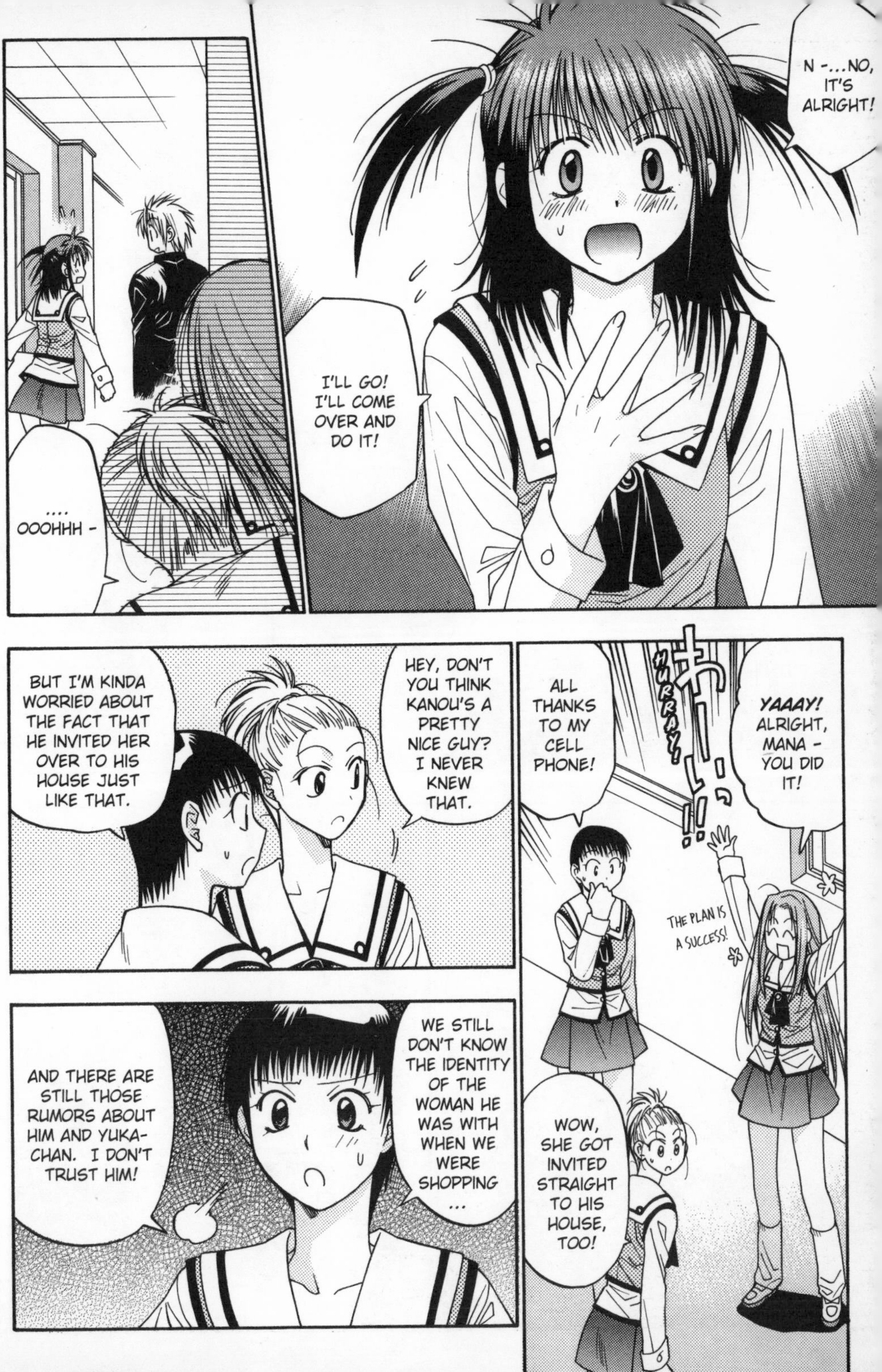
N -...NO, IT'S ALRIGHT!
I'LL GO! I'LL COME OVER AND DO IT!
.... OOOHHH -
YAAAY! ALRIGHT, MANA - YOU DID IT!
HURRAY!
ALL THANKS TO MY CELL PHONE!
THE PLAN IS A SUCCESS!
WOW, SHE GOT INVITED STRAIGHT TO HIS HOUSE, TOO!
HEY, DON'T YOU THINK KANOU'S A PRETTY NICE GUY? I NEVER KNEW THAT.
BUT I'M KINDA WORRIED ABOUT THE FACT THAT HE INVITED HER OVER TO HIS HOUSE JUST LIKE THAT.
WE STILL DON'T KNOW THE IDENTITY OF THE WOMAN HE WAS WITH WHEN WE WERE SHOPPING ...
AND THERE ARE STILL THOSE RUMORS ABOUT HIM AND YUKA-CHAN. I DON'T TRUST HIM!

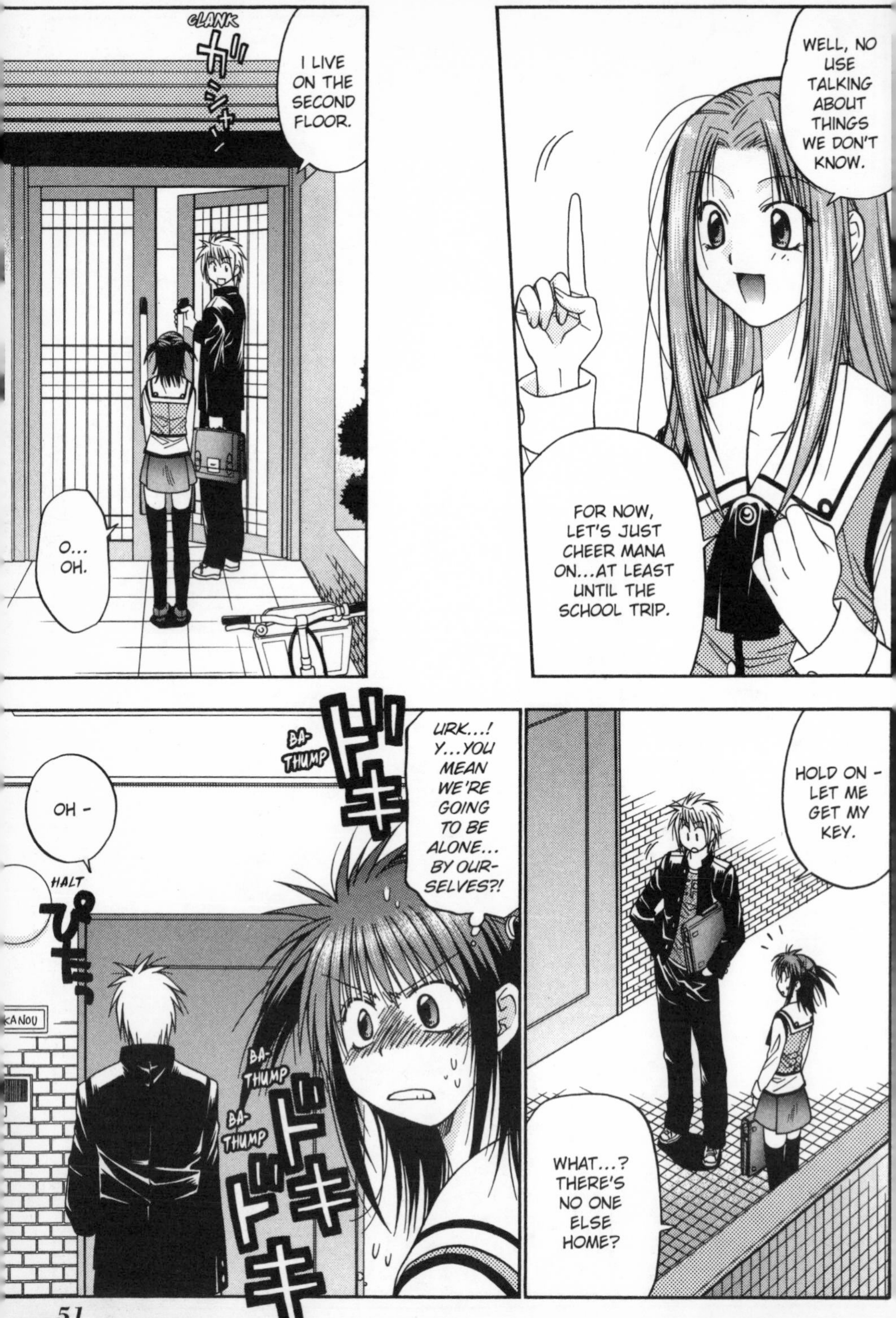
WELL, NO USE TALKING ABOUT THINGS WE DON'T KNOW.
FOR NOW, LET'S JUST CHEER MANA ON...AT LEAST UNTIL THE SCHOOL TRIP.
CLANK
I LIVE ON THE SECOND FLOOR.
O... OH.
HOLD ON - LET ME GET MY KEY.
WHAT...? THERE'S NO ONE ELSE HOME?
BA-THUMP
URK...! Y...YOU MEAN WE'RE GOING TO BE ALONE... BY OUR-SELVES?!
OH -
HALT
KANOU
BA-THUMP
BA-THUMP

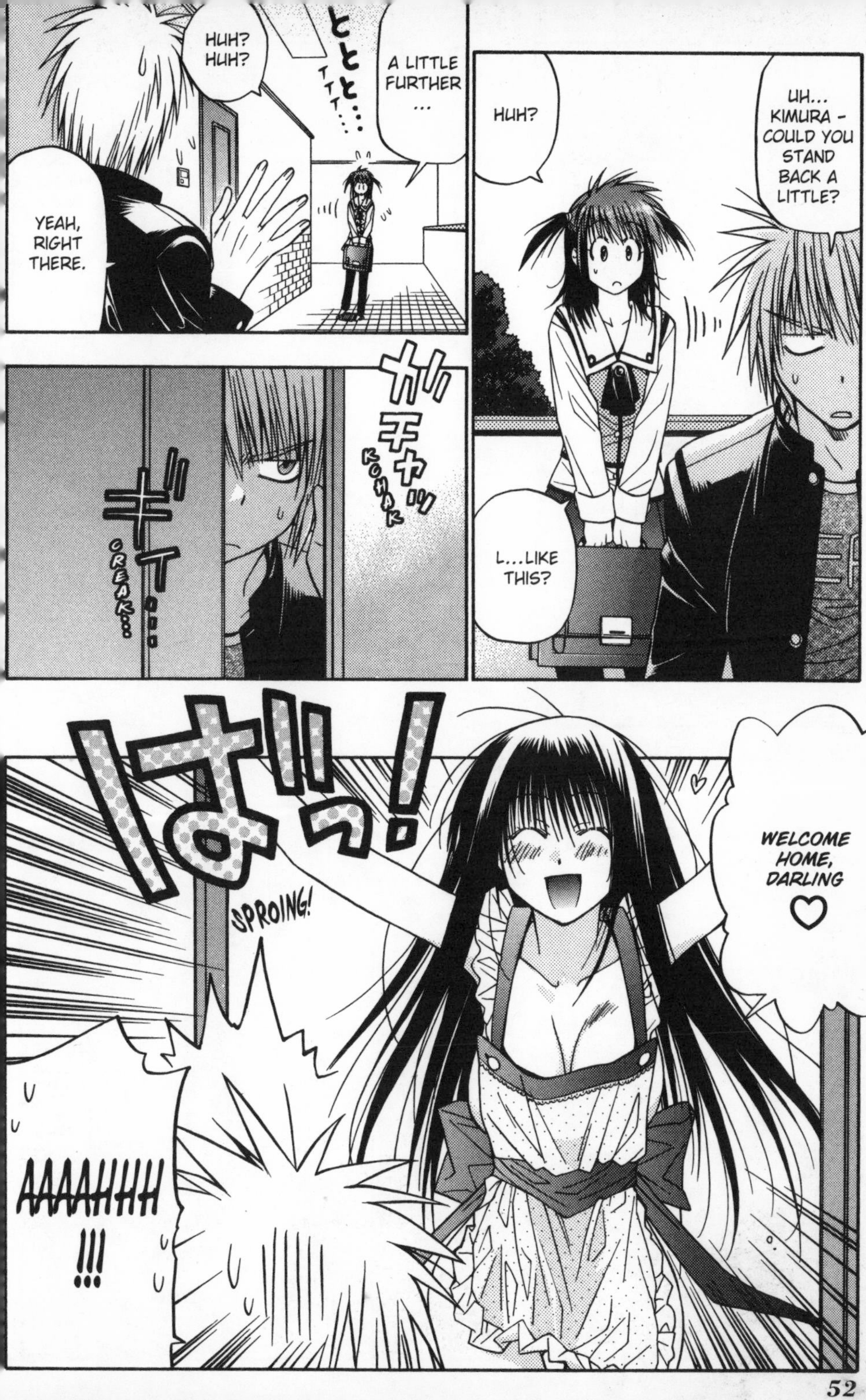
UH... KIMURA - COULD YOU STAND BACK A LITTLE?
HUH?
L...LIKE THIS?
A LITTLE FURTHER ...
とと...
TTT...
HUH? HUH?
YEAH, RIGHT THERE.
ガチャッ
KCHAK
ギイ...
CREAK...
ばっ!
WELCOME HOME, DARLING ♡
SPROING!
AAAAHHH !!!

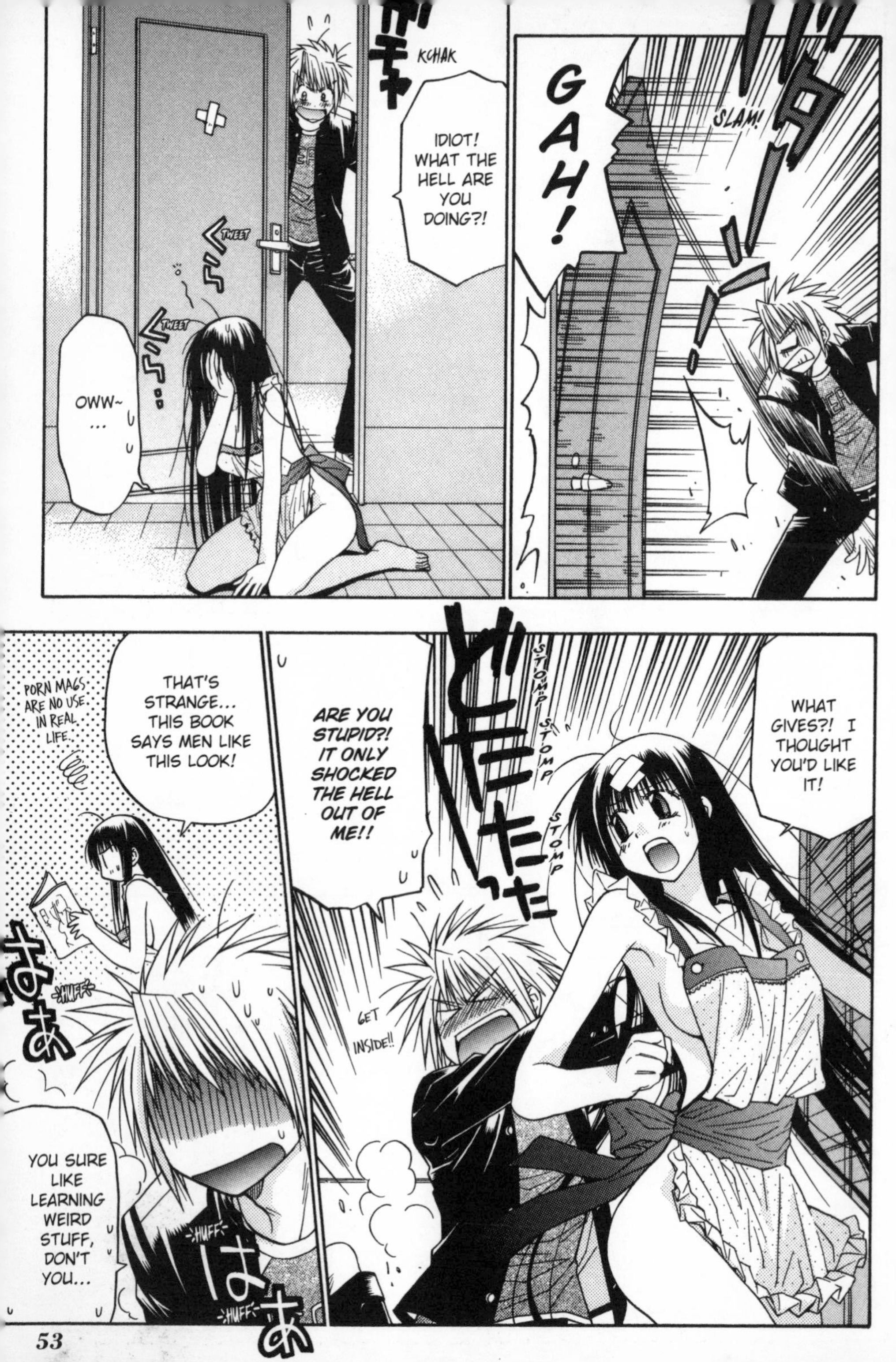
GAH!
SLAM!
KCHAK
IDIOT! WHAT THE HELL ARE YOU DOING?!
TWEET
TWEET
OWW~ ...
WHAT GIVES?! I THOUGHT YOU'D LIKE IT!
STOMP STOMP STOMP
ARE YOU STUPID?! IT ONLY SHOCKED THE HELL OUT OF ME!!
GET INSIDE!!
THAT'S STRANGE... THIS BOOK SAYS MEN LIKE THIS LOOK!
PORN MAGS ARE NO USE IN REAL LIFE.
HUFF
HUFF
HUFF
YOU SURE LIKE LEARNING WEIRD STUFF, DON'T YOU...

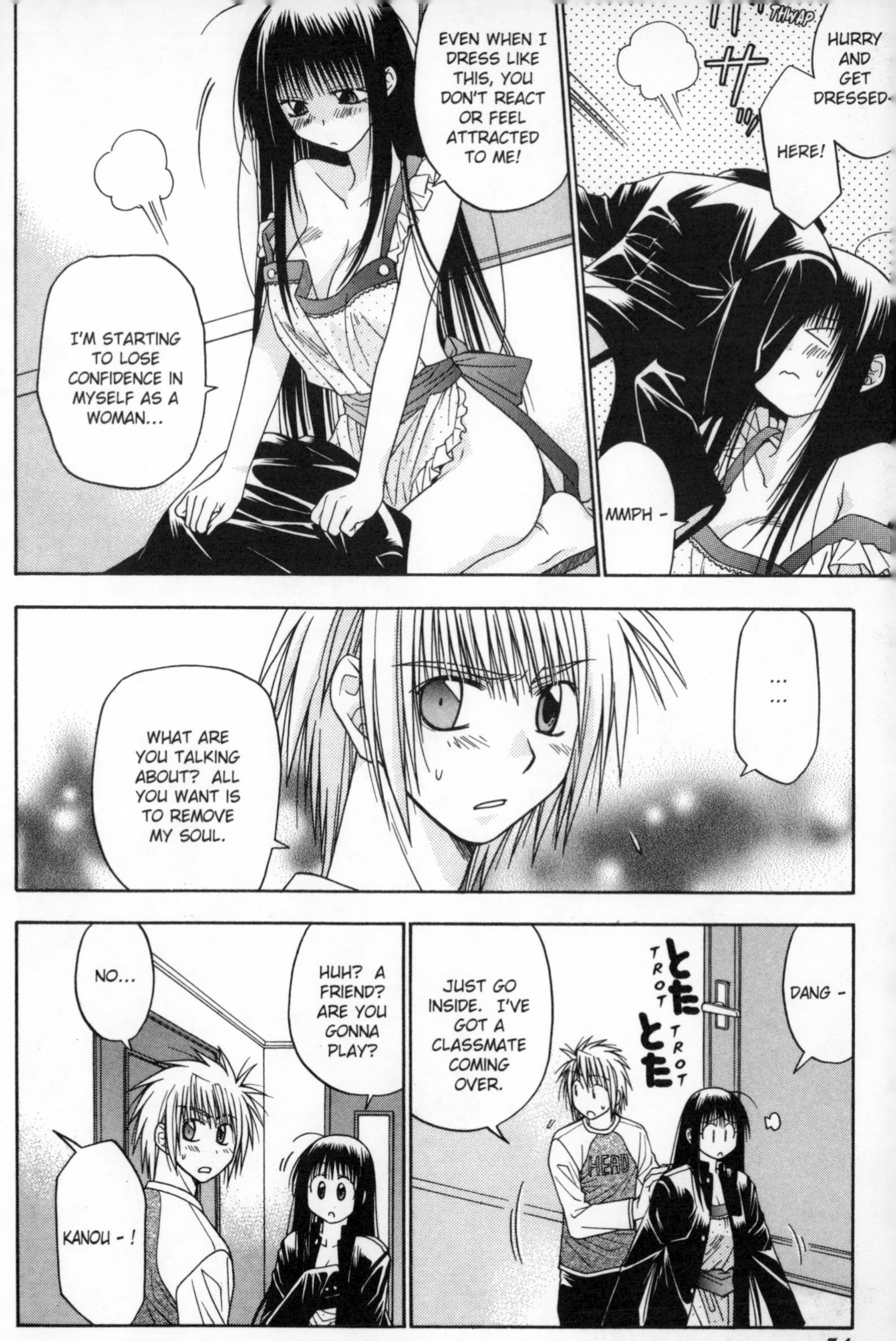
THWAP
HURRY AND GET DRESSED.
HERE!
MMPH -
EVEN WHEN I DRESS LIKE THIS, YOU DON'T REACT OR FEEL ATTRACTED TO ME!
I'M STARTING TO LOSE CONFIDENCE IN MYSELF AS A WOMAN...
… …
WHAT ARE YOU TALKING ABOUT? ALL YOU WANT IS TO REMOVE MY SOUL.
DANG -
とたとた TROT TROT
JUST GO INSIDE. I'VE GOT A CLASSMATE COMING OVER.
HEAD
HUH? A FRIEND? ARE YOU GONNA PLAY?
NO...
KANOU - !

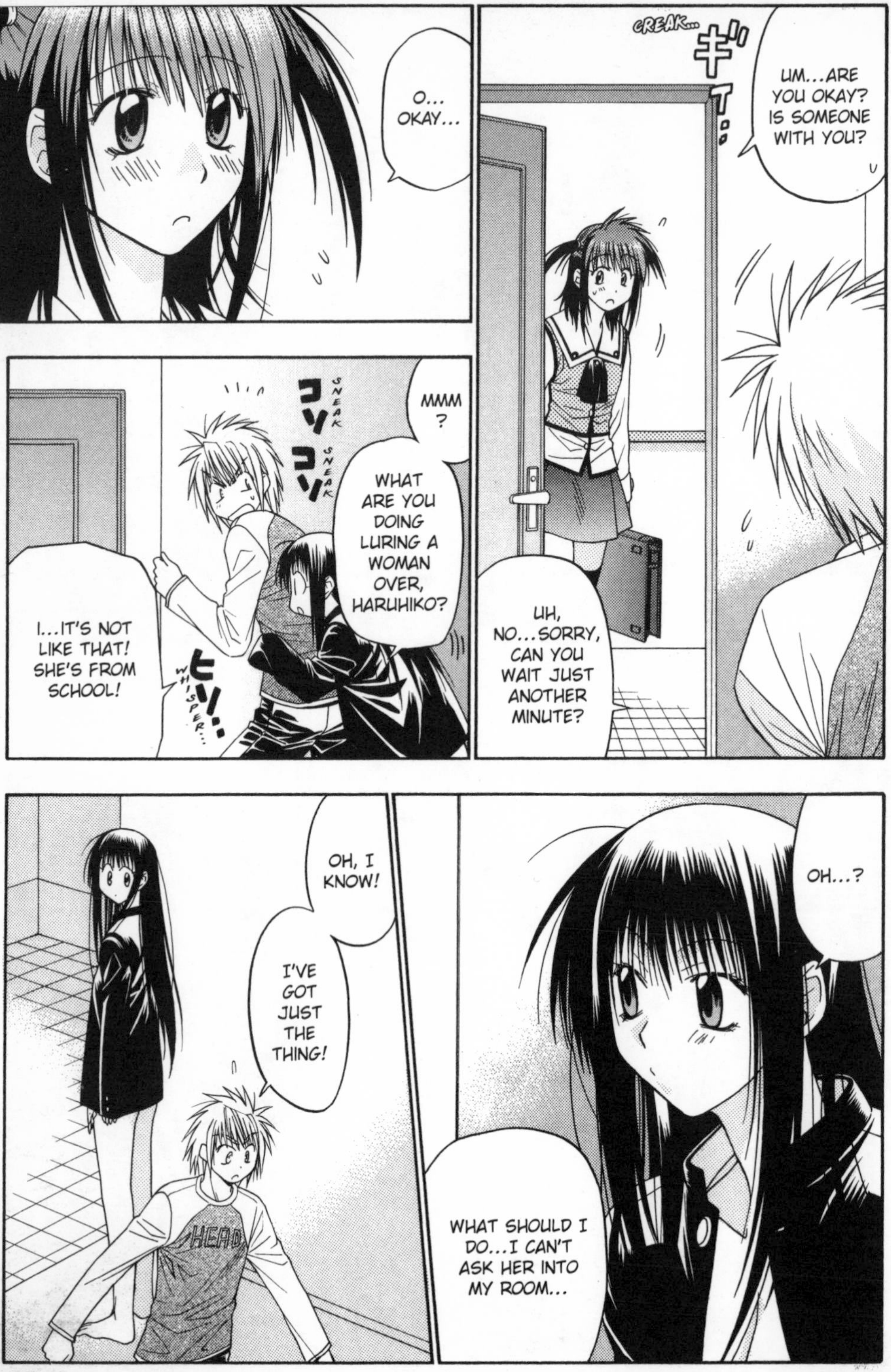
CREAK...
ギイ
UM...ARE YOU OKAY? IS SOMEONE WITH YOU?
UH, NO...SORRY, CAN YOU WAIT JUST ANOTHER MINUTE?
O... OKAY...
MMM ?
コソ SNEAK
コソ SNEAK
WHAT ARE YOU DOING LURING A WOMAN OVER, HARUHIKO?
I...IT'S NOT LIKE THAT! SHE'S FROM SCHOOL!
ヒソ WHISPER...
OH...?
WHAT SHOULD I DO...I CAN'T ASK HER INTO MY ROOM...
OH, I KNOW!
I'VE GOT JUST THE THING!
HEAD

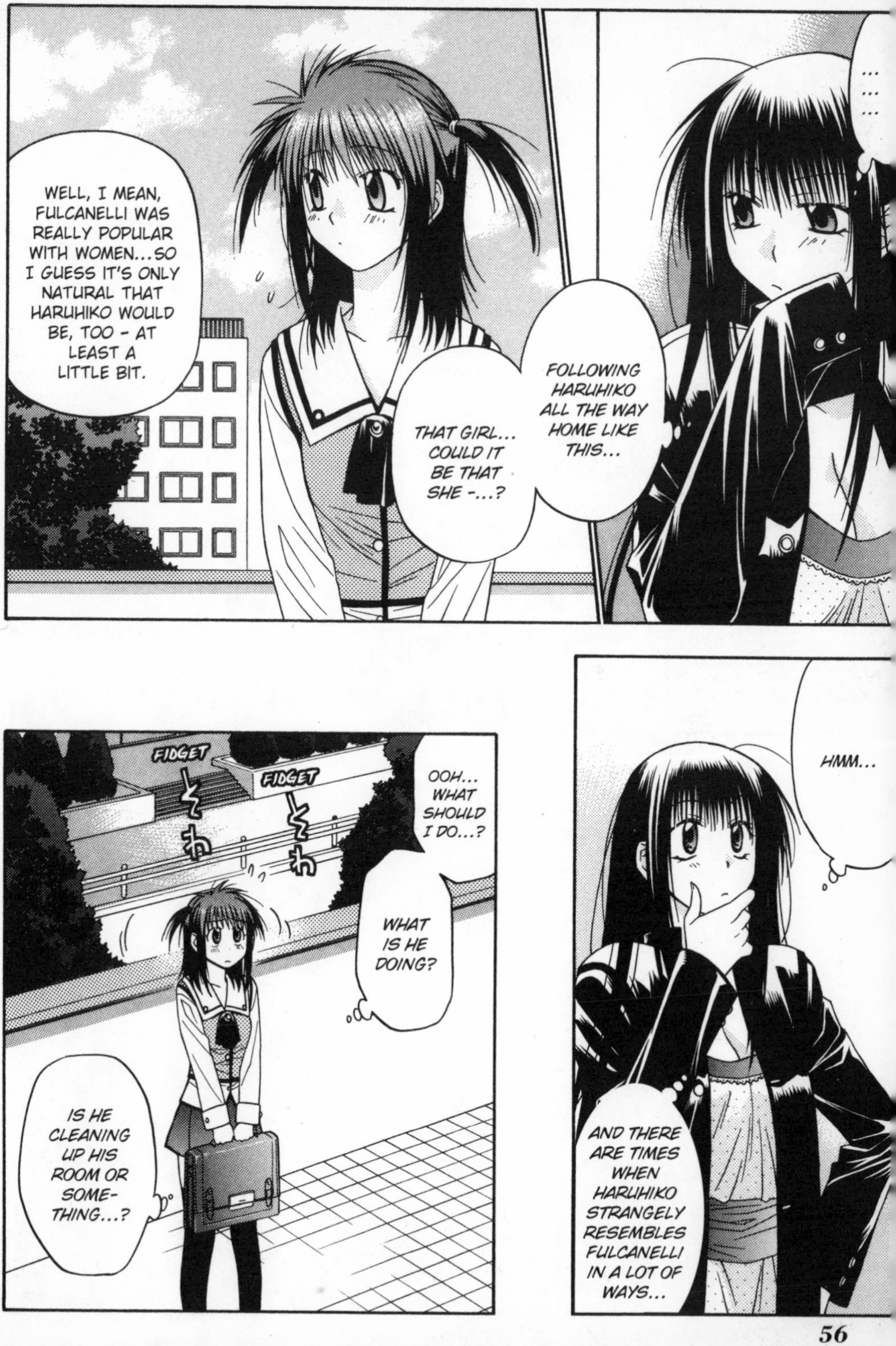
...
...
...
FOLLOWING HARUHIKO ALL THE WAY HOME LIKE THIS...
THAT GIRL... COULD IT BE THAT SHE -...?
WELL, I MEAN, FULCANELLI WAS REALLY POPULAR WITH WOMEN...SO I GUESS IT'S ONLY NATURAL THAT HARUHIKO WOULD BE, TOO - AT LEAST A LITTLE BIT.
HMM...
AND THERE ARE TIMES WHEN HARUHIKO STRANGELY RESEMBLES FULCANELLI IN A LOT OF WAYS...
OOH... WHAT SHOULD I DO...?
FIDGET
FIDGET
WHAT IS HE DOING?
IS HE CLEANING UP HIS ROOM OR SOME-THING...?

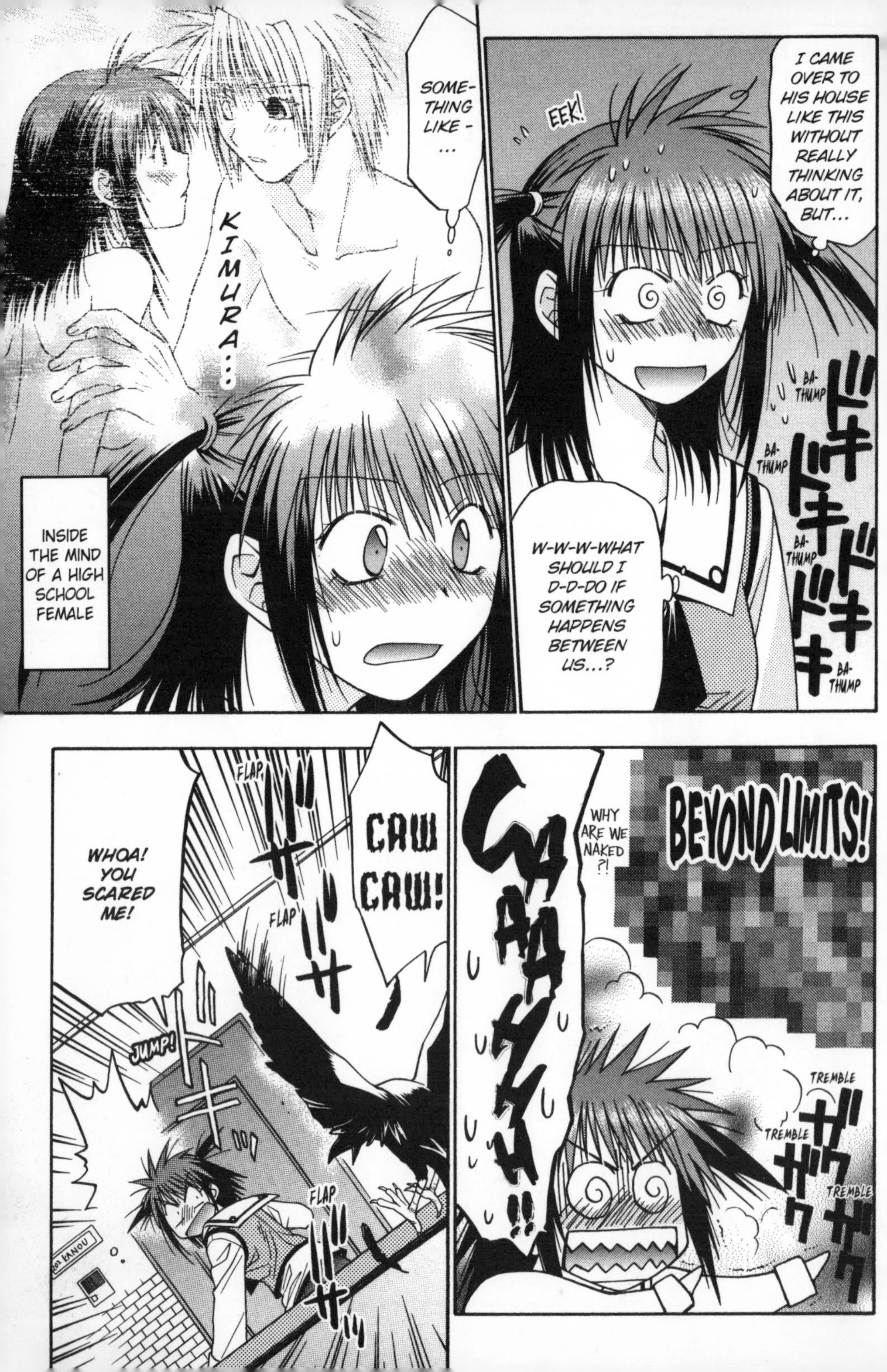
I CAME OVER TO HIS HOUSE LIKE THIS WITHOUT REALLY THINKING ABOUT IT, BUT...
EEK!
W-W-W-WHAT SHOULD I D-D-DO IF SOMETHING HAPPENS BETWEEN US...?
BA-THUMP
BA-THUMP
BA-THUMP
BA-THUMP
SOME-THING LIKE - ...
KIMURA...
INSIDE THE MIND OF A HIGH SCHOOL FEMALE
BEYOND LIMITS!
WHY ARE WE NAKED ?!
TREMBLE
TREMBLE
TREMBLE
CAW CAW!
FLAP
FLAP
FLAP
WHOA! YOU SCARED ME!
JUMP!

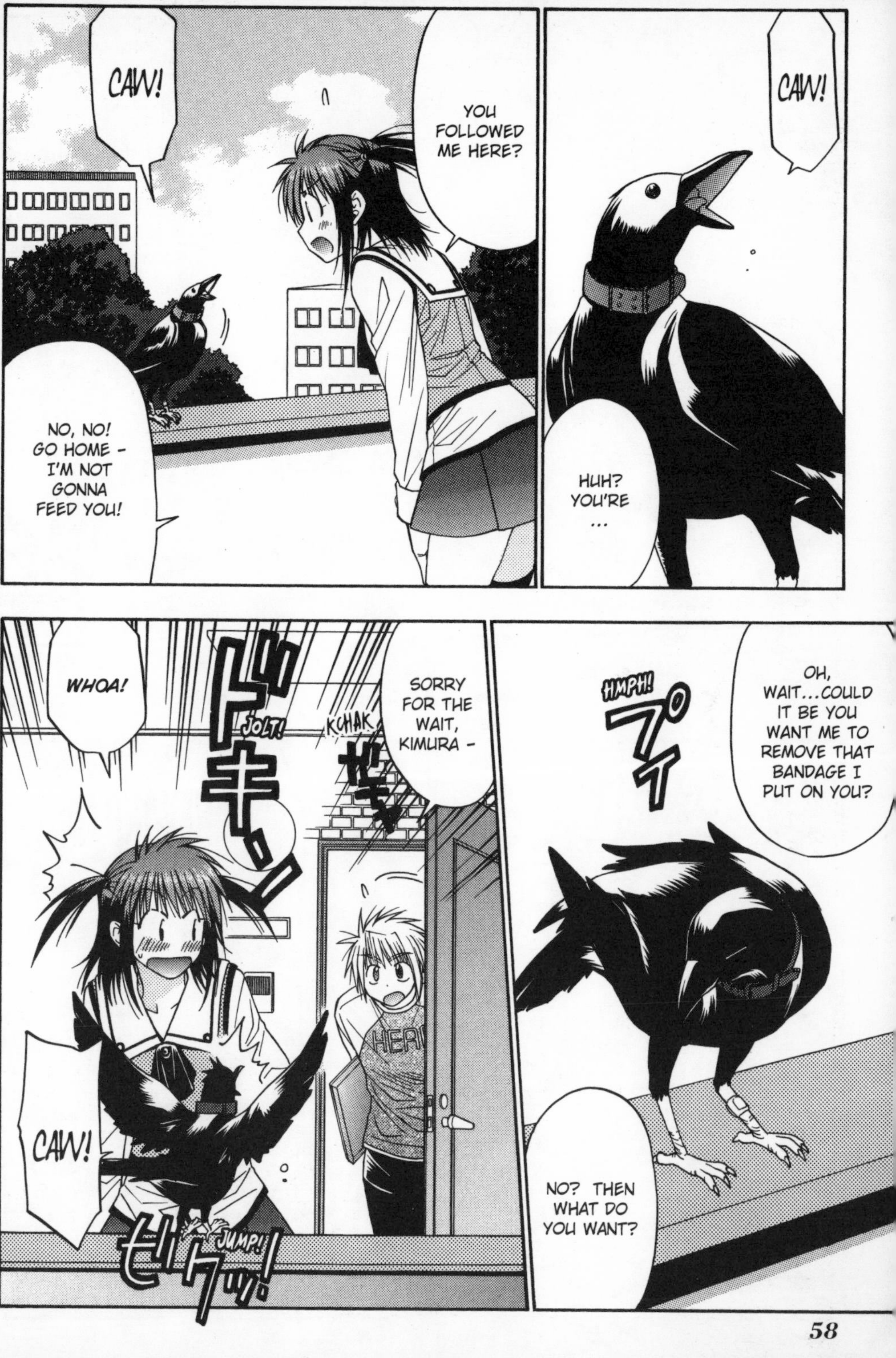
CAW!
HUH? YOU'RE ...
YOU FOLLOWED ME HERE?
CAW!
NO, NO! GO HOME - I'M NOT GONNA FEED YOU!
OH, WAIT...COULD IT BE YOU WANT ME TO REMOVE THAT BANDAGE I PUT ON YOU?
HMPH!
NO? THEN WHAT DO YOU WANT?
SORRY FOR THE WAIT, KIMURA -
KCHAK
JOLT!
WHOA!
CAW!
JUMP!

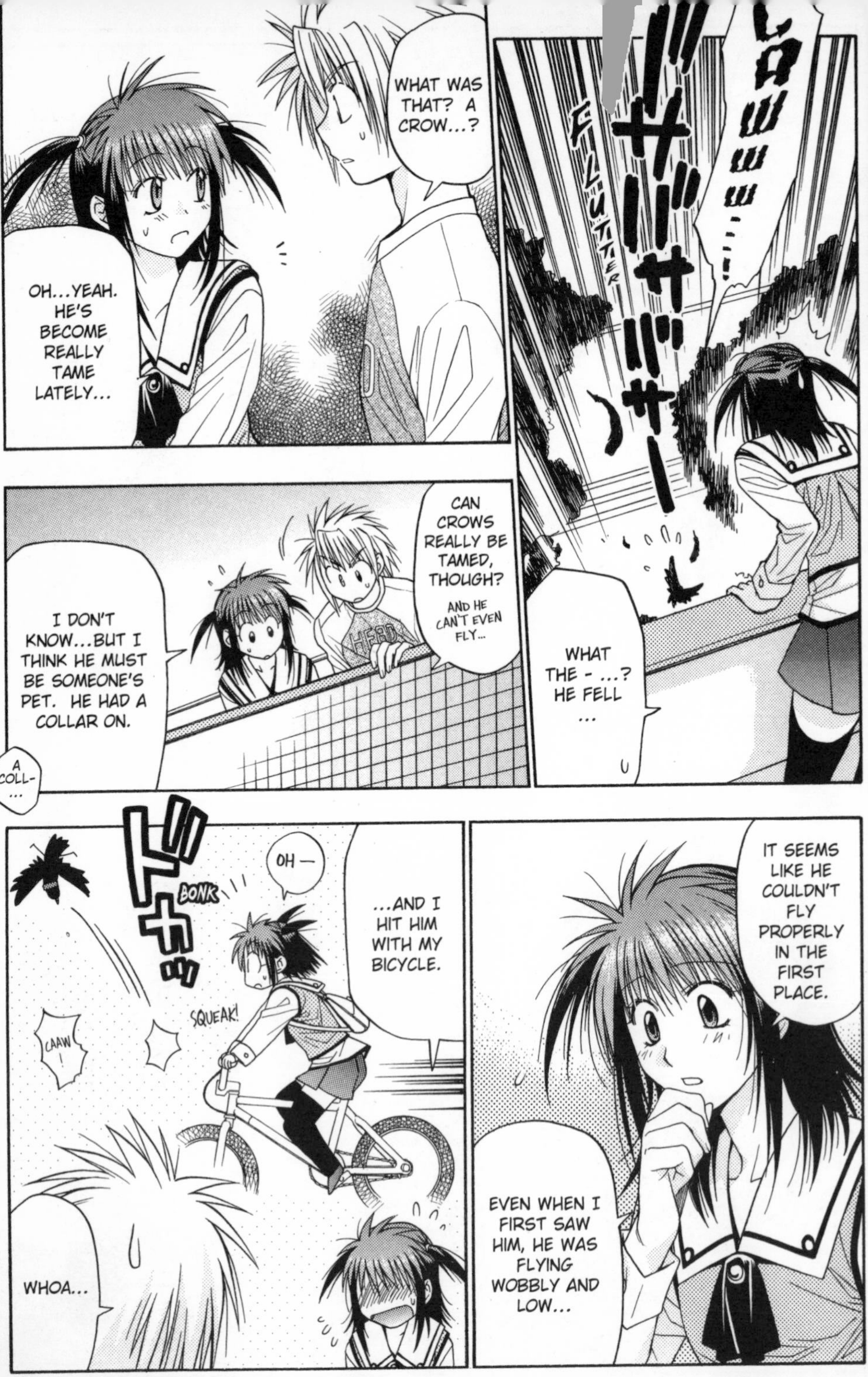
FLUTTER
WHAT THE - ...? HE FELL ...
WHAT WAS THAT? A CROW...?
OH...YEAH. HE'S BECOME REALLY TAME LATELY...
CAN CROWS REALLY BE TAMED, THOUGH?
AND HE CAN'T EVEN FLY...
I DON'T KNOW...BUT I THINK HE MUST BE SOMEONE'S PET. HE HAD A COLLAR ON.
A COLL-...
IT SEEMS LIKE HE COULDN'T FLY PROPERLY IN THE FIRST PLACE.
EVEN WHEN I FIRST SAW HIM, HE WAS FLYING WOBBLY AND LOW...
...AND I HIT HIM WITH MY BICYCLE.
OH —
BONK
SQUEAK!
CAAW!
WHOA...

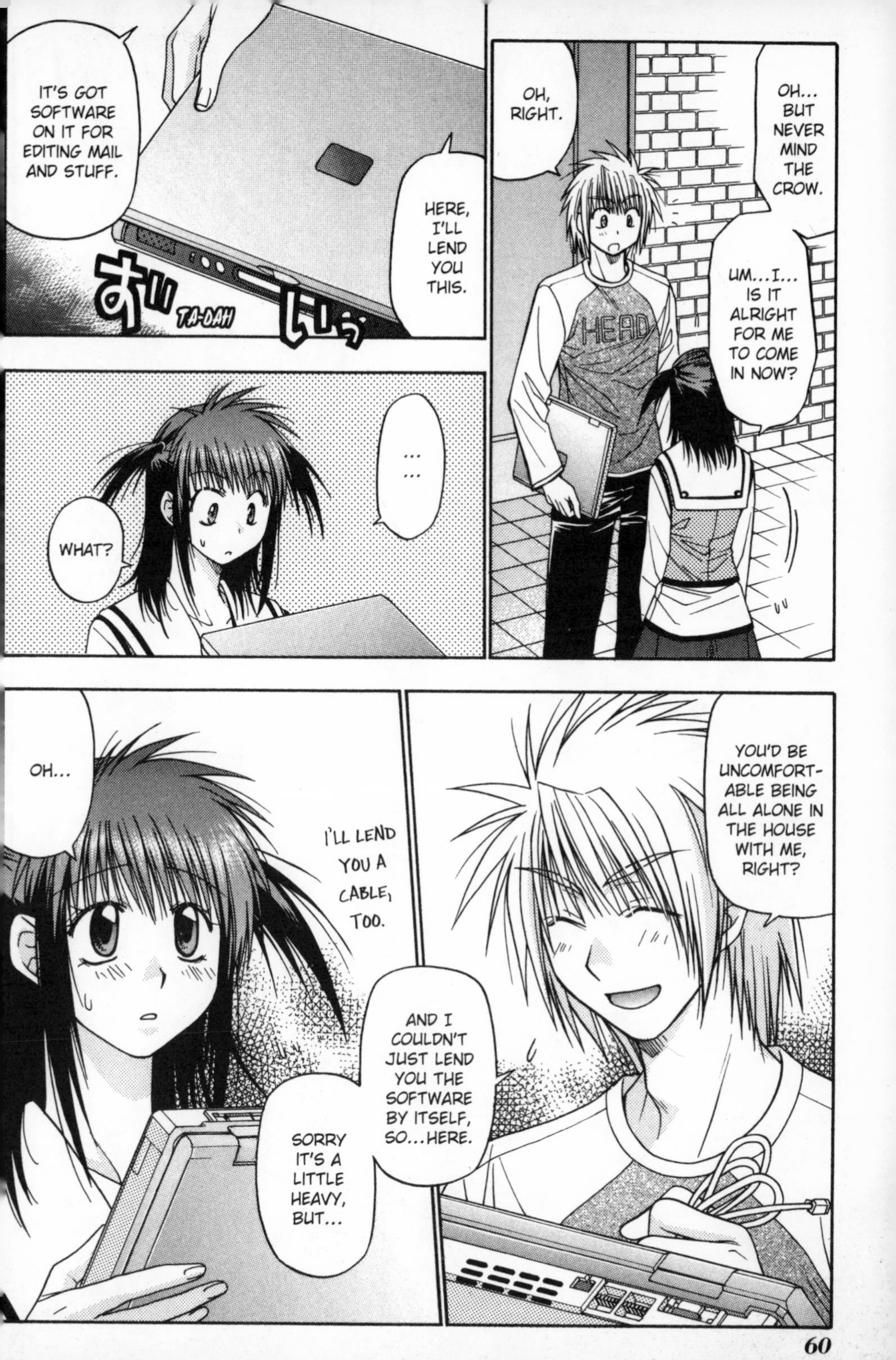
OH... BUT NEVER MIND THE CROW.
OH, RIGHT.
UM...I... IS IT ALRIGHT FOR ME TO COME IN NOW?
HERE, I'LL LEND YOU THIS.
IT'S GOT SOFTWARE ON IT FOR EDITING MAIL AND STUFF.
TA-DAH
......
WHAT?
YOU'D BE UNCOMFORT-ABLE BEING ALL ALONE IN THE HOUSE WITH ME, RIGHT?
AND I COULDN'T JUST LEND YOU THE SOFTWARE BY ITSELF, SO...HERE.
OH...
I'LL LEND YOU A CABLE, TOO.
SORRY IT'S A LITTLE HEAVY, BUT...

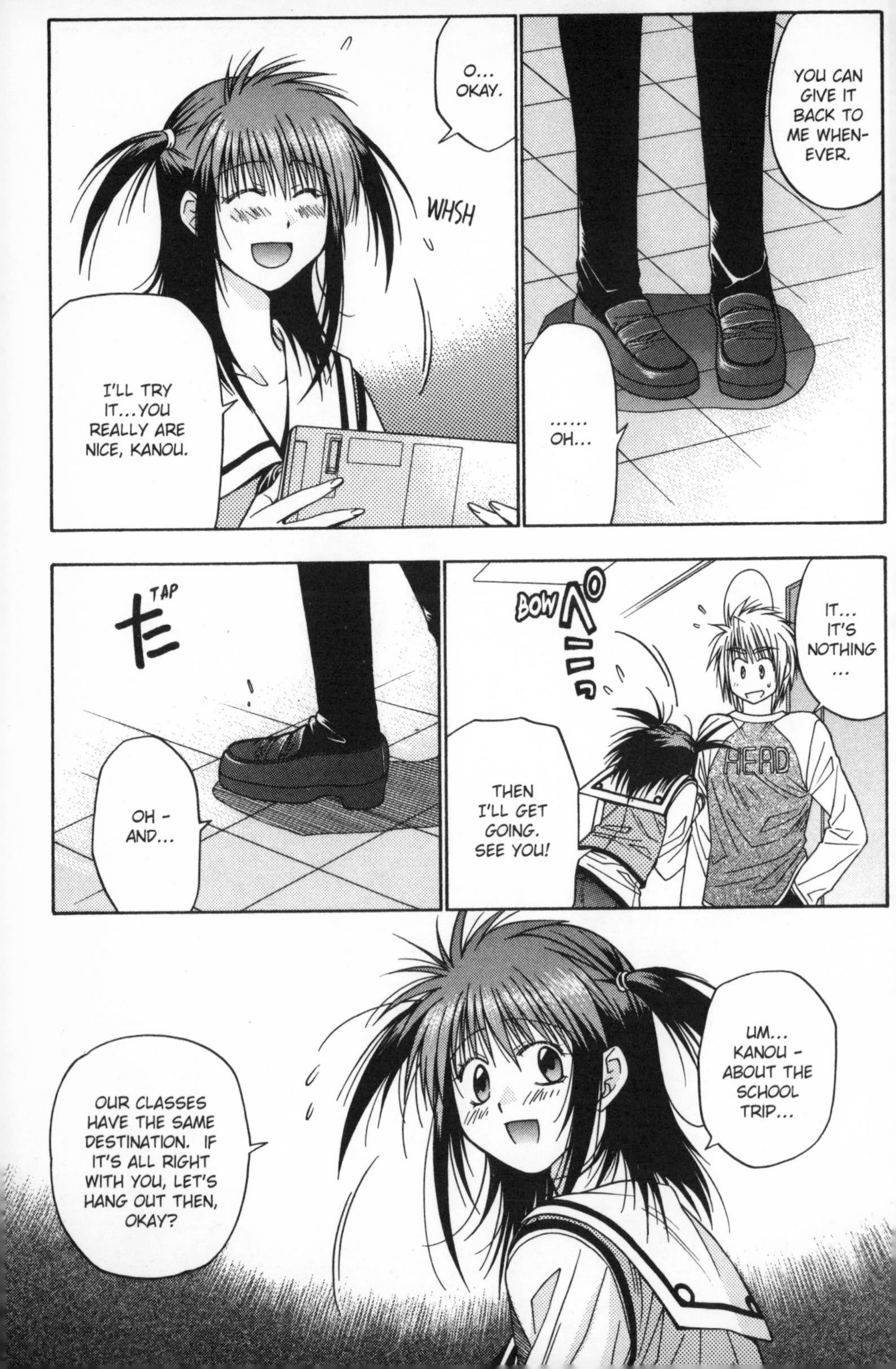
YOU CAN GIVE IT BACK TO ME WHEN-EVER.
...... OH...
O... OKAY.
WHSH
I'LL TRY IT...YOU REALLY ARE NICE, KANOU.
IT... IT'S NOTHING ...
BOW
THEN I'LL GET GOING. SEE YOU!
TAP
OH - AND...
UM... KANOU - ABOUT THE SCHOOL TRIP...
OUR CLASSES HAVE THE SAME DESTINATION. IF IT'S ALL RIGHT WITH YOU, LET'S HANG OUT THEN, OKAY?

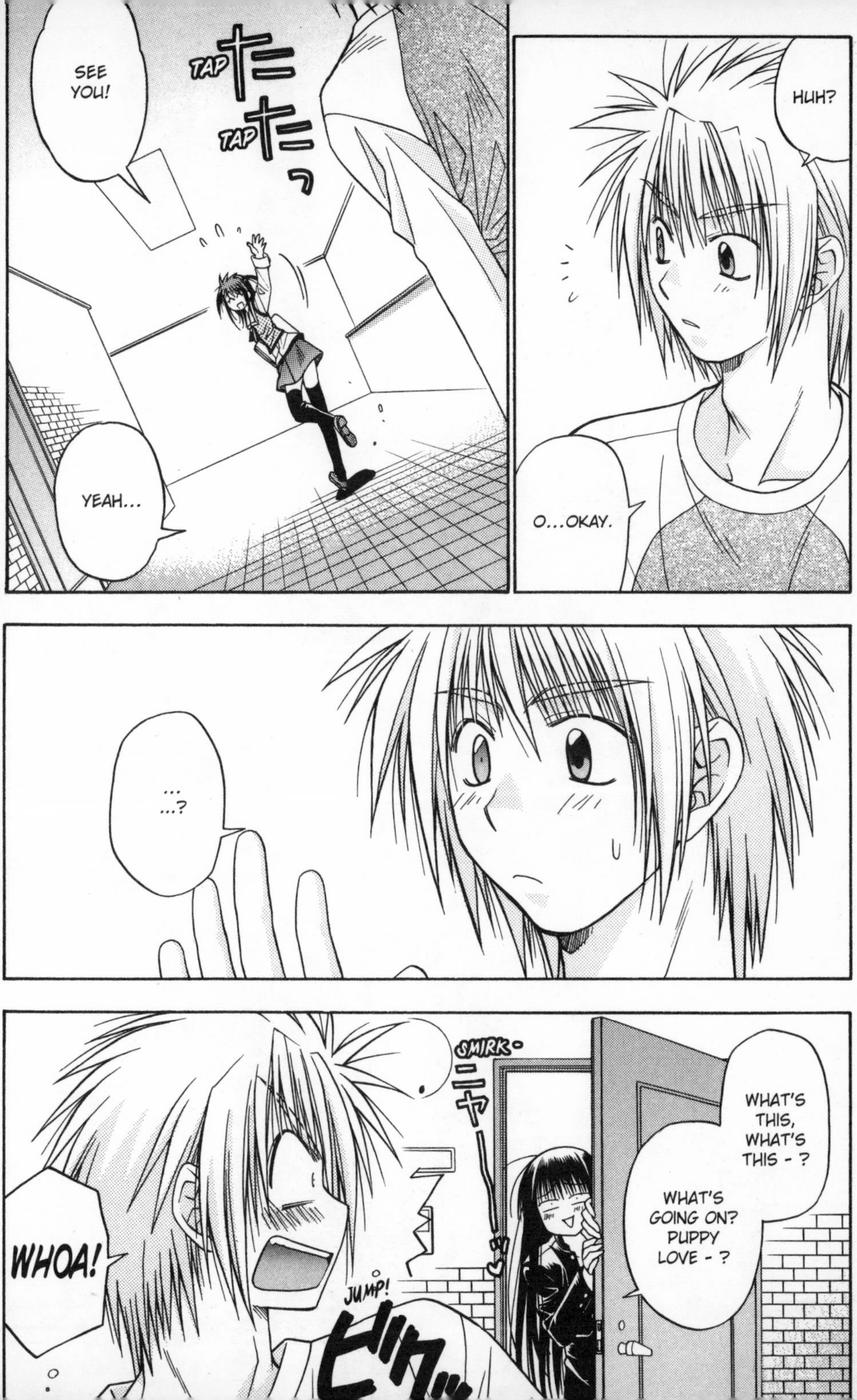
HUH?
O...OKAY.
SEE YOU!
TAP
TAP
YEAH...
...
...?
WHAT'S THIS, WHAT'S THIS - ?
WHAT'S GOING ON? PUPPY LOVE - ?
SMIRK
JUMP!
WHOA!

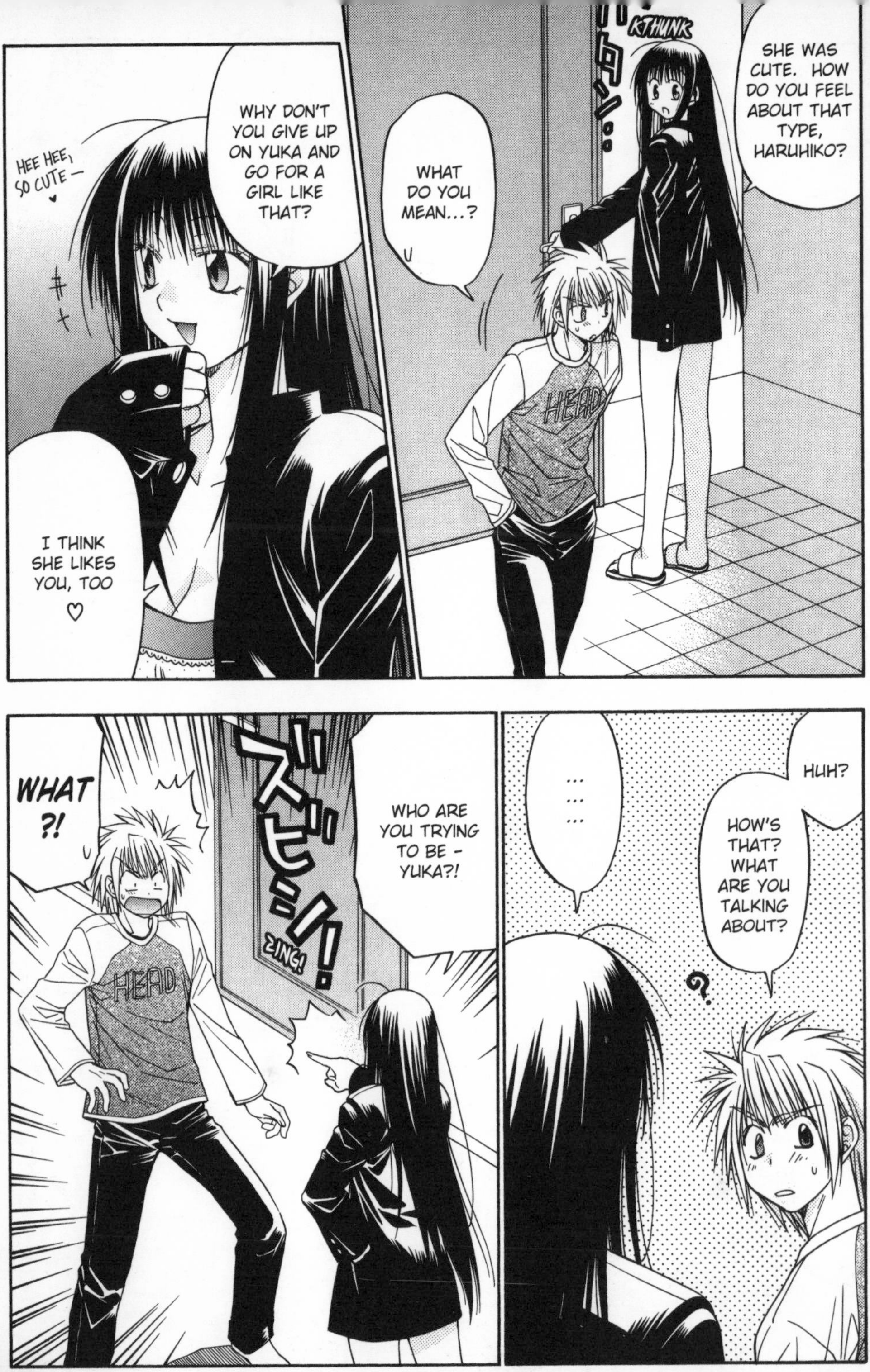
KTHUNK
SHE WAS CUTE. HOW DO YOU FEEL ABOUT THAT TYPE, HARUHIKO?
WHAT DO YOU MEAN...?
WHY DON'T YOU GIVE UP ON YUKA AND GO FOR A GIRL LIKE THAT?
HEE HEE, SO CUTE — ♥
I THINK SHE LIKES YOU, TOO ♡
HUH?
HOW'S THAT? WHAT ARE YOU TALKING ABOUT?
... ...
WHO ARE YOU TRYING TO BE - YUKA?!
ZING!
WHAT ?!

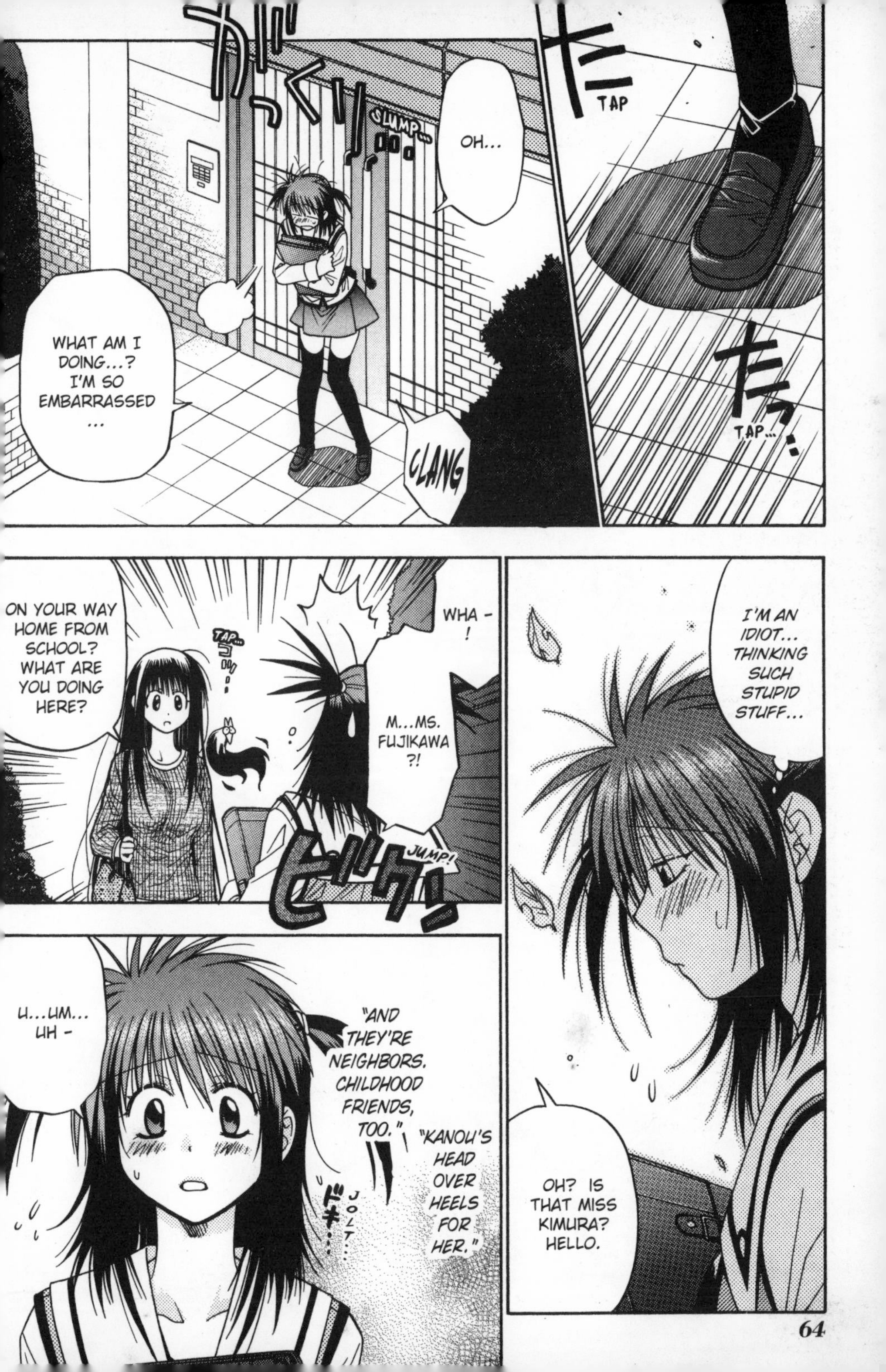
TAP
TAP...
OH...
SLUMP...
WHAT AM I DOING...? I'M SO EMBARRASSED ...
CLANG
I'M AN IDIOT... THINKING SUCH STUPID STUFF...
OH? IS THAT MISS KIMURA? HELLO.
WHA - !
M...MS. FUJIKAWA ?!
TAP...
ON YOUR WAY HOME FROM SCHOOL? WHAT ARE YOU DOING HERE?
JUMP!
"AND THEY'RE NEIGHBORS. CHILDHOOD FRIENDS, TOO."
"KANOU'S HEAD OVER HEELS FOR HER."
JOLT...
U...UM... UH -

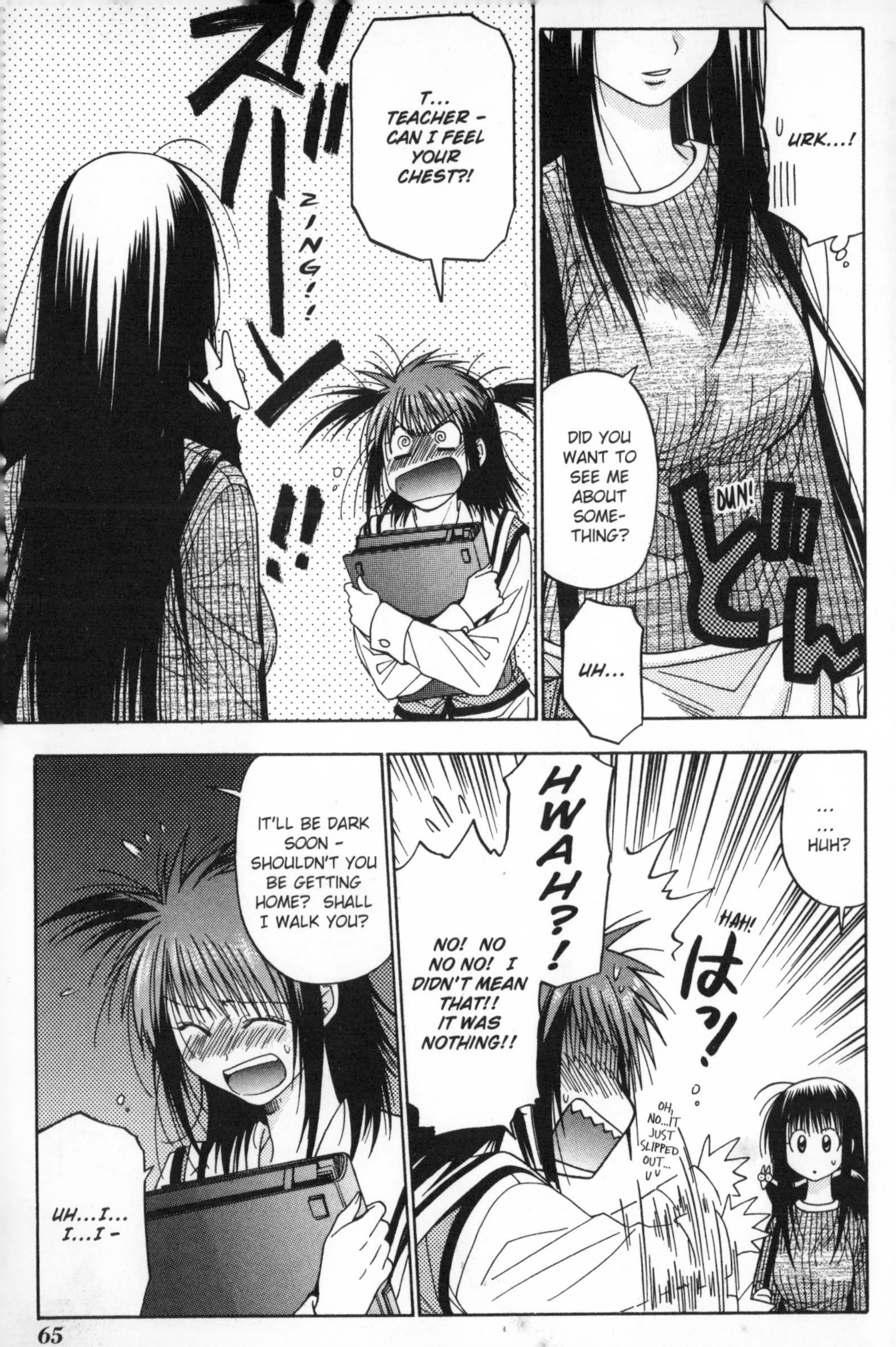
URK...!
DID YOU WANT TO SEE ME ABOUT SOME-THING?
DUN!
UH...
T... TEACHER - CAN I FEEL YOUR CHEST?!
ZING!!
... ... HUH?
HAH!
HWAH?!
NO! NO NO NO! I DIDN'T MEAN THAT!! IT WAS NOTHING!!
OH, NO...IT JUST SLIPPED OUT...
IT'LL BE DARK SOON - SHOULDN'T YOU BE GETTING HOME? SHALL I WALK YOU?
UH...I... I...I -

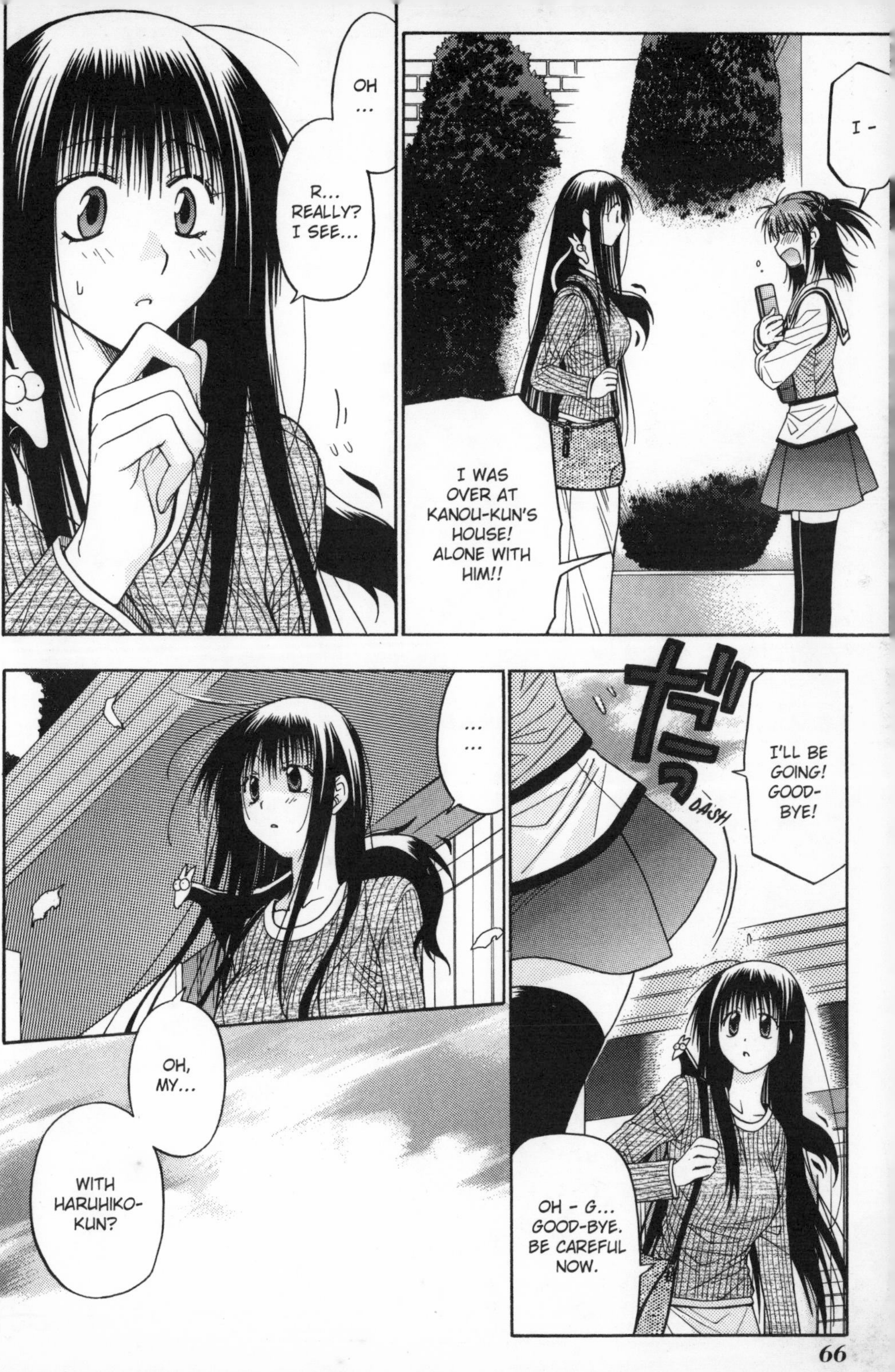
I -
I WAS OVER AT KANOU-KUN'S HOUSE! ALONE WITH HIM!!
OH ...
R... REALLY? I SEE...
DASH
I'LL BE GOING! GOOD-BYE!
OH - G... GOOD-BYE. BE CAREFUL NOW.
... ...
OH, MY...
WITH HARUHIKO-KUN?

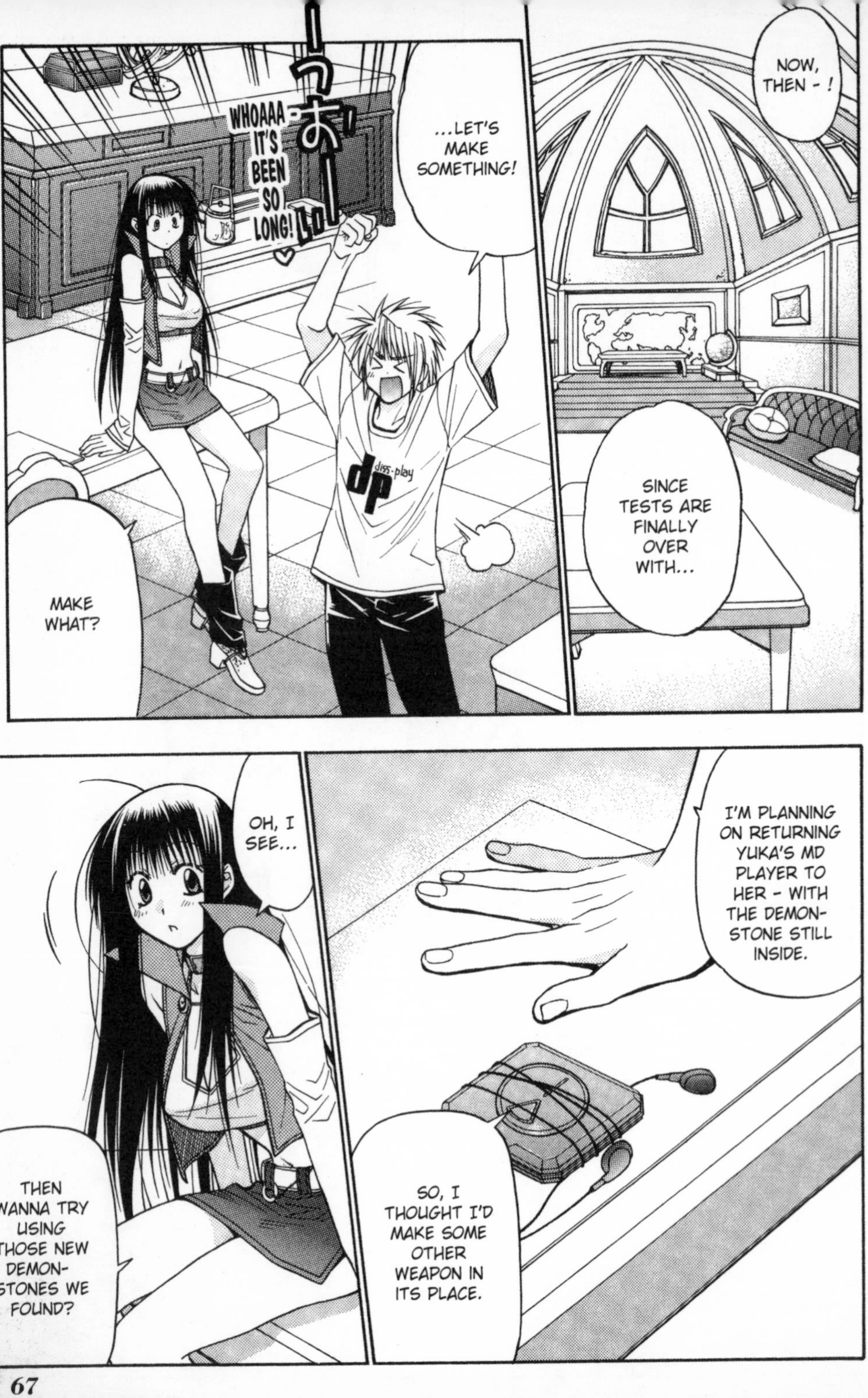
NOW, THEN - !
SINCE TESTS ARE FINALLY OVER WITH...
...LET'S MAKE SOMETHING!
WHOAAA IT'S BEEN SO LONG!
dp diss-play
MAKE WHAT?
I'M PLANNING ON RETURNING YUKA'S MD PLAYER TO HER - WITH THE DEMON-STONE STILL INSIDE.
SO, I THOUGHT I'D MAKE SOME OTHER WEAPON IN ITS PLACE.
OH, I SEE...
THEN WANNA TRY USING THOSE NEW DEMON-STONES WE FOUND?

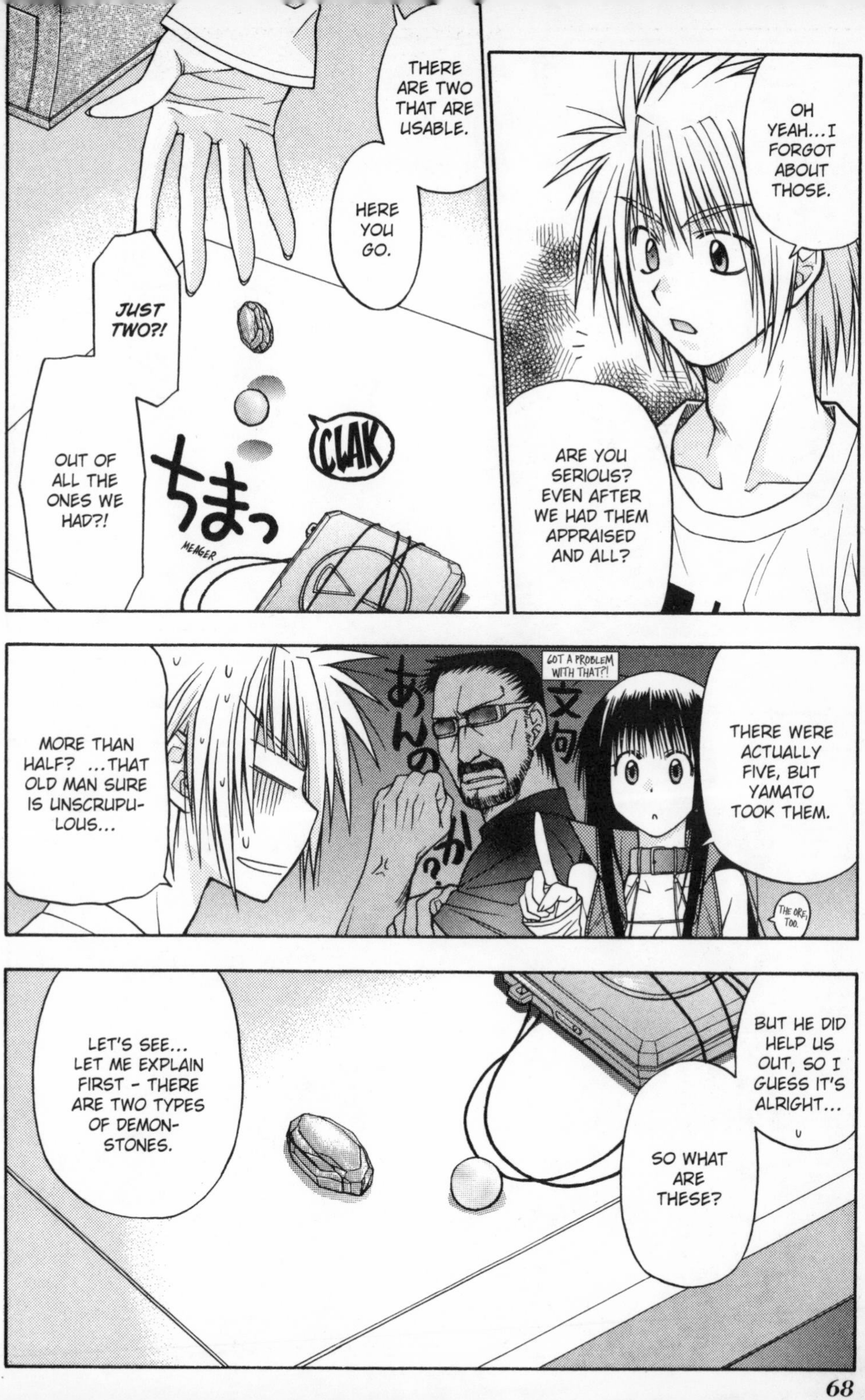
OH YEAH...I FORGOT ABOUT THOSE.
ARE YOU SERIOUS? EVEN AFTER WE HAD THEM APPRAISED AND ALL?
THERE ARE TWO THAT ARE USABLE.
HERE YOU GO.
JUST TWO?!
CLAK
ちまっ
MEAGER
OUT OF ALL THE ONES WE HAD?!
THERE WERE ACTUALLY FIVE, BUT YAMATO TOOK THEM.
THE ORE, TOO.
文句あんのか?
GOT A PROBLEM WITH THAT?!
MORE THAN HALF? ...THAT OLD MAN SURE IS UNSCRUPULOUS...
BUT HE DID HELP US OUT, SO I GUESS IT'S ALRIGHT...
SO WHAT ARE THESE?
LET'S SEE... LET ME EXPLAIN FIRST - THERE ARE TWO TYPES OF DEMON-STONES.

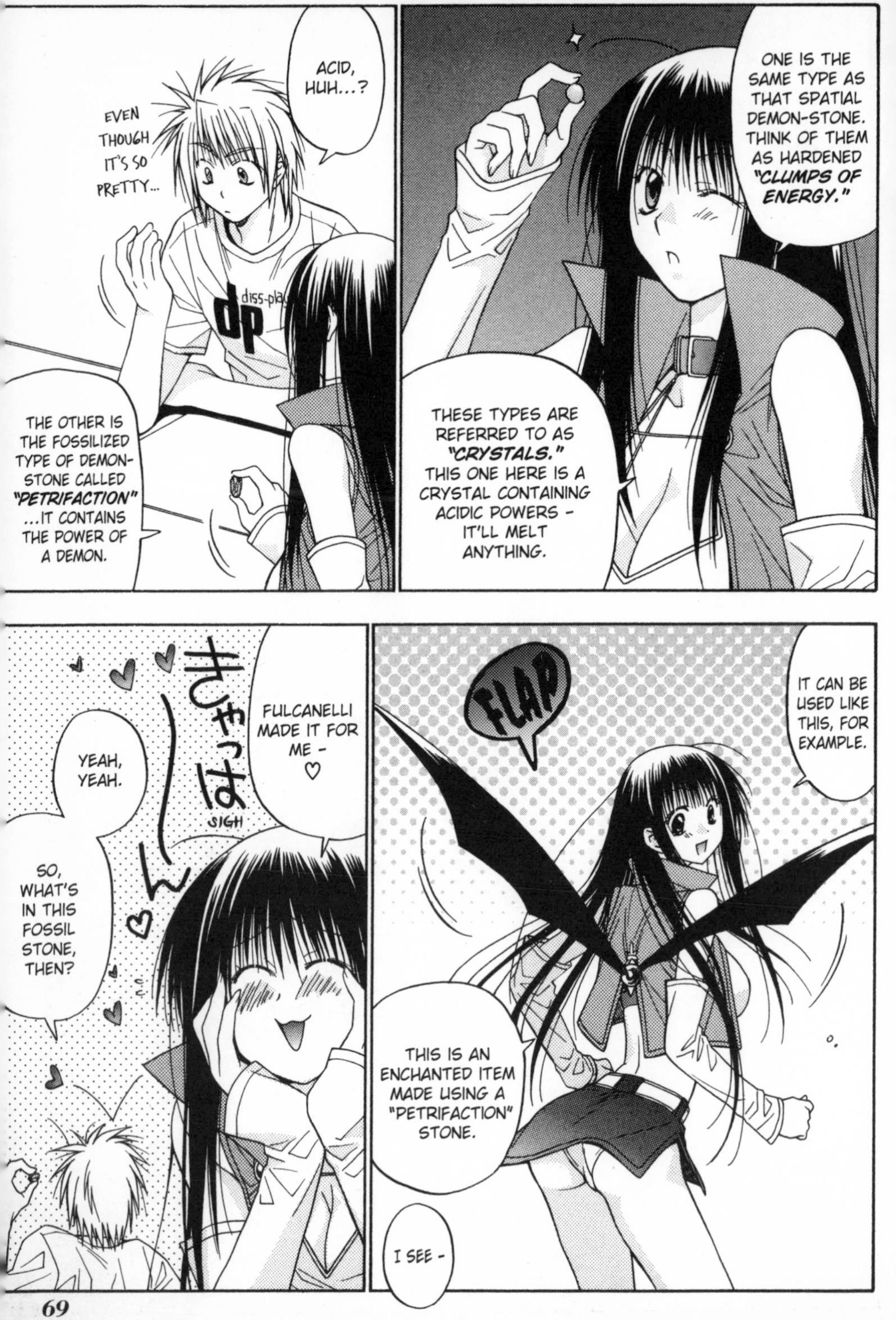

ONE IS THE SAME TYPE AS THAT SPATIAL DEMON-STONE. THINK OF THEM AS HARDENED ***"CLUMPS OF ENERGY."***
THESE TYPES ARE REFERRED TO AS ***"CRYSTALS."*** THIS ONE HERE IS A CRYSTAL CONTAINING ACIDIC POWERS - IT'LL MELT ANYTHING.
ACID, HUH...?
EVEN THOUGH IT'S SO PRETTY...
diss-play
dp
THE OTHER IS THE FOSSILIZED TYPE OF DEMON-STONE CALLED ***"PETRIFACTION"*** ...IT CONTAINS THE POWER OF A DEMON.
IT CAN BE USED LIKE THIS, FOR EXAMPLE.
FLAP
THIS IS AN ENCHANTED ITEM MADE USING A "PETRIFACTION" STONE.
I SEE -
FULCANELLI MADE IT FOR ME - ♡
きゃっは―ん
SIGH
YEAH, YEAH.
SO, WHAT'S IN THIS FOSSIL STONE, THEN?

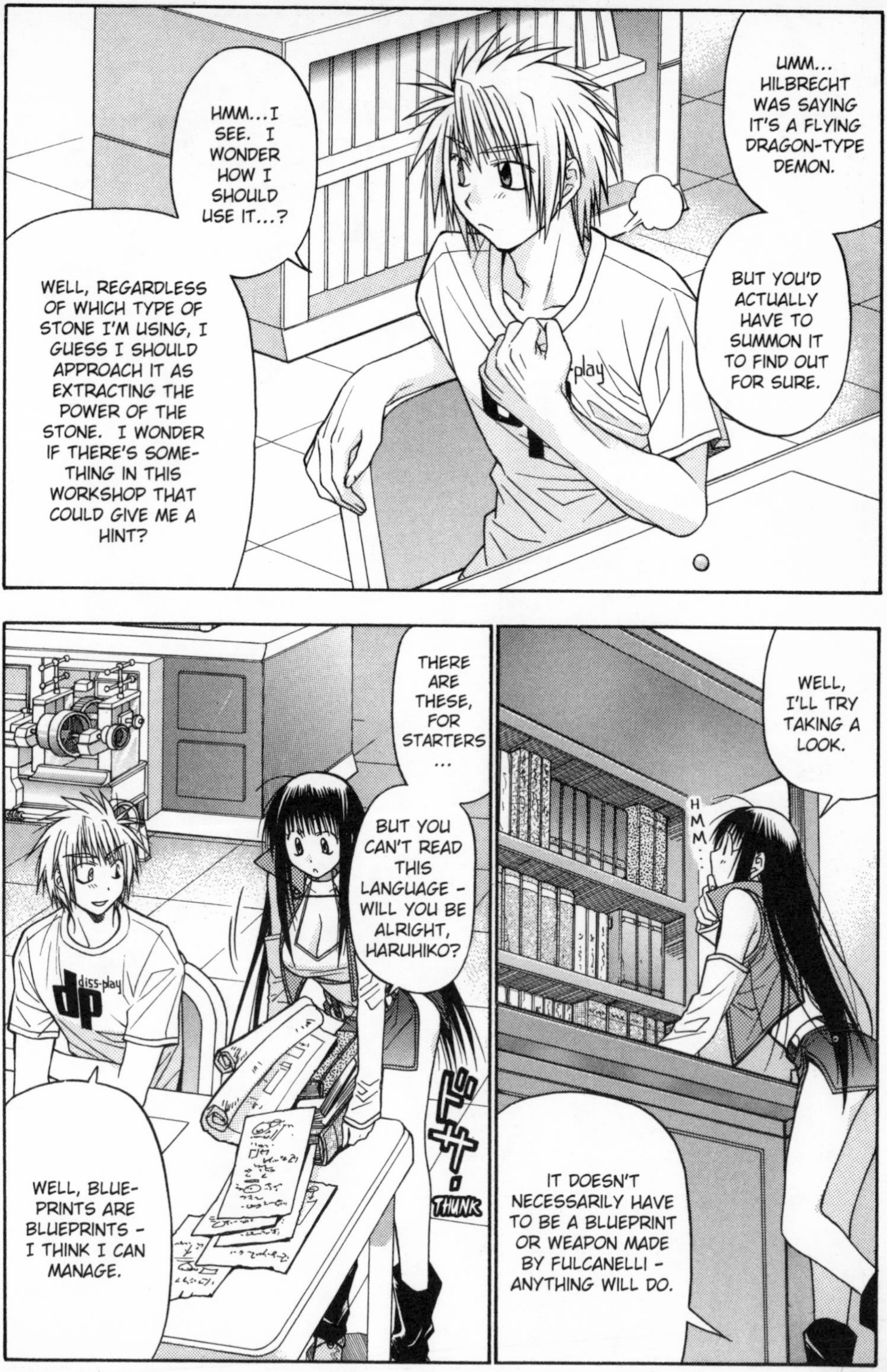
UMM... HILBRECHT WAS SAYING IT'S A FLYING DRAGON-TYPE DEMON.
BUT YOU'D ACTUALLY HAVE TO SUMMON IT TO FIND OUT FOR SURE.
HMM...I SEE. I WONDER HOW I SHOULD USE IT...?
WELL, REGARDLESS OF WHICH TYPE OF STONE I'M USING, I GUESS I SHOULD APPROACH IT AS EXTRACTING THE POWER OF THE STONE. I WONDER IF THERE'S SOME-THING IN THIS WORKSHOP THAT COULD GIVE ME A HINT?
WELL, I'LL TRY TAKING A LOOK.
HMM...
IT DOESN'T NECESSARILY HAVE TO BE A BLUEPRINT OR WEAPON MADE BY FULCANELLI - ANYTHING WILL DO.
THERE ARE THESE, FOR STARTERS...
BUT YOU CAN'T READ THIS LANGUAGE - WILL YOU BE ALRIGHT, HARUHIKO?
THUNK
WELL, BLUE-PRINTS ARE BLUEPRINTS - I THINK I CAN MANAGE.

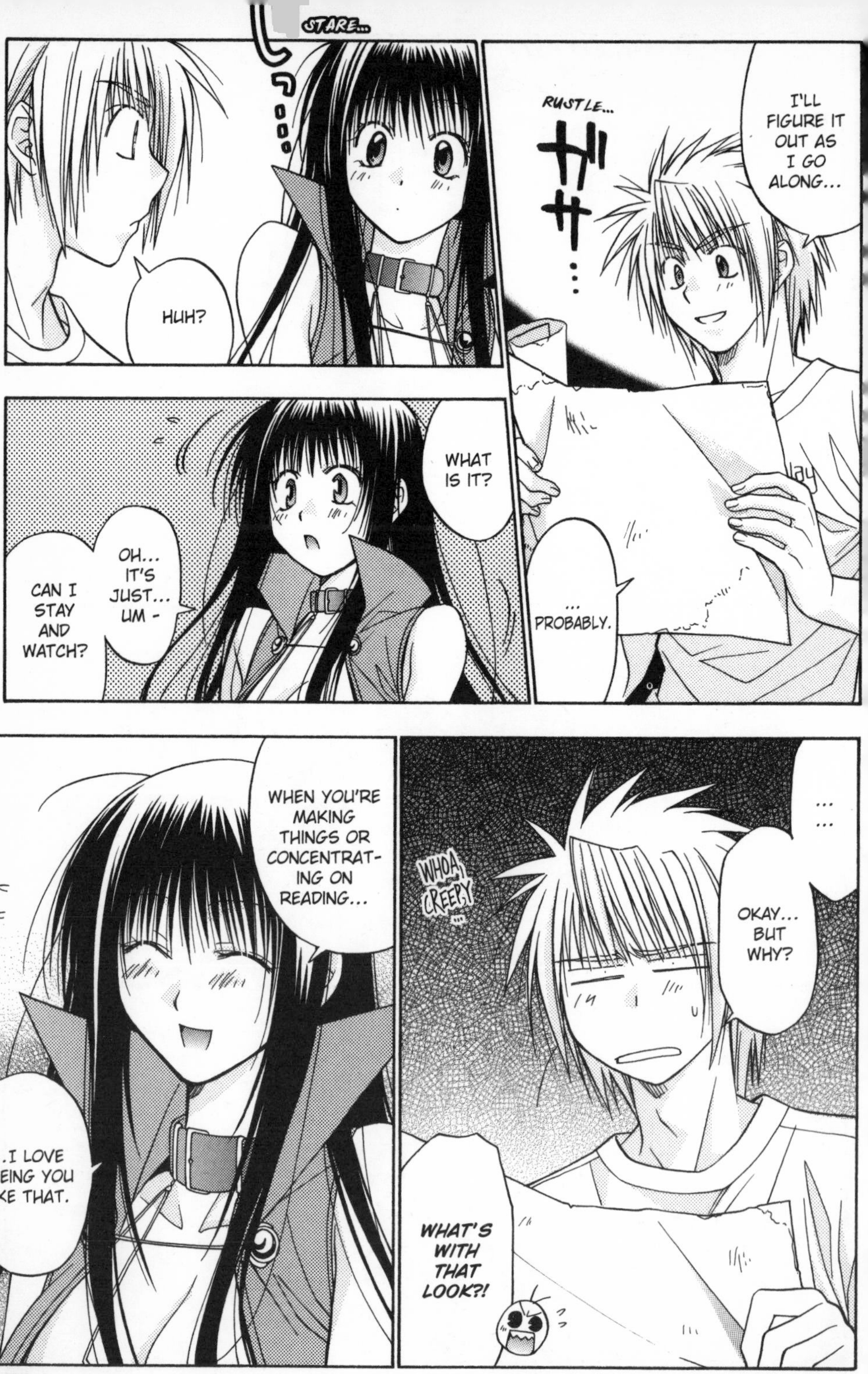

RUSTLE...
ガサ…
I'LL FIGURE IT OUT AS I GO ALONG...
... PROBABLY.
STARE...
HUH?
WHAT IS IT?
OH... IT'S JUST... UM -
CAN I STAY AND WATCH?
... ...
OKAY... BUT WHY?
WHOA, CREEPY...
WHAT'S WITH THAT LOOK?!
WHEN YOU'RE MAKING THINGS OR CONCENTRAT-ING ON READING...
...I LOVE SEEING YOU LIKE THAT.

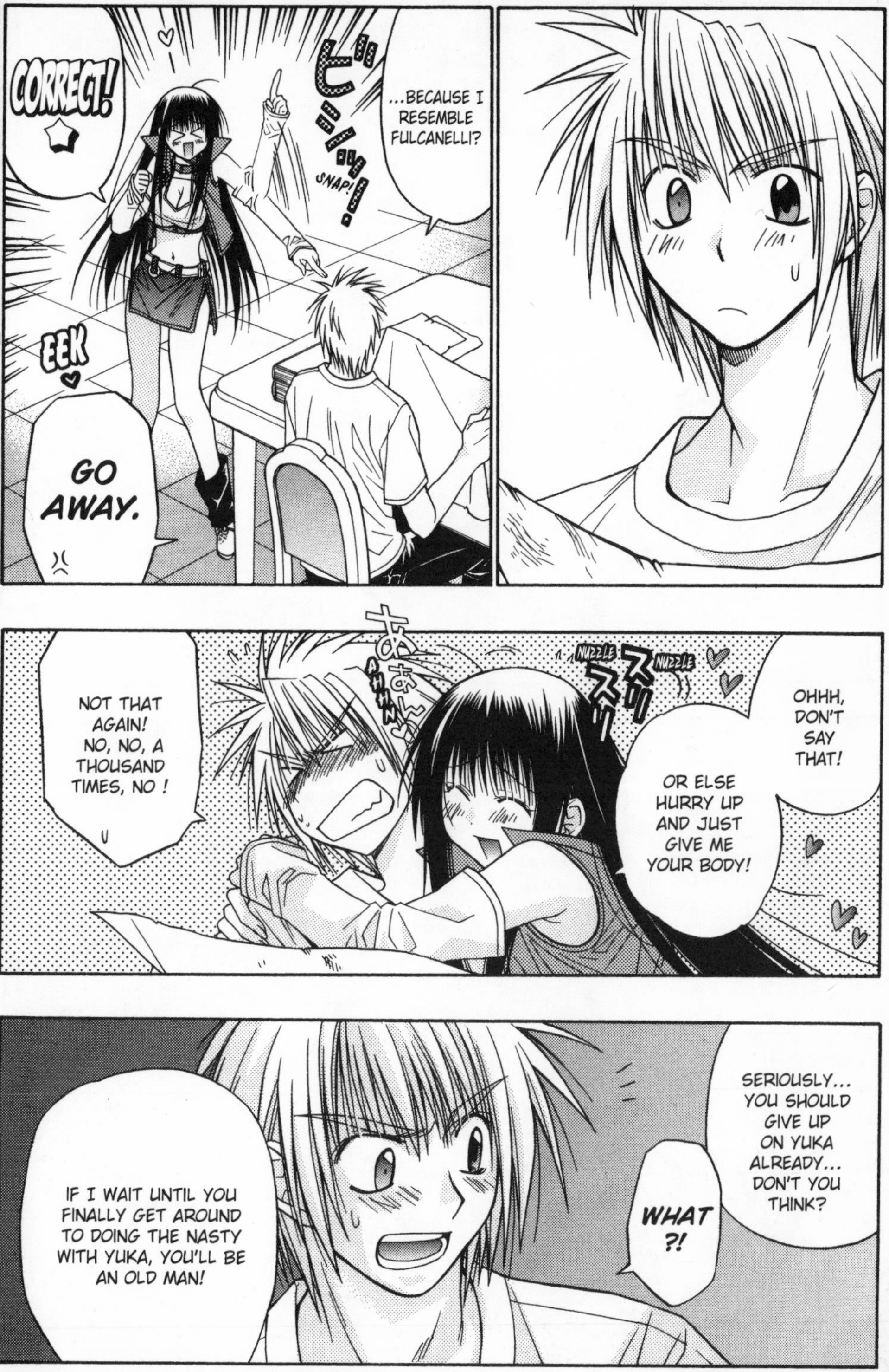
...BECAUSE I RESEMBLE FULCANELLI?
SNAP!
CORRECT!
EEK
GO AWAY.
OHHH, DON'T SAY THAT!
OR ELSE HURRY UP AND JUST GIVE ME YOUR BODY!
NUZZLE NUZZLE
AHHHN
NOT THAT AGAIN! NO, NO, A THOUSAND TIMES, NO !
SERIOUSLY... YOU SHOULD GIVE UP ON YUKA ALREADY... DON'T YOU THINK?
WHAT ?!
IF I WAIT UNTIL YOU FINALLY GET AROUND TO DOING THE NASTY WITH YUKA, YOU'LL BE AN OLD MAN!

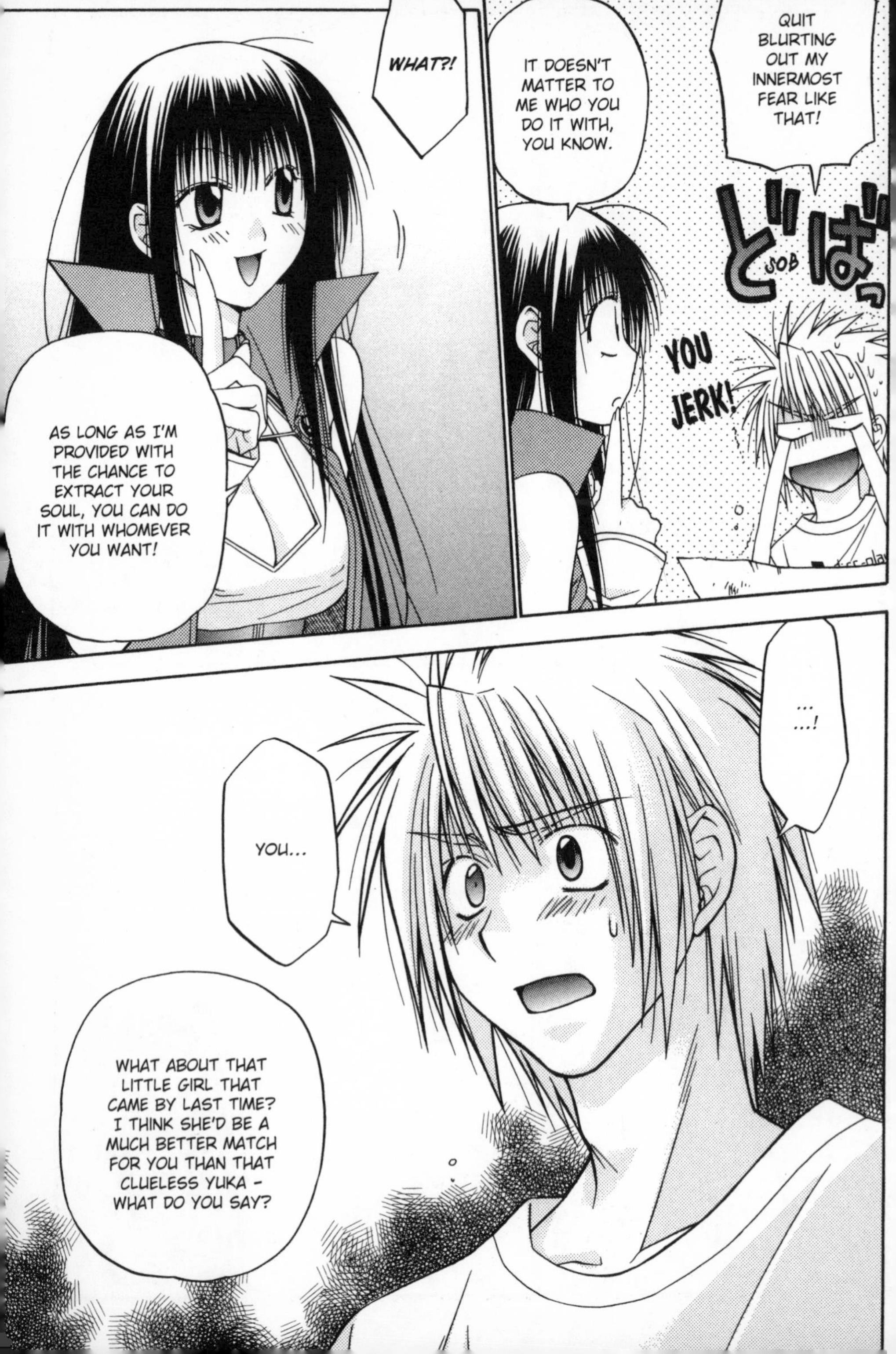
QUIT BLURTING OUT MY INNERMOST FEAR LIKE THAT!
どばっ
SOB
IT DOESN'T MATTER TO ME WHO YOU DO IT WITH, YOU KNOW.
YOU JERK!
WHAT?!
AS LONG AS I'M PROVIDED WITH THE CHANCE TO EXTRACT YOUR SOUL, YOU CAN DO IT WITH WHOMEVER YOU WANT!
... ...!
YOU...
WHAT ABOUT THAT LITTLE GIRL THAT CAME BY LAST TIME? I THINK SHE'D BE A MUCH BETTER MATCH FOR YOU THAN THAT CLUELESS YUKA - WHAT DO YOU SAY?

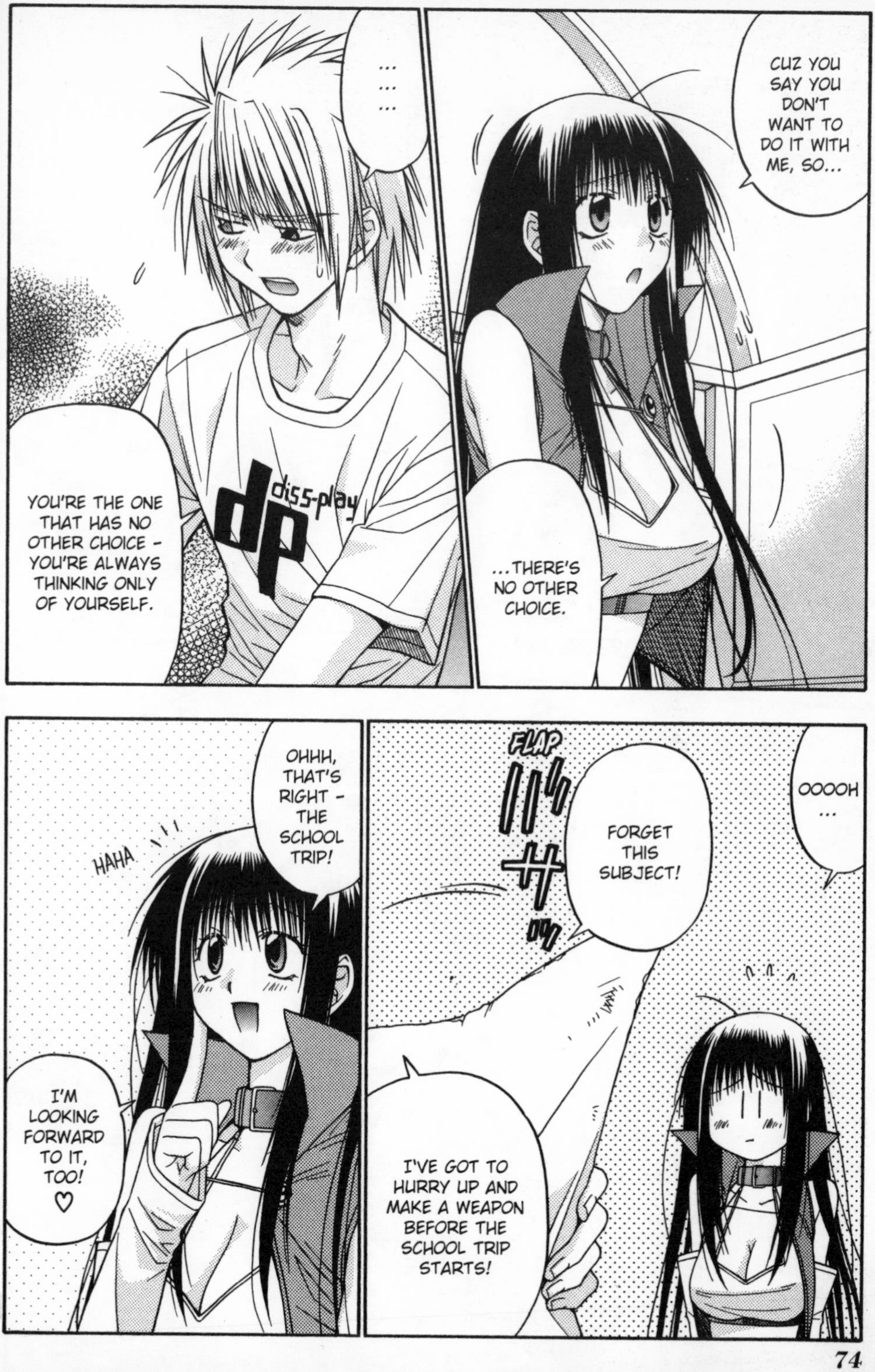
CUZ YOU SAY YOU DON'T WANT TO DO IT WITH ME, SO...
...THERE'S NO OTHER CHOICE.
...
...
...
dp diss-play
YOU'RE THE ONE THAT HAS NO OTHER CHOICE - YOU'RE ALWAYS THINKING ONLY OF YOURSELF.
OOOOH ...
FLAP
FORGET THIS SUBJECT!
I'VE GOT TO HURRY UP AND MAKE A WEAPON BEFORE THE SCHOOL TRIP STARTS!
OHHH, THAT'S RIGHT - THE SCHOOL TRIP!
HAHA
I'M LOOKING FORWARD TO IT, TOO! ♡

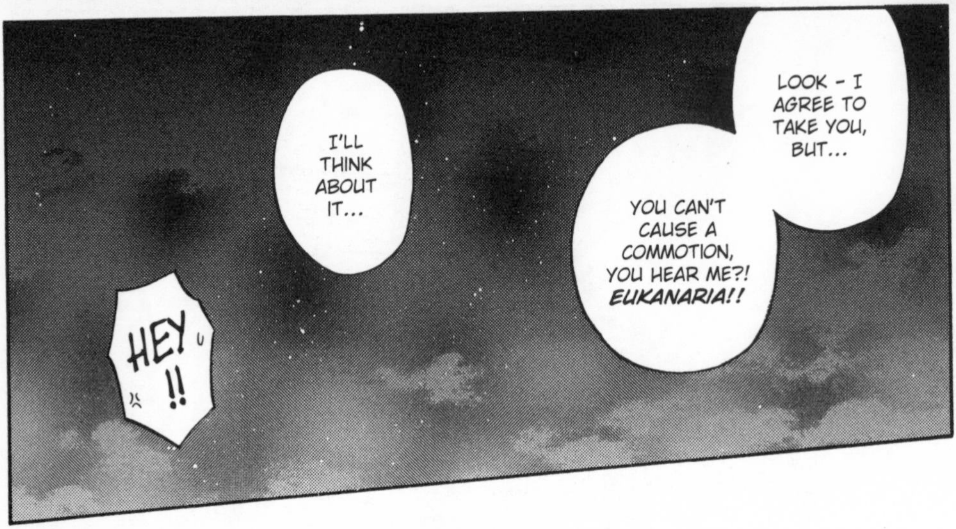
LOOK - I AGREE TO TAKE YOU, BUT...
YOU CAN'T CAUSE A COMMOTION, YOU HEAR ME?! *EUKANARIA!!*
I'LL THINK ABOUT IT...
HEY!!

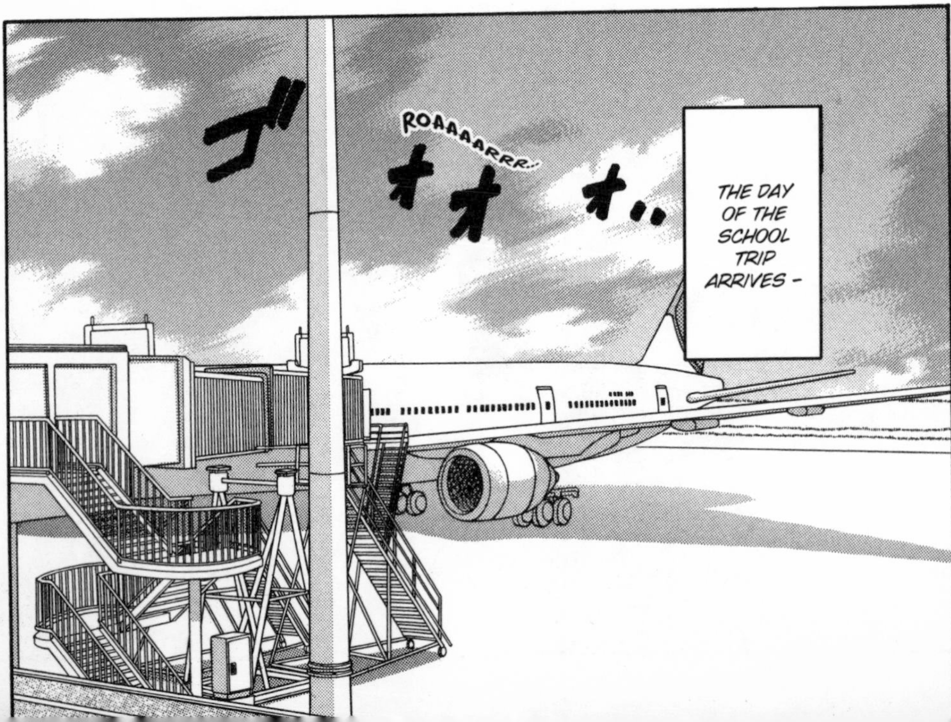
THE DAY OF THE SCHOOL TRIP ARRIVES -
ゴオオオ..
ROAAAAARRR..

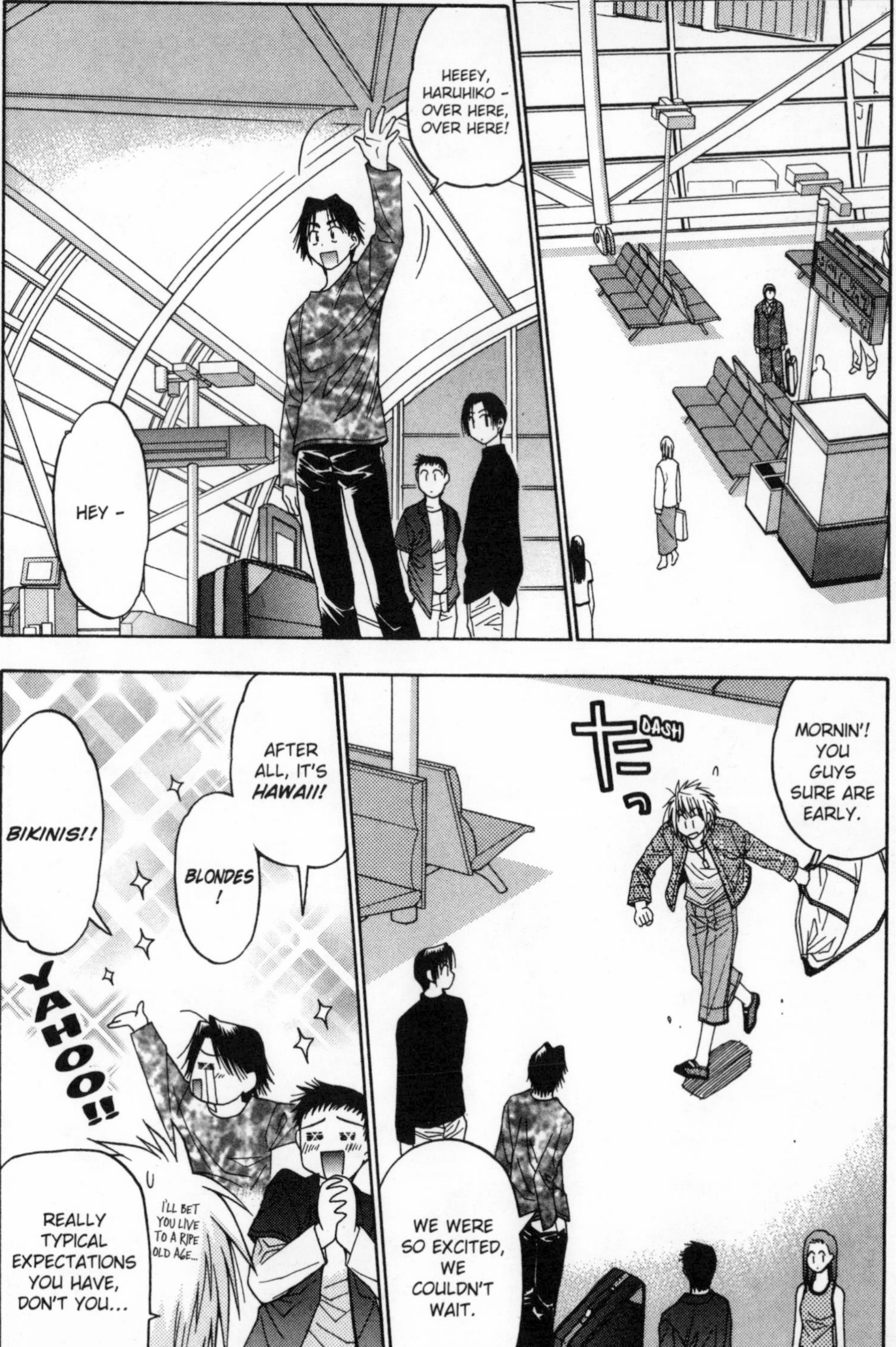
HEEEY, HARUHIKO - OVER HERE, OVER HERE!
HEY -
DASH
MORNIN'! YOU GUYS SURE ARE EARLY.
WE WERE SO EXCITED, WE COULDN'T WAIT.
AFTER ALL, IT'S HAWAII!
BLONDES!
BIKINIS!!
YAHOO!!
I'LL BET YOU LIVE TO A RIPE OLD AGE...
REALLY TYPICAL EXPECTATIONS YOU HAVE, DON'T YOU...

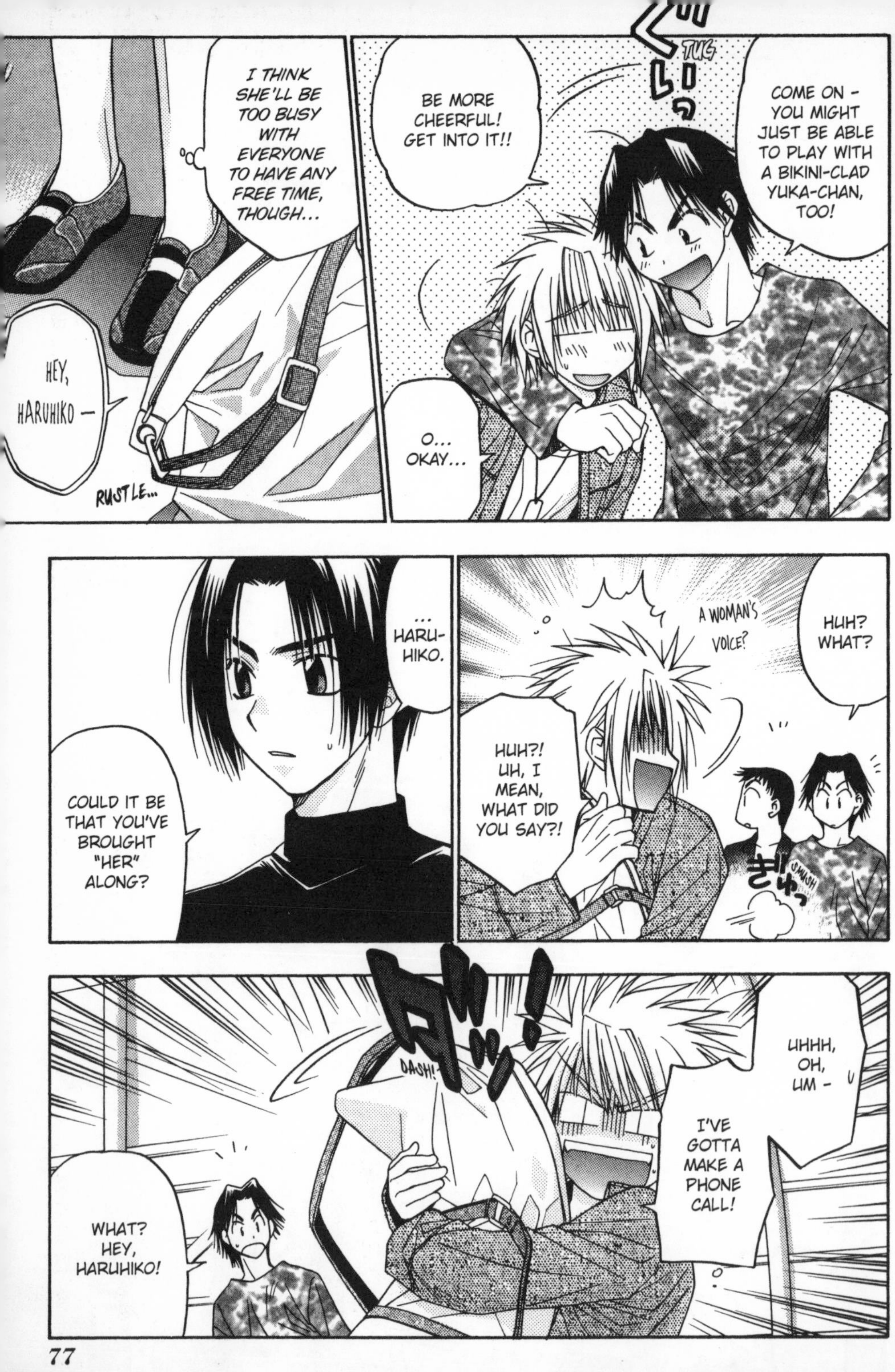
COME ON - YOU MIGHT JUST BE ABLE TO PLAY WITH A BIKINI-CLAD YUKA-CHAN, TOO!
TUG
BE MORE CHEERFUL! GET INTO IT!!
O... OKAY...
I THINK SHE'LL BE TOO BUSY WITH EVERYONE TO HAVE ANY FREE TIME, THOUGH...
HEY, HARUHIKO —
RUSTLE...
HUH? WHAT?
A WOMAN'S VOICE?
HUH?! UH, I MEAN, WHAT DID YOU SAY?!
SMASH
... HARU-HIKO.
COULD IT BE THAT YOU'VE BROUGHT "HER" ALONG?
UHHH, OH, UM -
I'VE GOTTA MAKE A PHONE CALL!
DASH!
WHAT? HEY, HARUHIKO!

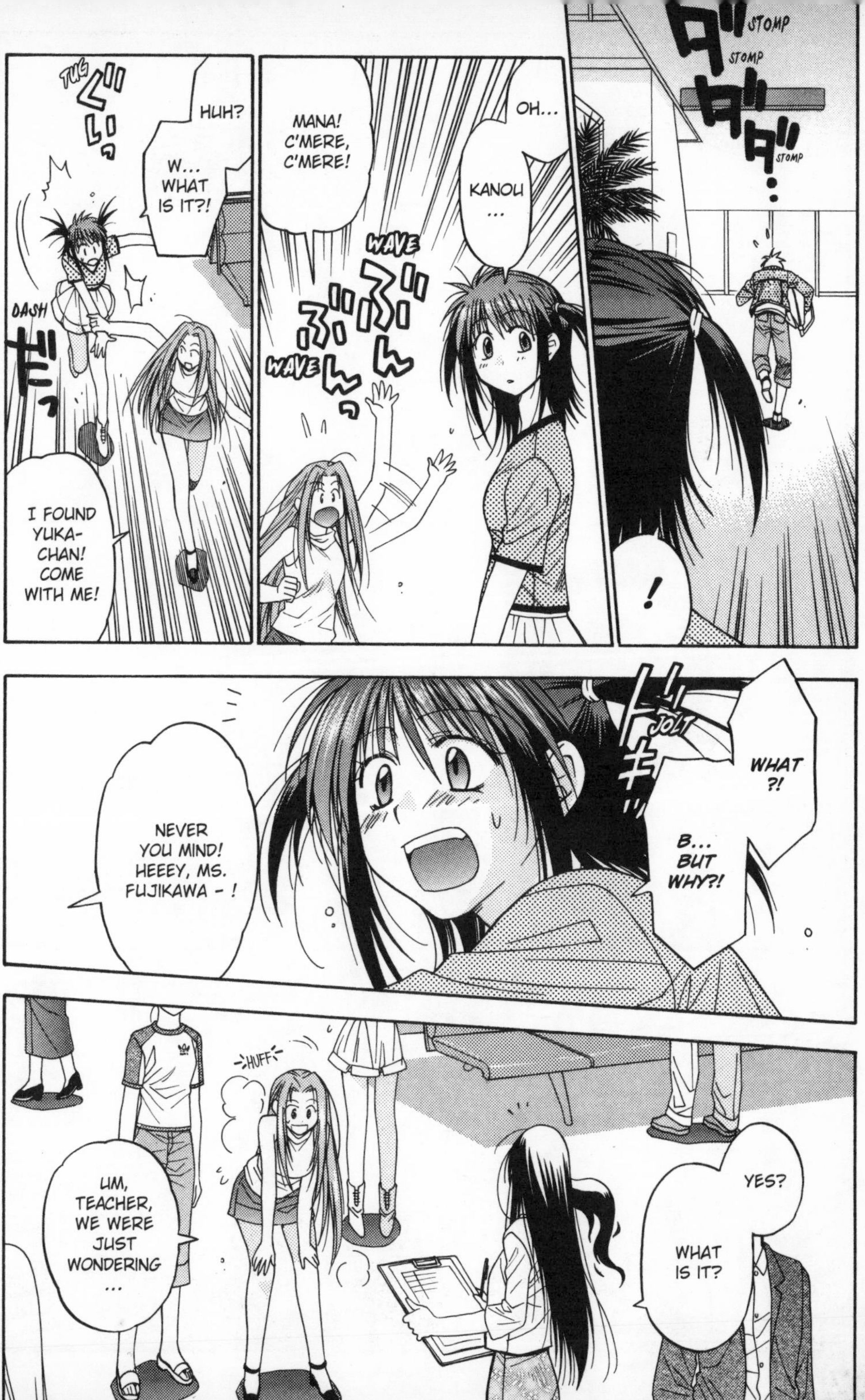
STOMP
STOMP
STOMP
!
OH...
KANOU ...
MANA! C'MERE, C'MERE!
WAVE
WAVE
HUH?
W... WHAT IS IT?!
TUG
DASH
I FOUND YUKA-CHAN! COME WITH ME!
WHAT ?!
B... BUT WHY?!
JOLT
NEVER YOU MIND! HEEEY, MS. FUJIKAWA - !
YES?
WHAT IS IT?
HUFF
UM, TEACHER, WE WERE JUST WONDERING ...

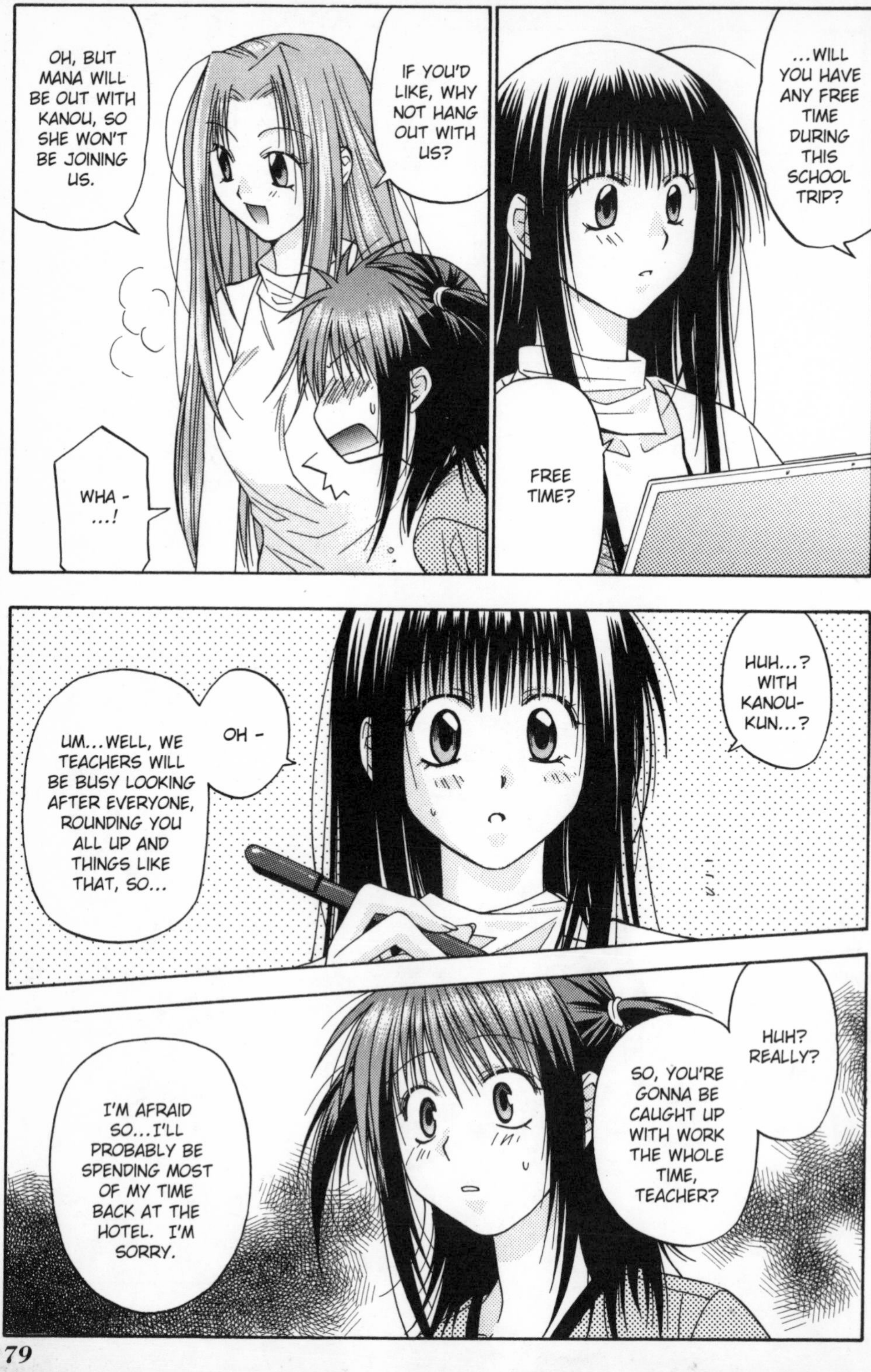
...WILL YOU HAVE ANY FREE TIME DURING THIS SCHOOL TRIP?
FREE TIME?
IF YOU'D LIKE, WHY NOT HANG OUT WITH US?
OH, BUT MANA WILL BE OUT WITH KANOU, SO SHE WON'T BE JOINING US.
WHA - ...!
HUH...? WITH KANOU-KUN...?
OH -
UM...WELL, WE TEACHERS WILL BE BUSY LOOKING AFTER EVERYONE, ROUNDING YOU ALL UP AND THINGS LIKE THAT, SO...
HUH? REALLY?
SO, YOU'RE GONNA BE CAUGHT UP WITH WORK THE WHOLE TIME, TEACHER?
I'M AFRAID SO...I'LL PROBABLY BE SPENDING MOST OF MY TIME BACK AT THE HOTEL. I'M SORRY.

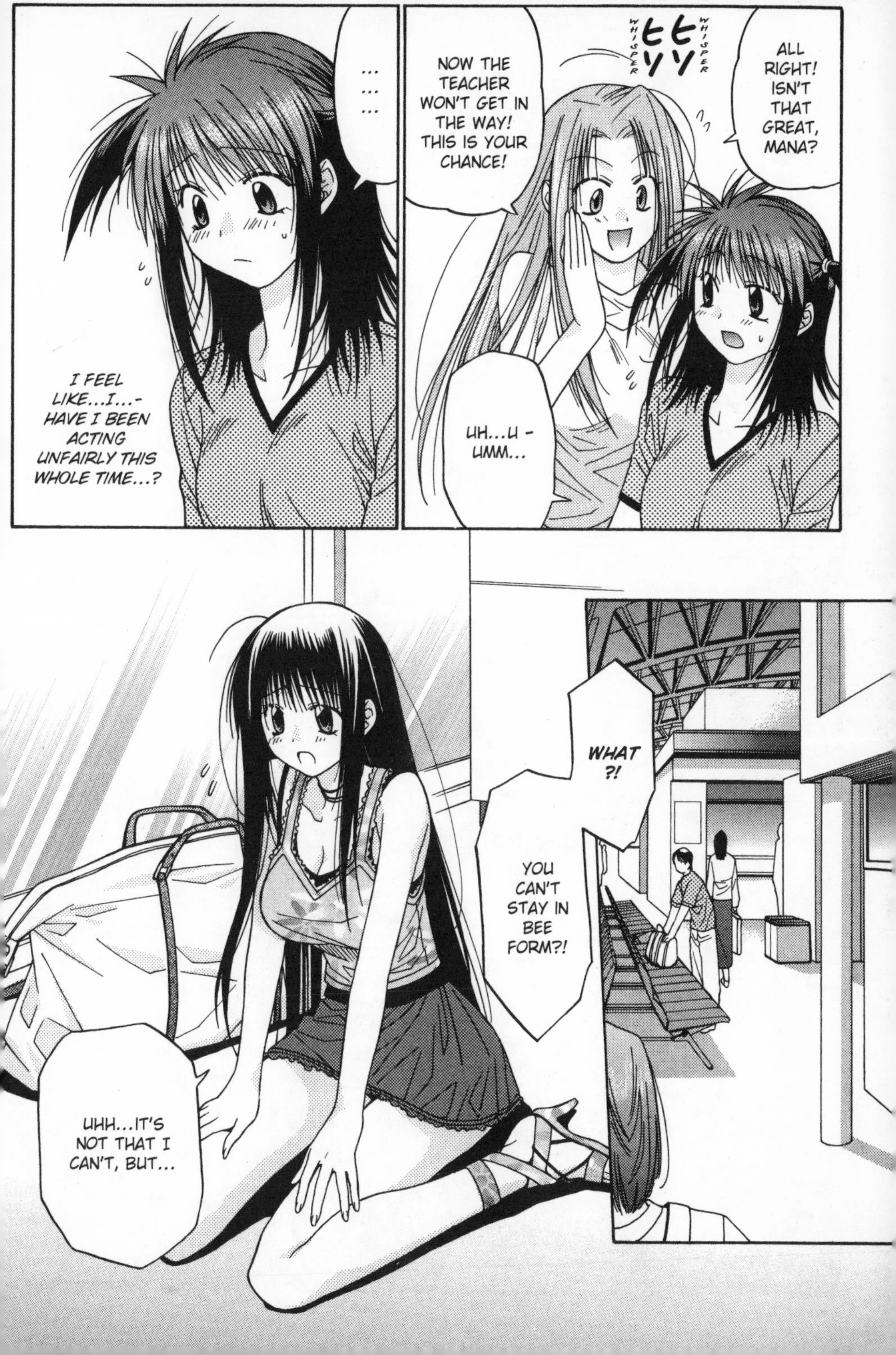
ALL RIGHT! ISN'T THAT GREAT, MANA?
ヒソヒソ
WHISPER WHISPER
NOW THE TEACHER WON'T GET IN THE WAY! THIS IS YOUR CHANCE!
UH...U - UMM...
... ...
I FEEL LIKE...I...- HAVE I BEEN ACTING UNFAIRLY THIS WHOLE TIME...?
WHAT?!
YOU CAN'T STAY IN BEE FORM?!
UHH...IT'S NOT THAT I CAN'T, BUT...

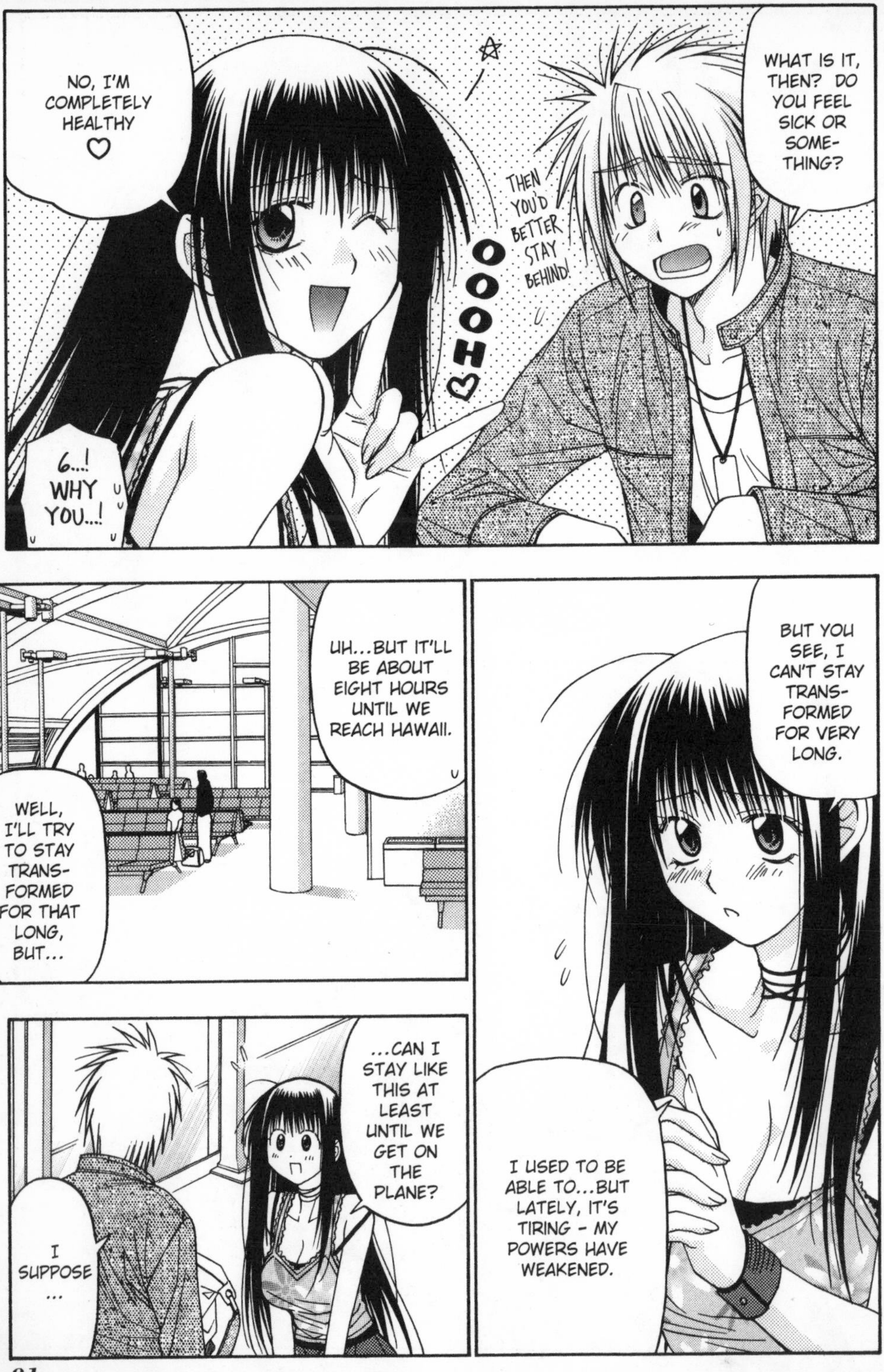
WHAT IS IT, THEN? DO YOU FEEL SICK OR SOME-THING?
THEN YOU'D BETTER STAY BEHIND!
OOOOH ♡
NO, I'M COMPLETELY HEALTHY ♡
G...! WHY YOU...!
BUT YOU SEE, I CAN'T STAY TRANS-FORMED FOR VERY LONG.
I USED TO BE ABLE TO...BUT LATELY, IT'S TIRING – MY POWERS HAVE WEAKENED.
UH...BUT IT'LL BE ABOUT EIGHT HOURS UNTIL WE REACH HAWAII.
WELL, I'LL TRY TO STAY TRANS-FORMED FOR THAT LONG, BUT...
...CAN I STAY LIKE THIS AT LEAST UNTIL WE GET ON THE PLANE?
I SUPPOSE ...

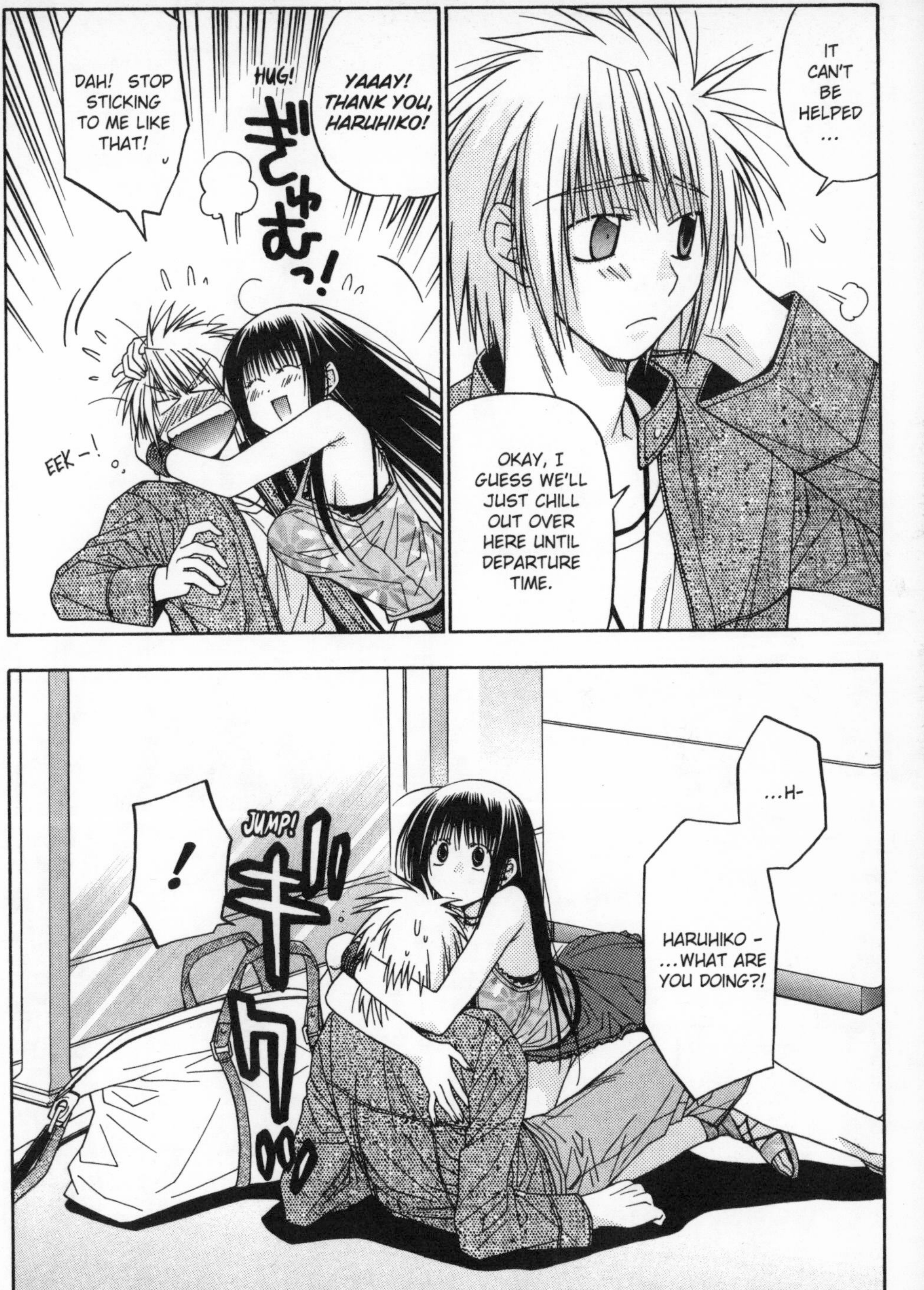
IT CAN'T BE HELPED ...
OKAY, I GUESS WE'LL JUST CHILL OUT OVER HERE UNTIL DEPARTURE TIME.
YAAAY! THANK YOU, HARUHIKO!
HUG!
ぎゅむっ!
DAH! STOP STICKING TO ME LIKE THAT!
EEK -!
...H-
HARUHIKO - ...WHAT ARE YOU DOING?!
JUMP!
!

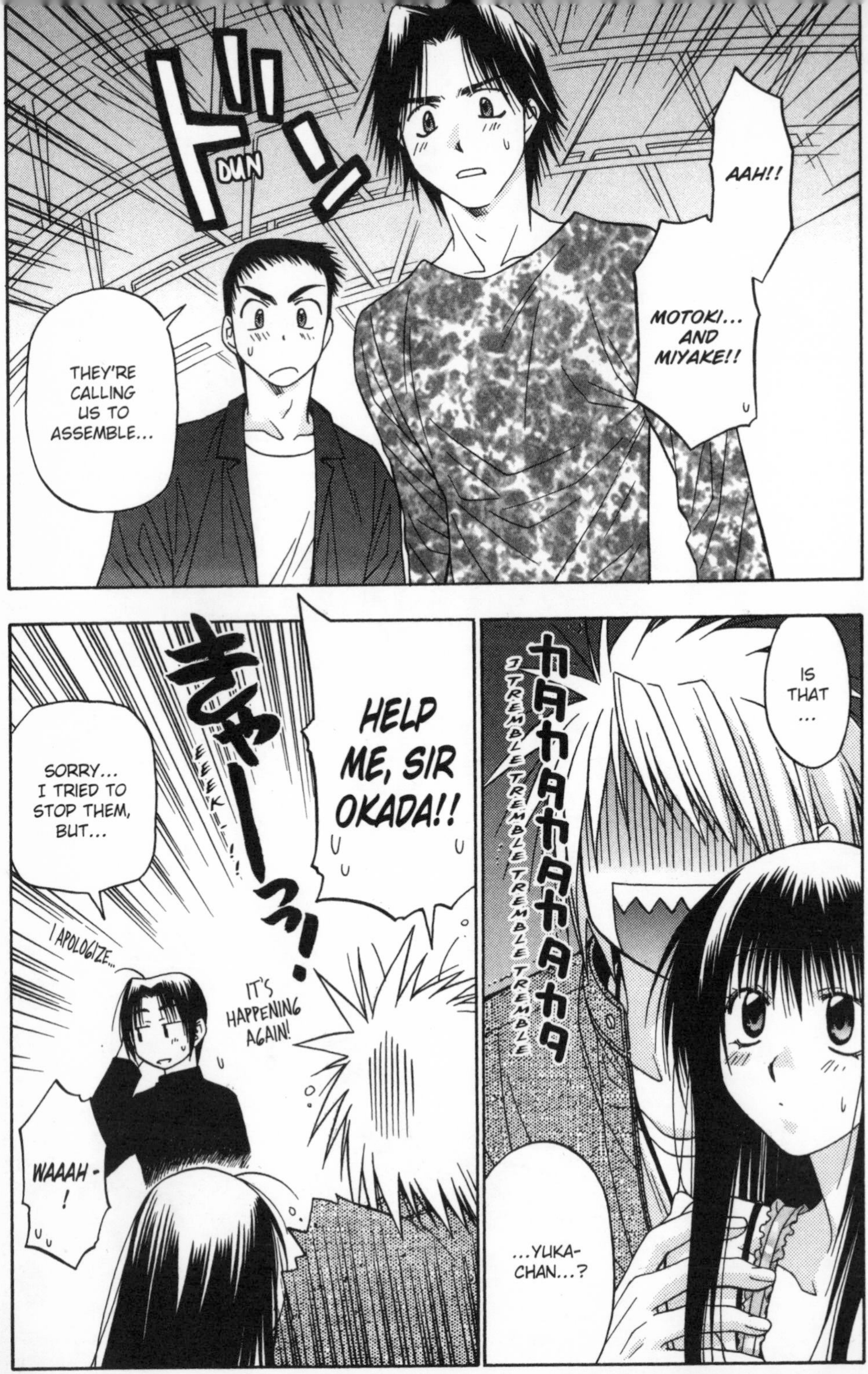
AAH!!
MOTOKI... AND MIYAKE!!
ドーン
DUN
THEY'RE CALLING US TO ASSEMBLE...
IS THAT...
カタカタカタカタカタカタ
TREMBLE TREMBLE TREMBLE TREMBLE
...YUKA-CHAN...?
HELP ME, SIR OKADA!!
きゃーっ!
EEEK!!
SORRY... I TRIED TO STOP THEM, BUT...
IT'S HAPPENING AGAIN!
I APOLOGIZE...
WAAAH-!

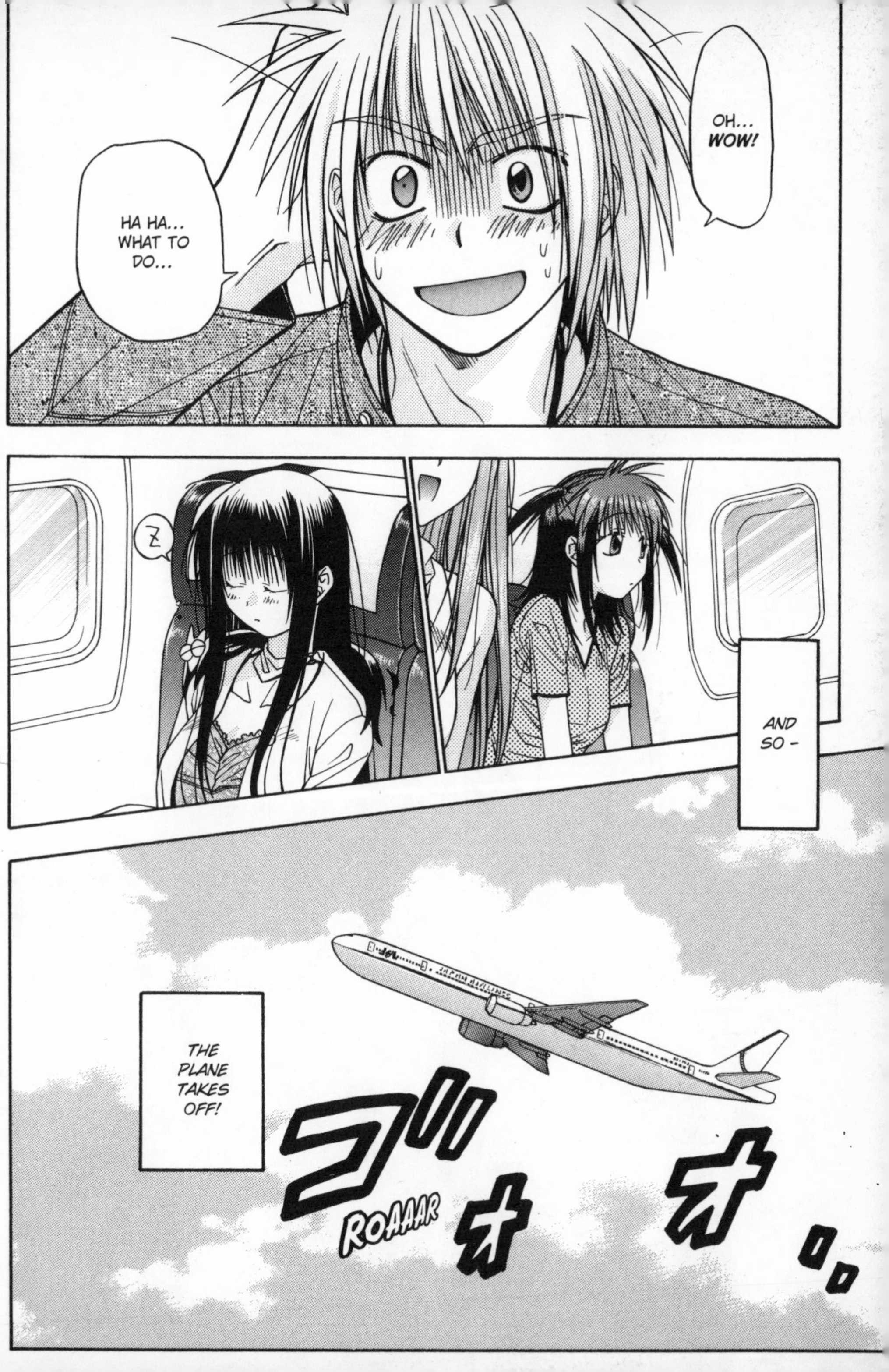
OH... WOW!
HA HA... WHAT TO DO...
AND SO -
Z
THE PLANE TAKES OFF!
ROAAAR

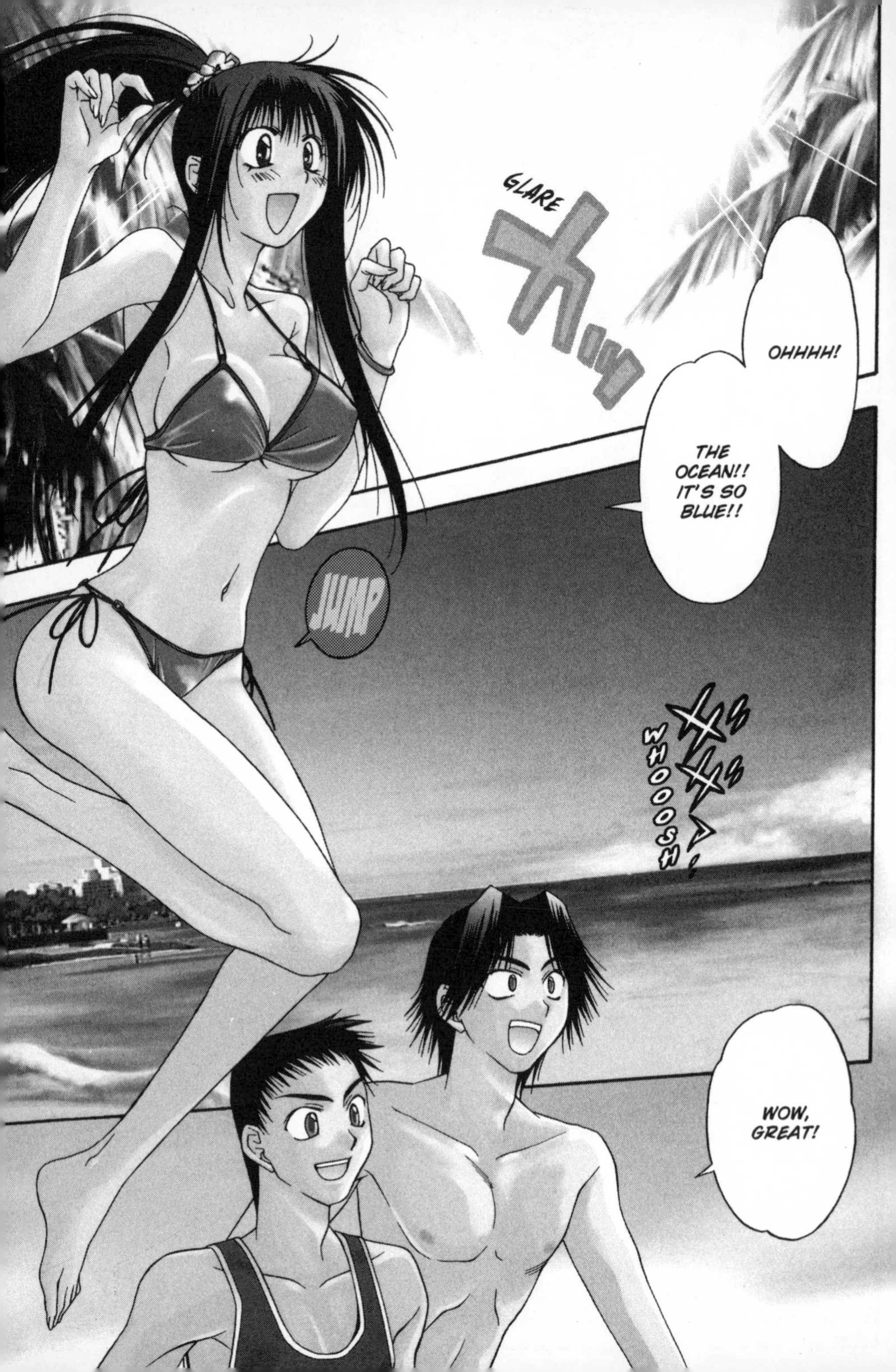
OHHHH!
GLARE
THE OCEAN!! IT'S SO BLUE!!
JUMP
WHOOOSH
WOW, GREAT!

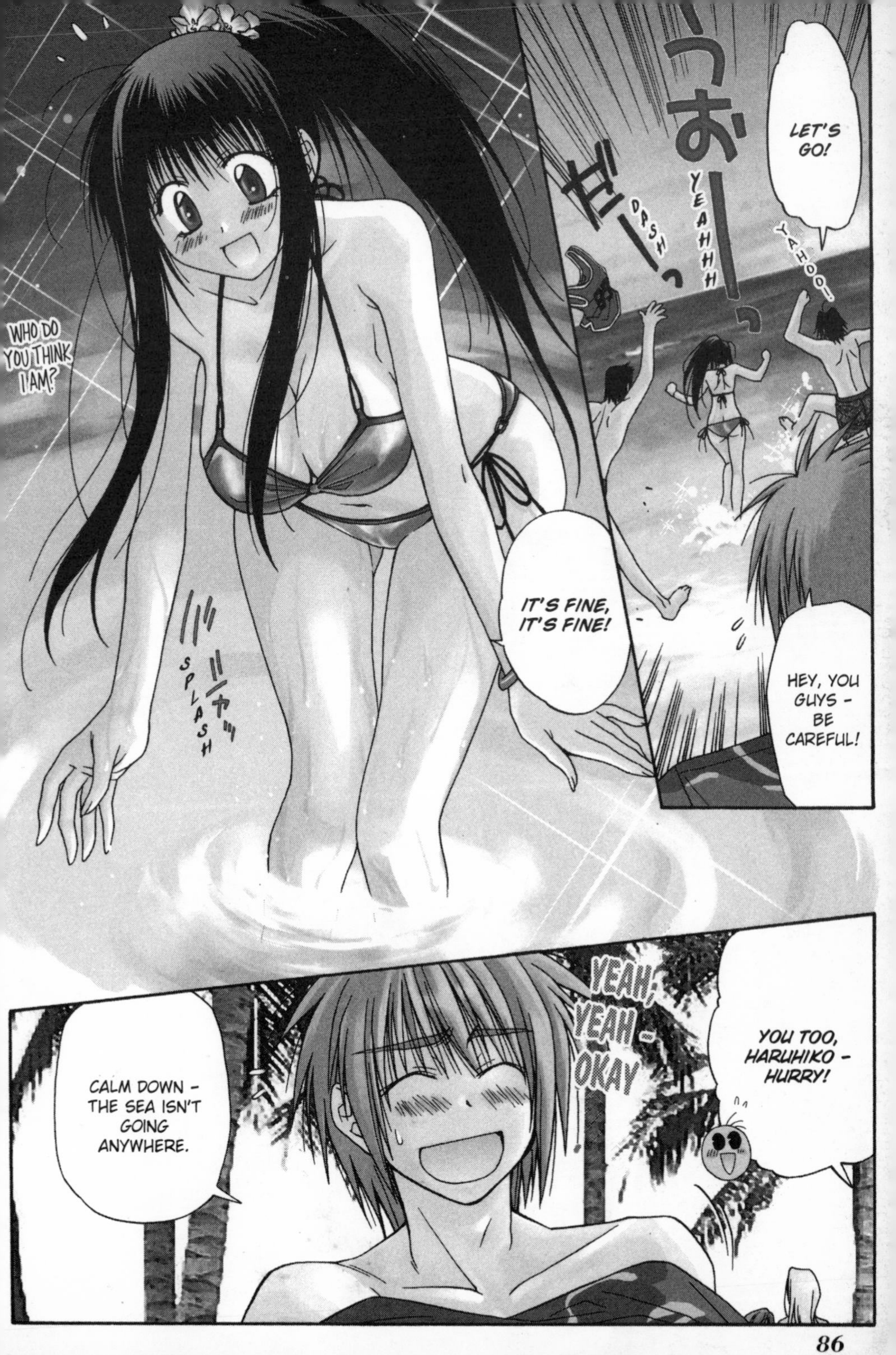
LET'S GO!
YEAHHH
DASH
YAHOO!
HEY, YOU GUYS - BE CAREFUL!
IT'S FINE, IT'S FINE!
SPLASH
WHO DO YOU THINK I AM?
YOU TOO, HARUHIKO - HURRY!
YEAH, YEAH... OKAY
CALM DOWN - THE SEA ISN'T GOING ANYWHERE.

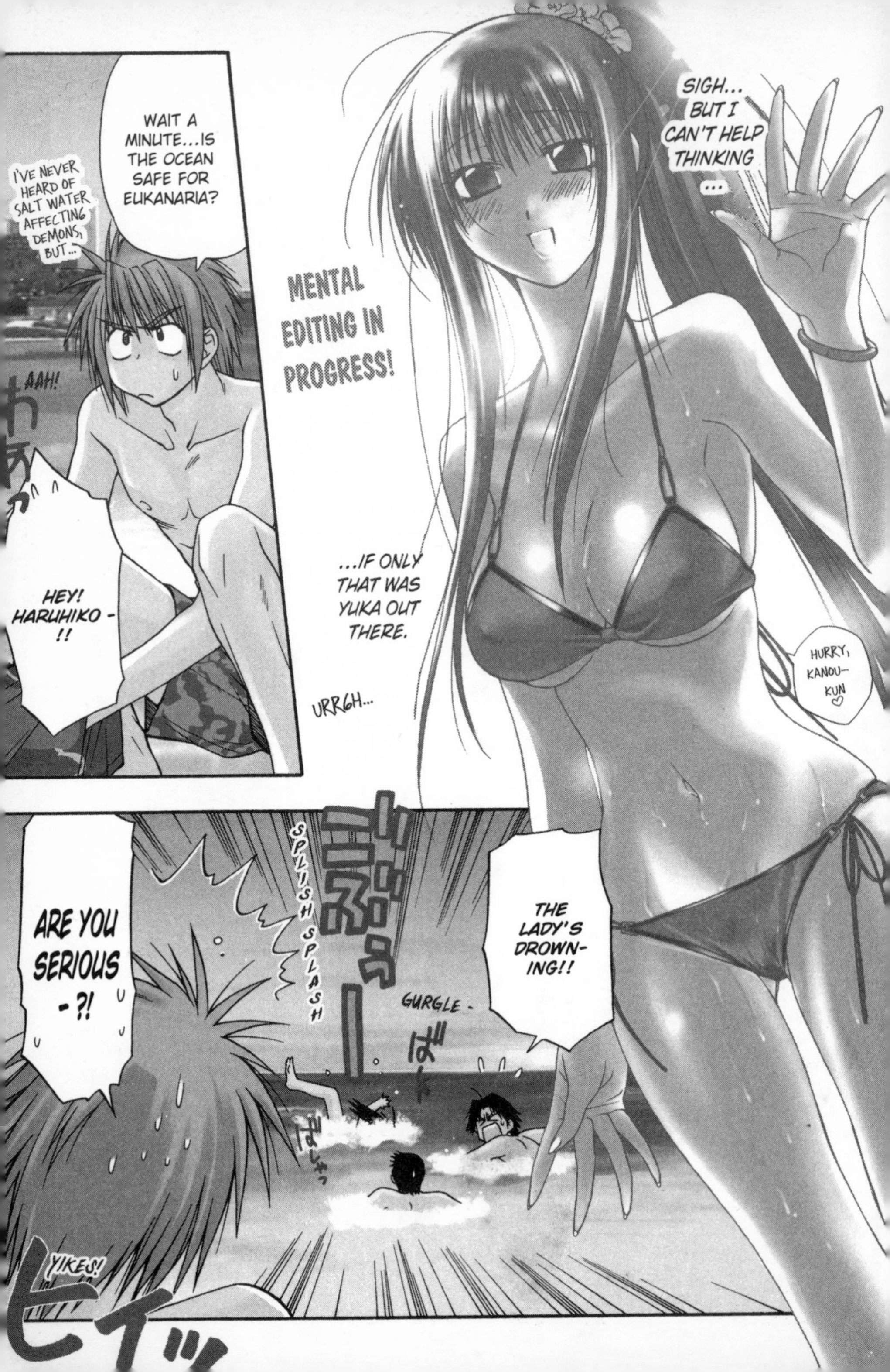
SIGH... BUT I CAN'T HELP THINKING ...
...IF ONLY THAT WAS YUKA OUT THERE.
MENTAL EDITING IN PROGRESS!
HURRY, KANOU-KUN ♡
URRGH...
WAIT A MINUTE...IS THE OCEAN SAFE FOR EUKANARIA?
I'VE NEVER HEARD OF SALT WATER AFFECTING DEMONS, BUT...
AAH!
HEY! HARUHIKO-!!
THE LADY'S DROWNING!!
GURGLE-
SPLISH SPLASH
ARE YOU SERIOUS-?!
YIKES!

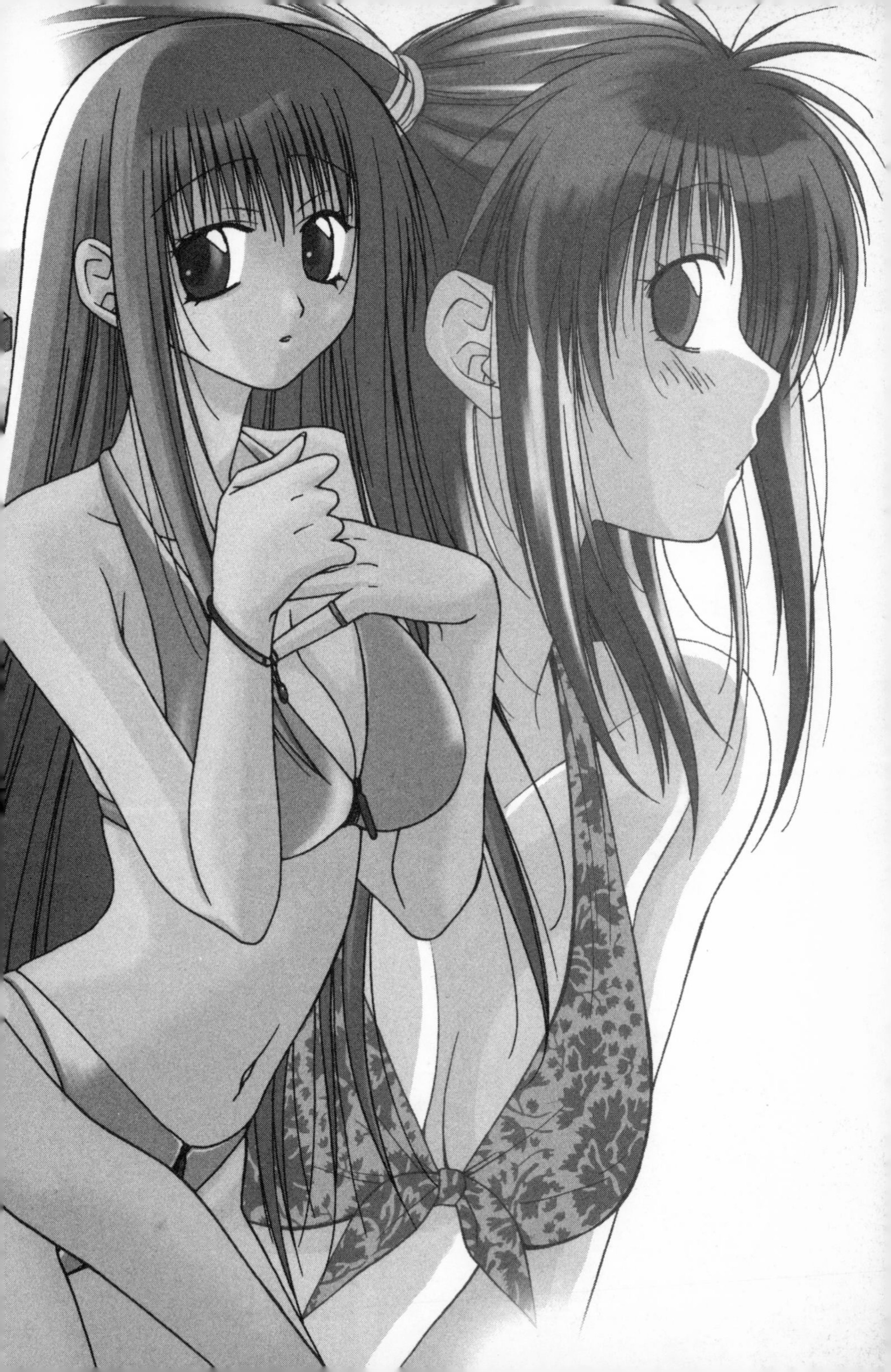

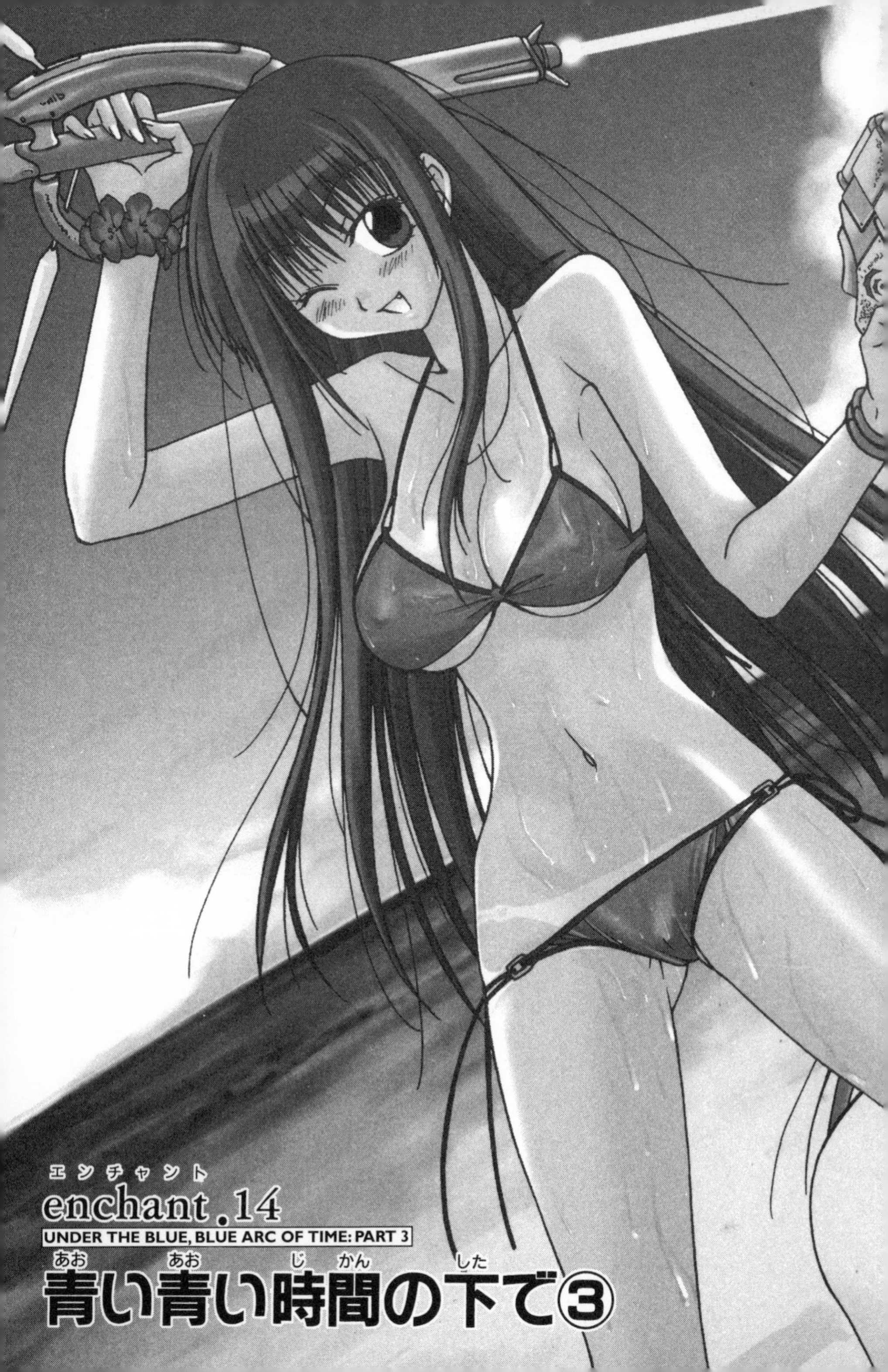

エンチャント
enchant.14
UNDER THE BLUE, BLUE ARC OF TIME: PART 3
青い青い時間の下で③

IDLE CHATTER 1/2

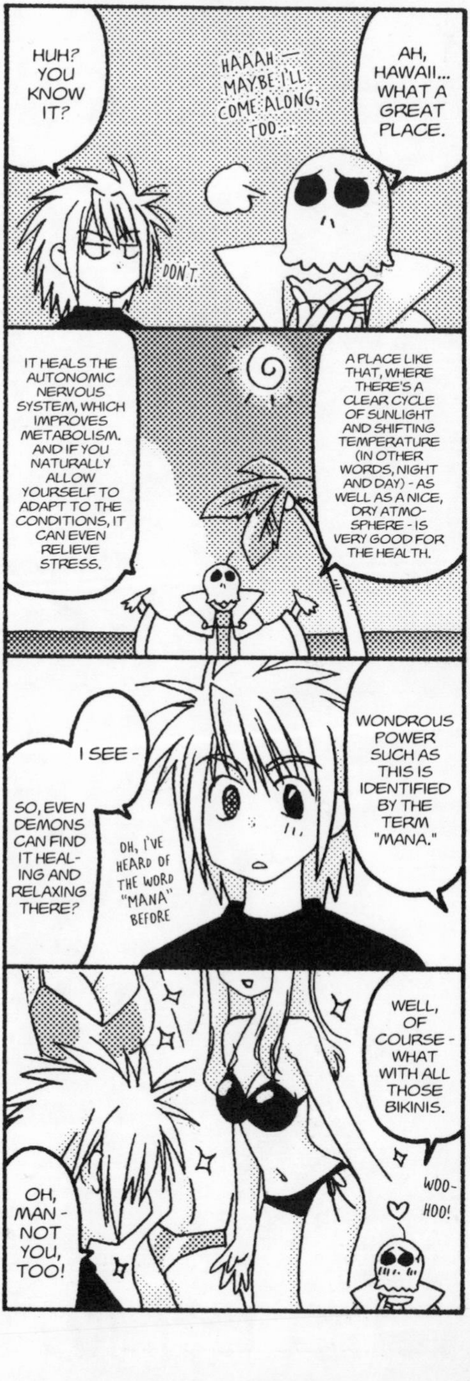
AH, HAWAII... WHAT A GREAT PLACE.
HAAAH— MAYBE I'LL COME ALONG, TOO...
HUH? YOU KNOW IT?
DON'T.
A PLACE LIKE THAT, WHERE THERE'S A CLEAR CYCLE OF SUNLIGHT AND SHIFTING TEMPERATURE (IN OTHER WORDS, NIGHT AND DAY) - AS WELL AS A NICE, DRY ATMO-SPHERE - IS VERY GOOD FOR THE HEALTH.
IT HEALS THE AUTONOMIC NERVOUS SYSTEM, WHICH IMPROVES METABOLISM. AND IF YOU NATURALLY ALLOW YOURSELF TO ADAPT TO THE CONDITIONS, IT CAN EVEN RELIEVE STRESS.
WONDROUS POWER SUCH AS THIS IS IDENTIFIED BY THE TERM "MANA."
I SEE - SO, EVEN DEMONS CAN FIND IT HEAL-ING AND RELAXING THERE?
OH, I'VE HEARD OF THE WORD "MANA" BEFORE
WELL, OF COURSE - WHAT WITH ALL THOSE BIKINIS.
WOO-HOO!
OH, MAN - NOT YOU, TOO!

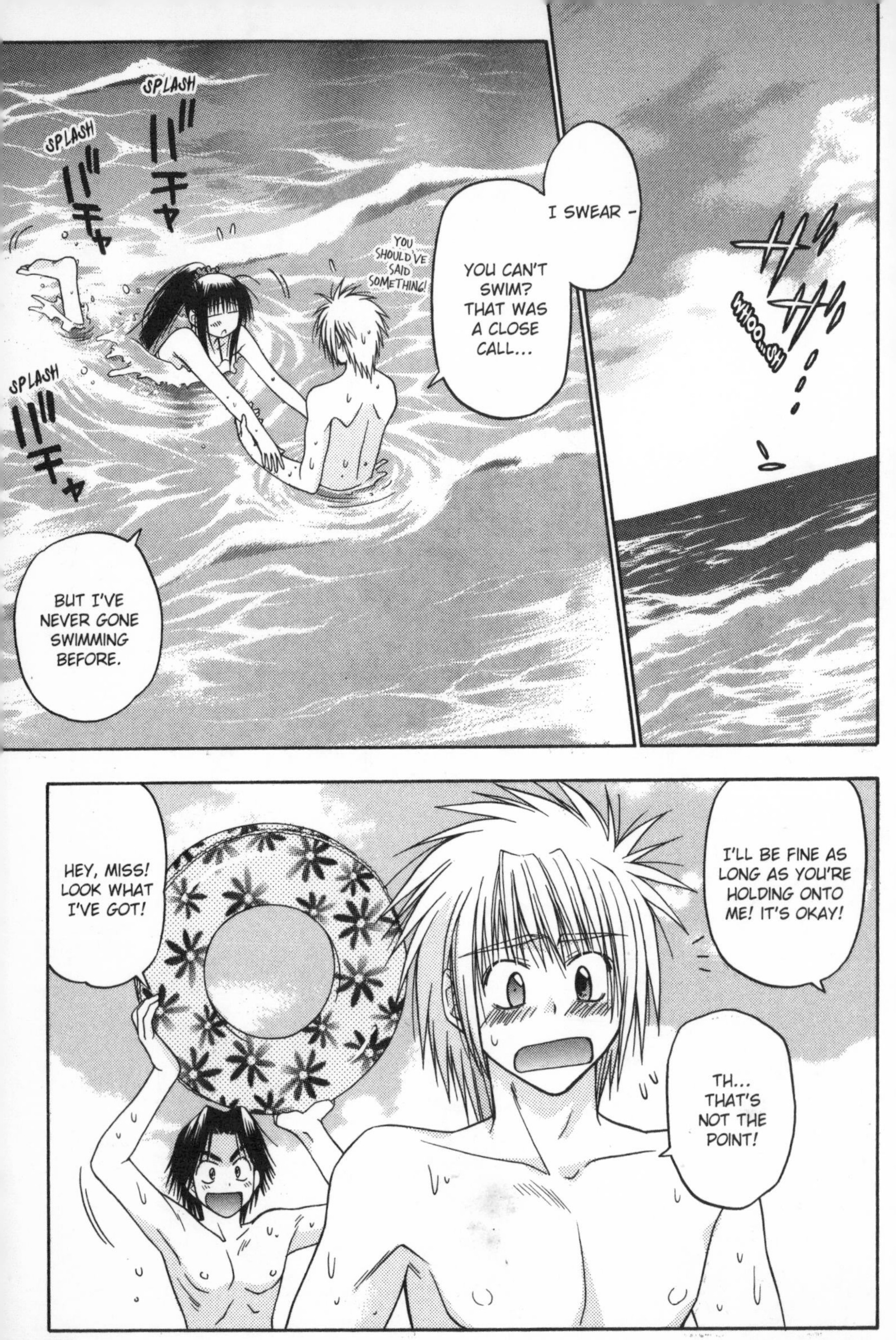
WHOO...SH
I SWEAR –
YOU CAN'T SWIM? THAT WAS A CLOSE CALL...
SPLASH
SPLASH
YOU SHOULD'VE SAID SOMETHING!
SPLASH
BUT I'VE NEVER GONE SWIMMING BEFORE.
I'LL BE FINE AS LONG AS YOU'RE HOLDING ONTO ME! IT'S OKAY!
HEY, MISS! LOOK WHAT I'VE GOT!
TH... THAT'S NOT THE POINT!

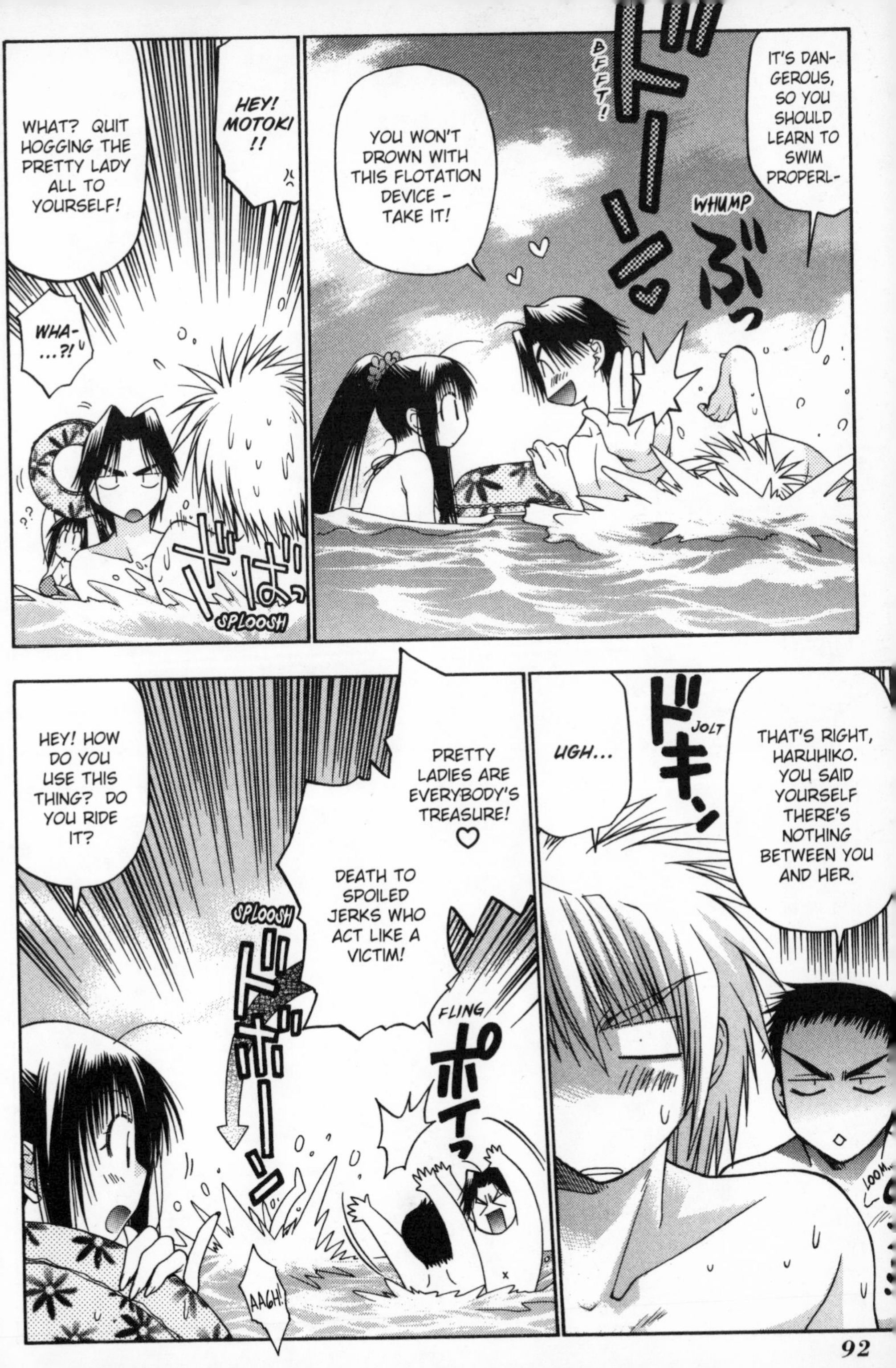
IT'S DANGEROUS, SO YOU SHOULD LEARN TO SWIM PROPERL-
BFFT!
WHUMP
YOU WON'T DROWN WITH THIS FLOTATION DEVICE - TAKE IT!
HEY! MOTOKI!!
WHAT? QUIT HOGGING THE PRETTY LADY ALL TO YOURSELF!
WHA-...?!
SPLOOSH
THAT'S RIGHT, HARUHIKO. YOU SAID YOURSELF THERE'S NOTHING BETWEEN YOU AND HER.
JOLT
UGH...
LOOM...
PRETTY LADIES ARE EVERYBODY'S TREASURE! ♡
DEATH TO SPOILED JERKS WHO ACT LIKE A VICTIM!
FLING
SPLOOSH
HEY! HOW DO YOU USE THIS THING? DO YOU RIDE IT?
AAGH!

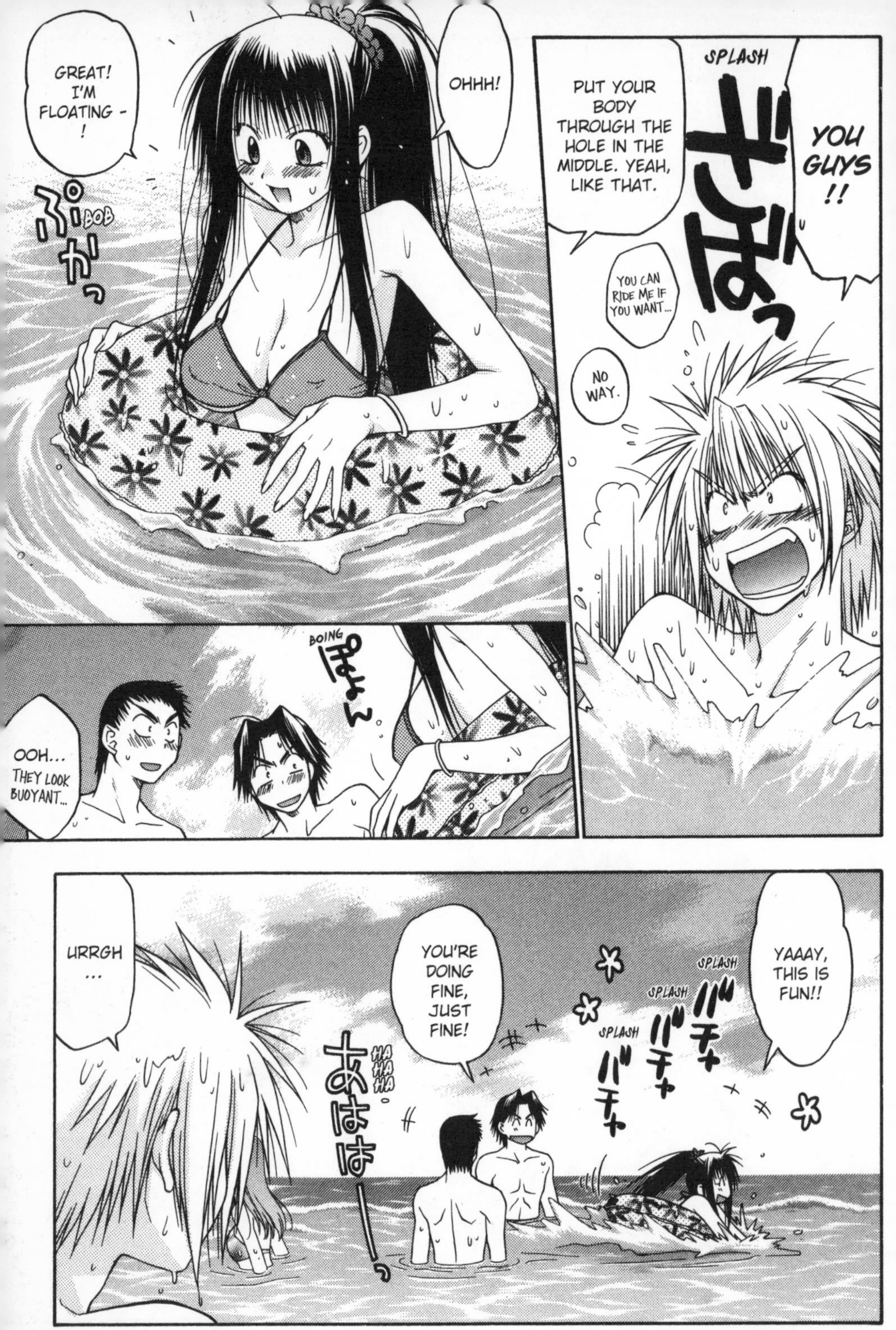
SPLASH
YOU GUYS!!
PUT YOUR BODY THROUGH THE HOLE IN THE MIDDLE. YEAH, LIKE THAT.
YOU CAN RIDE ME IF YOU WANT...
NO WAY.
OHHH!
GREAT! I'M FLOATING -!
BOB
BOING
OOH... THEY LOOK BUOYANT...
YAAAY, THIS IS FUN!!
SPLASH
SPLASH
SPLASH
YOU'RE DOING FINE, JUST FINE!
HA HA HA
URRGH ...

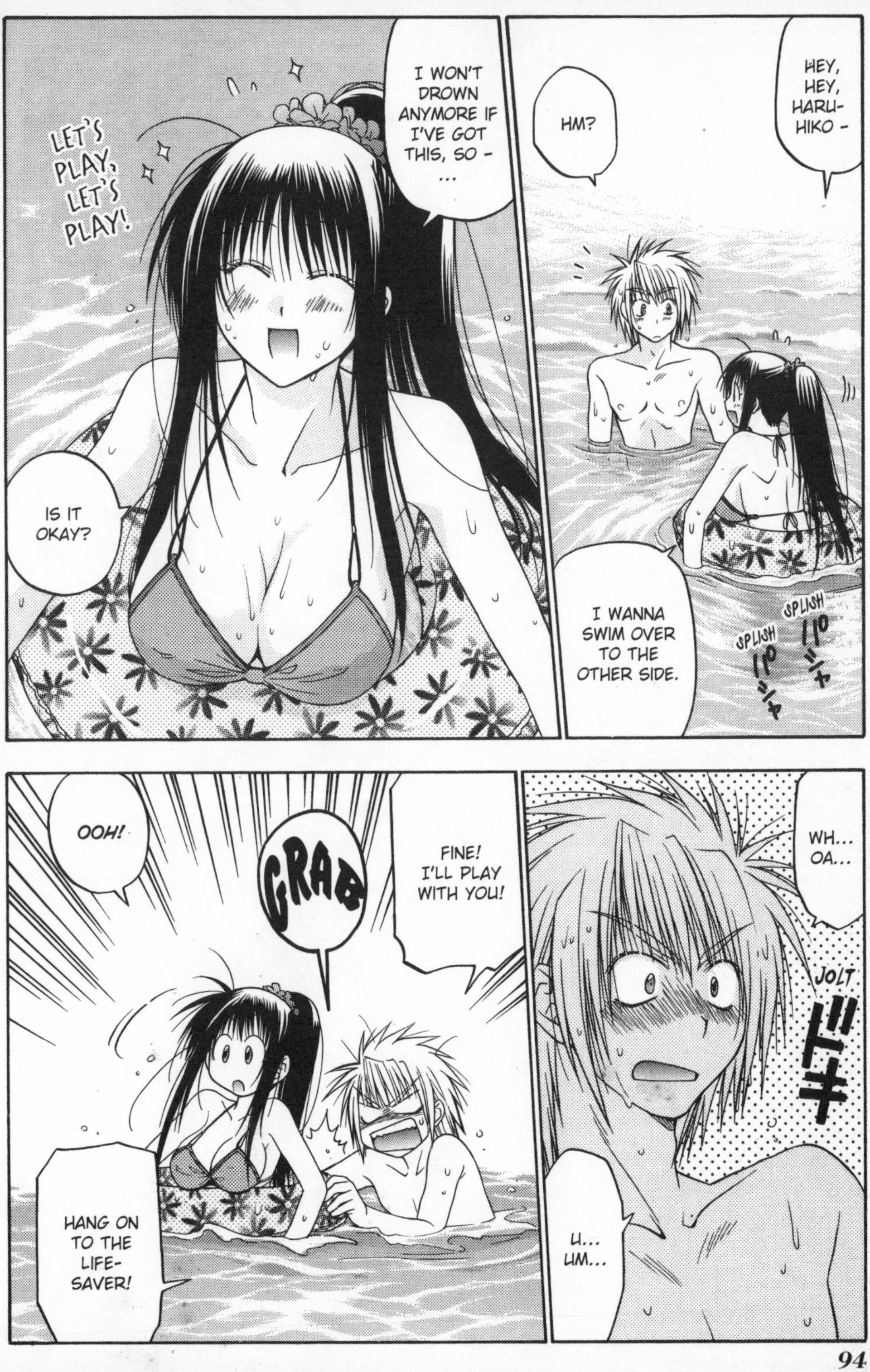
HEY, HEY, HARU-HIKO -
HM?
I WANNA SWIM OVER TO THE OTHER SIDE.
SPLISH パシャ
SPLISH パシャ
I WON'T DROWN ANYMORE IF I'VE GOT THIS, SO - ...
LET'S PLAY, LET'S PLAY!
IS IT OKAY?
WH... OA...
JOLT ドキ
U... UM...
FINE! I'LL PLAY WITH YOU!
GRAB
OOH!
HANG ON TO THE LIFE-SAVER!

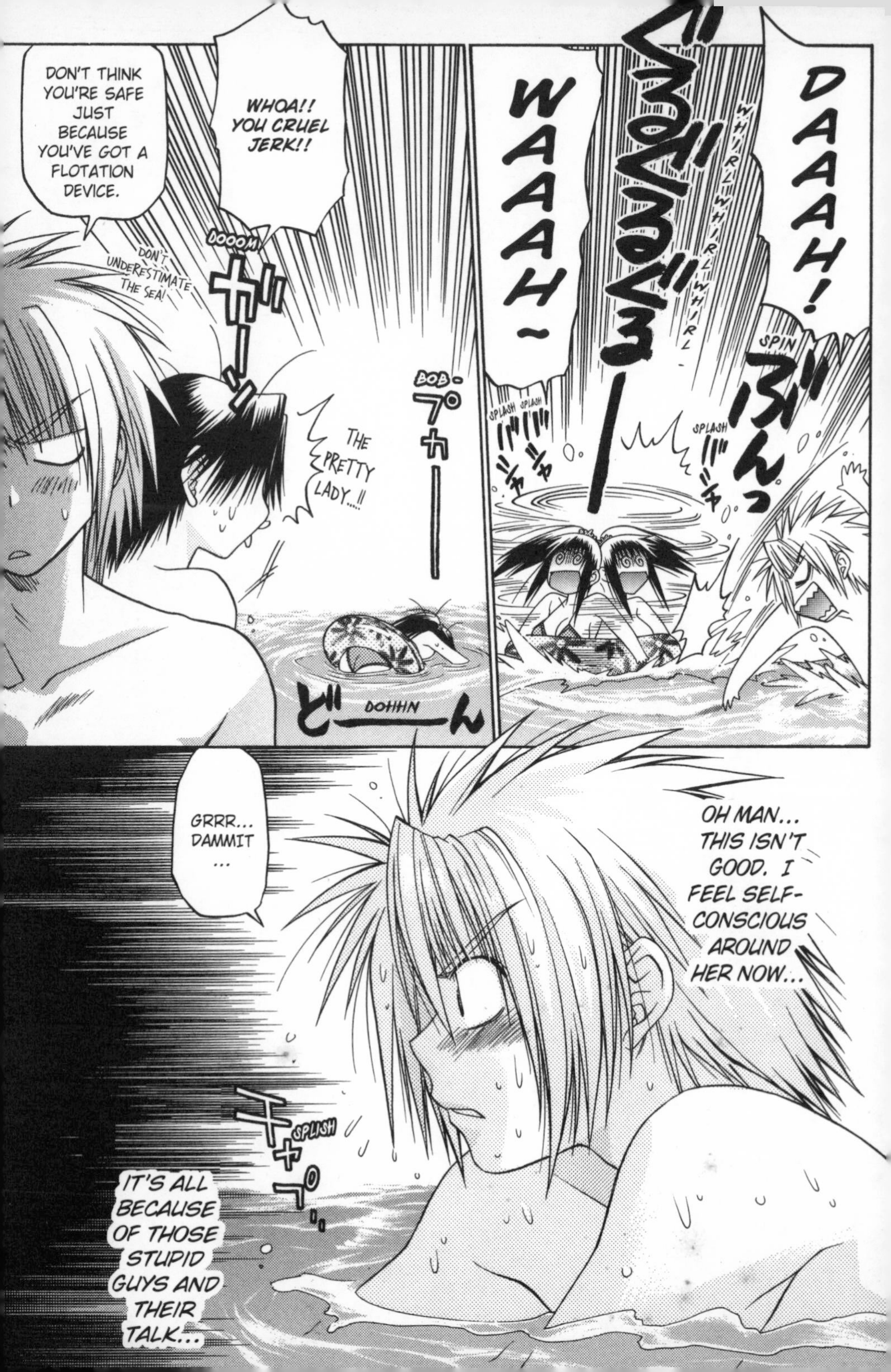

DAAAAH!
WAAAAH~
ぐるぐるぐるー
WHIRL WHIRL WHIRL
SPIN
ぶんっ
SPLASH
バシャ
SPLASH SPLASH
バシャバシャ
WHOA!! YOU CRUEL JERK!!
DON'T THINK YOU'RE SAFE JUST BECAUSE YOU'VE GOT A FLOTATION DEVICE.
DOOOM
ガーン
DON'T UNDERESTIMATE THE SEA!
BOB
プカー
THE PRETTY LADY...!!
どーん
DOHHN
OH MAN... THIS ISN'T GOOD. I FEEL SELF-CONSCIOUS AROUND HER NOW...
GRRR... DAMMIT ...
SPLISH
チャプ
IT'S ALL BECAUSE OF THOSE STUPID GUYS AND THEIR TALK...

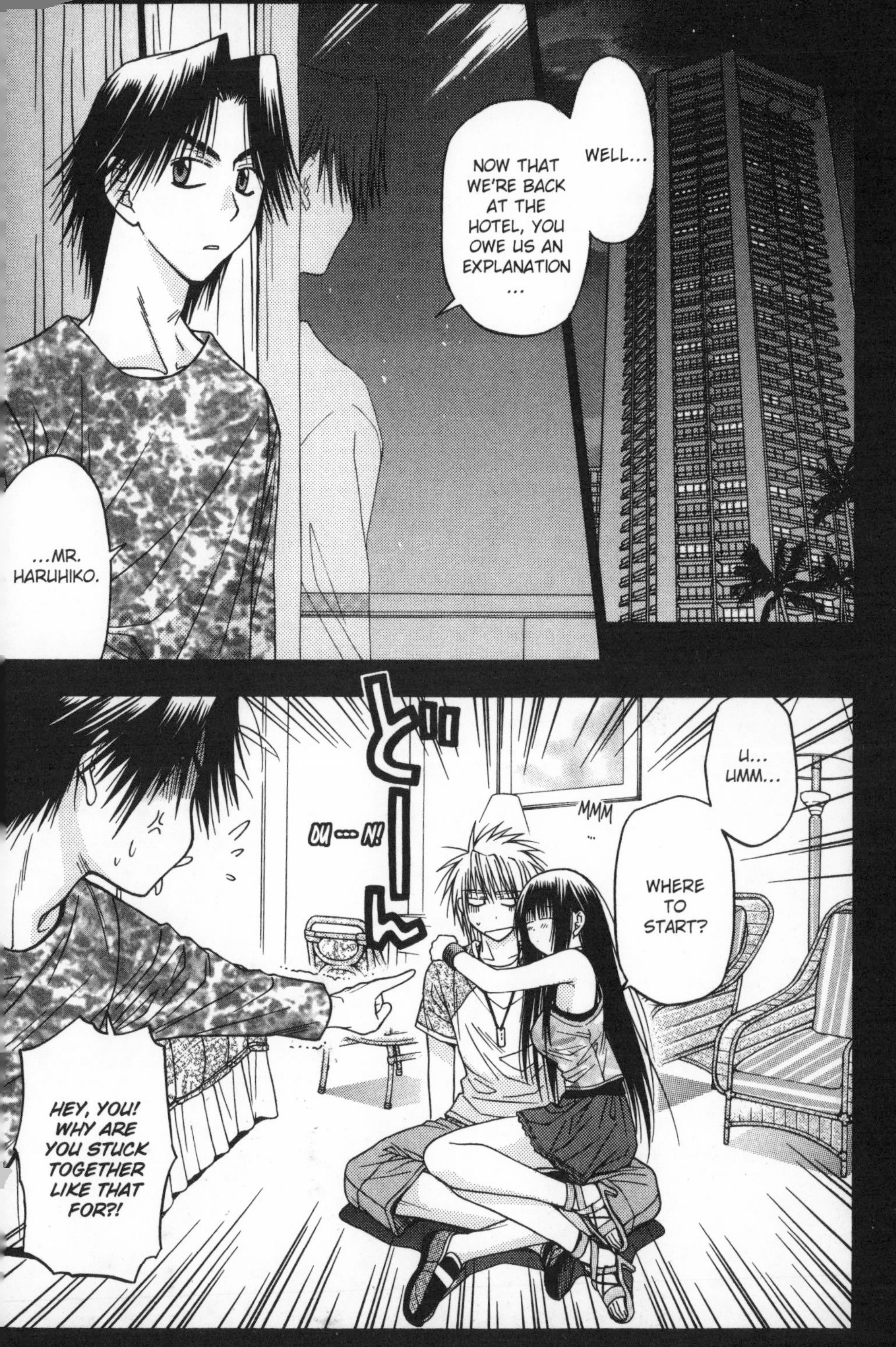
WELL...
NOW THAT WE'RE BACK AT THE HOTEL, YOU OWE US AN EXPLANATION ...
...MR. HARUHIKO.
U... UMMM...
どーん
DU---N!
MMM ...
WHERE TO START?
HEY, YOU! WHY ARE YOU STUCK TOGETHER LIKE THAT FOR?!

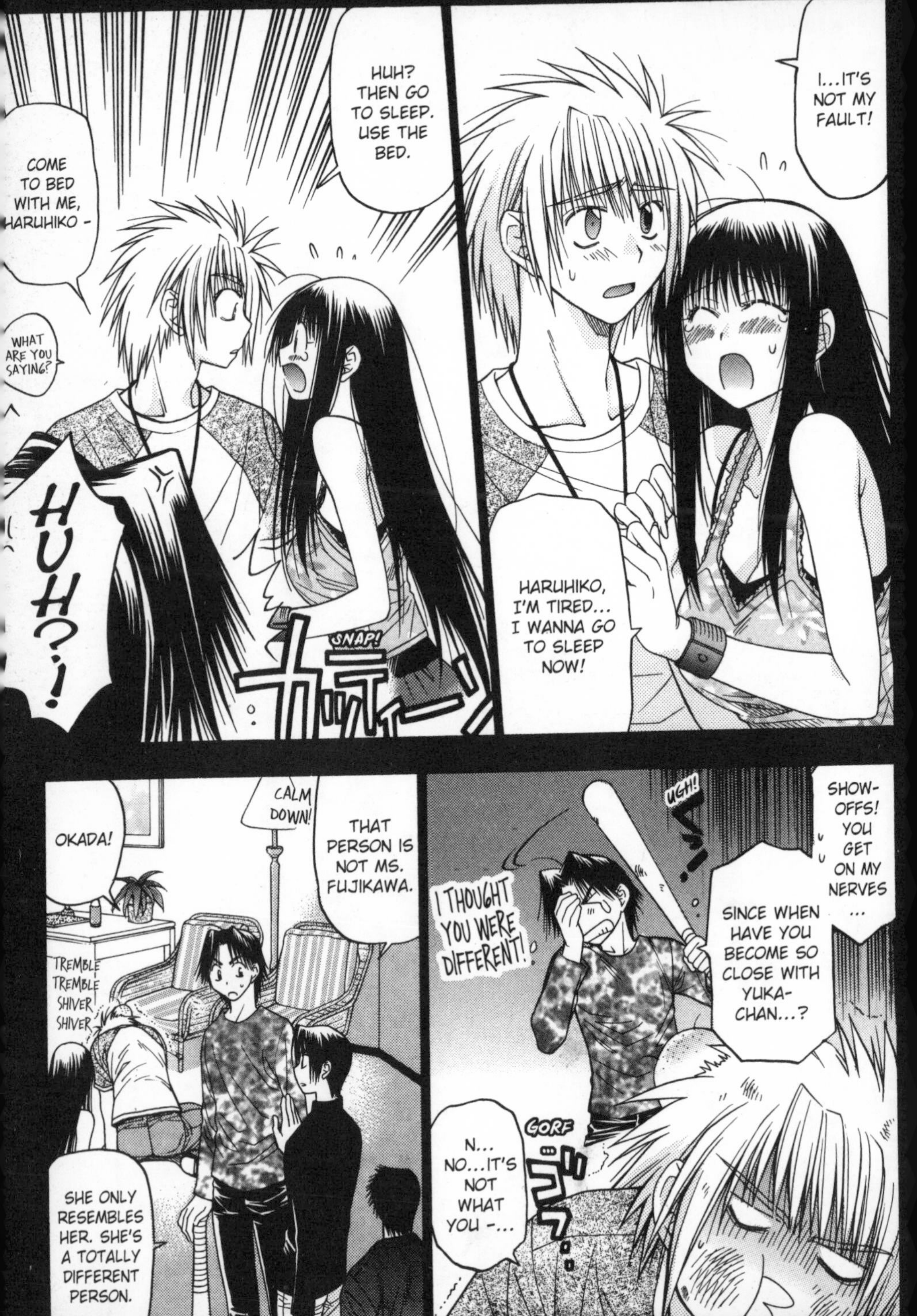
I...IT'S NOT MY FAULT!
HARUHIKO, I'M TIRED... I WANNA GO TO SLEEP NOW!
HUH? THEN GO TO SLEEP. USE THE BED.
COME TO BED WITH ME, HARUHIKO -
WHAT ARE YOU SAYING?
HUH?!
SNAP!
SHOW-OFFS! YOU GET ON MY NERVES...
UGH!
SINCE WHEN HAVE YOU BECOME SO CLOSE WITH YUKA-CHAN...?
I THOUGHT YOU WERE DIFFERENT!
GORF
N... NO...IT'S NOT WHAT YOU -...
CALM DOWN!
THAT PERSON IS NOT MS. FUJIKAWA.
OKADA!
TREMBLE TREMBLE SHIVER SHIVER
SHE ONLY RESEMBLES HER. SHE'S A TOTALLY DIFFERENT PERSON.

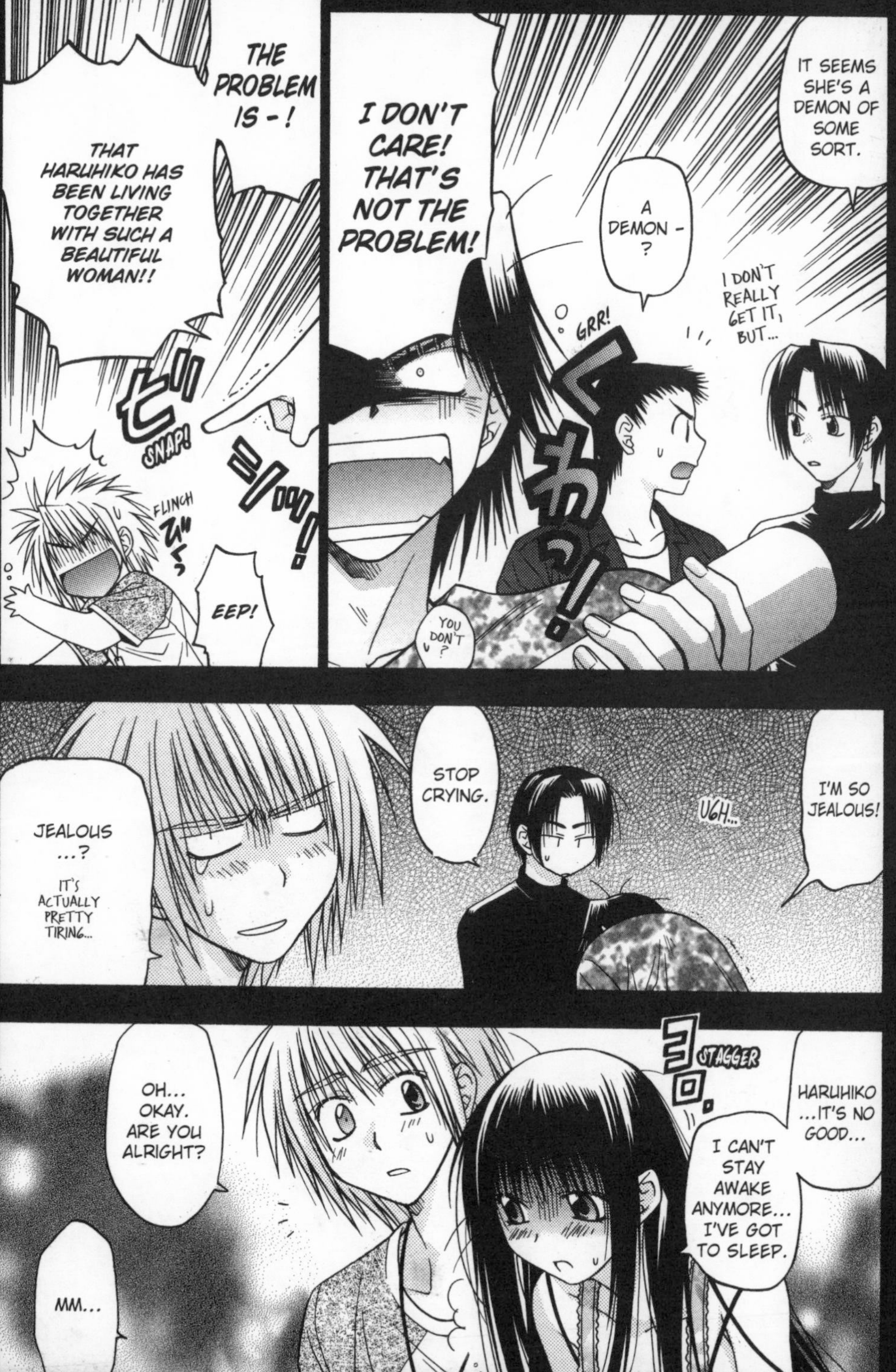
IT SEEMS SHE'S A DEMON OF SOME SORT.
A DEMON -?
I DON'T REALLY GET IT, BUT...
GRR!
I DON'T CARE! THAT'S NOT THE PROBLEM!
YOU DON'T?
THE PROBLEM IS -!
THAT HARUHIKO HAS BEEN LIVING TOGETHER WITH SUCH A BEAUTIFUL WOMAN!!
SNAP!
FLINCH
EEP!
I'M SO JEALOUS!
UGH...
STOP CRYING.
JEALOUS ...?
IT'S ACTUALLY PRETTY TIRING...
STAGGER
HARUHIKO ...IT'S NO GOOD...
I CAN'T STAY AWAKE ANYMORE... I'VE GOT TO SLEEP.
OH... OKAY. ARE YOU ALRIGHT?
MM...

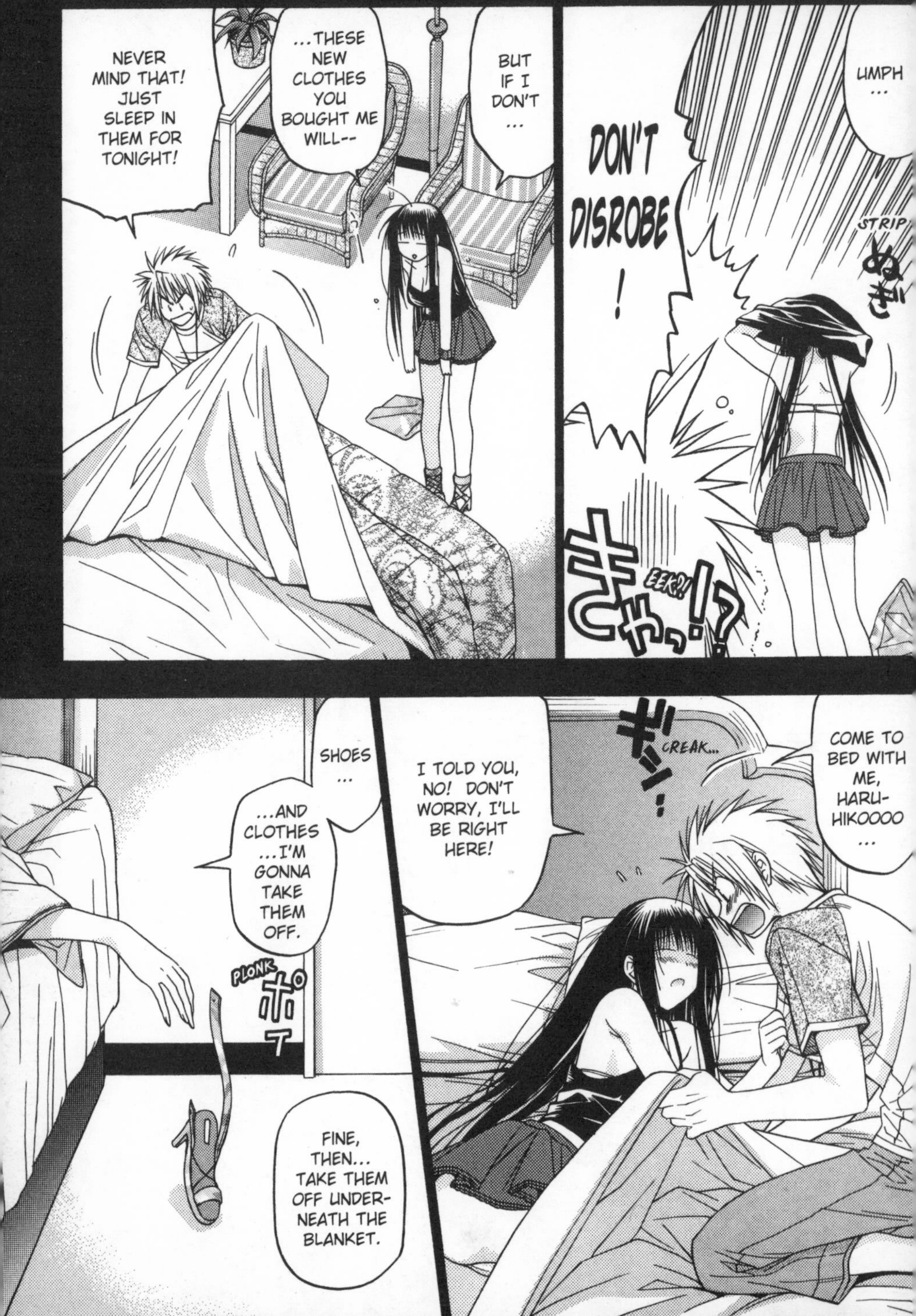
UMPH ...
DON'T DISROBE !
STRIP
ぬぎ
きゃっ!?
EEK?!
BUT IF I DON'T ...
...THESE NEW CLOTHES YOU BOUGHT ME WILL--
NEVER MIND THAT! JUST SLEEP IN THEM FOR TONIGHT!
COME TO BED WITH ME, HARU-HIKOOOO ...
ギシッ
CREAK...
I TOLD YOU, NO! DON'T WORRY, I'LL BE RIGHT HERE!
SHOES ...
...AND CLOTHES ...I'M GONNA TAKE THEM OFF.
PLONK
ポテ
FINE, THEN... TAKE THEM OFF UNDER-NEATH THE BLANKET.

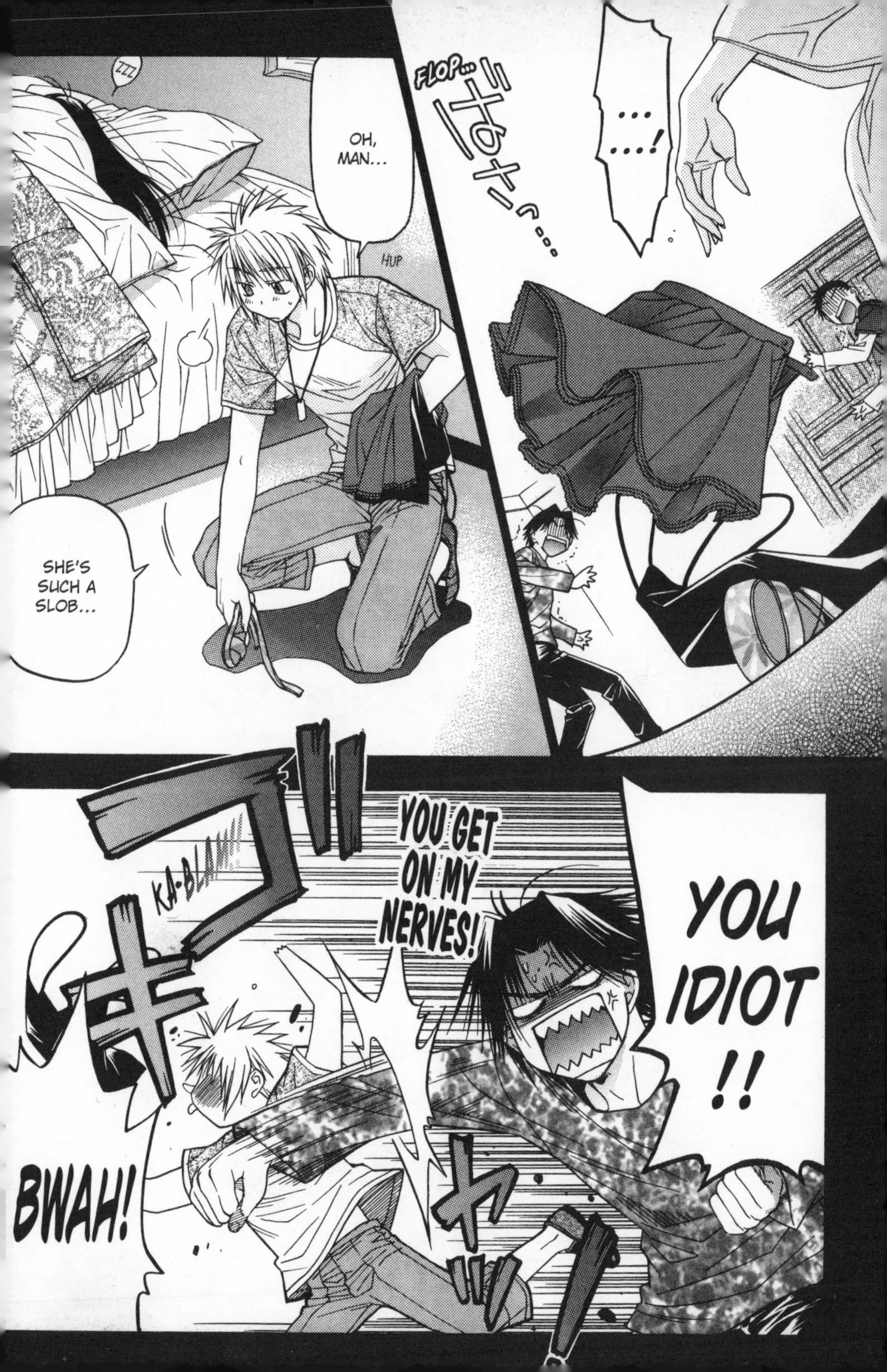

FLOP...
......!
ZZZ
OH, MAN...
HUP
SHE'S SUCH A SLOB...
YOU IDIOT!!
YOU GET ON MY NERVES!
KA-BLAM!!
BWAH!

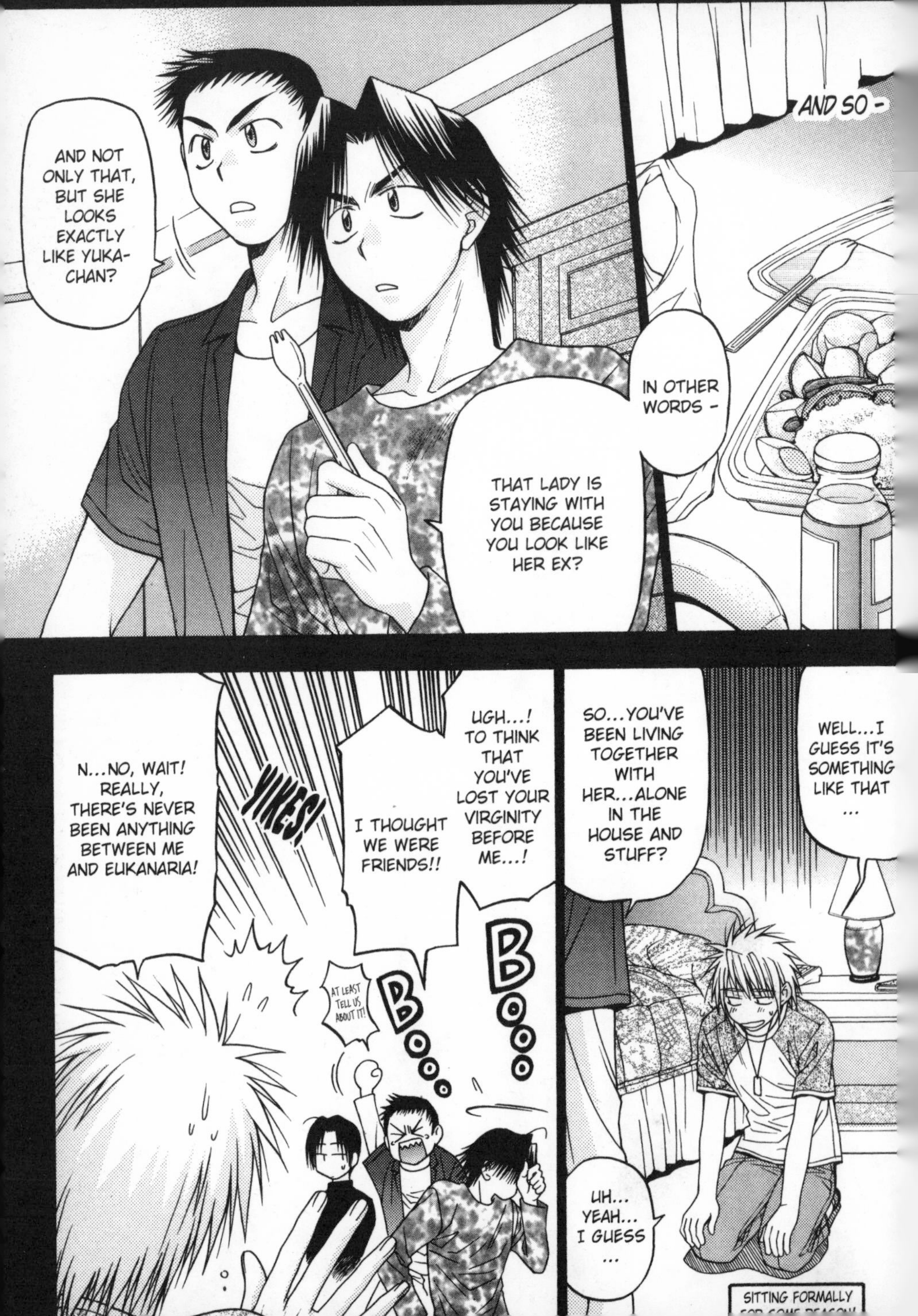
AND SO -
IN OTHER WORDS -
THAT LADY IS STAYING WITH YOU BECAUSE YOU LOOK LIKE HER EX?
AND NOT ONLY THAT, BUT SHE LOOKS EXACTLY LIKE YUKA-CHAN?
WELL...I GUESS IT'S SOMETHING LIKE THAT ...
SO...YOU'VE BEEN LIVING TOGETHER WITH HER...ALONE IN THE HOUSE AND STUFF?
UH... YEAH... I GUESS ...
SITTING FORMALLY FOR SOME REASON!
UGH...! TO THINK THAT YOU'VE LOST YOUR VIRGINITY BEFORE ME...!
I THOUGHT WE WERE FRIENDS!!
YIKES!
BOOO
BOOO
AT LEAST TELL US ABOUT IT!
N...NO, WAIT! REALLY, THERE'S NEVER BEEN ANYTHING BETWEEN ME AND EUKANARIA!

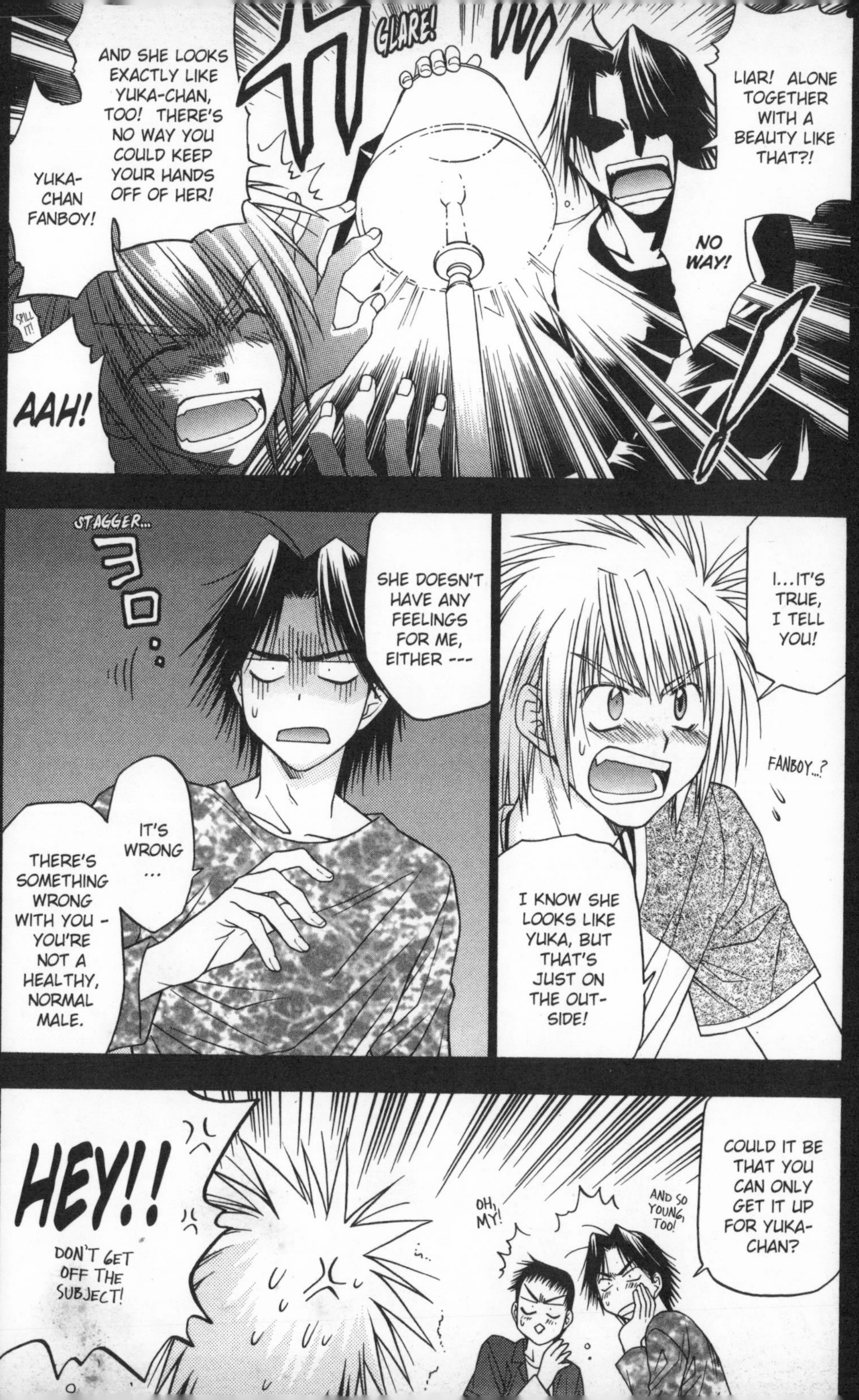
LIAR! ALONE TOGETHER WITH A BEAUTY LIKE THAT?!
NO WAY!
GLARE!
AND SHE LOOKS EXACTLY LIKE YUKA-CHAN, TOO! THERE'S NO WAY YOU COULD KEEP YOUR HANDS OFF OF HER!
YUKA-CHAN FANBOY!
SPILL IT!
AAH!
I...IT'S TRUE, I TELL YOU!
FANBOY...?
I KNOW SHE LOOKS LIKE YUKA, BUT THAT'S JUST ON THE OUT-SIDE!
SHE DOESN'T HAVE ANY FEELINGS FOR ME, EITHER ---
STAGGER...
IT'S WRONG ...
THERE'S SOMETHING WRONG WITH YOU - YOU'RE NOT A HEALTHY, NORMAL MALE.
COULD IT BE THAT YOU CAN ONLY GET IT UP FOR YUKA-CHAN?
AND SO YOUNG, TOO!
OH, MY!
HEY!!
DON'T GET OFF THE SUBJECT!

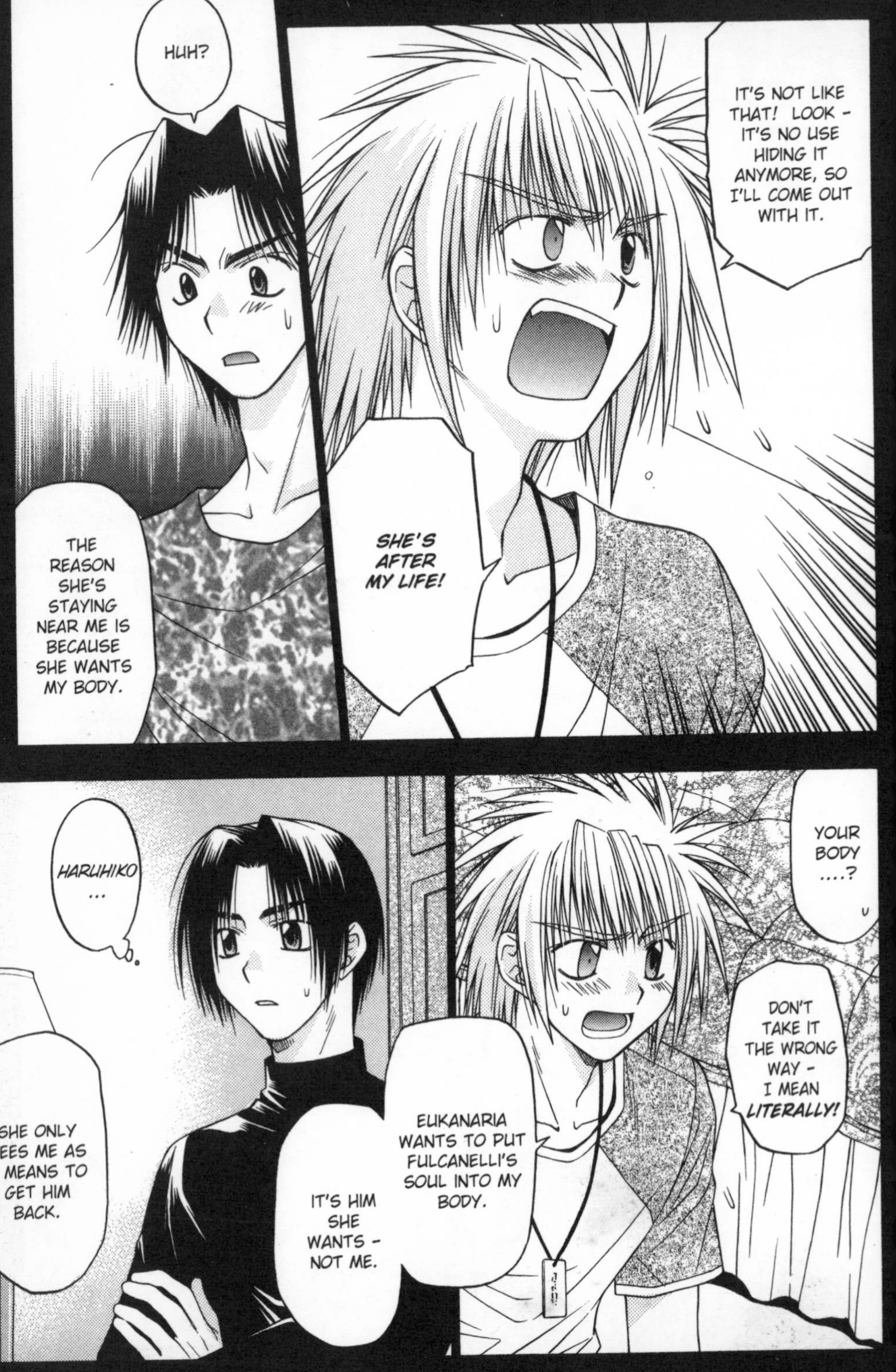
IT'S NOT LIKE THAT! LOOK - IT'S NO USE HIDING IT ANYMORE, SO I'LL COME OUT WITH IT.
SHE'S AFTER MY LIFE!
HUH?
THE REASON SHE'S STAYING NEAR ME IS BECAUSE SHE WANTS MY BODY.
YOUR BODY ....?
DON'T TAKE IT THE WRONG WAY - I MEAN *LITERALLY!*
EUKANARIA WANTS TO PUT FULCANELLI'S SOUL INTO MY BODY.
IT'S HIM SHE WANTS - NOT ME.
HARUHIKO ...
SHE ONLY SEES ME AS A MEANS TO GET HIM BACK.

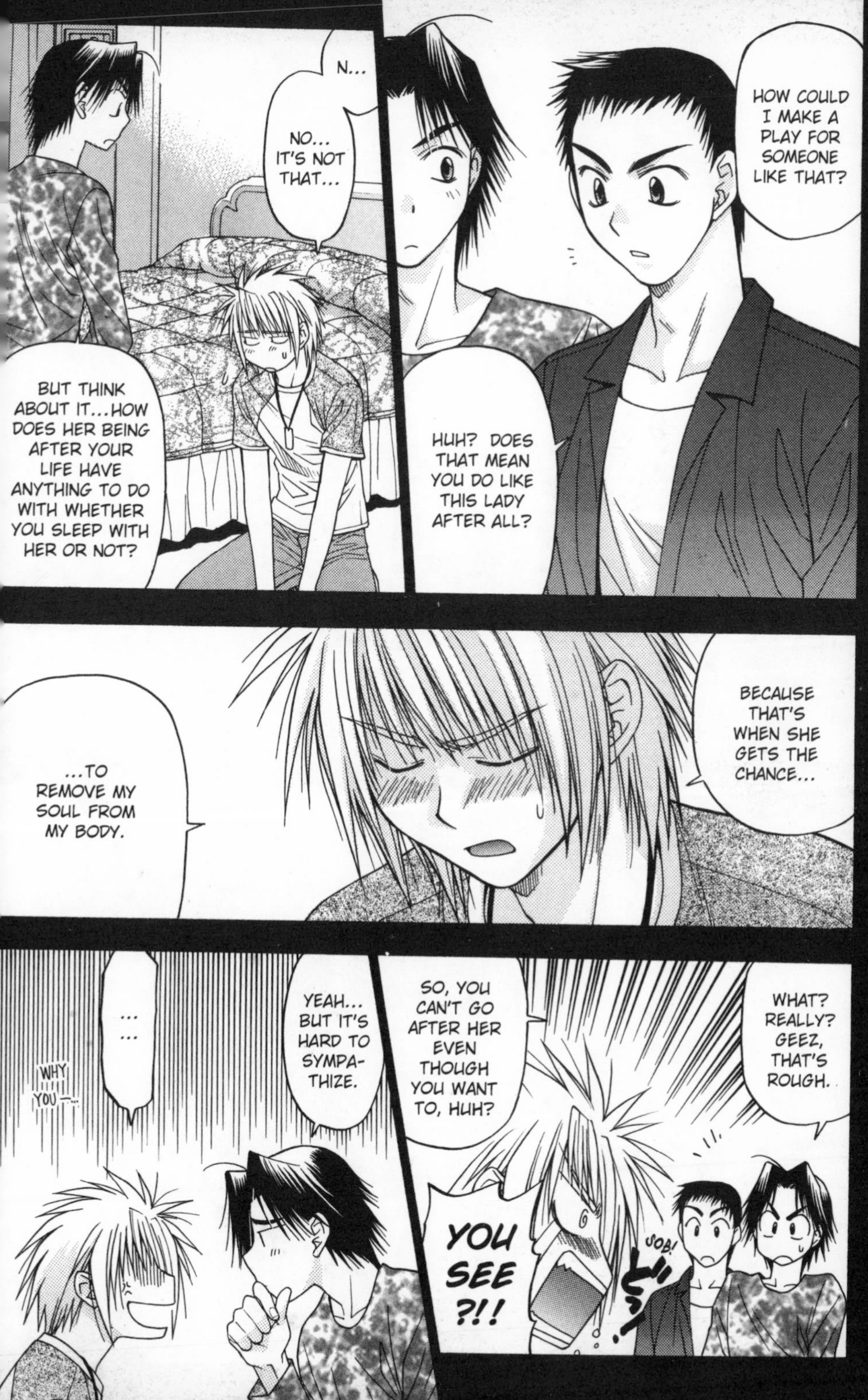
HOW COULD I MAKE A PLAY FOR SOMEONE LIKE THAT?
HUH? DOES THAT MEAN YOU DO LIKE THIS LADY AFTER ALL?
N...
NO... IT'S NOT THAT...
BUT THINK ABOUT IT...HOW DOES HER BEING AFTER YOUR LIFE HAVE ANYTHING TO DO WITH WHETHER YOU SLEEP WITH HER OR NOT?
BECAUSE THAT'S WHEN SHE GETS THE CHANCE...
...TO REMOVE MY SOUL FROM MY BODY.
WHAT? REALLY? GEEZ, THAT'S ROUGH.
YOU SEE ?!!
SOB!
SO, YOU CAN'T GO AFTER HER EVEN THOUGH YOU WANT TO, HUH?
YEAH... BUT IT'S HARD TO SYMPA-THIZE.
... ...
WHY YOU—...

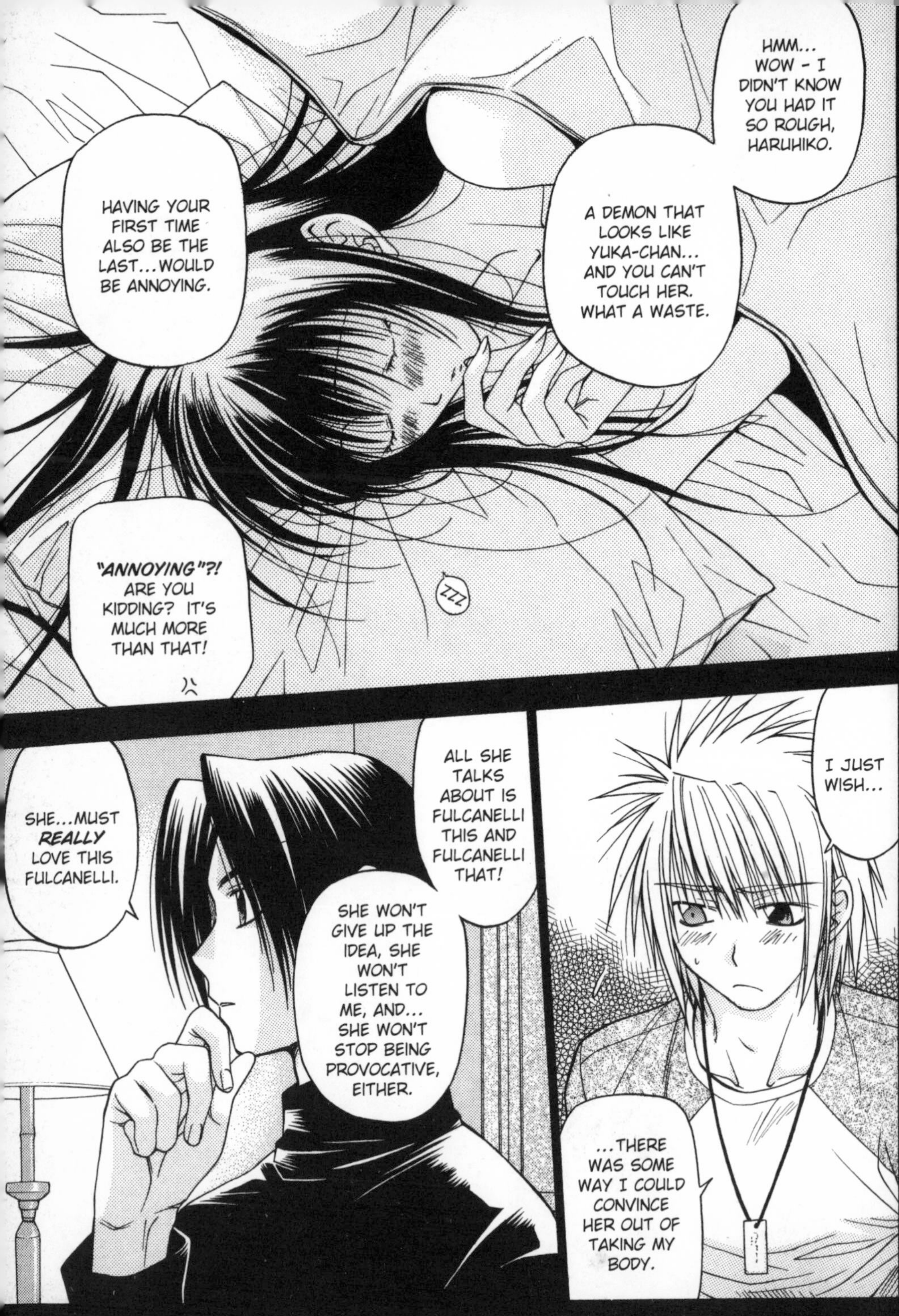
HMM... WOW - I DIDN'T KNOW YOU HAD IT SO ROUGH, HARUHIKO.
A DEMON THAT LOOKS LIKE YUKA-CHAN... AND YOU CAN'T TOUCH HER. WHAT A WASTE.
HAVING YOUR FIRST TIME ALSO BE THE LAST...WOULD BE ANNOYING.
ZZZ
"ANNOYING"?! ARE YOU KIDDING? IT'S MUCH MORE THAN THAT!
I JUST WISH...
...THERE WAS SOME WAY I COULD CONVINCE HER OUT OF TAKING MY BODY.
ALL SHE TALKS ABOUT IS FULCANELLI THIS AND FULCANELLI THAT!
SHE WON'T GIVE UP THE IDEA, SHE WON'T LISTEN TO ME, AND... SHE WON'T STOP BEING PROVOCATIVE, EITHER.
SHE...MUST *REALLY* LOVE THIS FULCANELLI.

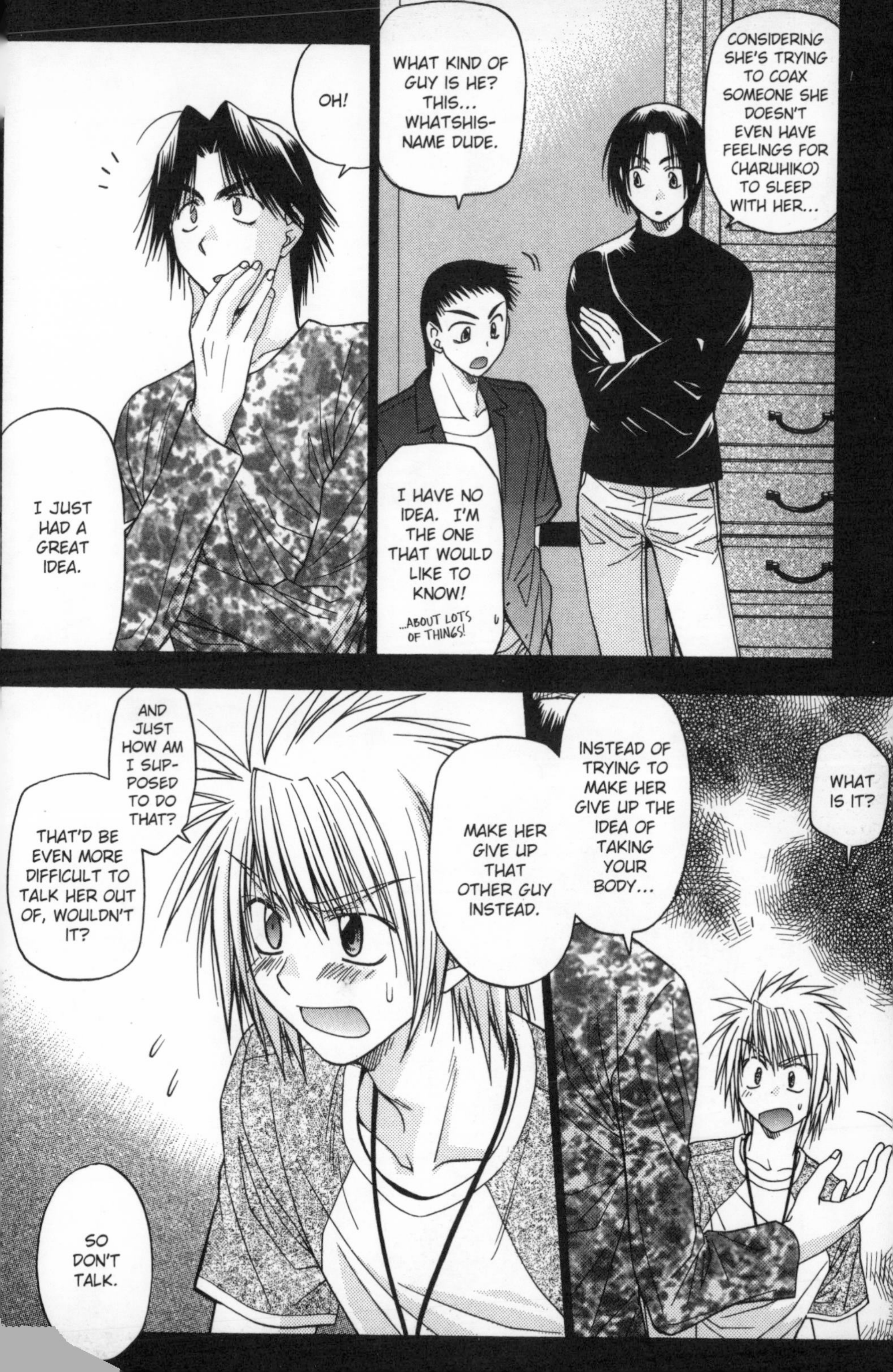
CONSIDERING SHE'S TRYING TO COAX SOMEONE SHE DOESN'T EVEN HAVE FEELINGS FOR (HARUHIKO) TO SLEEP WITH HER...
WHAT KIND OF GUY IS HE? THIS... WHATSHIS-NAME DUDE.
I HAVE NO IDEA. I'M THE ONE THAT WOULD LIKE TO KNOW!
...ABOUT LOTS OF THINGS!
OH!
I JUST HAD A GREAT IDEA.
WHAT IS IT?
INSTEAD OF TRYING TO MAKE HER GIVE UP THE IDEA OF TAKING YOUR BODY...
MAKE HER GIVE UP THAT OTHER GUY INSTEAD.
AND JUST HOW AM I SUP-POSED TO DO THAT?
THAT'D BE EVEN MORE DIFFICULT TO TALK HER OUT OF, WOULDN'T IT?
SO DON'T TALK.

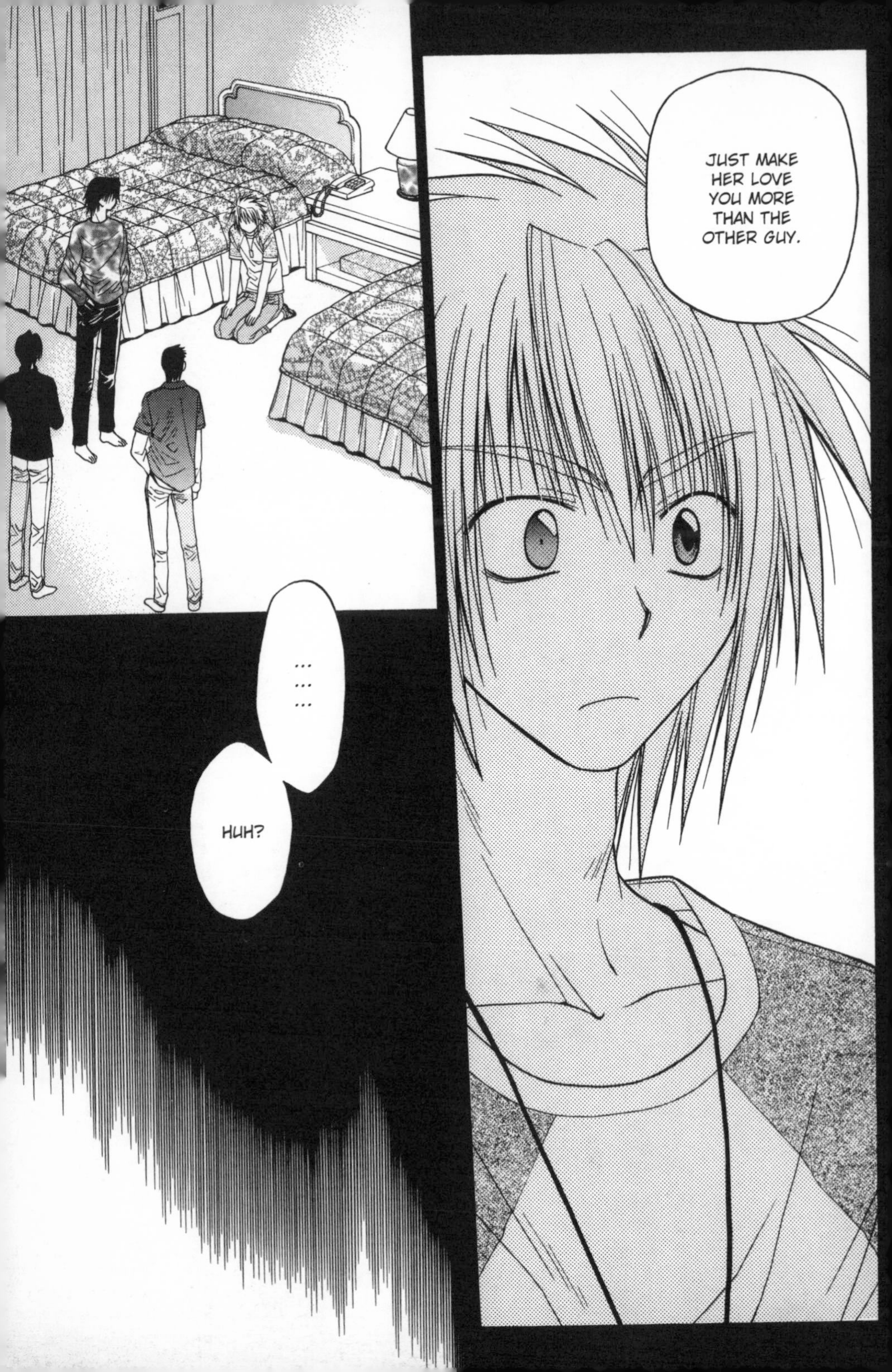
JUST MAKE HER LOVE YOU MORE THAN THE OTHER GUY.
... ...
HUH?

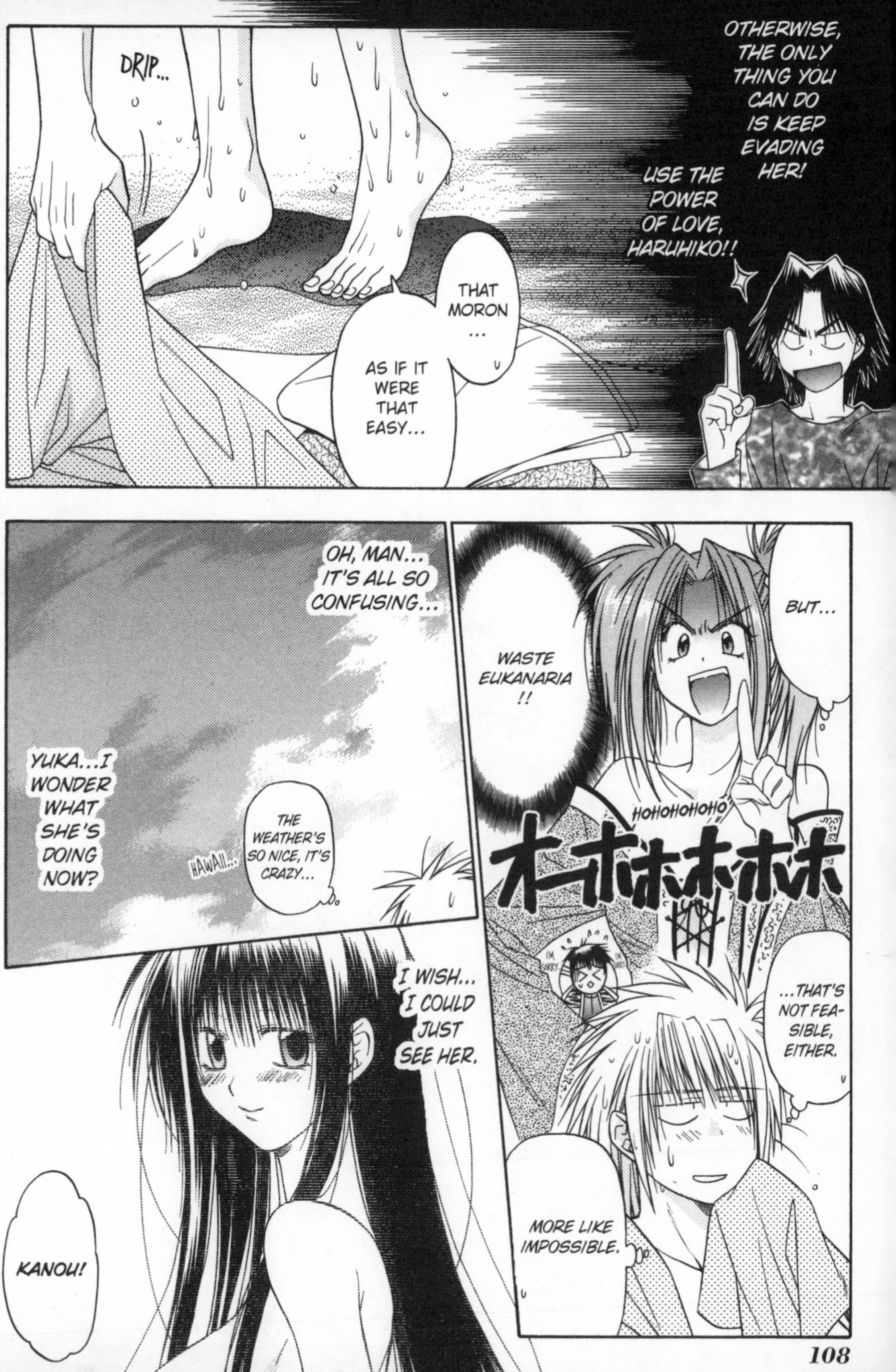
OTHERWISE, THE ONLY THING YOU CAN DO IS KEEP EVADING HER!
USE THE POWER OF LOVE, HARUHIKO!!
DRIP...
THAT MORON...
AS IF IT WERE THAT EASY...
BUT...
WASTE EUKANARIA!!
HOHOHOHOHO
オーホホホホホ
I'M SORRY
I'M SORRY
...THAT'S NOT FEA-SIBLE, EITHER.
MORE LIKE IMPOSSIBLE.
OH, MAN... IT'S ALL SO CONFUSING...
THE WEATHER'S SO NICE, IT'S CRAZY...
HAWAII...
YUKA...I WONDER WHAT SHE'S DOING NOW?
I WISH... I COULD JUST SEE HER.
KANOU!

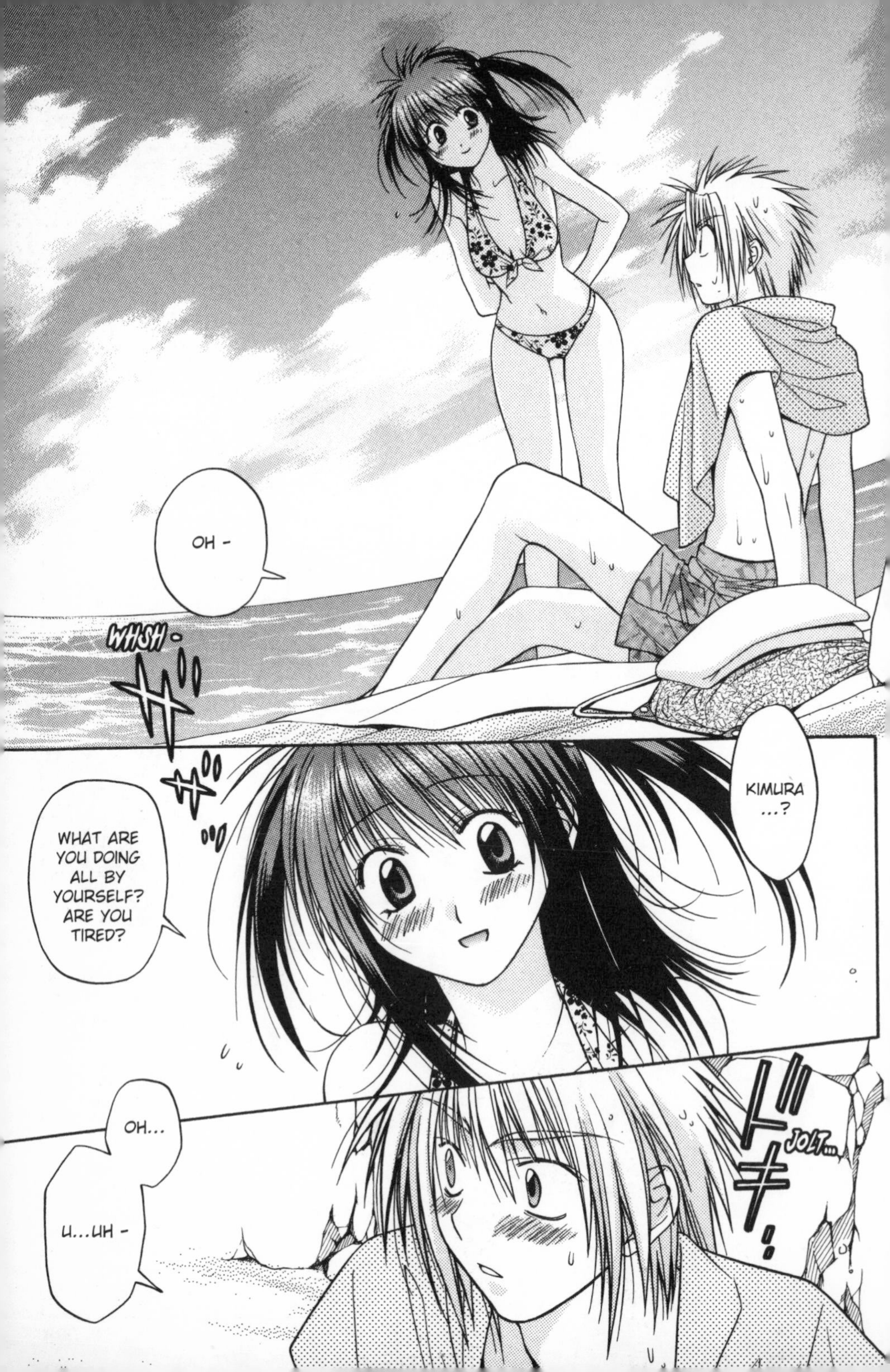
OH -
WHSH -
KIMURA ...?
WHAT ARE YOU DOING ALL BY YOURSELF? ARE YOU TIRED?
JOLT...
OH...
U...UH -

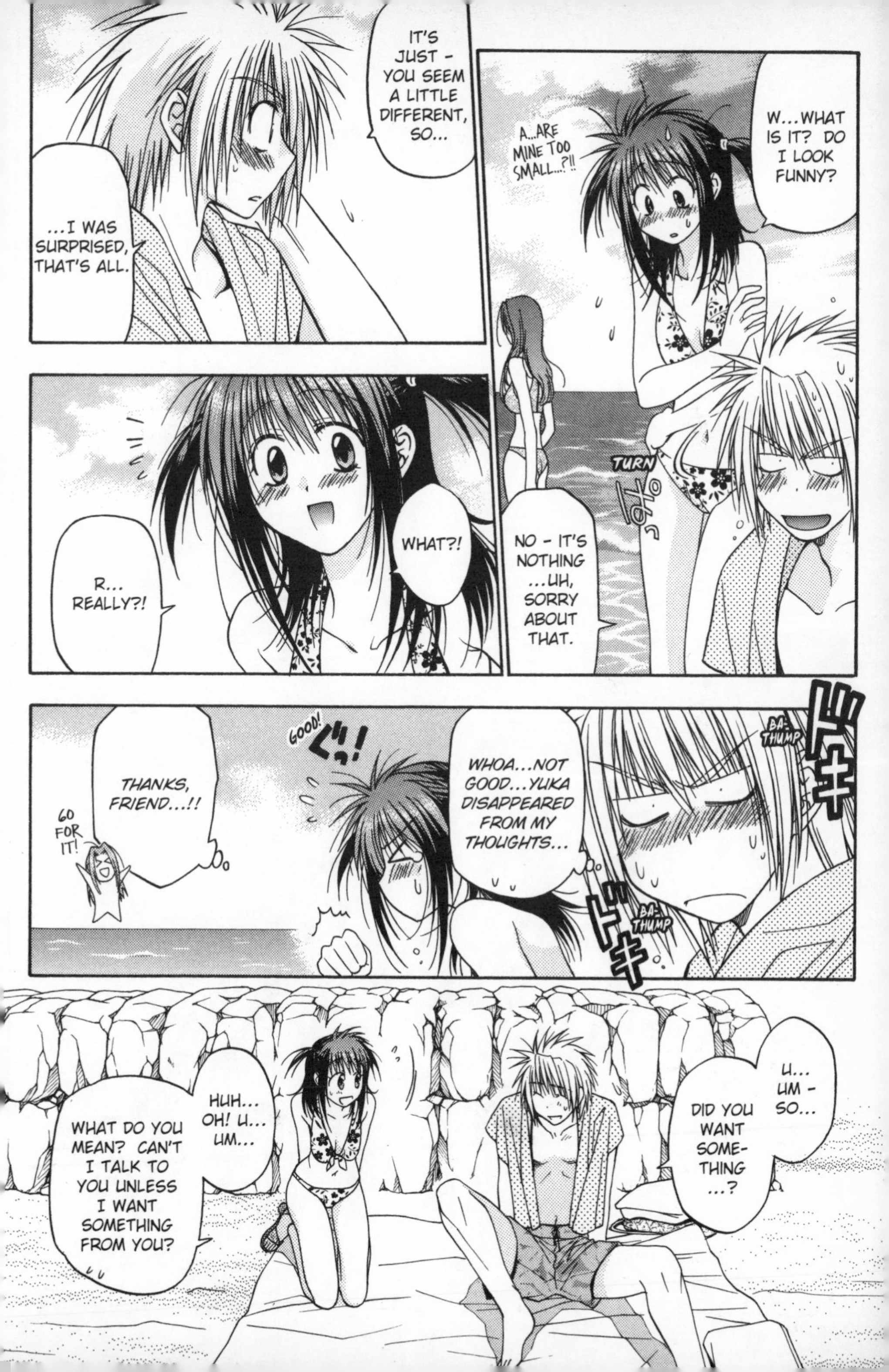
W...WHAT IS IT? DO I LOOK FUNNY?
A...ARE MINE TOO SMALL...?!!
TURN
NO - IT'S NOTHING ...UH, SORRY ABOUT THAT.
IT'S JUST - YOU SEEM A LITTLE DIFFERENT, SO...
...I WAS SURPRISED, THAT'S ALL.
WHAT?!
R... REALLY?!
BA-THUMP
BA-THUMP
WHOA...NOT GOOD...YUKA DISAPPEARED FROM MY THOUGHTS...
GOOD!
THANKS, FRIEND...!!
GO FOR IT!
U... UM - SO...
DID YOU WANT SOME-THING ...?
HUH... OH! U... UM...
WHAT DO YOU MEAN? CAN'T I TALK TO YOU UNLESS I WANT SOMETHING FROM YOU?

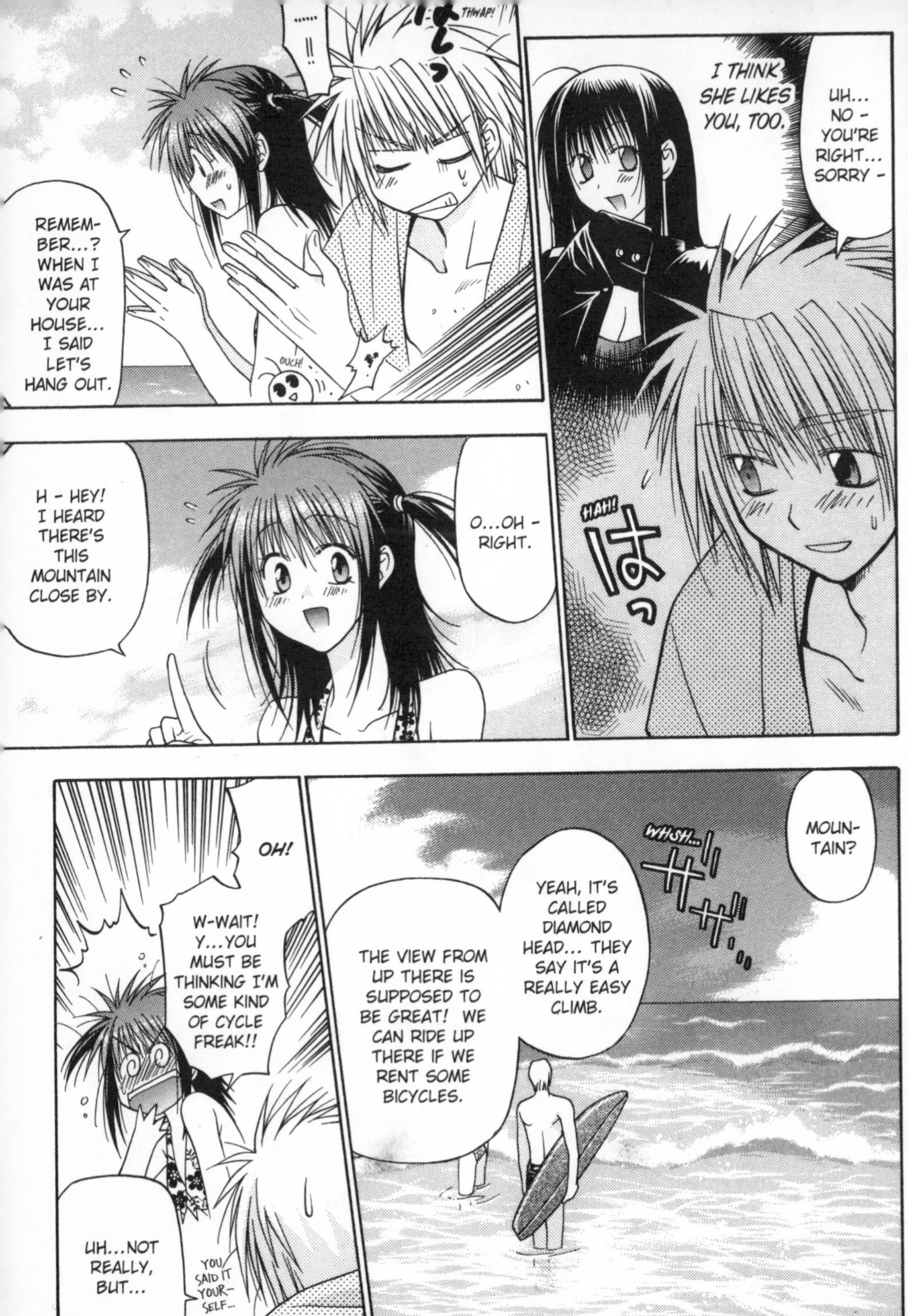
I THINK SHE LIKES YOU, TOO.
UH... NO - YOU'RE RIGHT... SORRY -
HAH!
......
!!
THWAP!
REMEM-BER...? WHEN I WAS AT YOUR HOUSE... I SAID LET'S HANG OUT.
OUCH!
O...OH - RIGHT.
H - HEY! I HEARD THERE'S THIS MOUNTAIN CLOSE BY.
MOUN-TAIN?
WHSH...
YEAH, IT'S CALLED DIAMOND HEAD... THEY SAY IT'S A REALLY EASY CLIMB.
THE VIEW FROM UP THERE IS SUPPOSED TO BE GREAT! WE CAN RIDE UP THERE IF WE RENT SOME BICYCLES.
OH!
W-WAIT! Y...YOU MUST BE THINKING I'M SOME KIND OF CYCLE FREAK!!
UH...NOT REALLY, BUT...
YOU SAID IT YOUR-SELF...

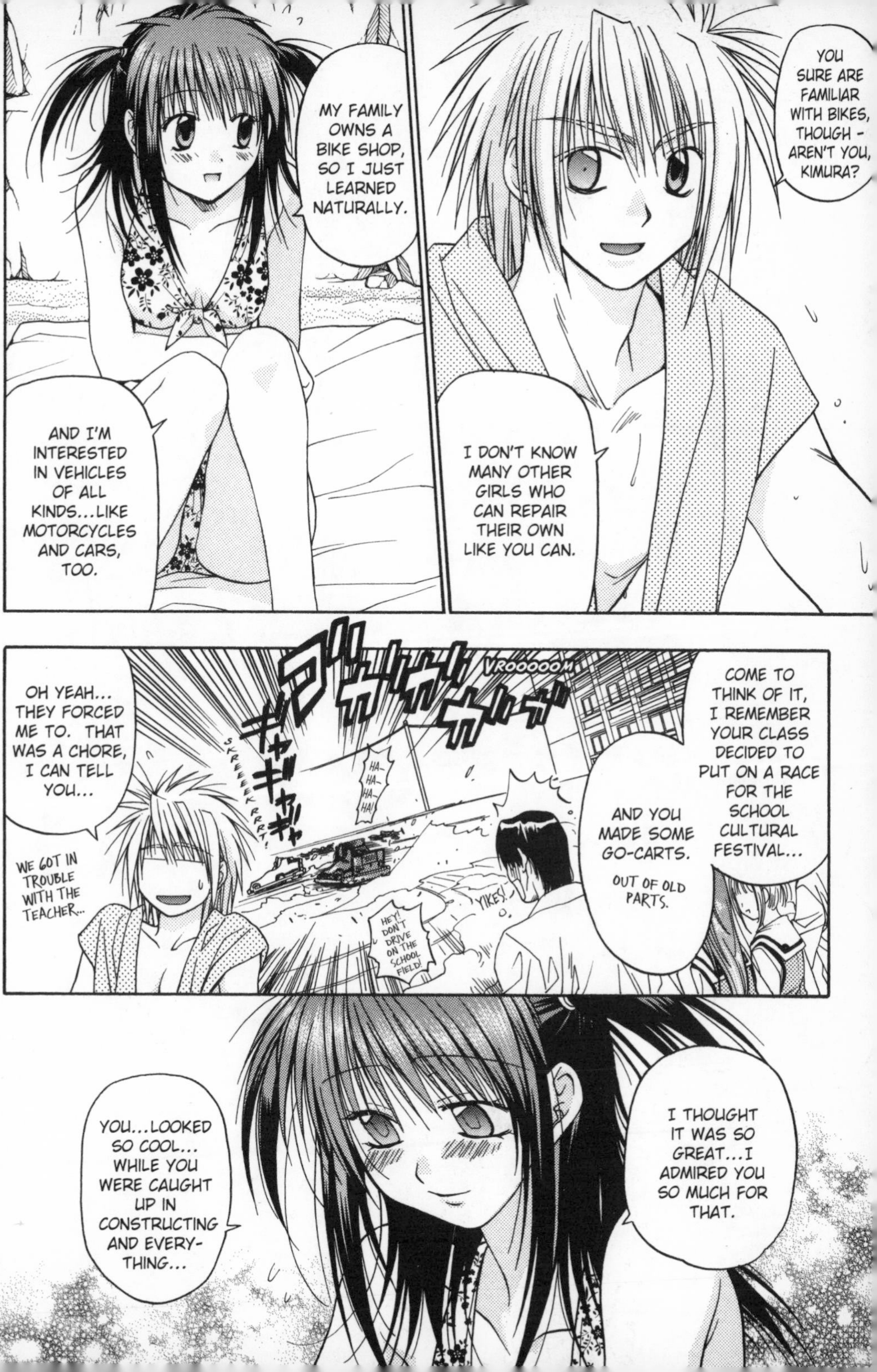

YOU SURE ARE FAMILIAR WITH BIKES, THOUGH - AREN'T YOU, KIMURA?
I DON'T KNOW MANY OTHER GIRLS WHO CAN REPAIR THEIR OWN LIKE YOU CAN.
MY FAMILY OWNS A BIKE SHOP, SO I JUST LEARNED NATURALLY.
AND I'M INTERESTED IN VEHICLES OF ALL KINDS...LIKE MOTORCYCLES AND CARS, TOO.
COME TO THINK OF IT, I REMEMBER YOUR CLASS DECIDED TO PUT ON A RACE FOR THE SCHOOL CULTURAL FESTIVAL...
AND YOU MADE SOME GO-CARTS.
OUT OF OLD PARTS.
VROOOOOM
YIKES!
HEY! DON'T DRIVE ON THE SCHOOL FIELD!
HA-HA-HA-HA!
SKREEEEK RRRT!
OH YEAH... THEY FORCED ME TO. THAT WAS A CHORE, I CAN TELL YOU...
WE GOT IN TROUBLE WITH THE TEACHER...
I THOUGHT IT WAS SO GREAT...I ADMIRED YOU SO MUCH FOR THAT.
YOU...LOOKED SO COOL... WHILE YOU WERE CAUGHT UP IN CONSTRUCTING AND EVERY-THING...

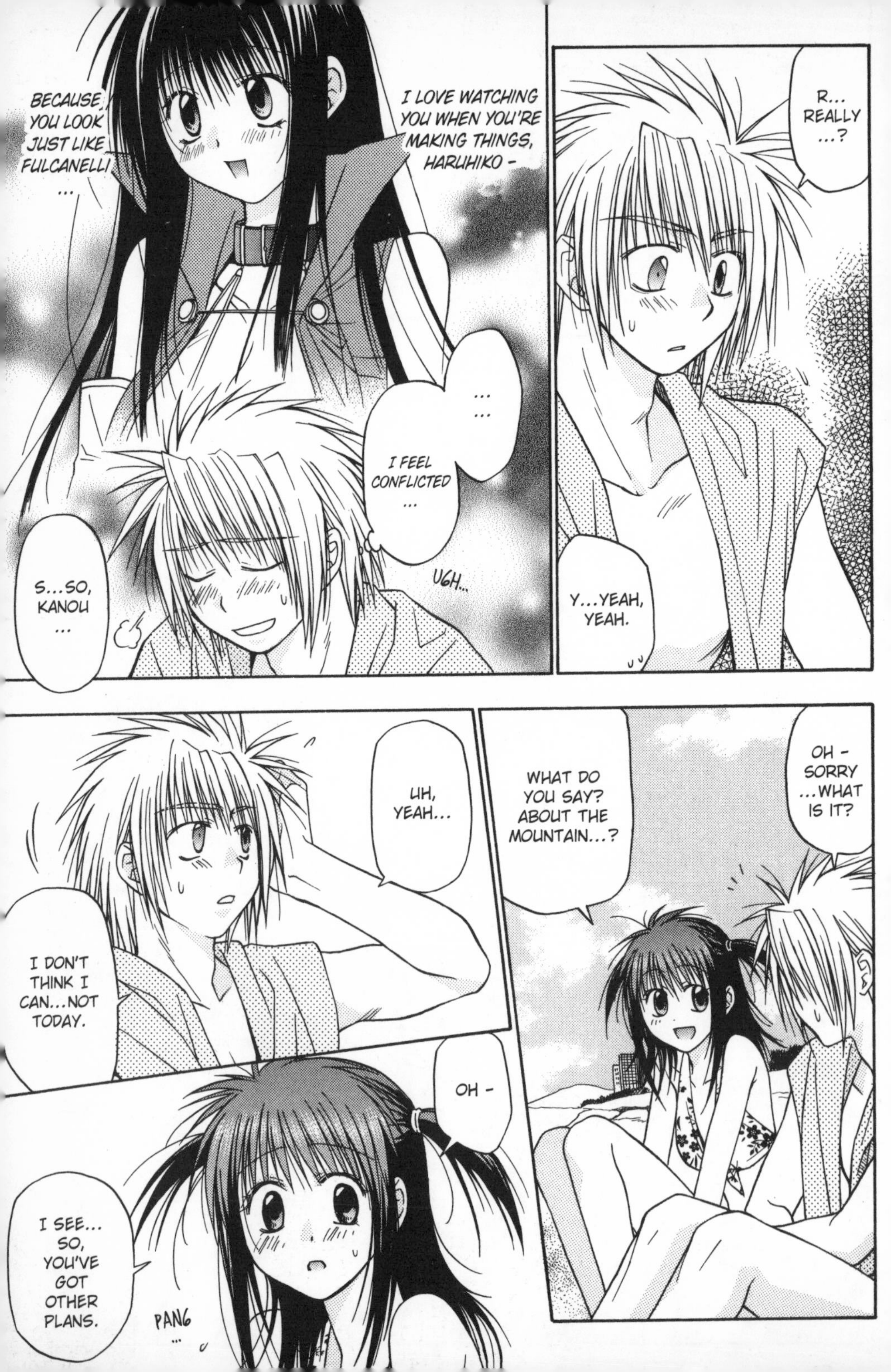
R... REALLY ...?
Y...YEAH, YEAH.
I LOVE WATCHING YOU WHEN YOU'RE MAKING THINGS, HARUHIKO -
BECAUSE YOU LOOK JUST LIKE FULCANELLI ...
... ... I FEEL CONFLICTED ...
UGH...
S...SO, KANOU ...
OH - SORRY ...WHAT IS IT?
WHAT DO YOU SAY? ABOUT THE MOUNTAIN...?
UH, YEAH...
I DON'T THINK I CAN...NOT TODAY.
OH -
I SEE... SO, YOU'VE GOT OTHER PLANS.
PANG ...

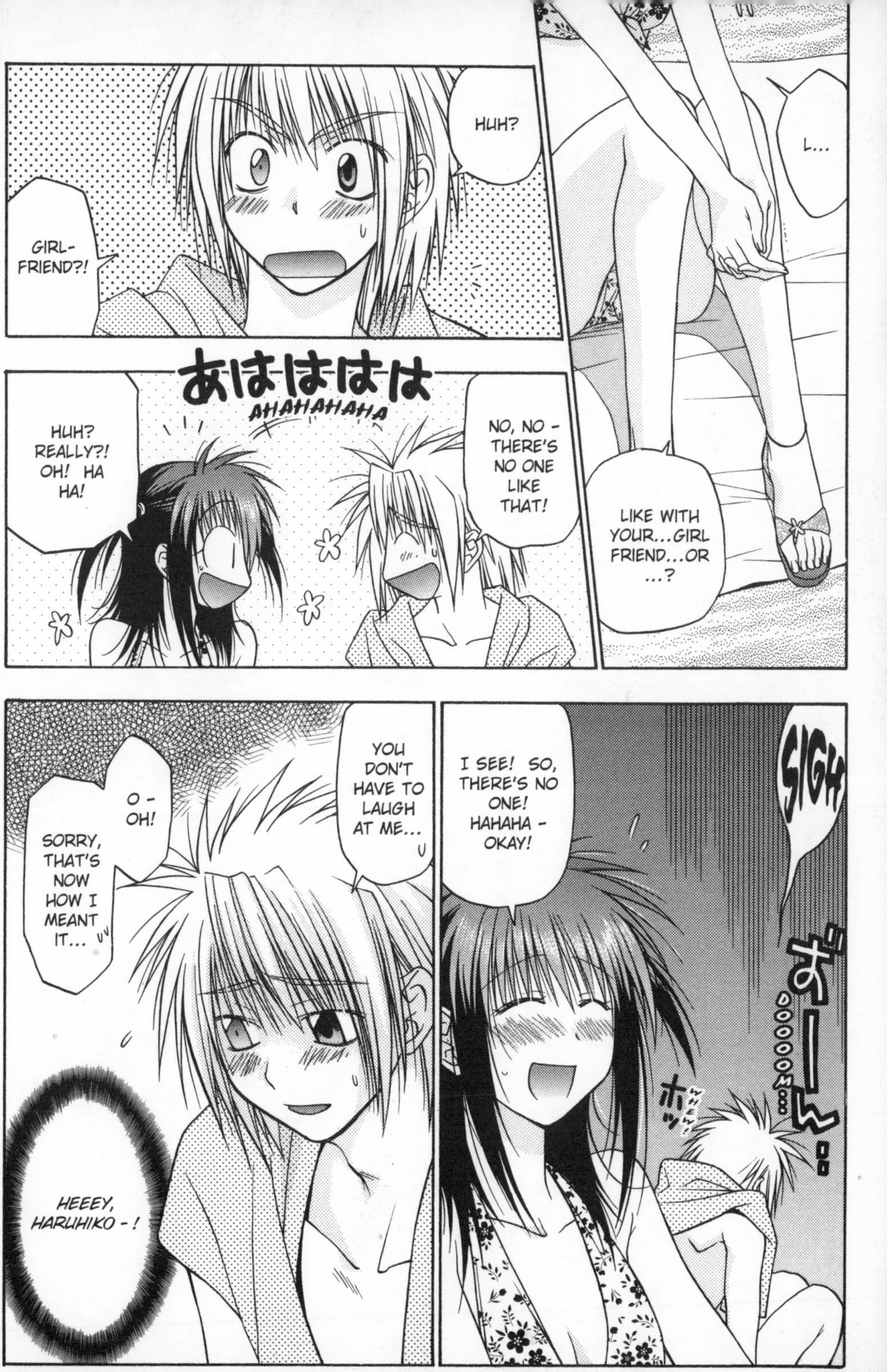
L...
LIKE WITH YOUR...GIRL FRIEND...OR ...?
HUH?
GIRL-FRIEND?!
あはははは
AHAHAHAHA
NO, NO - THERE'S NO ONE LIKE THAT!
HUH? REALLY?! OH! HA HA!
SIGH
I SEE! SO, THERE'S NO ONE! HAHAHA - OKAY!
ぼーん!!
DOOOOOM...
ホッ
WHEW!
YOU DON'T HAVE TO LAUGH AT ME...
O - OH!
SORRY, THAT'S NOW HOW I MEANT IT...
HEEEY, HARUHIKO - !

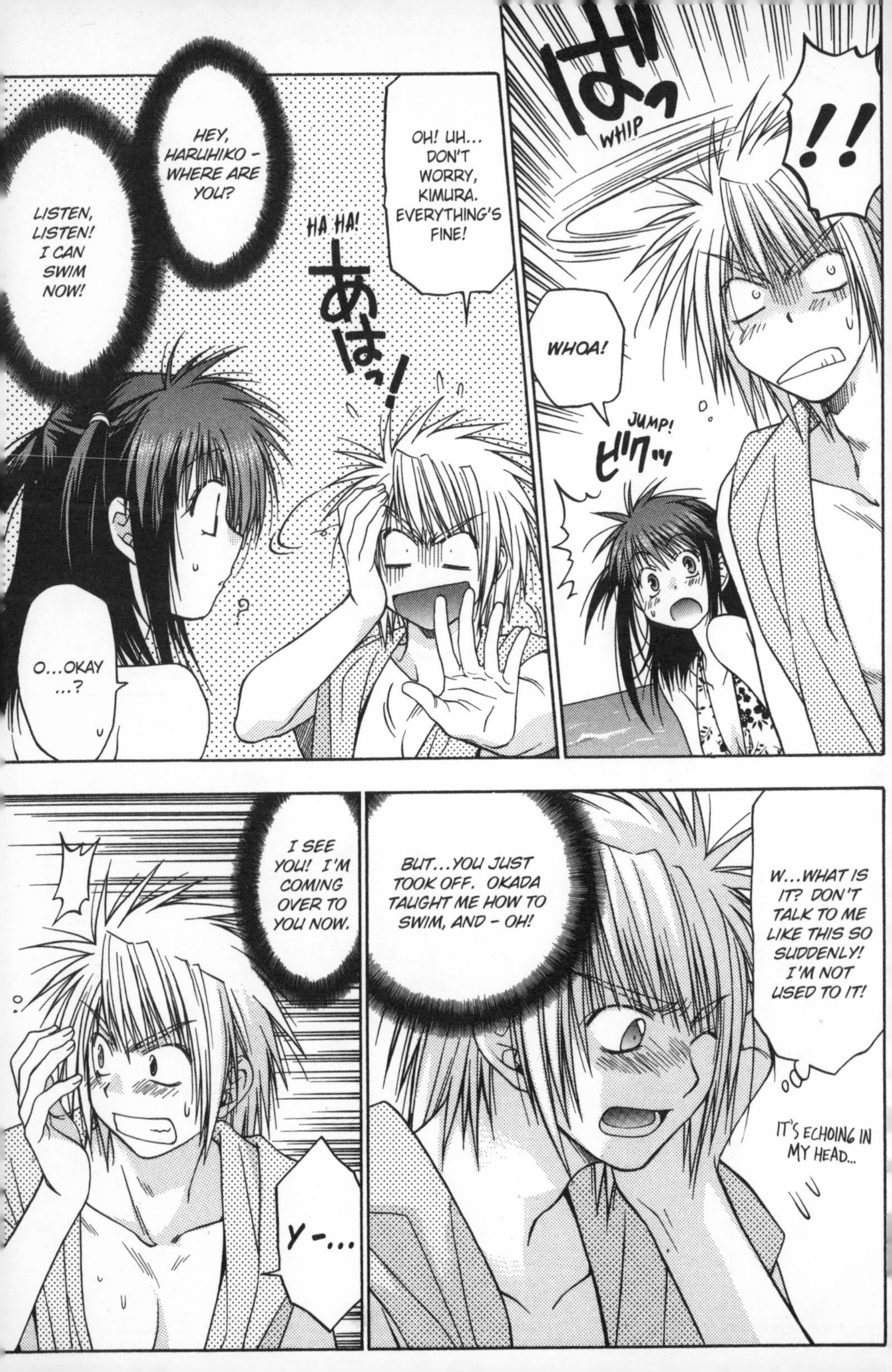

ぱっ
WHIP
!!
WHOA!
JUMP!
ビクッ
OH! UH... DON'T WORRY, KIMURA. EVERYTHING'S FINE!
HA HA!
あはっ!
HEY, HARUHIKO - WHERE ARE YOU?
LISTEN, LISTEN! I CAN SWIM NOW!
O...OKAY ...?
W...WHAT IS IT? DON'T TALK TO ME LIKE THIS SO SUDDENLY! I'M NOT USED TO IT!
BUT...YOU JUST TOOK OFF. OKADA TAUGHT ME HOW TO SWIM, AND - OH!
IT'S ECHOING IN MY HEAD...
I SEE YOU! I'M COMING OVER TO YOU NOW.
Y-...

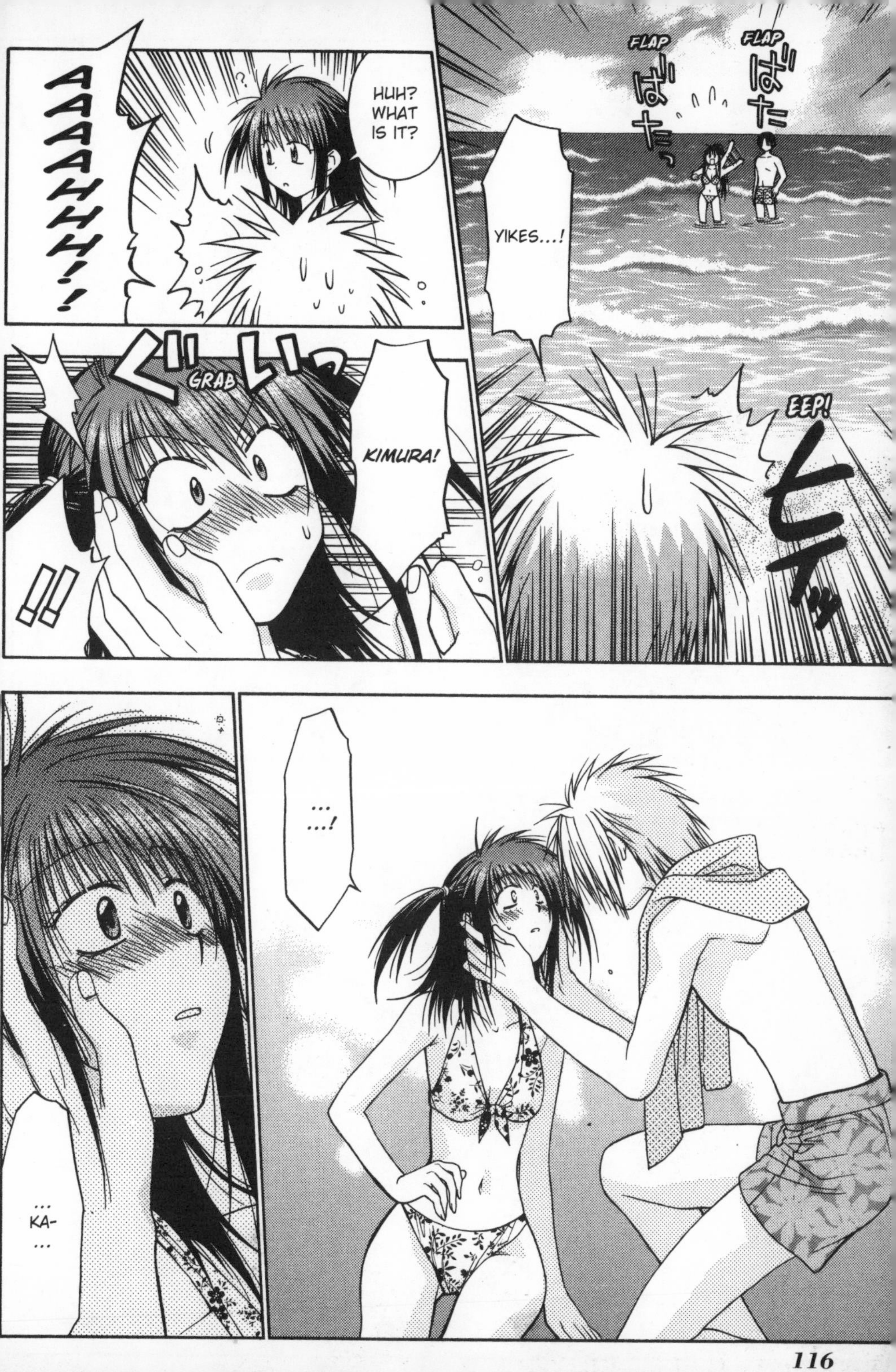
FLAP
ばた
FLAP
ばたっ
YIKES...!
EEP!
ヒィッ
HUH? WHAT IS IT?
AAAAAHHHH!!
ぐいっ
GRAB
KIMURA!
!!
...
...!
...
KA-
...

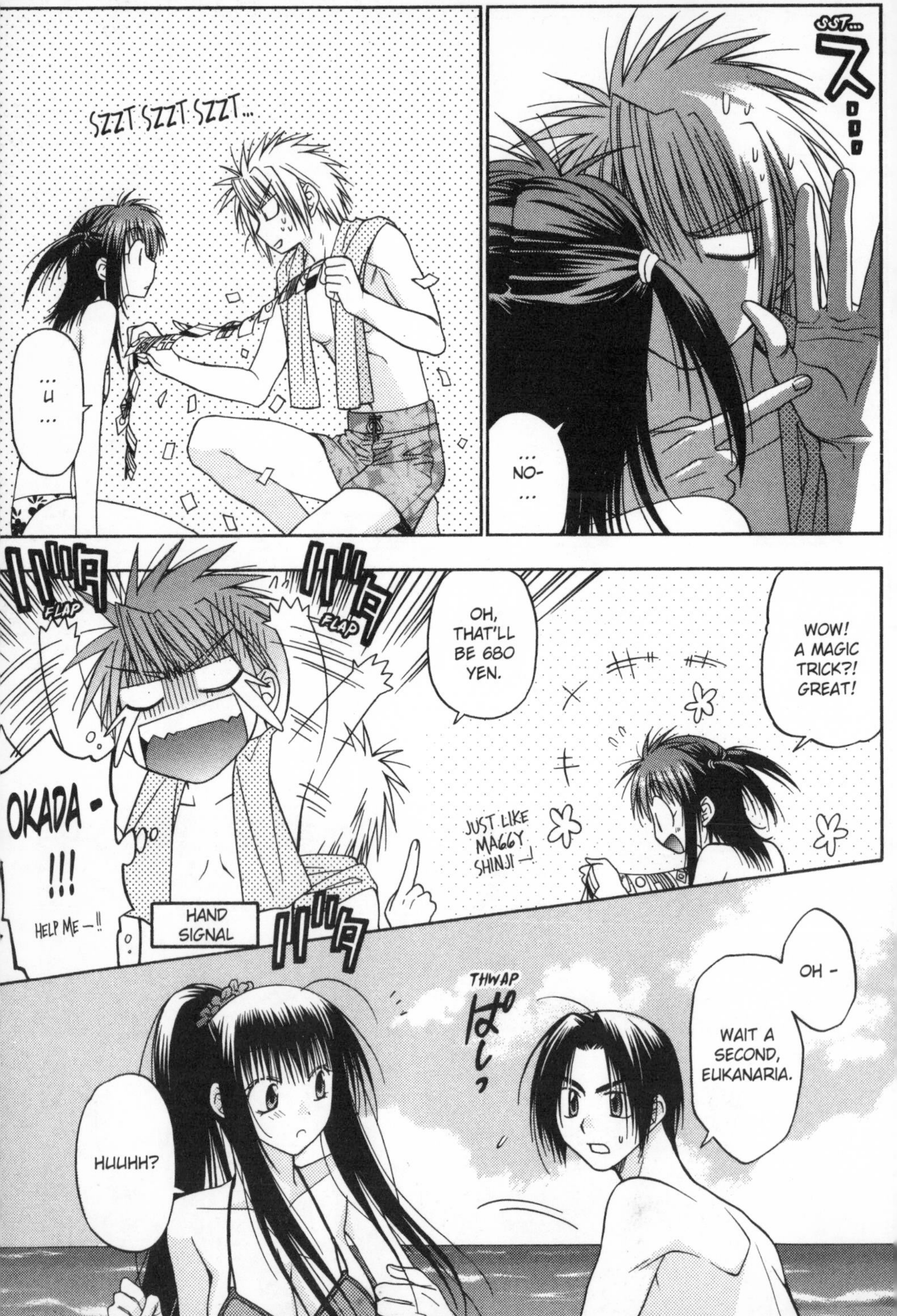
SST...
ス...
... NO- ...
SZZT SZZT SZZT...
... U ...
WOW! A MAGIC TRICK?! GREAT!
OH, THAT'LL BE 680 YEN.
JUST LIKE MAGGY SHINJI
FLAP
FLAP
OKADA- !!!
HELP ME-!!
HAND SIGNAL
OH -
WAIT A SECOND, EUKANARIA.
THWAP
ぱしっ
HUUHH?

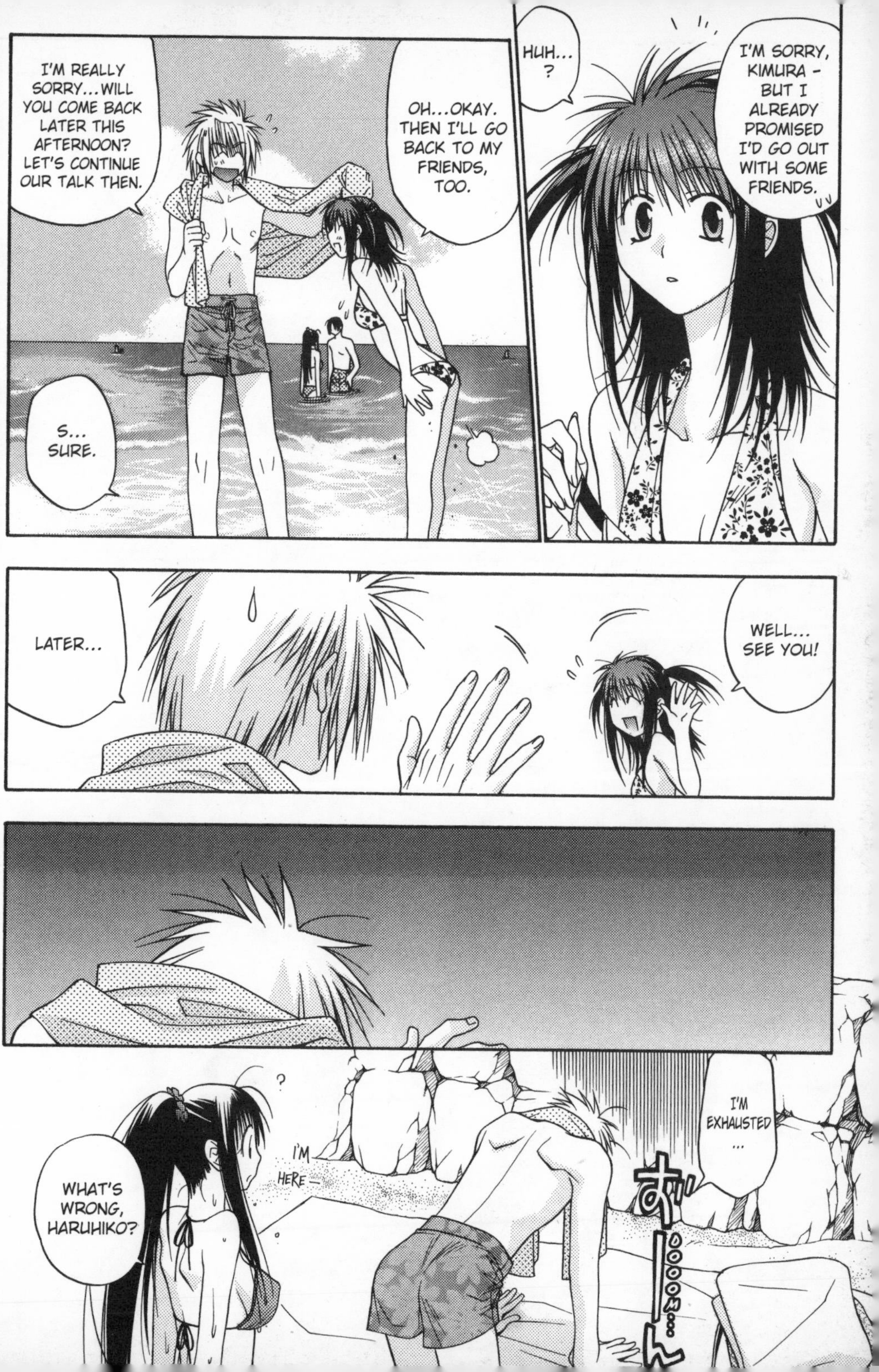
I'M SORRY, KIMURA - BUT I ALREADY PROMISED I'D GO OUT WITH SOME FRIENDS.
HUH...?
OH...OKAY. THEN I'LL GO BACK TO MY FRIENDS, TOO.
I'M REALLY SORRY...WILL YOU COME BACK LATER THIS AFTERNOON? LET'S CONTINUE OUR TALK THEN.
S... SURE.
WELL... SEE YOU!
LATER...
I'M EXHAUSTED ...
ず〜OOOOOM...ん
?
I'M HERE—
WHAT'S WRONG, HARUHIKO?

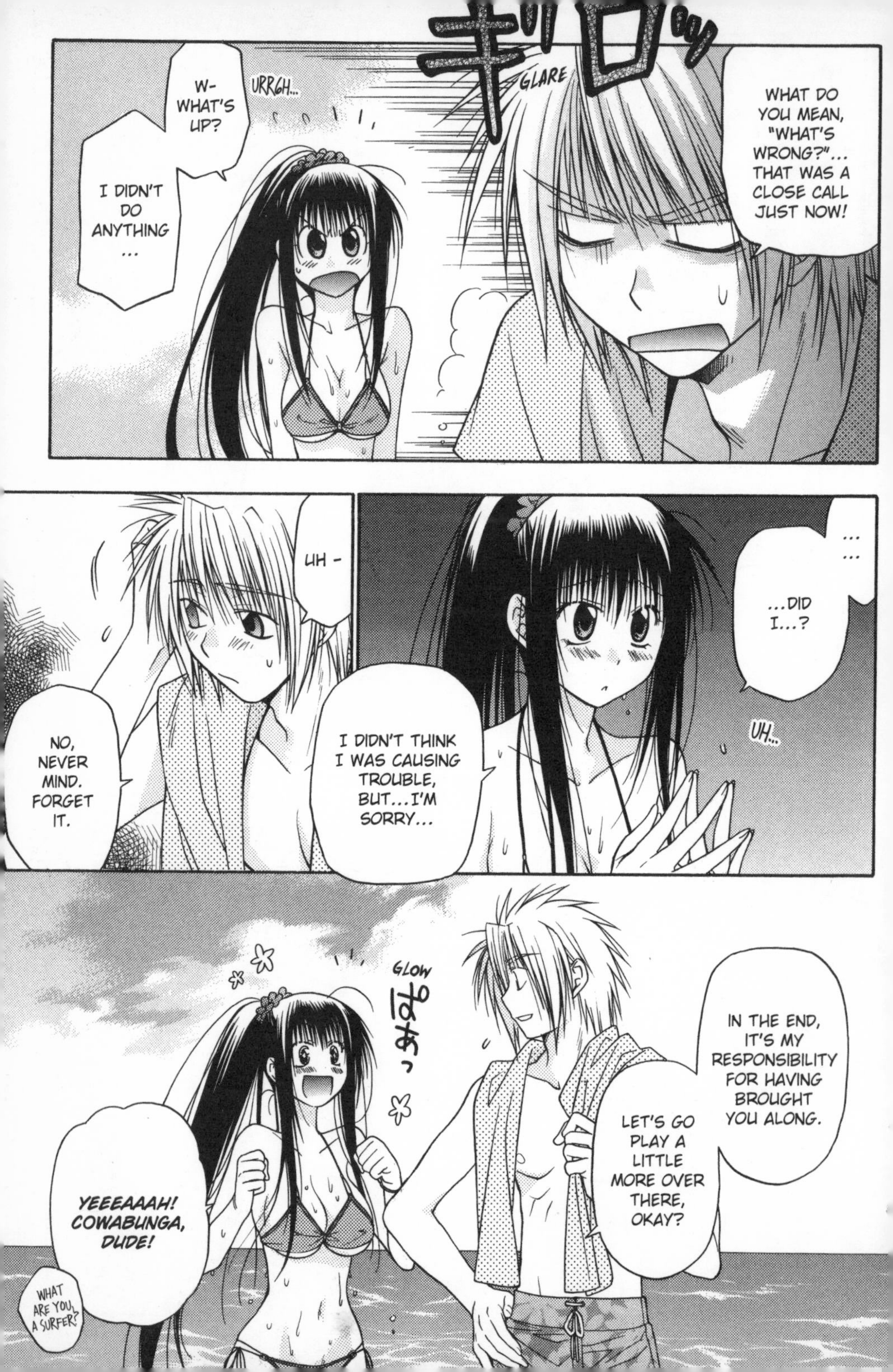

ギロッ
GLARE
WHAT DO YOU MEAN, "WHAT'S WRONG?"... THAT WAS A CLOSE CALL JUST NOW!
URRGH...
W-WHAT'S UP?
I DIDN'T DO ANYTHING...
......
...DID I...?
UH...
I DIDN'T THINK I WAS CAUSING TROUBLE, BUT...I'M SORRY...
UH -
NO, NEVER MIND. FORGET IT.
IN THE END, IT'S MY RESPONSIBILITY FOR HAVING BROUGHT YOU ALONG.
LET'S GO PLAY A LITTLE MORE OVER THERE, OKAY?
GLOW
ぱあっ
YEEEAAAH! COWABUNGA, DUDE!
WHAT ARE YOU, A SURFER?

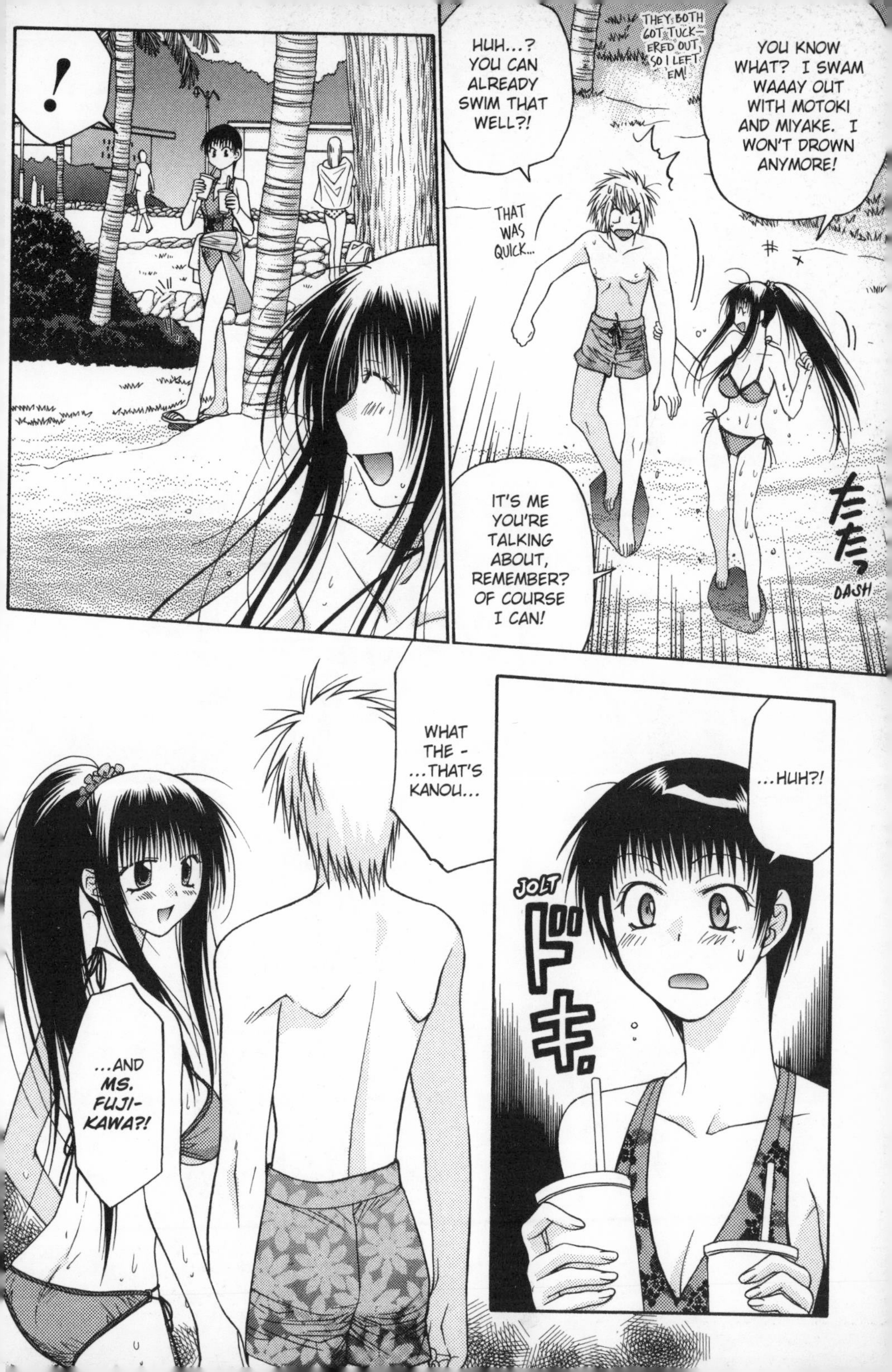
YOU KNOW WHAT? I SWAM WAAAY OUT WITH MOTOKI AND MIYAKE. I WON'T DROWN ANYMORE!
THEY BOTH GOT TUCK-ERED OUT, SO I LEFT 'EM!
HUH...? YOU CAN ALREADY SWIM THAT WELL?!
THAT WAS QUICK...
IT'S ME YOU'RE TALKING ABOUT, REMEMBER? OF COURSE I CAN!
DASH
!
...HUH?!
JOLT
WHAT THE - ...THAT'S KANOU...
...AND MS. FUJI-KAWA?!

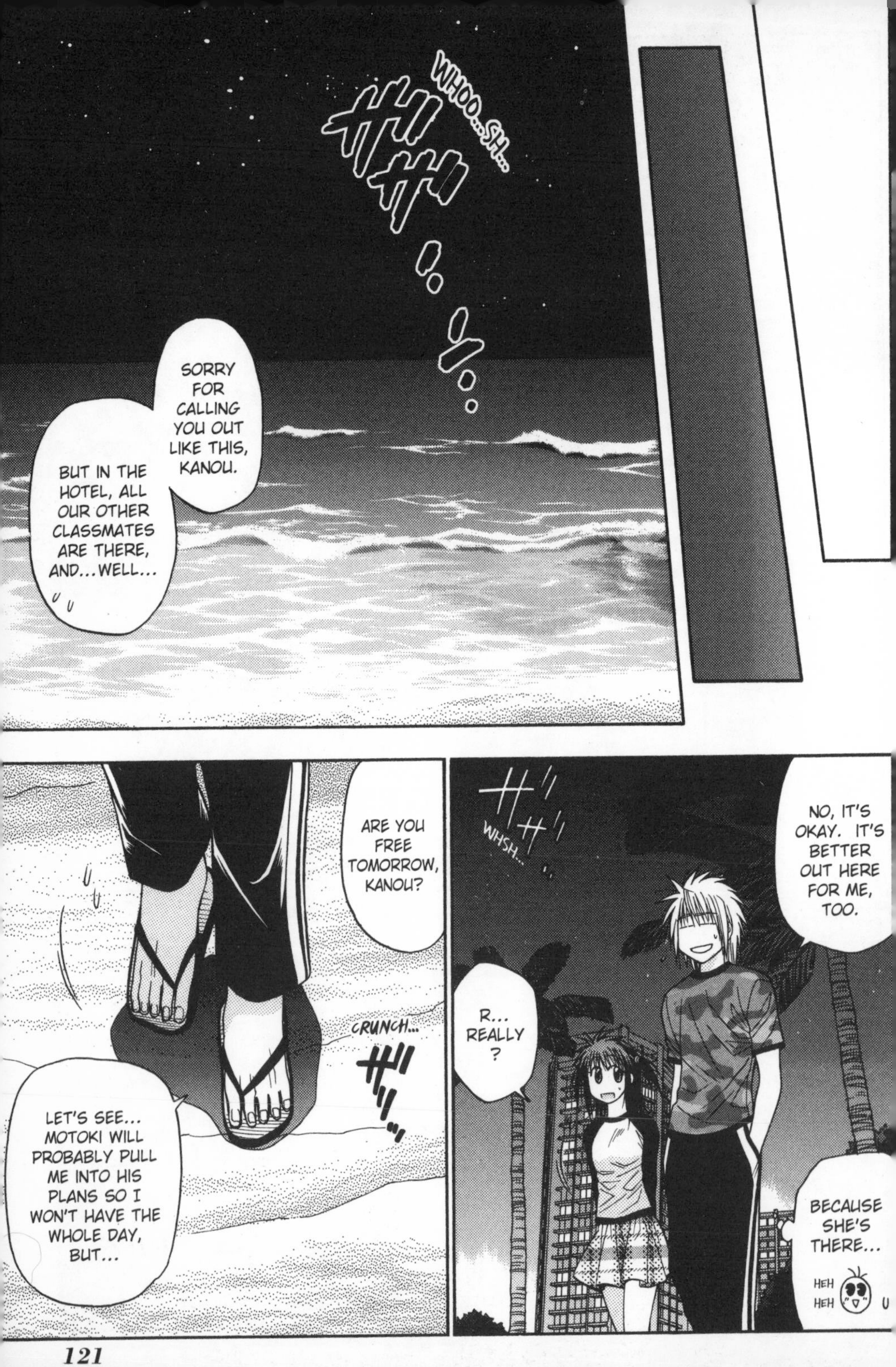
WHOO...SH...
SORRY FOR CALLING YOU OUT LIKE THIS, KANOU.
BUT IN THE HOTEL, ALL OUR OTHER CLASSMATES ARE THERE, AND...WELL...
WHSH...
NO, IT'S OKAY. IT'S BETTER OUT HERE FOR ME, TOO.
R... REALLY?
BECAUSE SHE'S THERE...
HEH HEH
ARE YOU FREE TOMORROW, KANOU?
CRUNCH...
LET'S SEE... MOTOKI WILL PROBABLY PULL ME INTO HIS PLANS SO I WON'T HAVE THE WHOLE DAY, BUT...

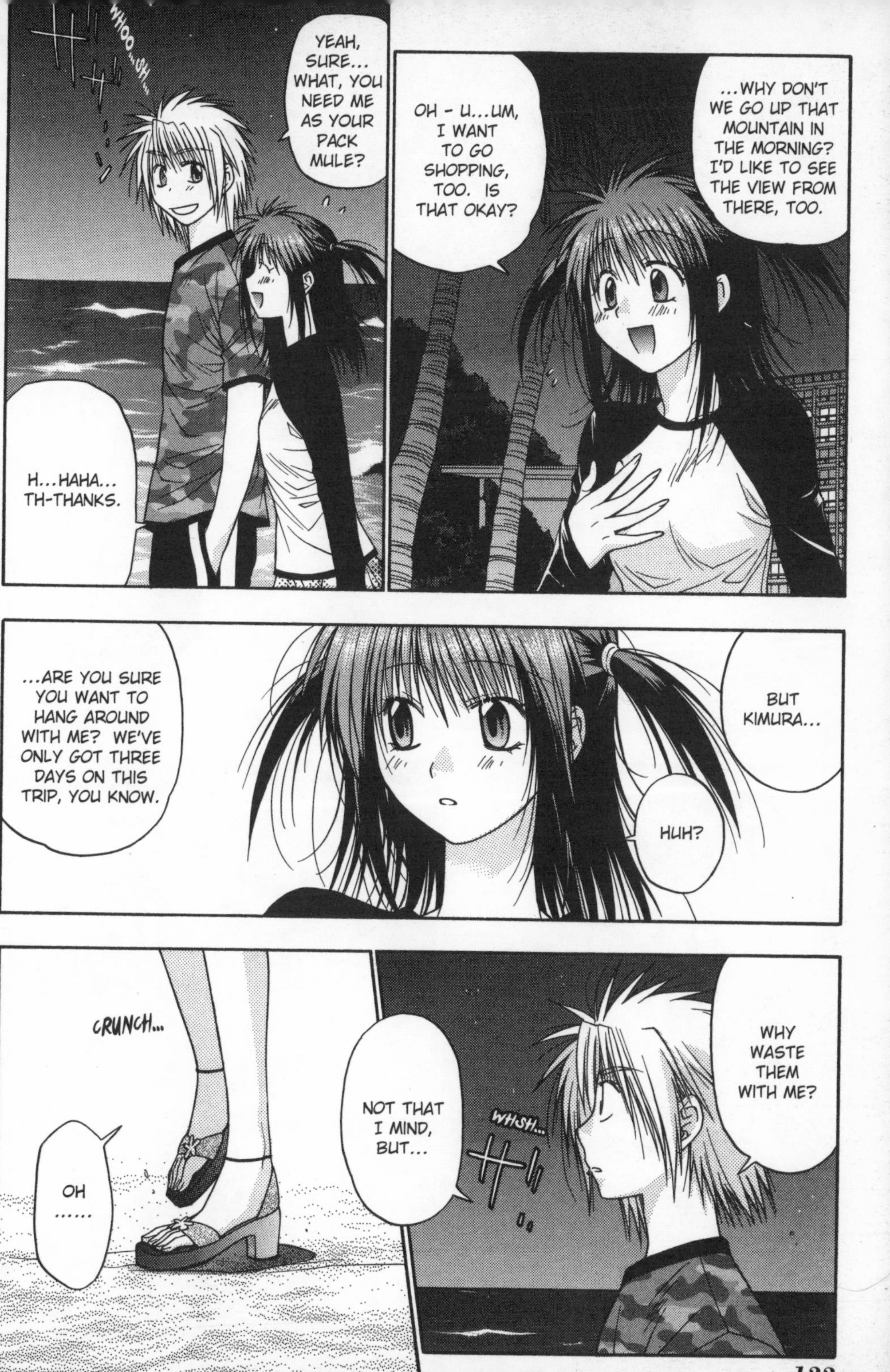
...WHY DON'T WE GO UP THAT MOUNTAIN IN THE MORNING? I'D LIKE TO SEE THE VIEW FROM THERE, TOO.
OH - U...UM, I WANT TO GO SHOPPING, TOO. IS THAT OKAY?
WHOO...SH...
YEAH, SURE... WHAT, YOU NEED ME AS YOUR PACK MULE?
H...HAHA... TH-THANKS.
BUT KIMURA...
HUH?
...ARE YOU SURE YOU WANT TO HANG AROUND WITH ME? WE'VE ONLY GOT THREE DAYS ON THIS TRIP, YOU KNOW.
WHY WASTE THEM WITH ME?
WHSH...
NOT THAT I MIND, BUT...
CRUNCH...
OH ......

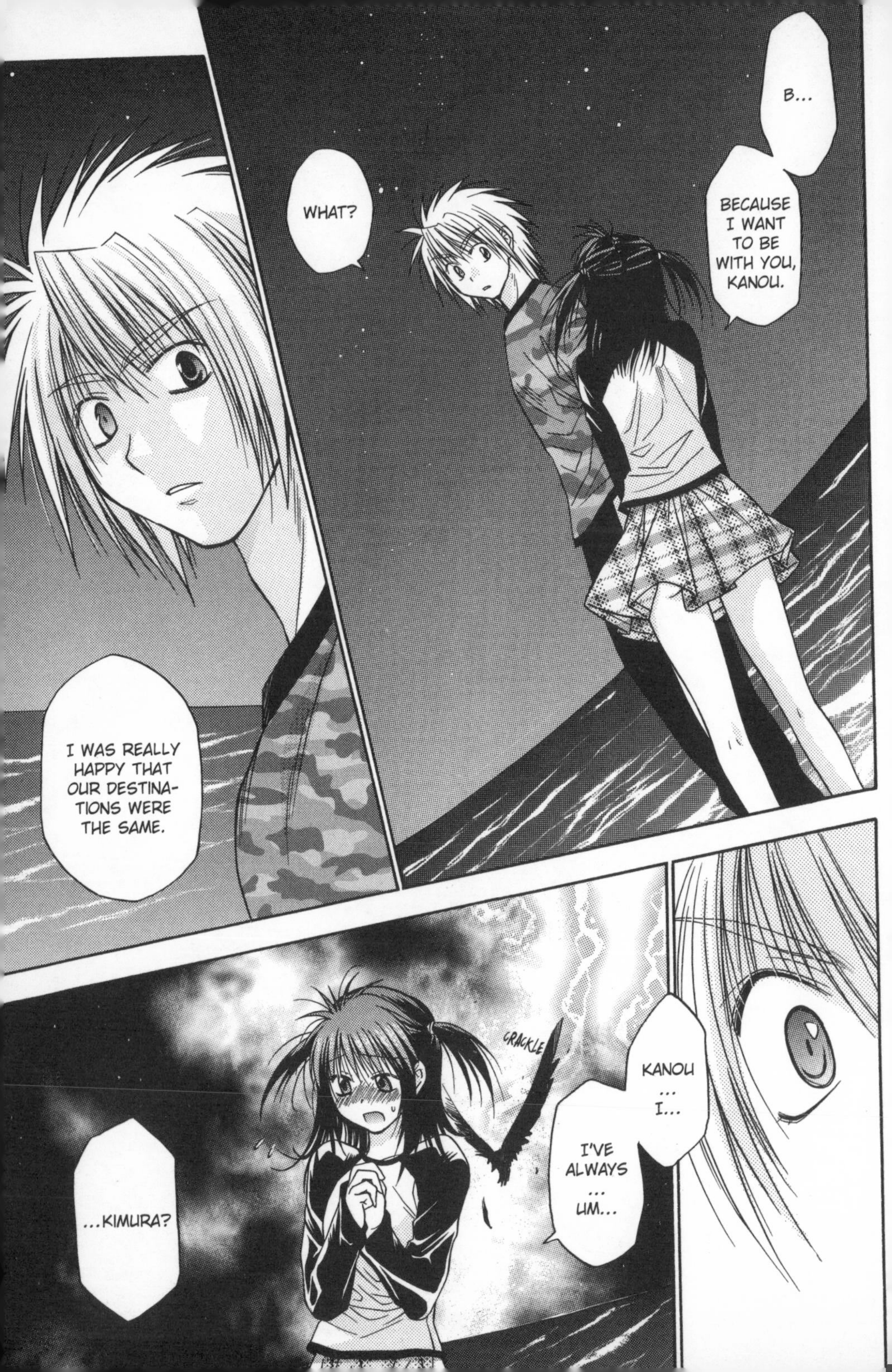
B...
BECAUSE I WANT TO BE WITH YOU, KANOU.
WHAT?
I WAS REALLY HAPPY THAT OUR DESTINATIONS WERE THE SAME.
CRACKLE
KANOU ... I...
I'VE ALWAYS ... UM...
...KIMURA?

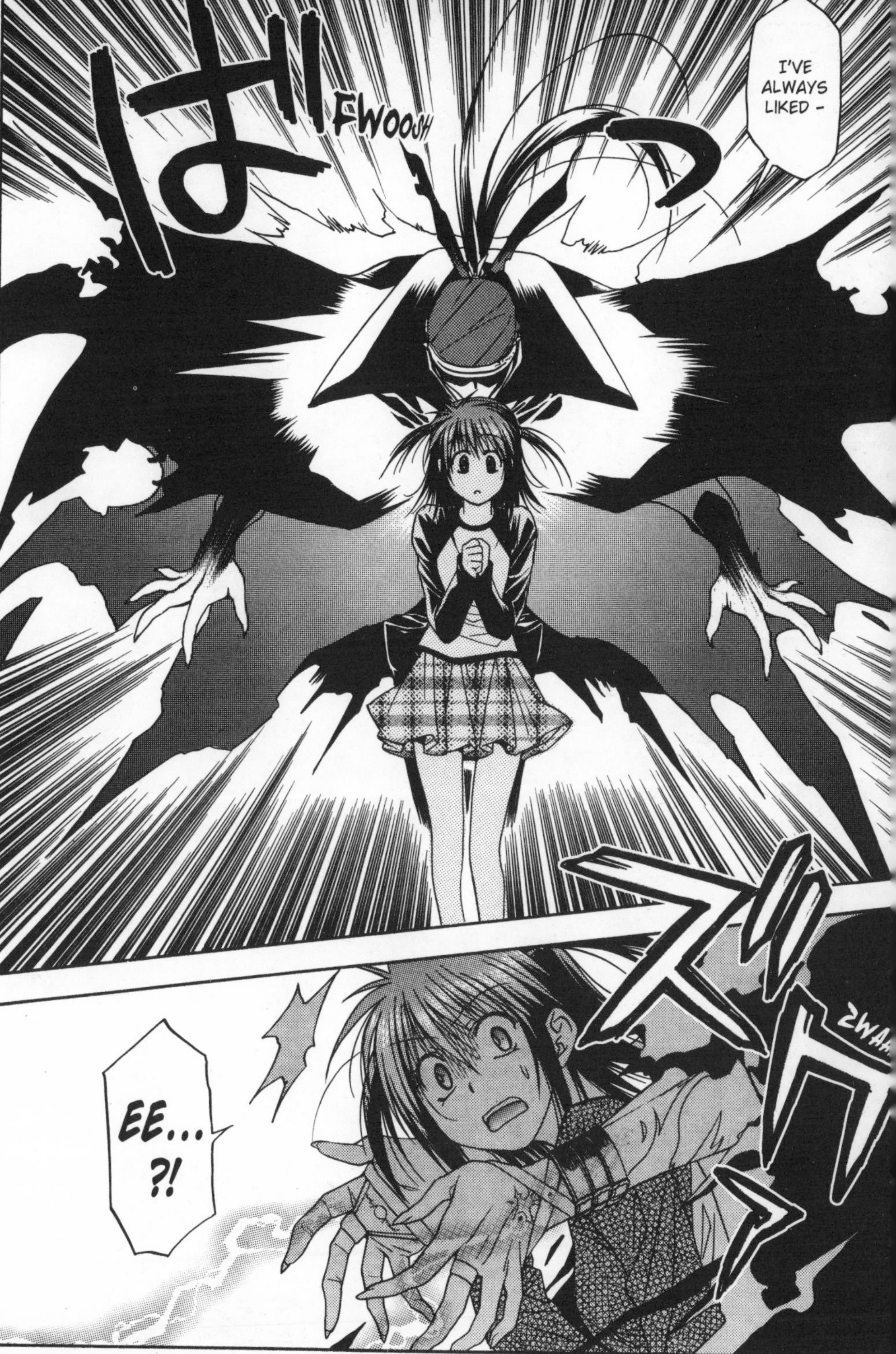
I'VE ALWAYS LIKED -
はっ
FWOOSH
ZWAA
EE... ?!

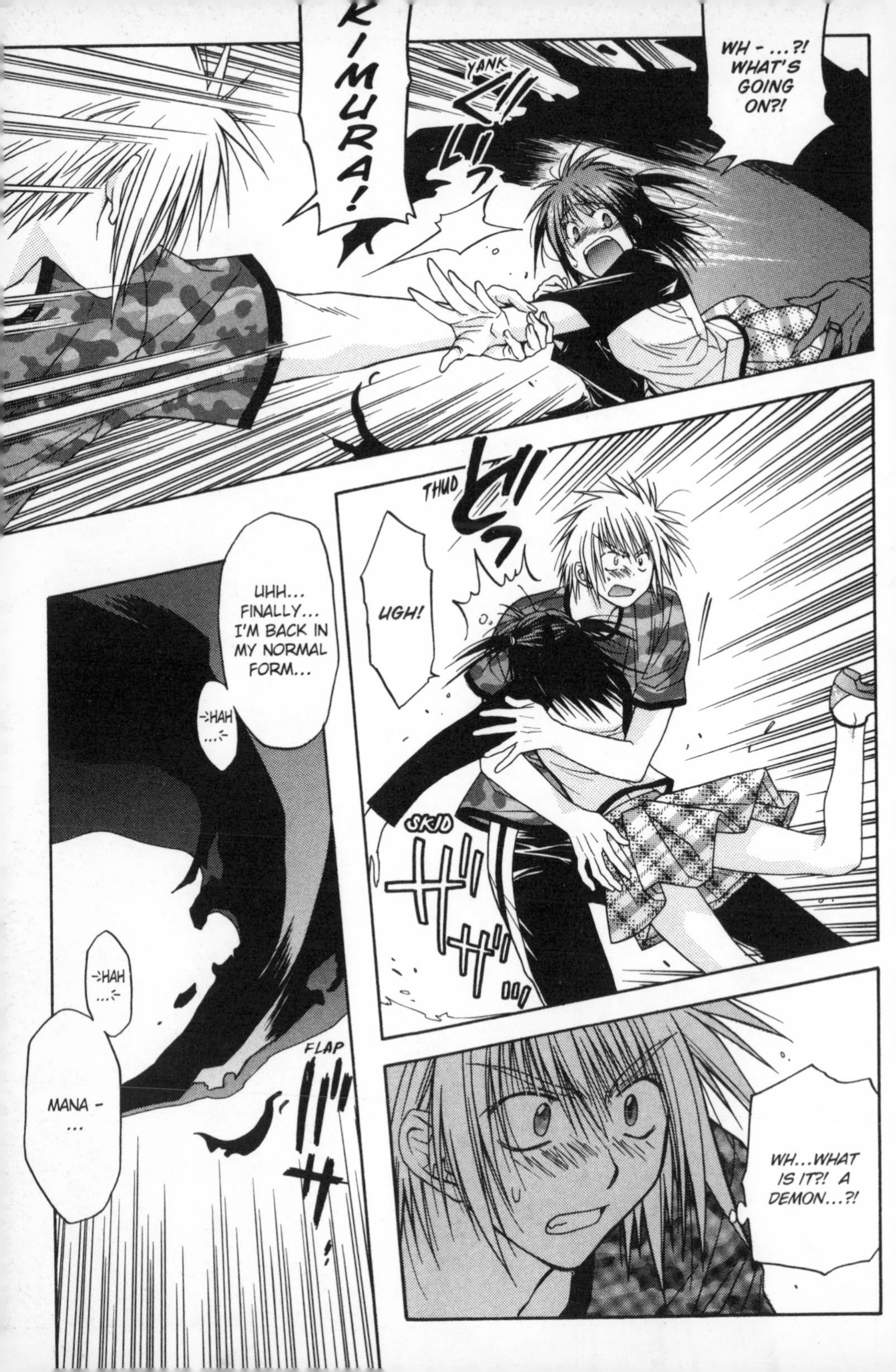
WH - ...?! WHAT'S GOING ON?!
YANK
KIMURA!
THUD
UGH!
SKID
WH...WHAT IS IT?! A DEMON...?!
UHH... FINALLY... I'M BACK IN MY NORMAL FORM...
HAH ...
HAH ...
MANA - ...
FLAP

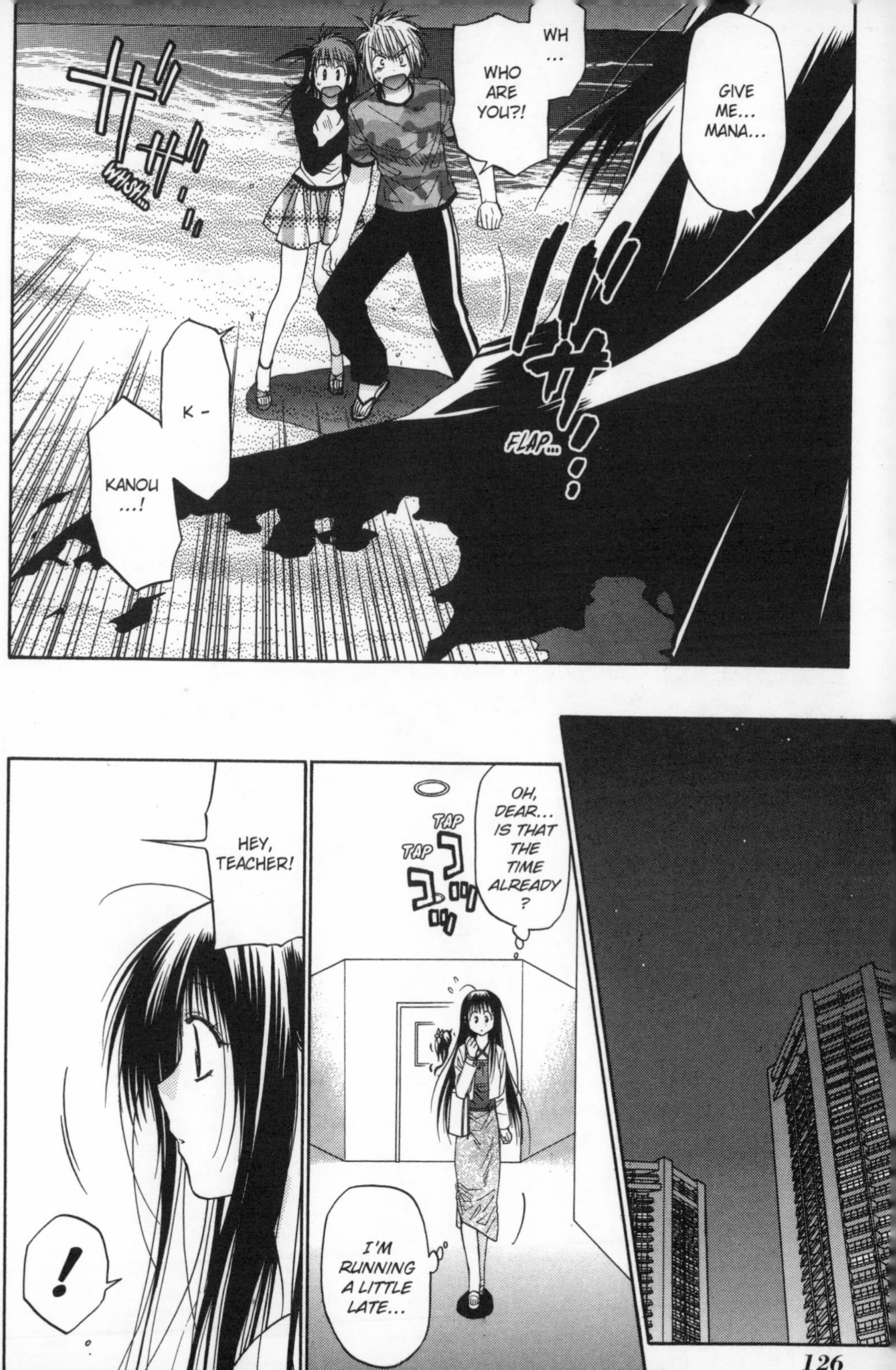
GIVE ME... MANA...
FLAP...
WH... WHO ARE YOU?!
WHSH...
K- KANOU...!
OH, DEAR... IS THAT THE TIME ALREADY?
TAP TAP
I'M RUNNING A LITTLE LATE...
HEY, TEACHER!
!

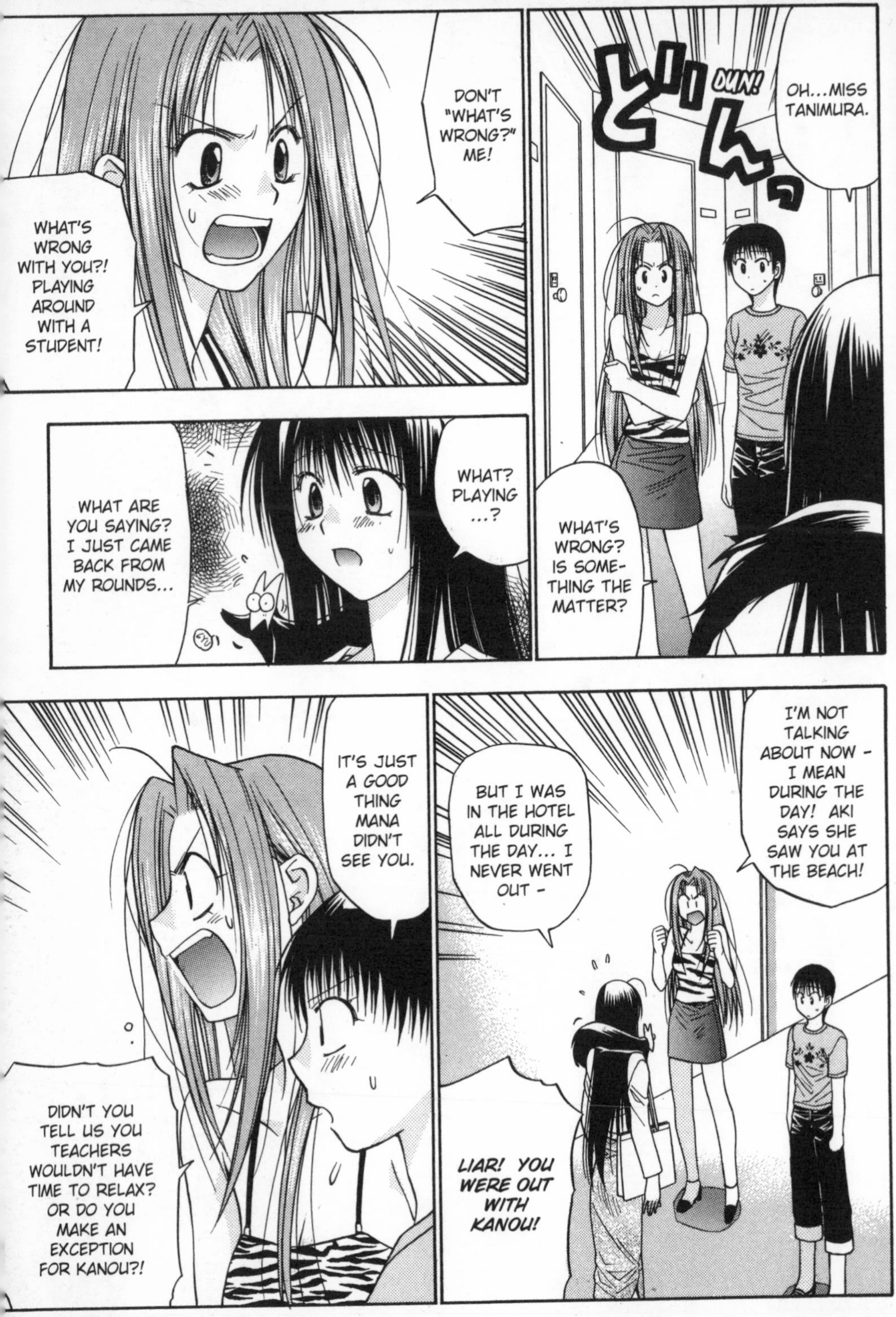
どーんっ
DUN!
OH...MISS TANIMURA.
WHAT'S WRONG? IS SOME-THING THE MATTER?
DON'T "WHAT'S WRONG?" ME!
WHAT'S WRONG WITH YOU?! PLAYING AROUND WITH A STUDENT!
WHAT? PLAYING ...?
WHAT ARE YOU SAYING? I JUST CAME BACK FROM MY ROUNDS...
GYU
I'M NOT TALKING ABOUT NOW - I MEAN DURING THE DAY! AKI SAYS SHE SAW YOU AT THE BEACH!
BUT I WAS IN THE HOTEL ALL DURING THE DAY... I NEVER WENT OUT -
LIAR! YOU WERE OUT WITH KANOU!
IT'S JUST A GOOD THING MANA DIDN'T SEE YOU.
DIDN'T YOU TELL US YOU TEACHERS WOULDN'T HAVE TIME TO RELAX? OR DO YOU MAKE AN EXCEPTION FOR KANOU?!

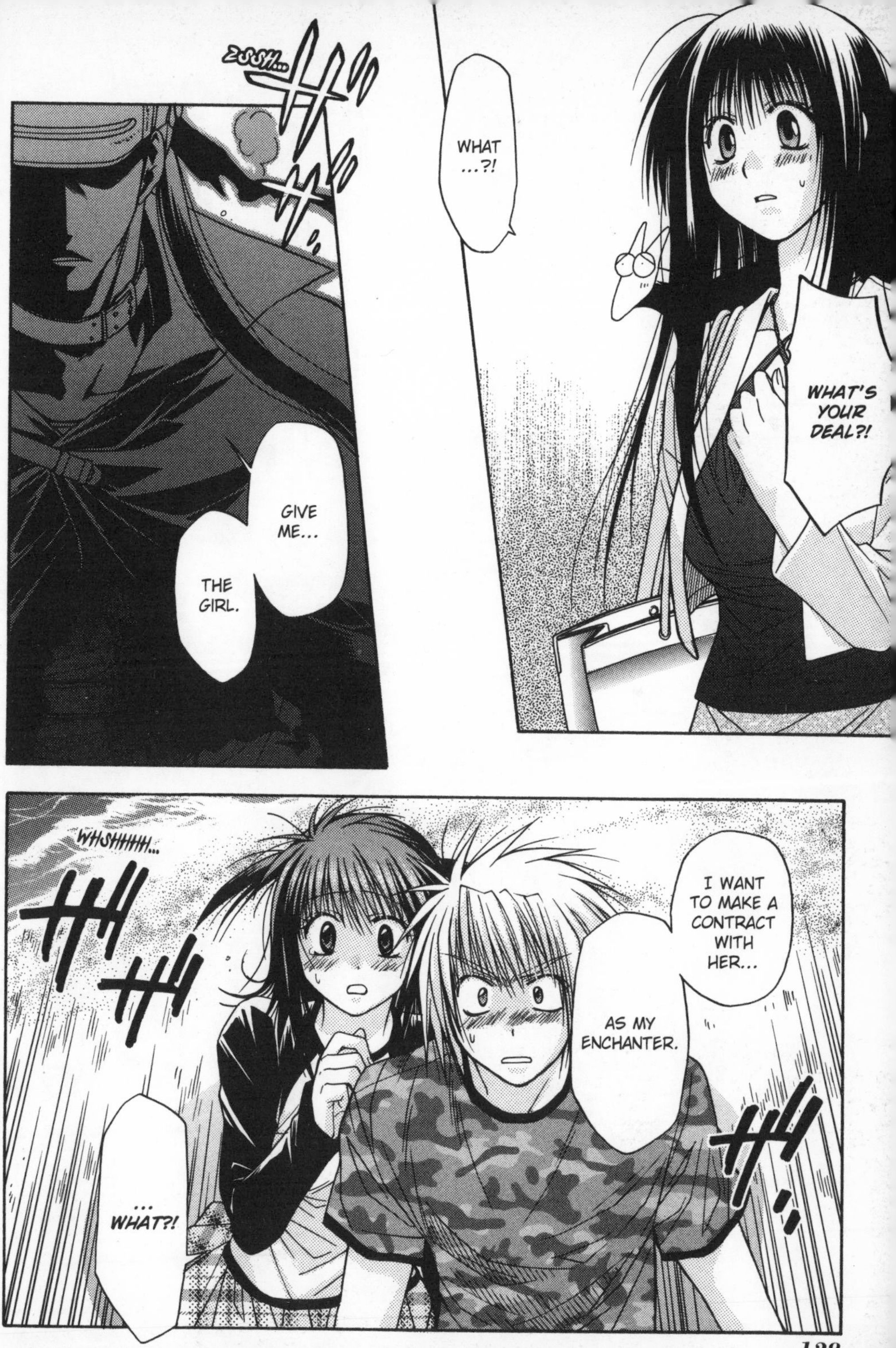
WHAT'S YOUR DEAL?!
WHAT ...?!
ZSSH...
GIVE ME...
THE GIRL.
I WANT TO MAKE A CONTRACT WITH HER...
AS MY ENCHANTER.
WHSHHHH...
... WHAT?!

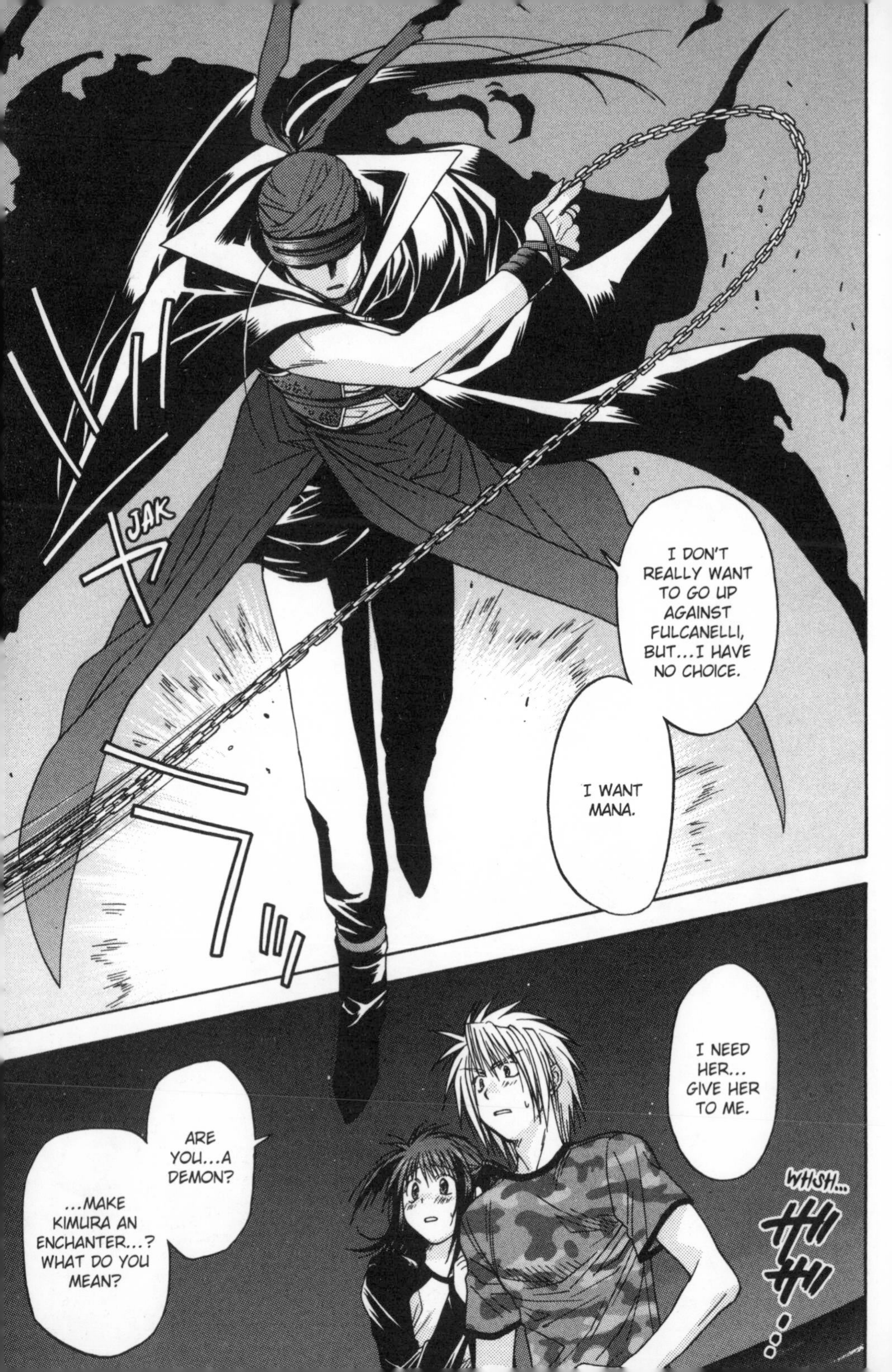
I DON'T REALLY WANT TO GO UP AGAINST FULCANELLI, BUT…I HAVE NO CHOICE.
I WANT MANA.
JAK
WHSH…
I NEED HER… GIVE HER TO ME.
ARE YOU…A DEMON?
…MAKE KIMURA AN ENCHANTER…? WHAT DO YOU MEAN?

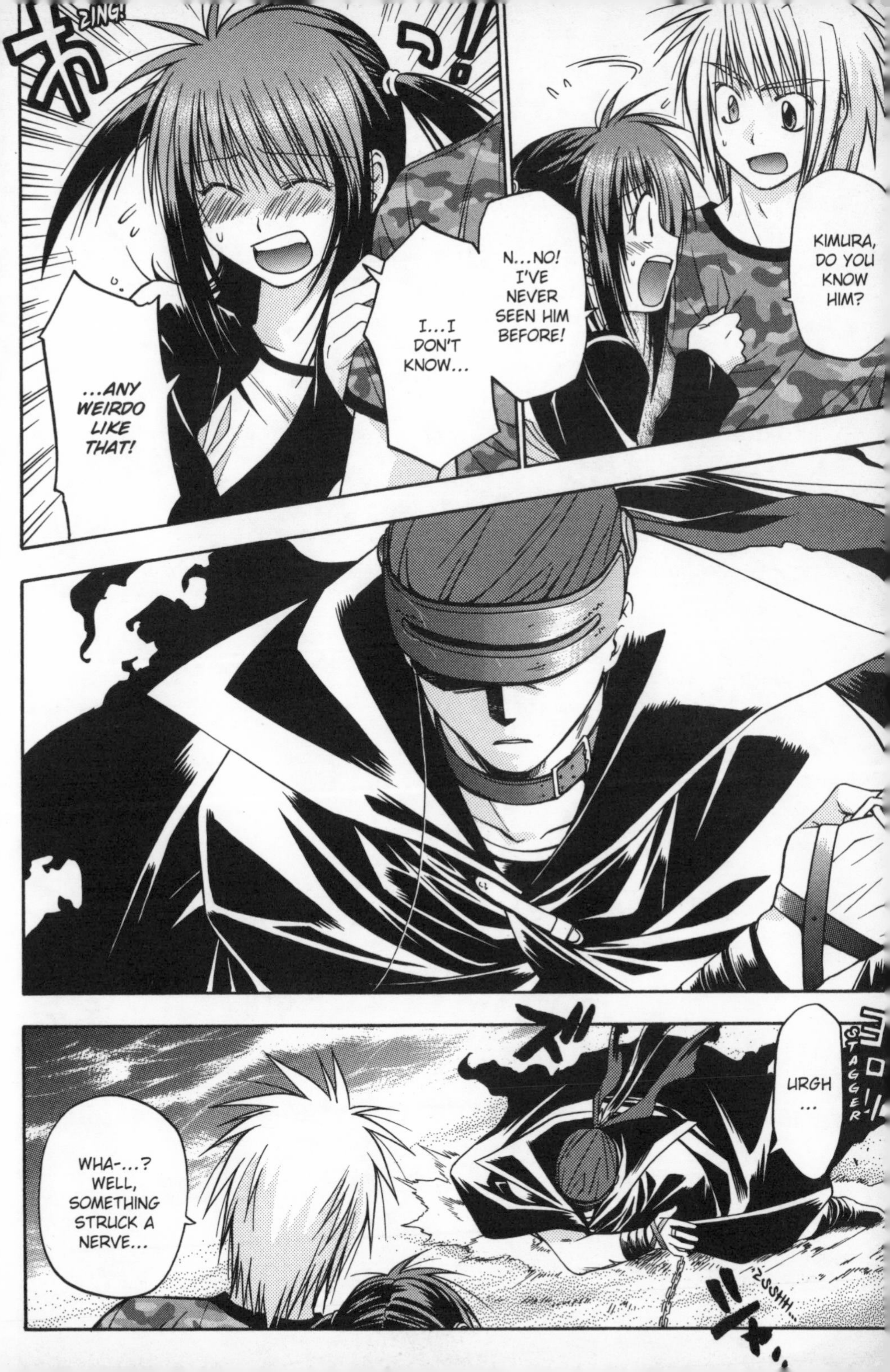
ZING!
KIMURA, DO YOU KNOW HIM?
N...NO! I'VE NEVER SEEN HIM BEFORE!
I...I DON'T KNOW...
...ANY WEIRDO LIKE THAT!
STAGGER
URGH ...
WHA-...? WELL, SOMETHING STRUCK A NERVE...
ZSSHH...

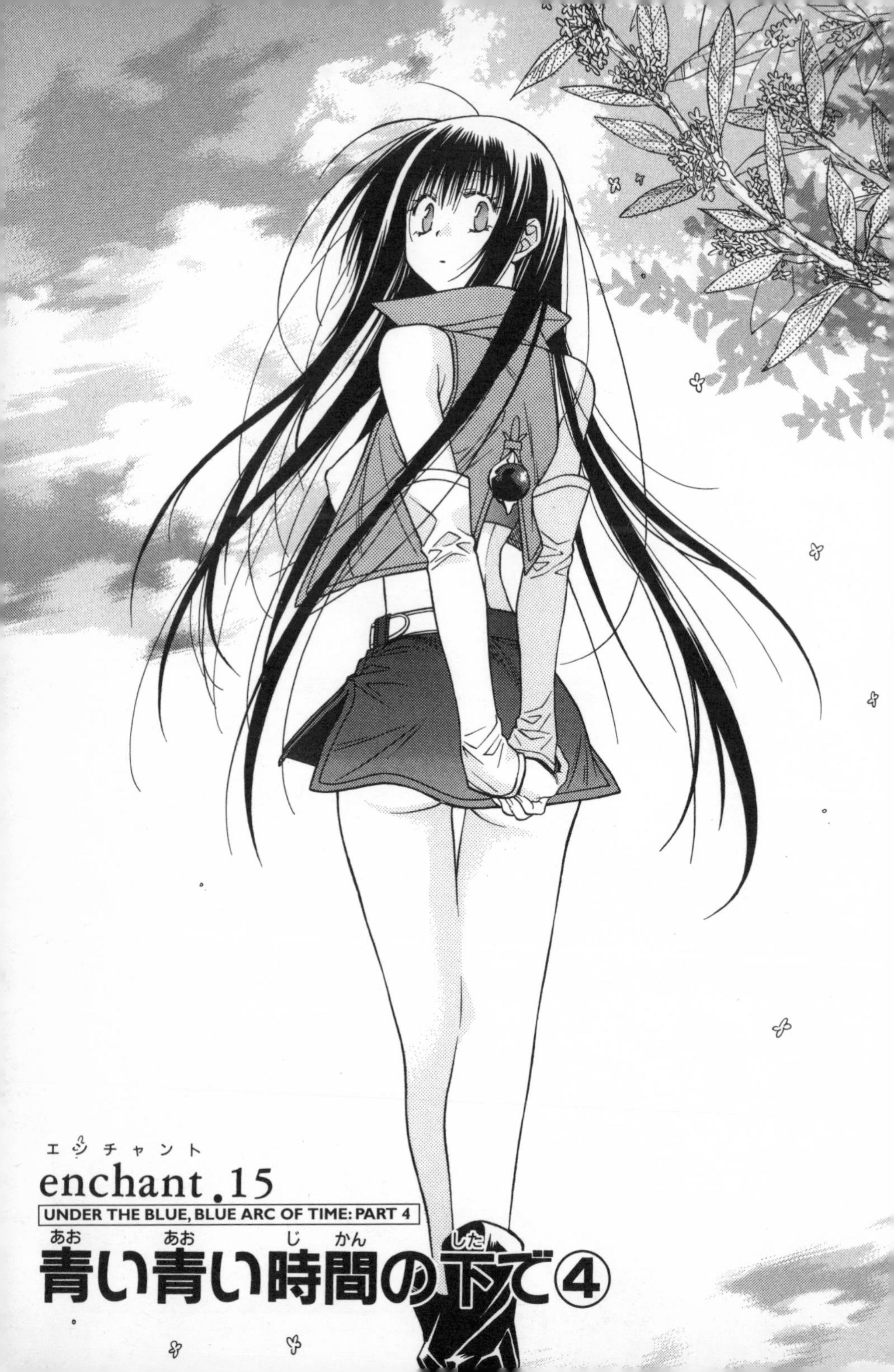
エンチャント
enchant.15
UNDER THE BLUE, BLUE ARC OF TIME: PART 4
青い青い時間の下で④

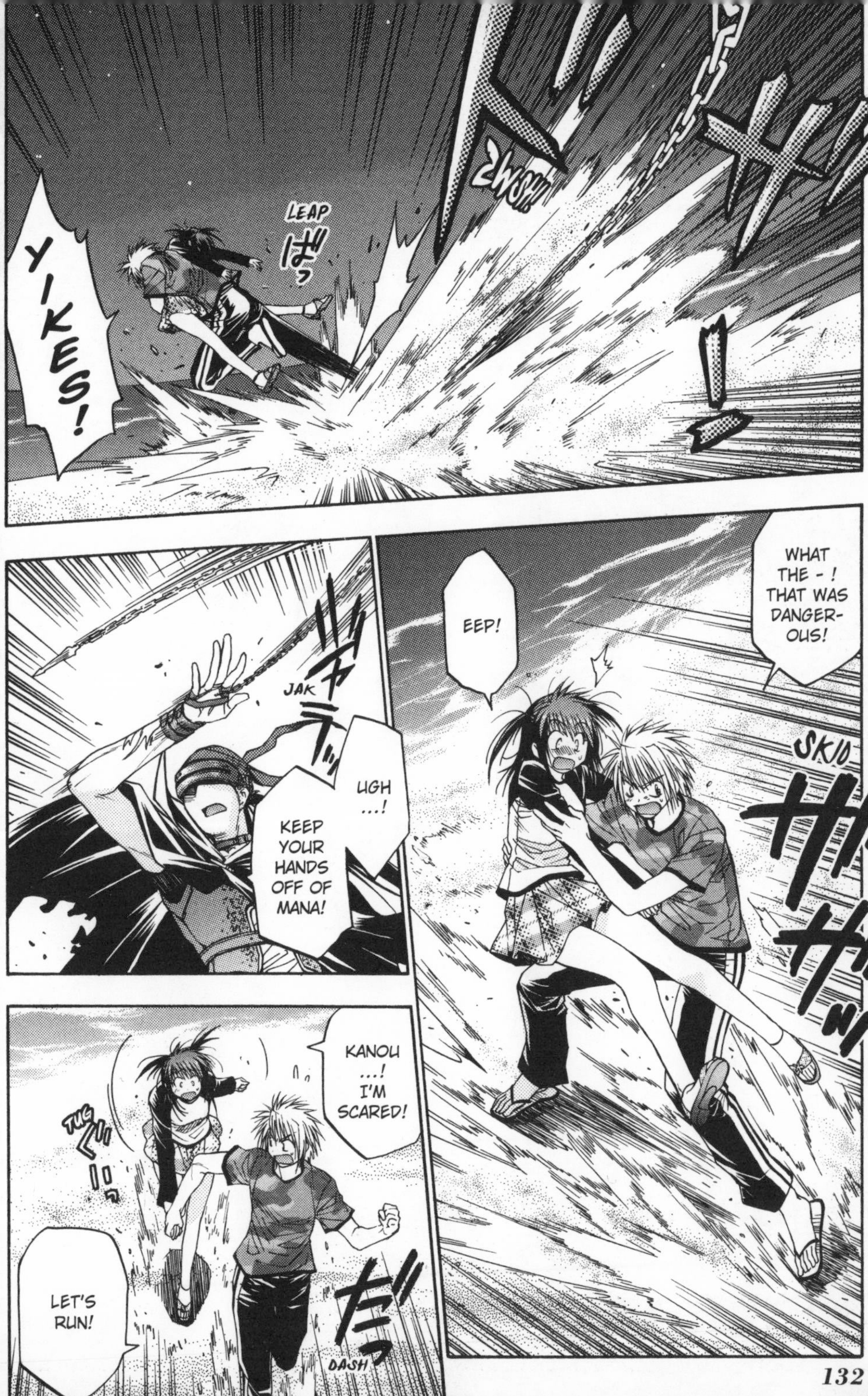
SMASH
LEAP
ぱっ
YIKES!
WHAT THE - ! THAT WAS DANGER-OUS!
EEP!
SKID
JAK
UGH ...!
KEEP YOUR HANDS OFF OF MANA!
KANOU ...! I'M SCARED!
TUG
LET'S RUN!
DASH
だっ

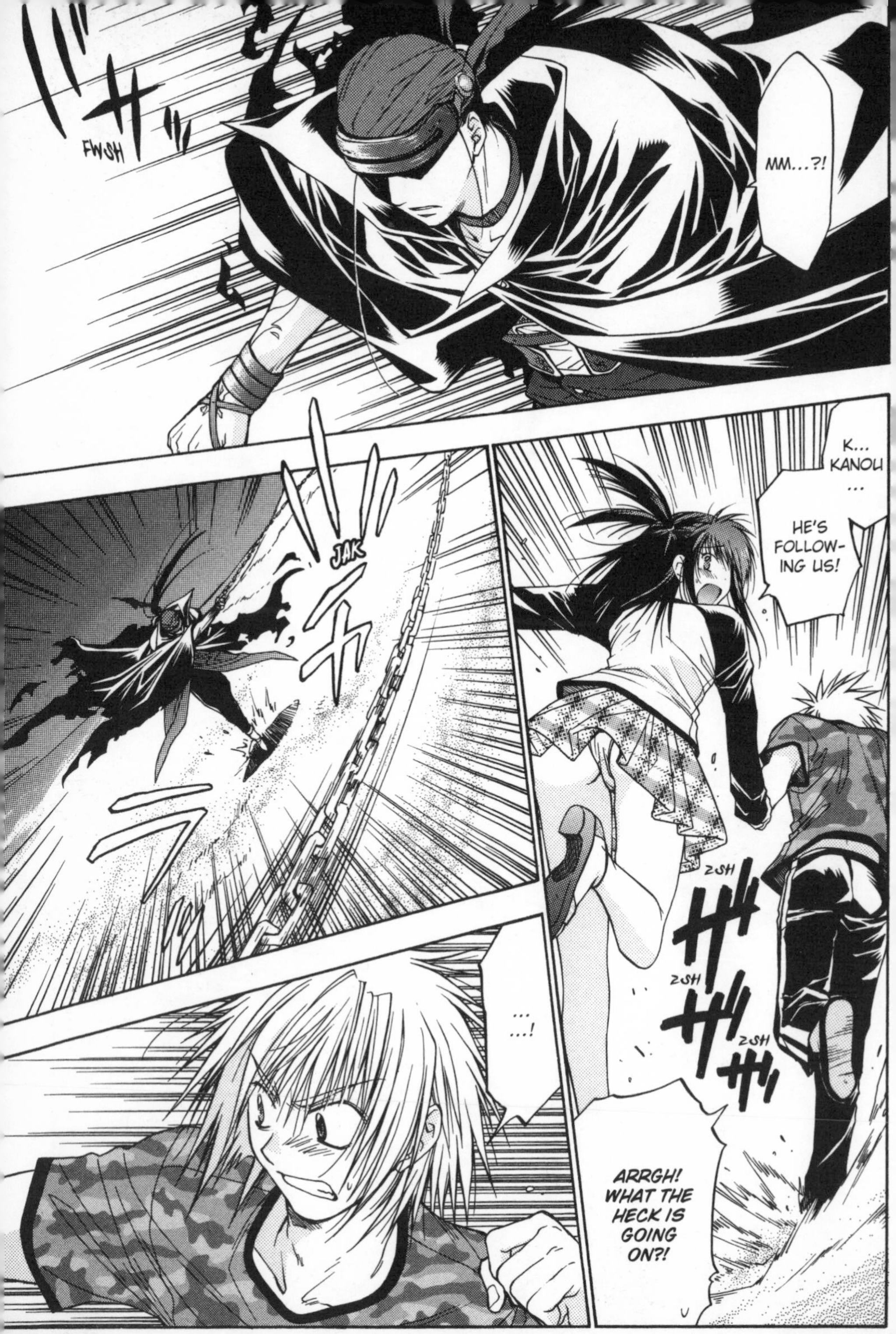
FWSH
MM...?!
K... KANOU ...
HE'S FOLLOWING US!
ZSH
ZSH
ZSH
JAK
... ...!
ARRGH! WHAT THE HECK IS GOING ON?!

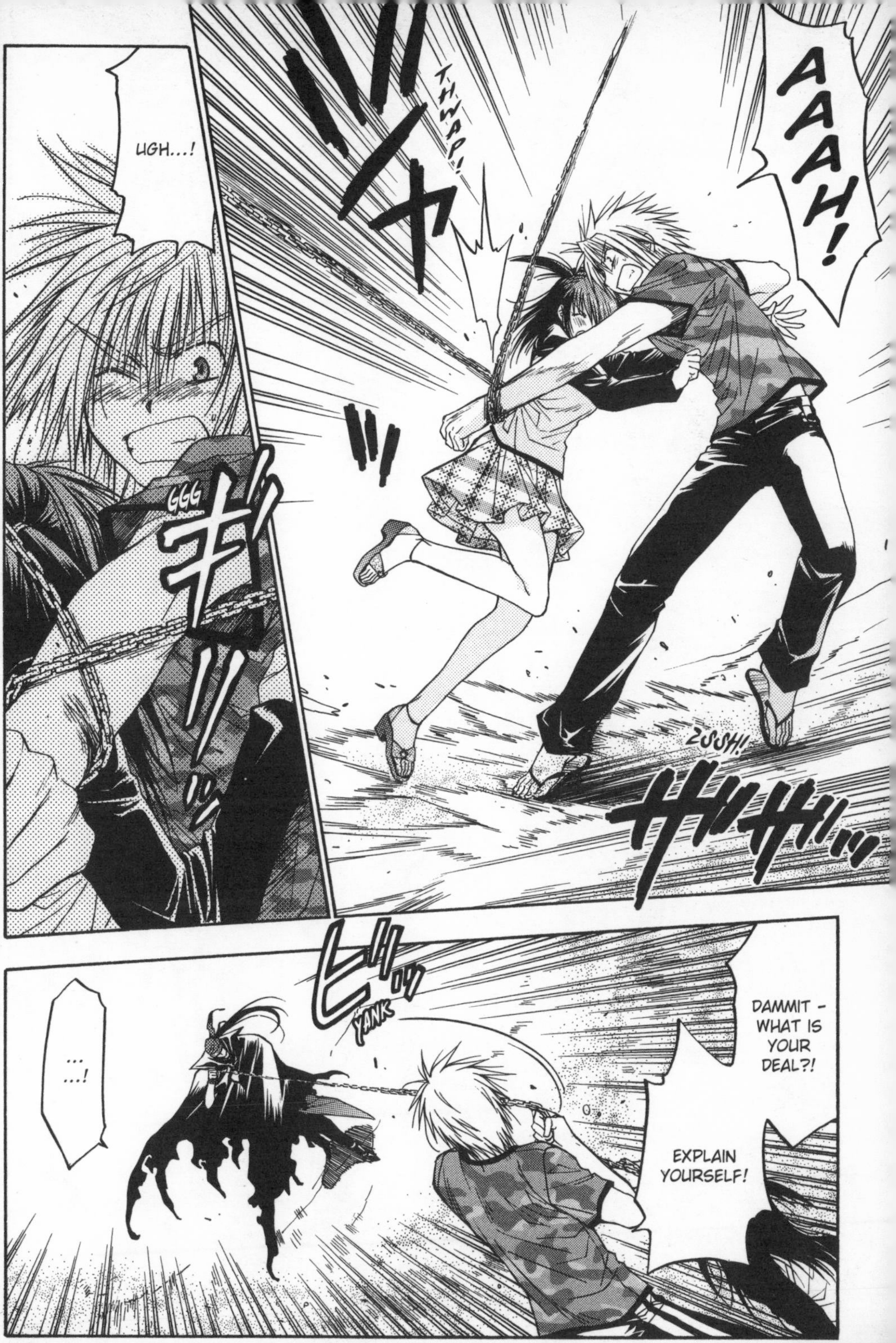
AAAAH!
THWAP!!
ZSSH!!
UGH...!
GGG
DAMMIT - WHAT IS YOUR DEAL?!
EXPLAIN YOURSELF!
YANK
...
...!

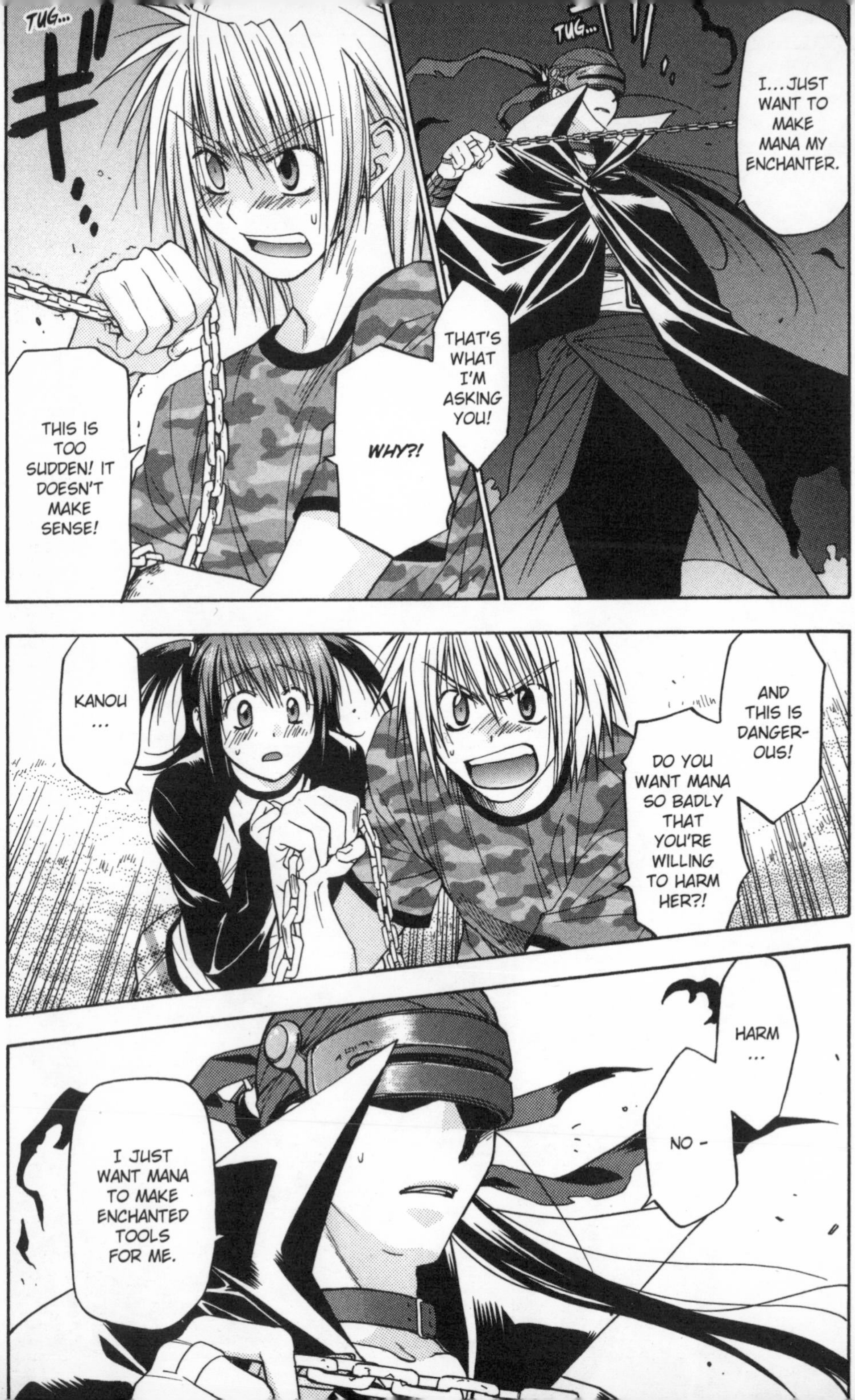
TUG...
I...JUST WANT TO MAKE MANA MY ENCHANTER.
TUG...
ギ
THAT'S WHAT I'M ASKING YOU!
WHY?!
THIS IS TOO SUDDEN! IT DOESN'T MAKE SENSE!
AND THIS IS DANGER-OUS!
DO YOU WANT MANA SO BADLY THAT YOU'RE WILLING TO HARM HER?!
KANOU ...
HARM ...
NO -
I JUST WANT MANA TO MAKE ENCHANTED TOOLS FOR ME.

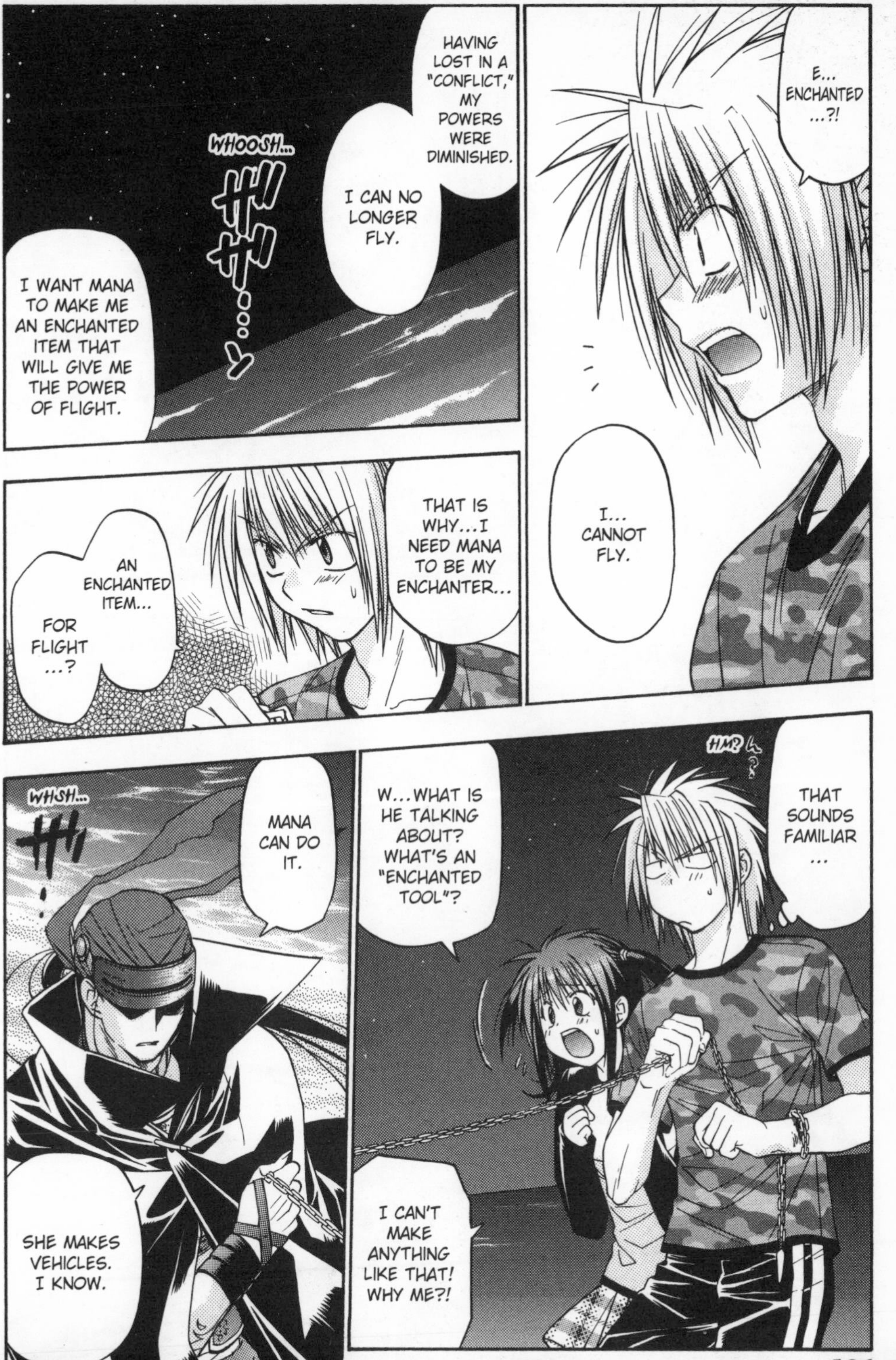
E... ENCHANTED ...?!
I... CANNOT FLY.
HAVING LOST IN A "CONFLICT," MY POWERS WERE DIMINISHED.
I CAN NO LONGER FLY.
WHOOSH...
I WANT MANA TO MAKE ME AN ENCHANTED ITEM THAT WILL GIVE ME THE POWER OF FLIGHT.
THAT IS WHY...I NEED MANA TO BE MY ENCHANTER...
AN ENCHANTED ITEM...
FOR FLIGHT ...?
HM?
THAT SOUNDS FAMILIAR ...
W...WHAT IS HE TALKING ABOUT? WHAT'S AN "ENCHANTED TOOL"?
I CAN'T MAKE ANYTHING LIKE THAT! WHY ME?!
WHSH...
MANA CAN DO IT.
SHE MAKES VEHICLES. I KNOW.

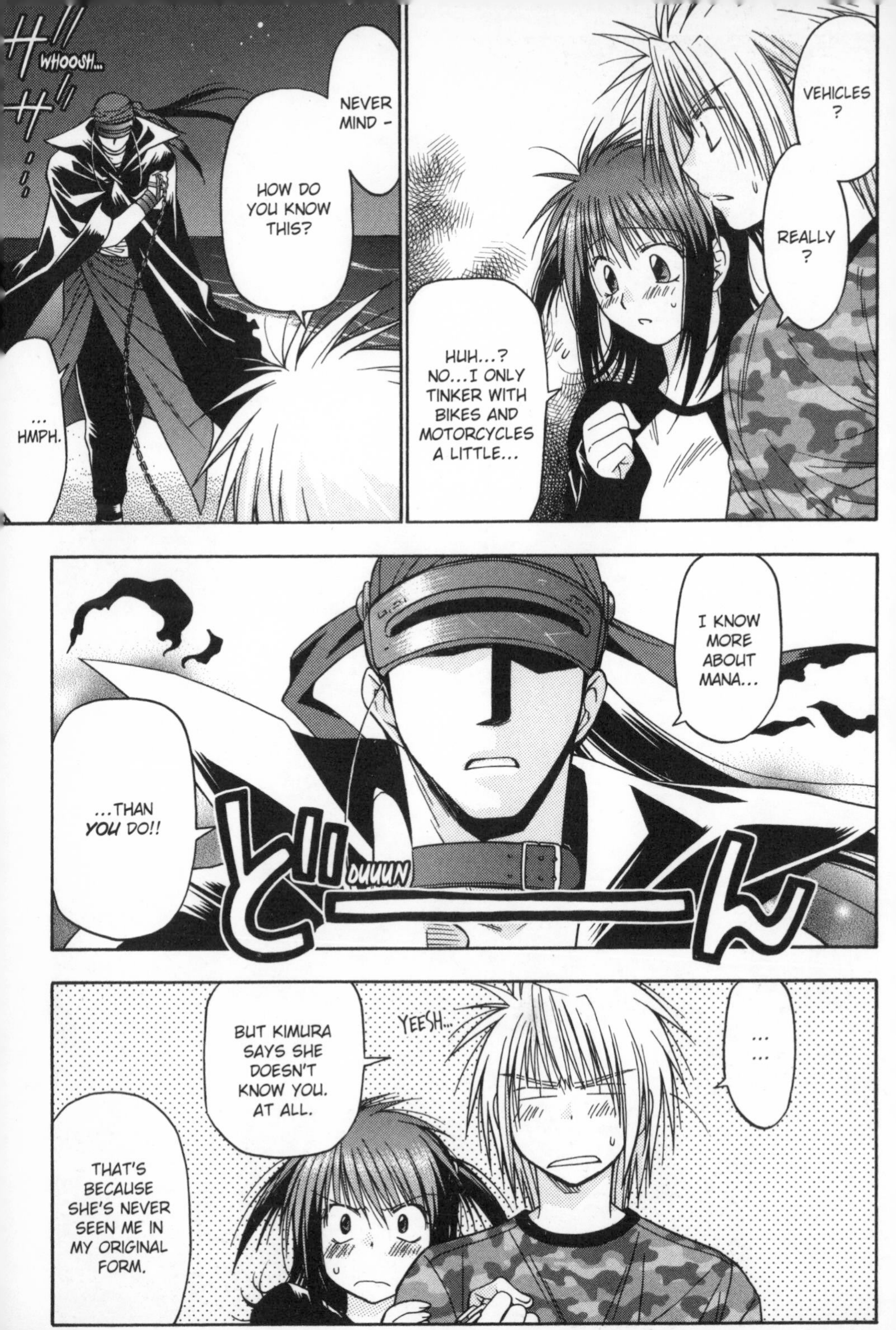
VEHICLES?
REALLY?
HUH...? NO...I ONLY TINKER WITH BIKES AND MOTORCYCLES A LITTLE...
NEVER MIND -
HOW DO YOU KNOW THIS?
WHOOSH...
...HMPH.
I KNOW MORE ABOUT MANA...
...THAN *YOU* DO!!
DUUUN
... ...
YEESH...
BUT KIMURA SAYS SHE DOESN'T KNOW YOU. AT ALL.
THAT'S BECAUSE SHE'S NEVER SEEN ME IN MY ORIGINAL FORM.

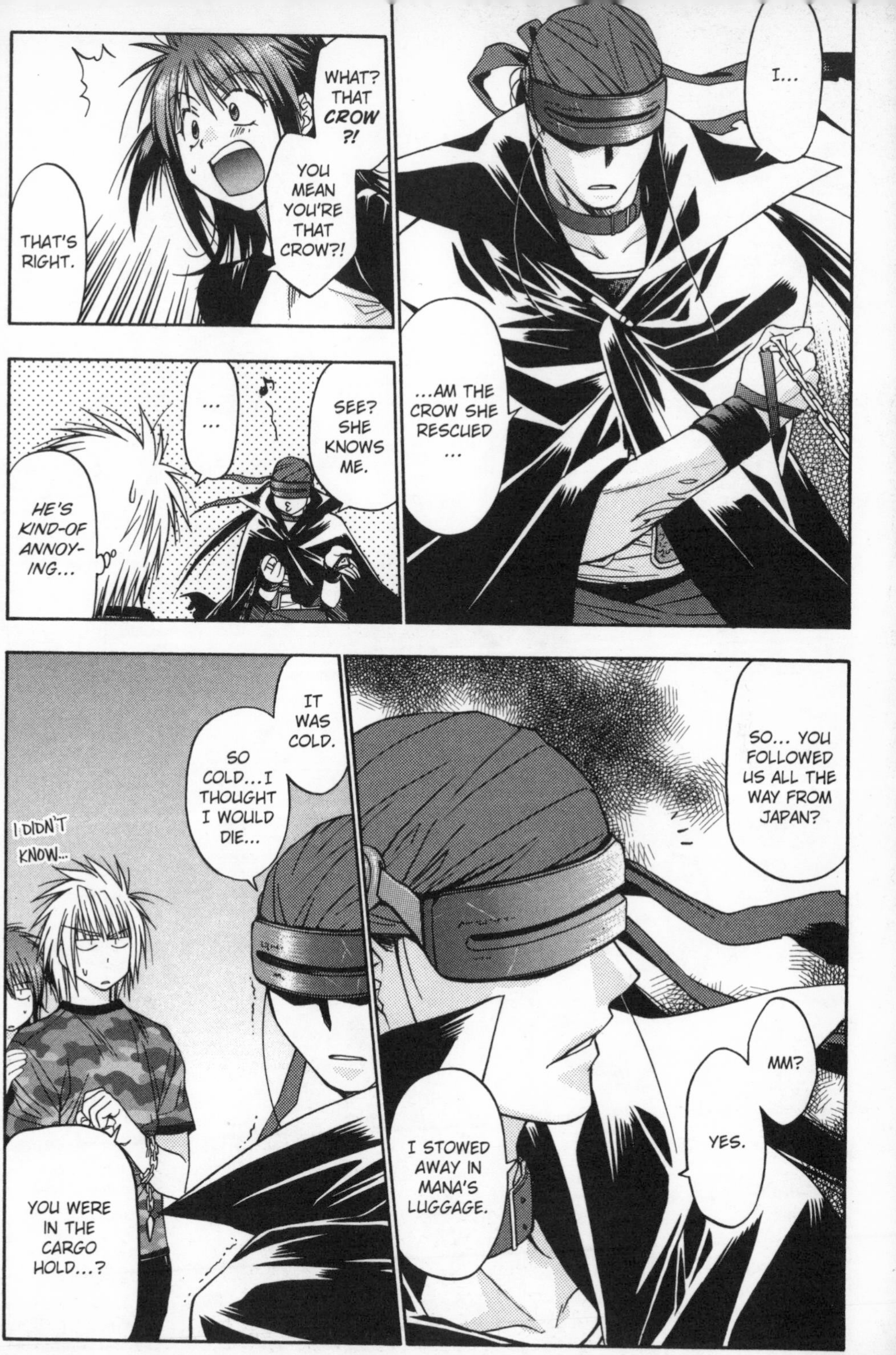
I...
...AM THE CROW SHE RESCUED ...
WHAT? THAT CROW?!
YOU MEAN YOU'RE THAT CROW?!
THAT'S RIGHT.
SEE? SHE KNOWS ME.
... ...
HE'S KIND-OF ANNOY-ING...
SO... YOU FOLLOWED US ALL THE WAY FROM JAPAN?
MM?
YES.
I STOWED AWAY IN MANA'S LUGGAGE.
IT WAS COLD.
SO COLD...I THOUGHT I WOULD DIE...
I DIDN'T KNOW...
YOU WERE IN THE CARGO HOLD...?

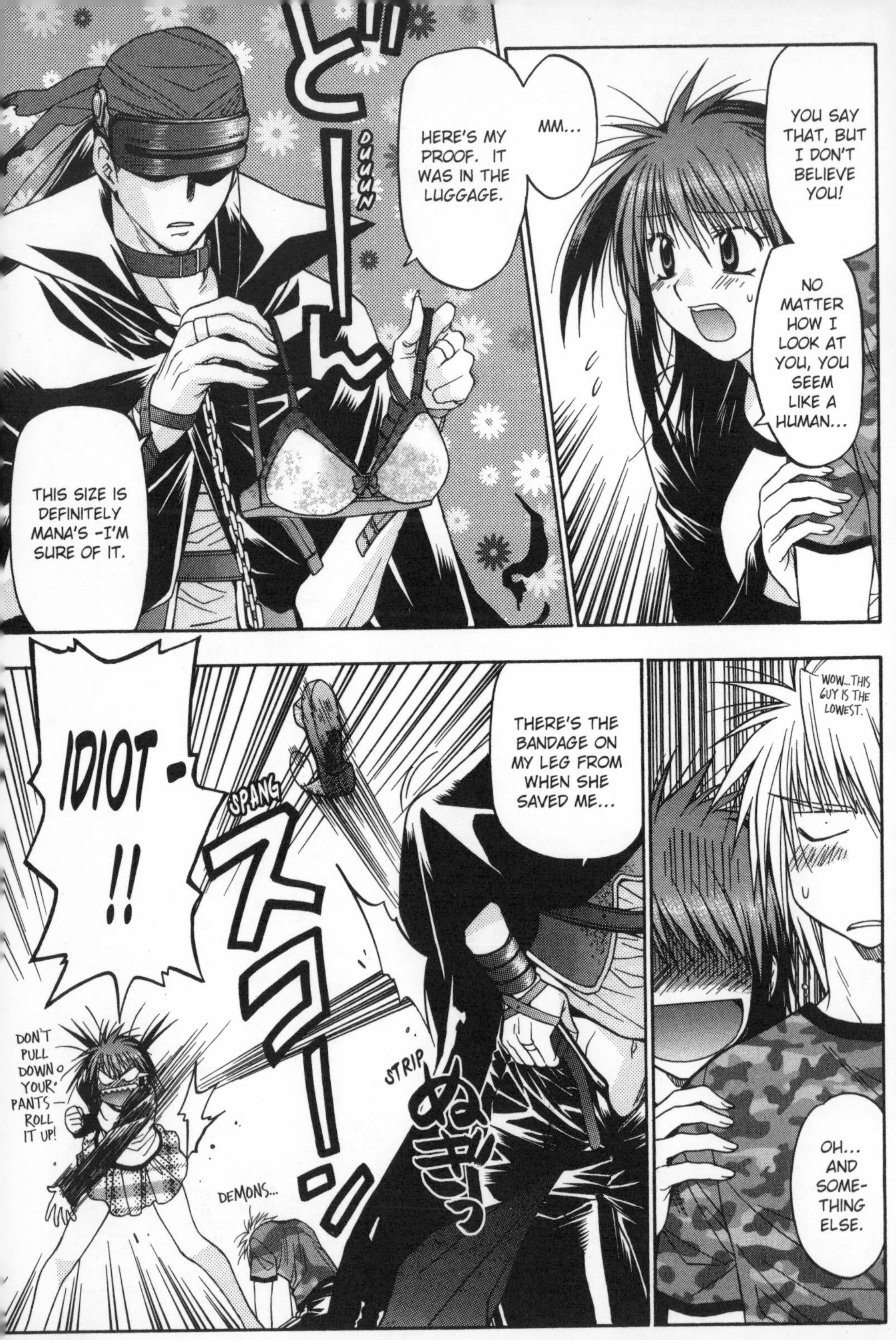
YOU SAY THAT, BUT I DON'T BELIEVE YOU!
NO MATTER HOW I LOOK AT YOU, YOU SEEM LIKE A HUMAN...
MM...
HERE'S MY PROOF. IT WAS IN THE LUGGAGE.
DUUUN
THIS SIZE IS DEFINITELY MANA'S -I'M SURE OF IT.
WOW...THIS GUY IS THE LOWEST.
OH... AND SOME-THING ELSE.
THERE'S THE BANDAGE ON MY LEG FROM WHEN SHE SAVED ME...
STRIP
SPANG
IDIOT - !!
DON'T PULL DOWN YOUR PANTS — ROLL IT UP!
DEMONS...

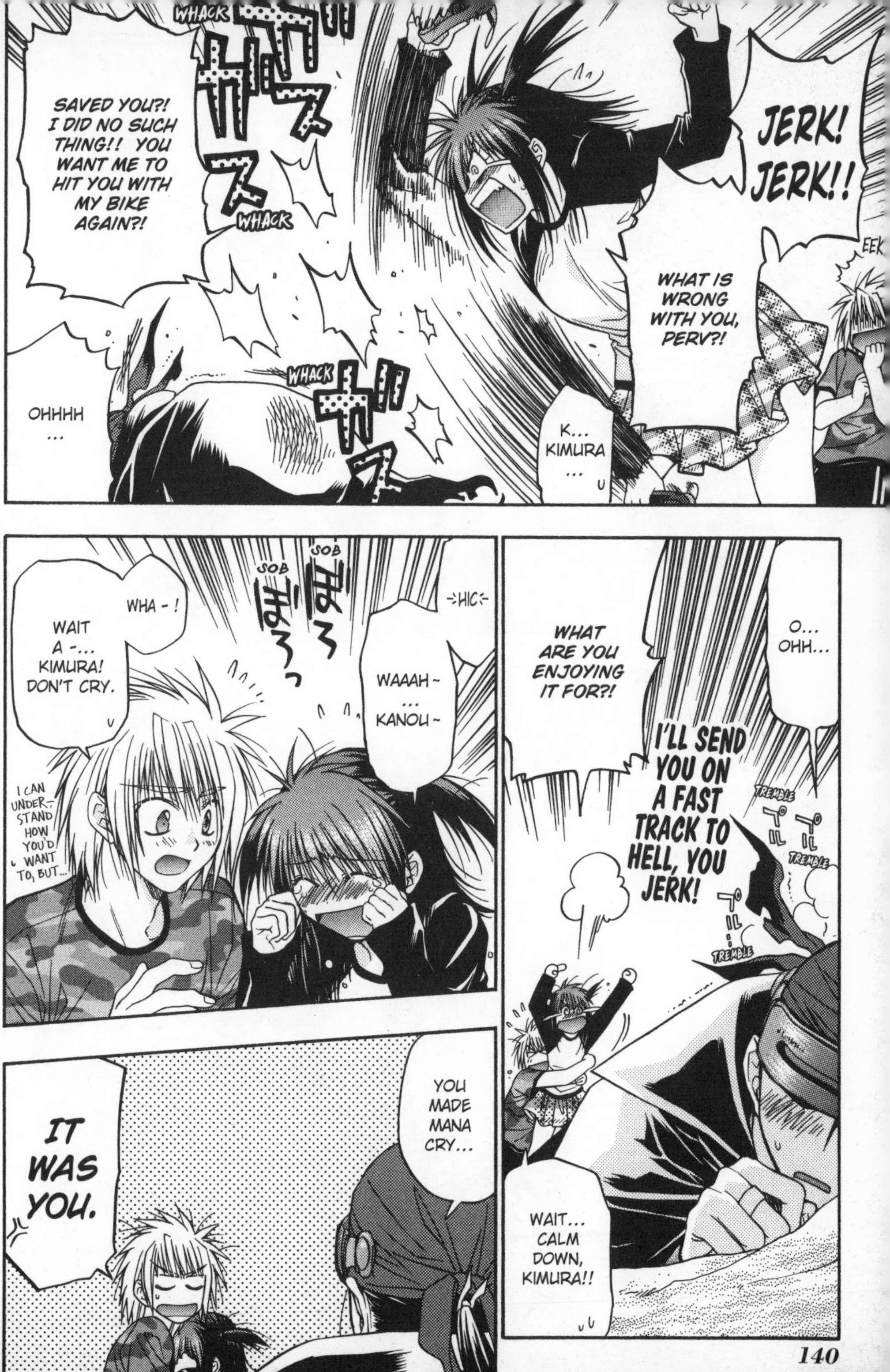
JERK! JERK!!
EEK
WHAT IS WRONG WITH YOU, PERV?!
K... KIMURA...
WHACK
WHACK
WHACK
SAVED YOU?! I DID NO SUCH THING!! YOU WANT ME TO HIT YOU WITH MY BIKE AGAIN?!
OHHHH...
O... OHH...
WHAT ARE YOU ENJOYING IT FOR?!
I'LL SEND YOU ON A FAST TRACK TO HELL, YOU JERK!
TREMBLE
TREMBLE
TREMBLE
WAIT... CALM DOWN, KIMURA!!
SOB
SOB
HIC
WAAAH~ ... KANOU~
WHA-!
WAIT A-... KIMURA! DON'T CRY.
I CAN UNDERSTAND HOW YOU'D WANT TO, BUT...
YOU MADE MANA CRY...
IT WAS YOU.

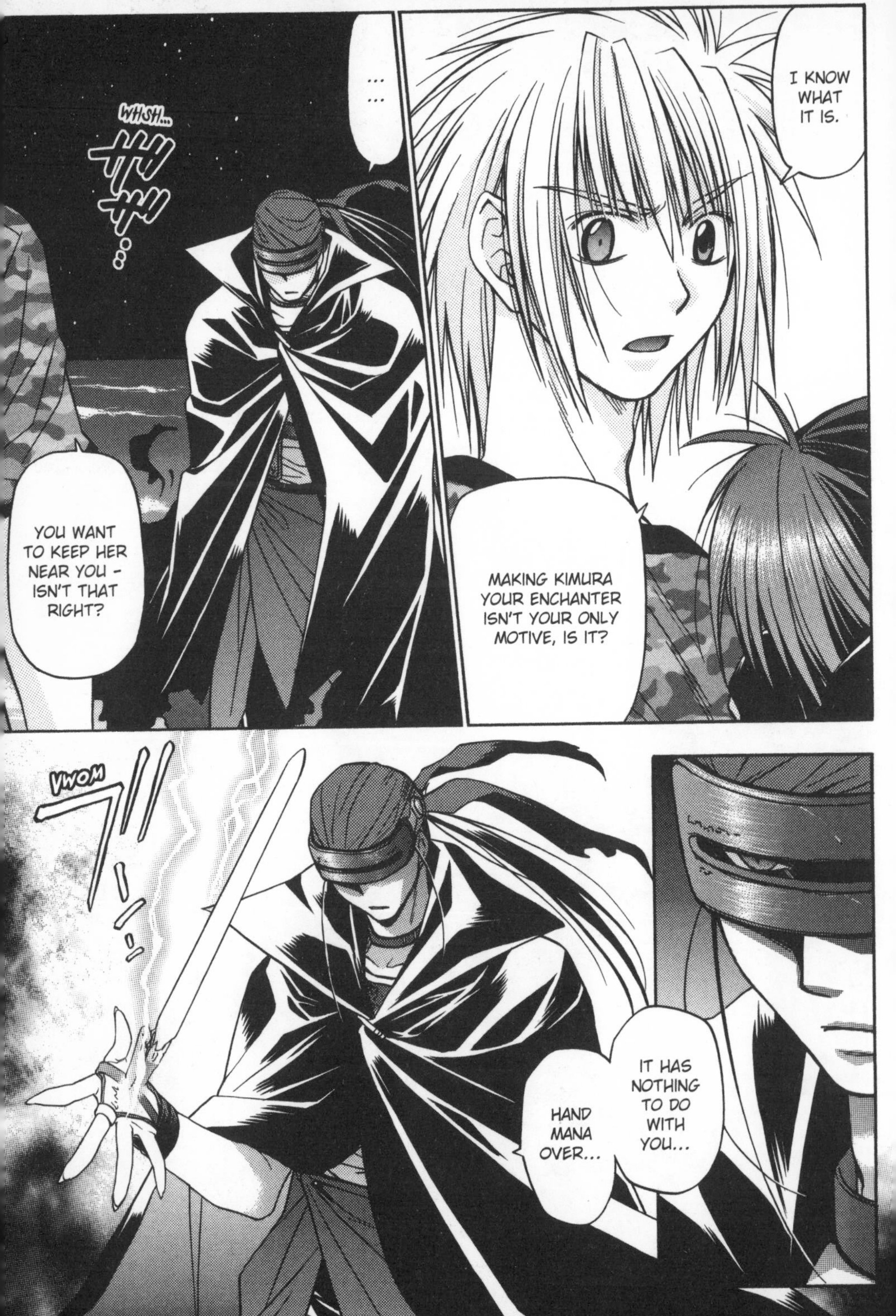
I KNOW WHAT IT IS.
MAKING KIMURA YOUR ENCHANTER ISN'T YOUR ONLY MOTIVE, IS IT?
……
WHSH...
YOU WANT TO KEEP HER NEAR YOU - ISN'T THAT RIGHT?
IT HAS NOTHING TO DO WITH YOU...
HAND MANA OVER...
VWOM

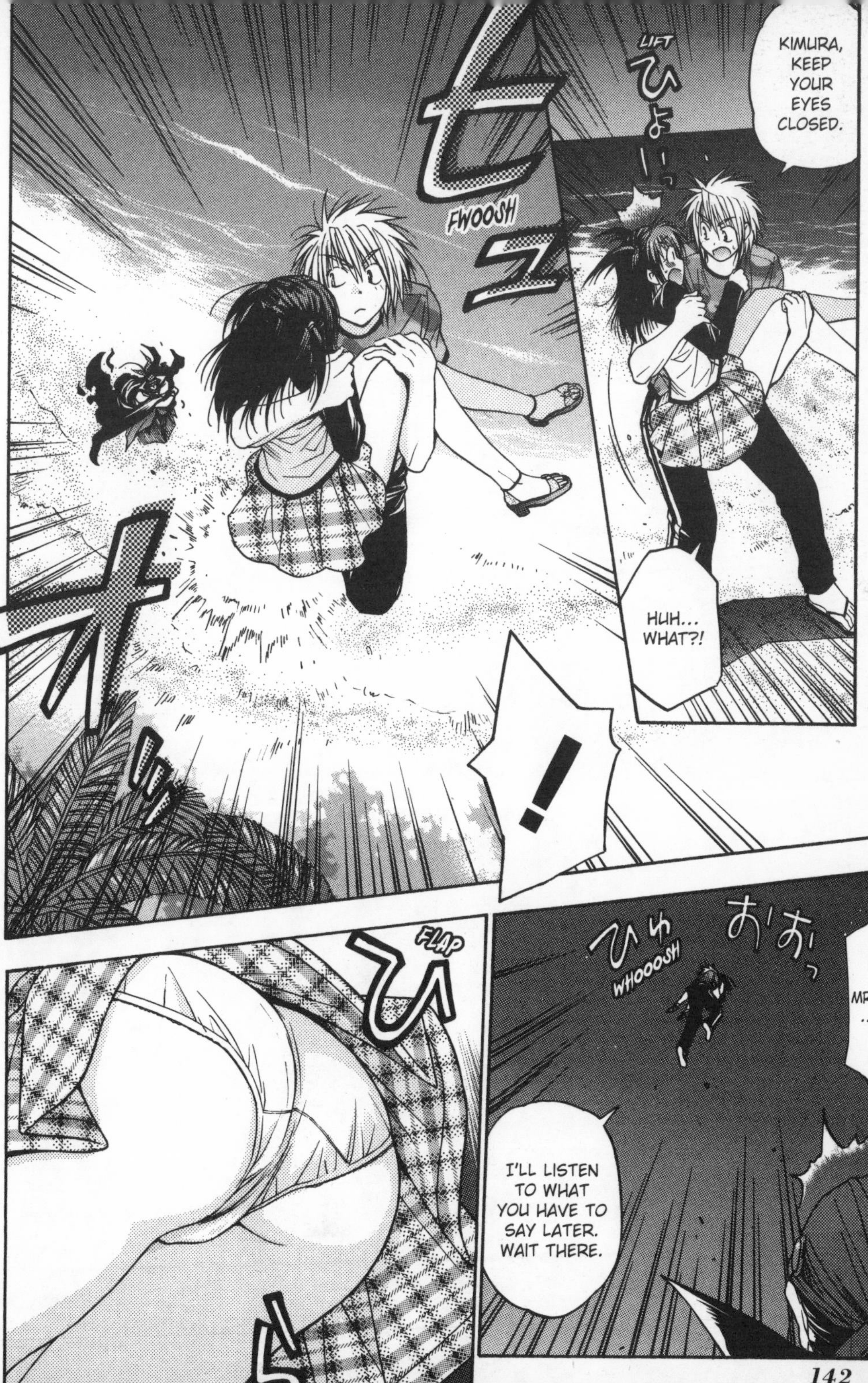

LIFT
KIMURA, KEEP YOUR EYES CLOSED.
HUH... WHAT?!
FWOOSH
!
WHOOOSH
MRGH ...!
I'LL LISTEN TO WHAT YOU HAVE TO SAY LATER. WAIT THERE.
FLAP

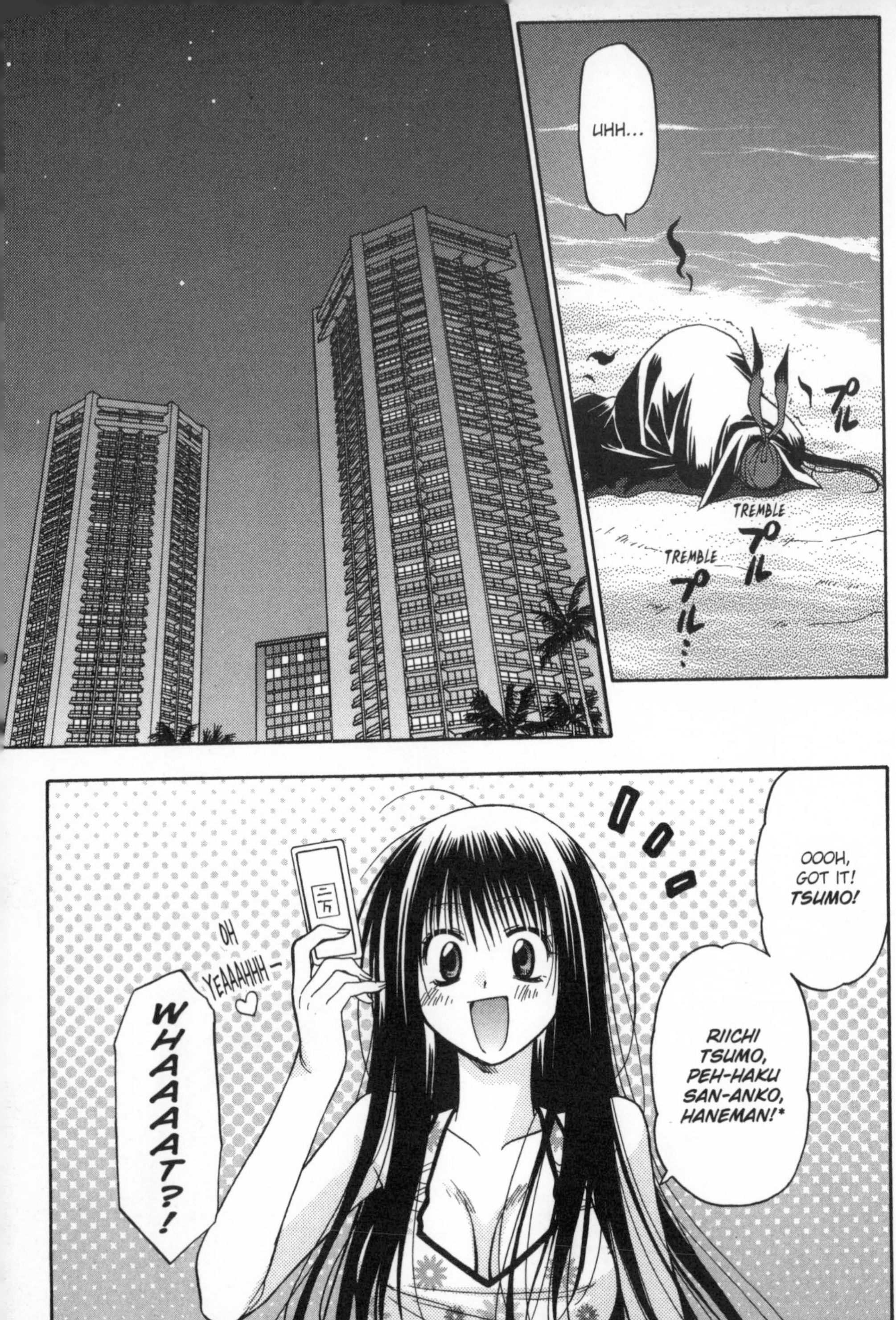
UHH...
プル
TREMBLE
プル
TREMBLE
プル...
OOOH, GOT IT! TSUMO!
RIICHI TSUMO, PEH-HAKU SAN-ANKO, HANEMAN!*
OH YEAAAHHH-♡
WHAAAAAT?!

*NOTE: MAHJONG TERMS. BASICALLY WHAT'S HAPPENING IN THIS SCENE IS THAT EUKANARIA IS RACKING UP A TREMENDOUS AMOUNT OF BONUS POINTS WITH AN IMPROBABLE SUCCESSION OF GREAT HANDS.

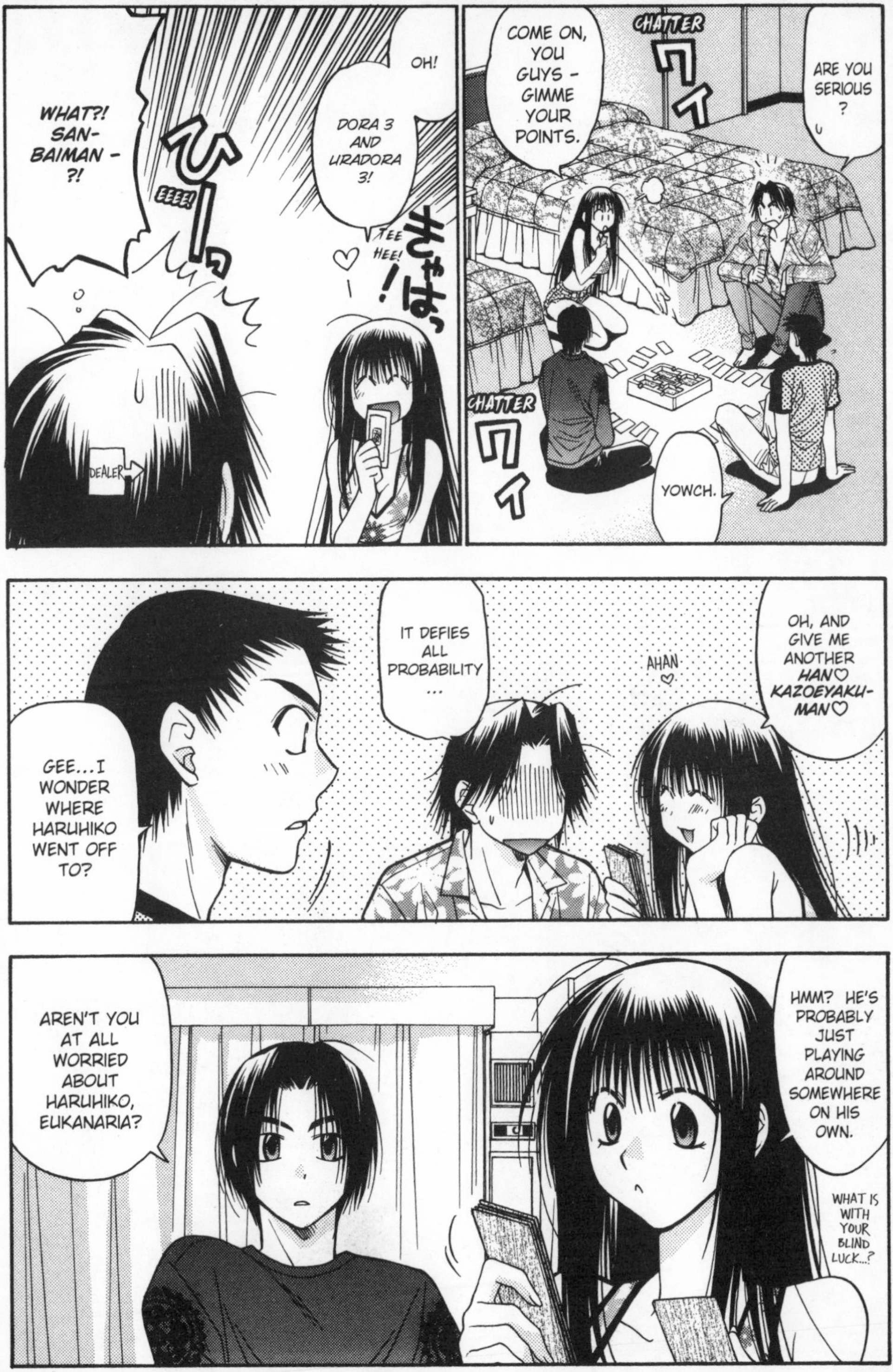
CHATTER
ワイ
COME ON, YOU GUYS - GIMME YOUR POINTS.
ARE YOU SERIOUS?
CHATTER
ワイ
YOWCH.
OH!
DORA 3 AND URADORA 3!
きゃはっ!
TEE HEE!
WHAT?! SAN-BAIMAN -?!
ひーっ
EEEE!
DEALER
OH, AND GIVE ME ANOTHER HAN♡ KAZOEYAKUMAN♡
AHAN♡
IT DEFIES ALL PROBABILITY...
GEE...I WONDER WHERE HARUHIKO WENT OFF TO?
HMM? HE'S PROBABLY JUST PLAYING AROUND SOMEWHERE ON HIS OWN.
WHAT IS WITH YOUR BLIND LUCK...?
AREN'T YOU AT ALL WORRIED ABOUT HARUHIKO, EUKANARIA?

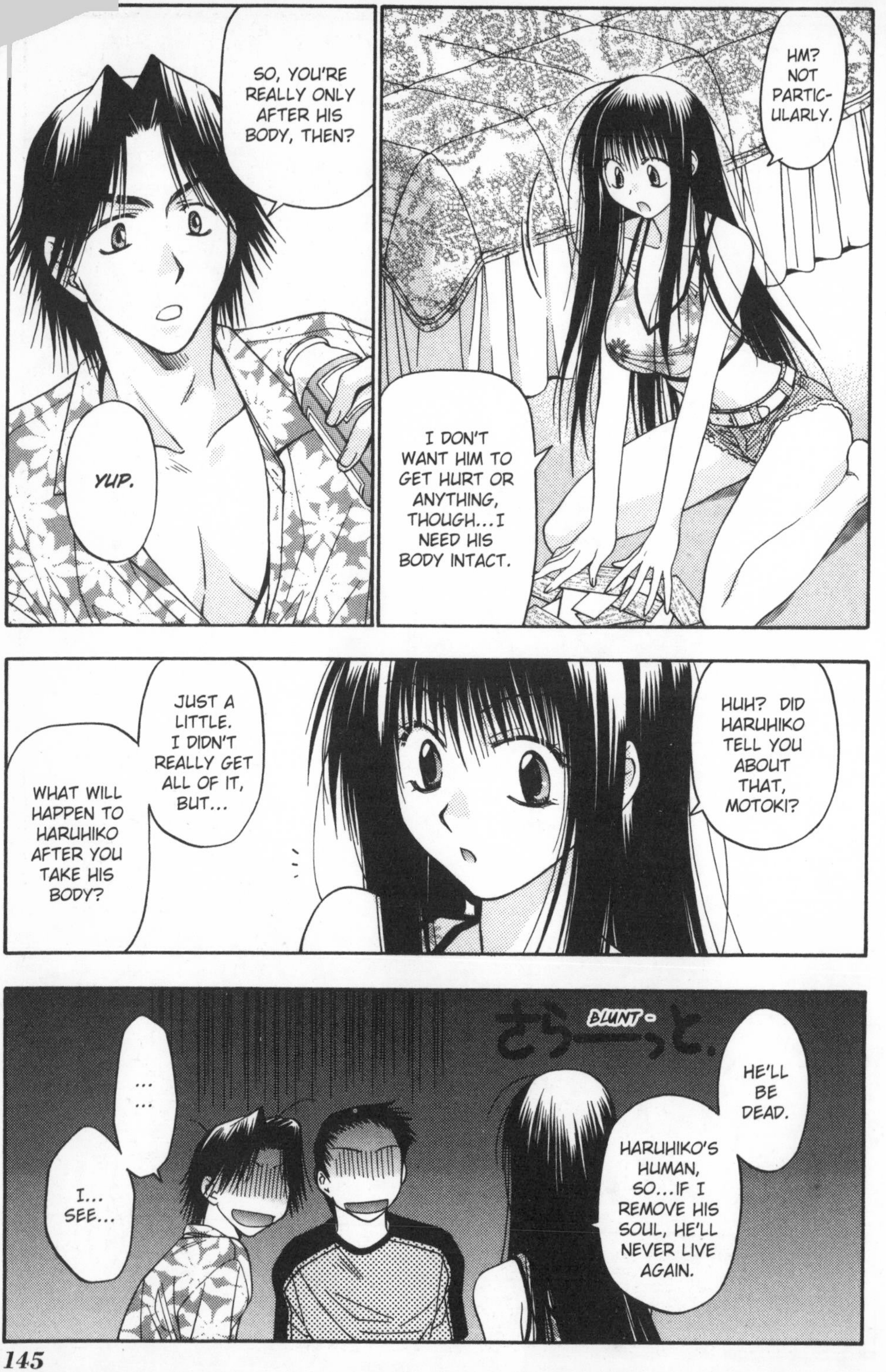
HM? NOT PARTIC-ULARLY.
I DON'T WANT HIM TO GET HURT OR ANYTHING, THOUGH...I NEED HIS BODY INTACT.
SO, YOU'RE REALLY ONLY AFTER HIS BODY, THEN?
YUP.
HUH? DID HARUHIKO TELL YOU ABOUT THAT, MOTOKI?
JUST A LITTLE. I DIDN'T REALLY GET ALL OF IT, BUT...
WHAT WILL HAPPEN TO HARUHIKO AFTER YOU TAKE HIS BODY?
BLUNT-
HE'LL BE DEAD.
HARUHIKO'S HUMAN, SO...IF I REMOVE HIS SOUL, HE'LL NEVER LIVE AGAIN.
......
I... SEE...

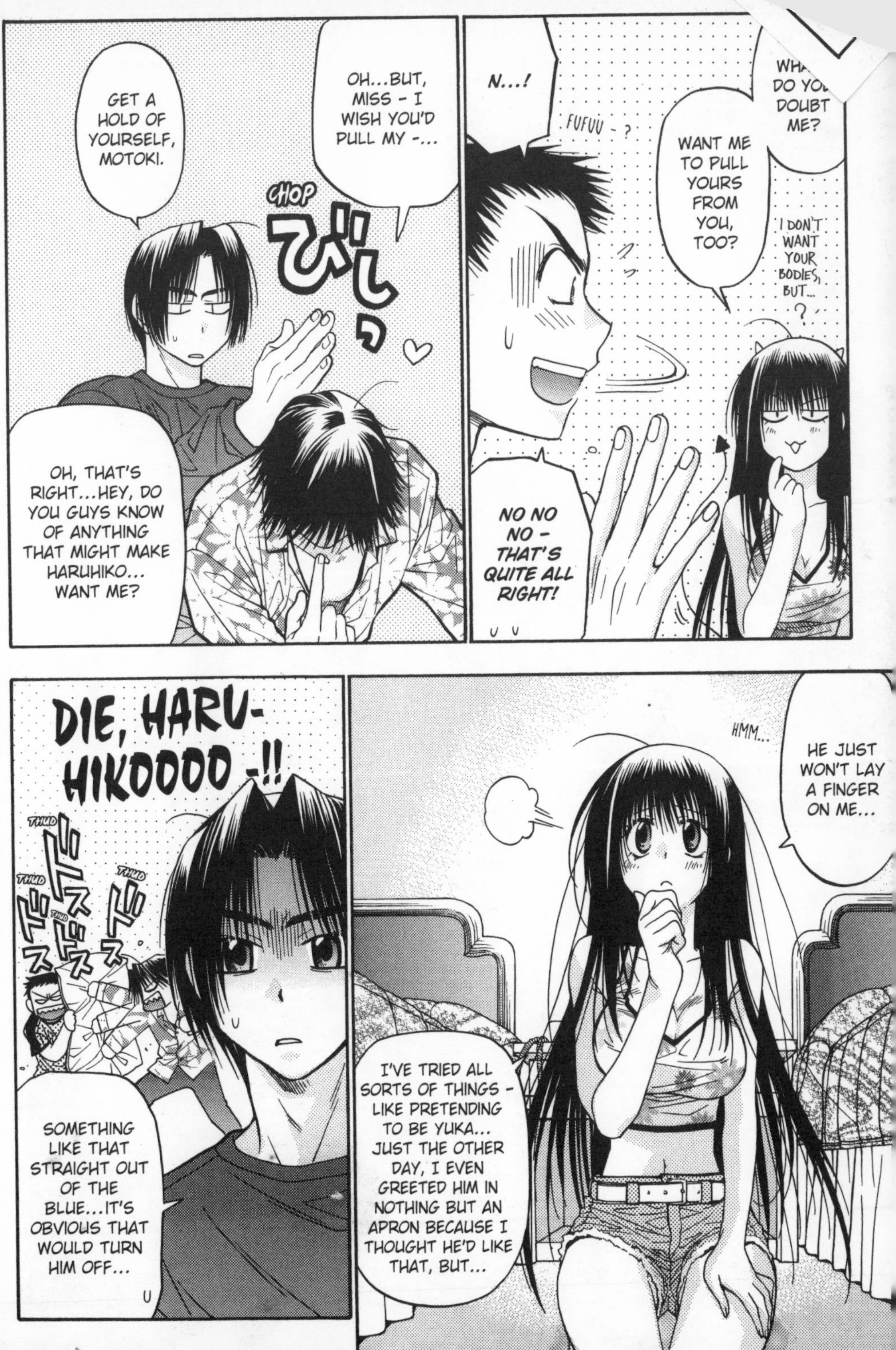
WHA DO YO DOUBT ME?
WANT ME TO PULL YOURS FROM YOU, TOO?
I DON'T WANT YOUR BODIES, BUT...
N...!
FUFUU - ?
NO NO NO - THAT'S QUITE ALL RIGHT!
OH...BUT, MISS - I WISH YOU'D PULL MY -...
GET A HOLD OF YOURSELF, MOTOKI.
CHOP
OH, THAT'S RIGHT...HEY, DO YOU GUYS KNOW OF ANYTHING THAT MIGHT MAKE HARUHIKO... WANT ME?
HMM...
HE JUST WON'T LAY A FINGER ON ME...
I'VE TRIED ALL SORTS OF THINGS - LIKE PRETENDING TO BE YUKA... JUST THE OTHER DAY, I EVEN GREETED HIM IN NOTHING BUT AN APRON BECAUSE I THOUGHT HE'D LIKE THAT, BUT...
DIE, HARU-HIKOOOO -!!
THUD
THUD
THUD
THUD
SOMETHING LIKE THAT STRAIGHT OUT OF THE BLUE...IT'S OBVIOUS THAT WOULD TURN HIM OFF...

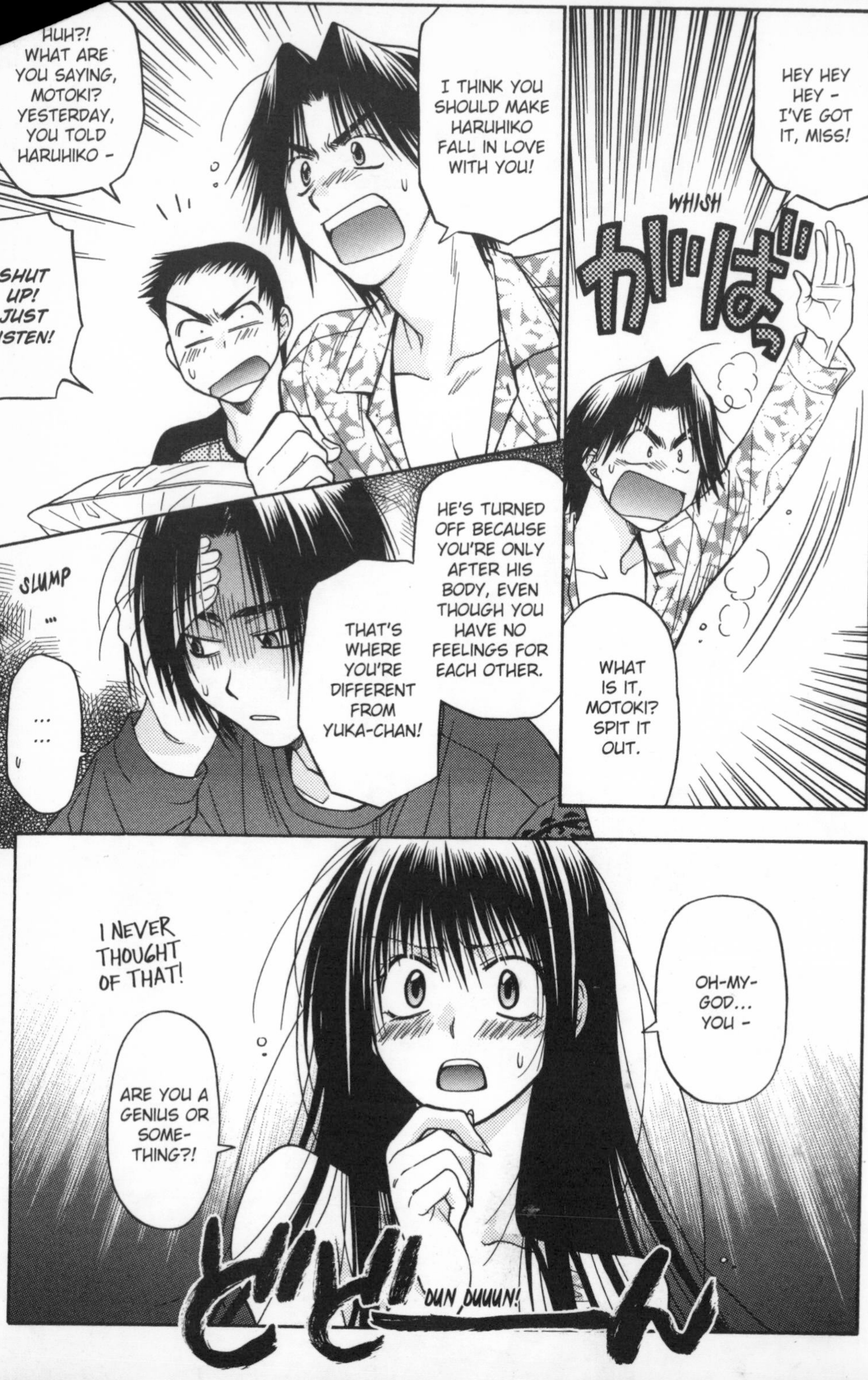

HEY HEY HEY - I'VE GOT IT, MISS!
WHISH
かばっ
WHAT IS IT, MOTOKI? SPIT IT OUT.
I THINK YOU SHOULD MAKE HARUHIKO FALL IN LOVE WITH YOU!
HUH?! WHAT ARE YOU SAYING, MOTOKI? YESTERDAY, YOU TOLD HARUHIKO -
SHUT UP! JUST LISTEN!
HE'S TURNED OFF BECAUSE YOU'RE ONLY AFTER HIS BODY, EVEN THOUGH YOU HAVE NO FEELINGS FOR EACH OTHER.
THAT'S WHERE YOU'RE DIFFERENT FROM YUKA-CHAN!
SLUMP
...
... ...
OH-MY-GOD... YOU -
I NEVER THOUGHT OF THAT!
ARE YOU A GENIUS OR SOME- THING?!
どどーん
DUN DUUUN!

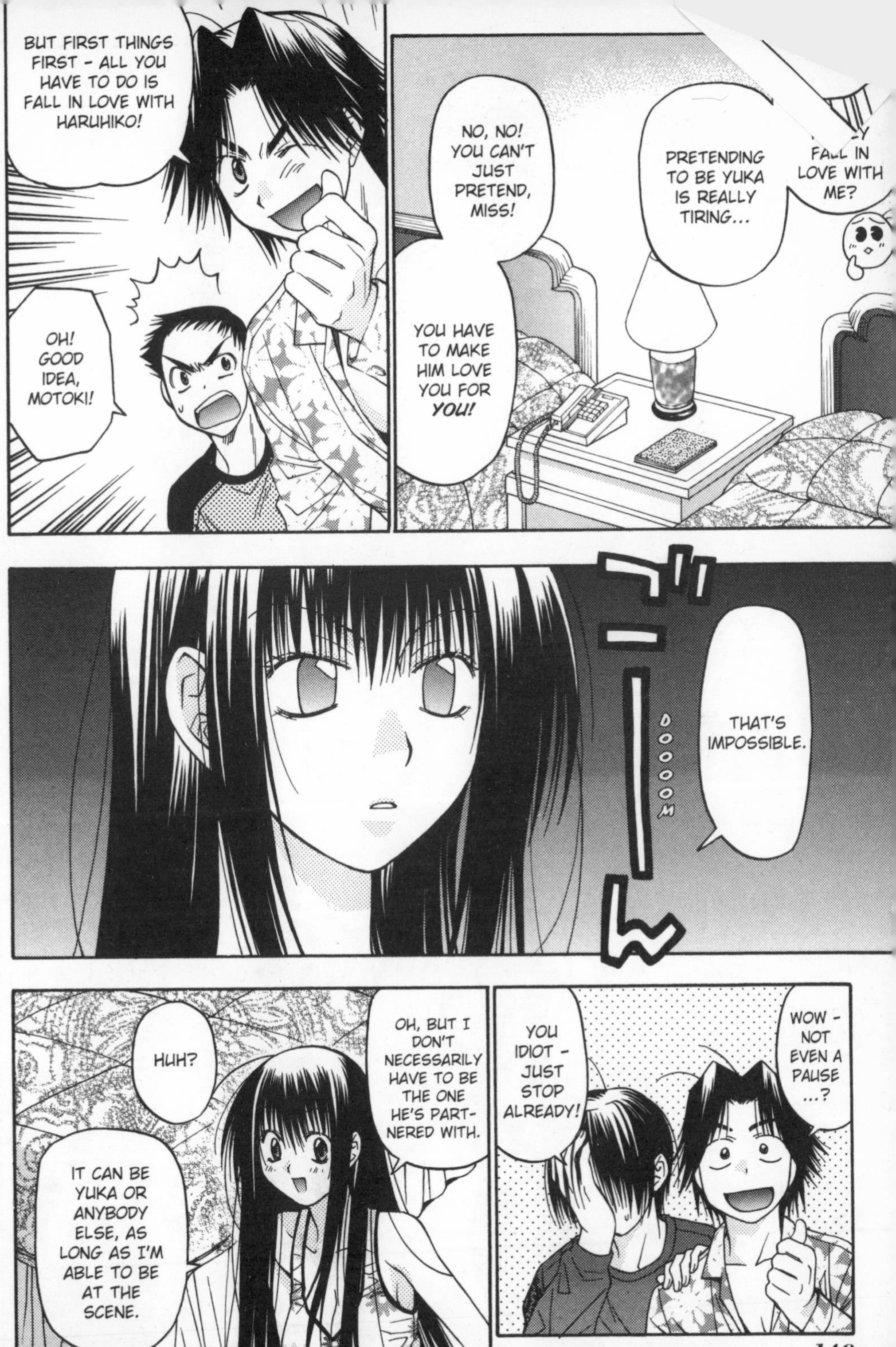
FALL IN LOVE WITH ME?
PRETENDING TO BE YUKA IS REALLY TIRING...
NO, NO! YOU CAN'T JUST PRETEND, MISS!
YOU HAVE TO MAKE HIM LOVE YOU FOR YOU!
BUT FIRST THINGS FIRST - ALL YOU HAVE TO DO IS FALL IN LOVE WITH HARUHIKO!
OH! GOOD IDEA, MOTOKI!
DOOOOOM
THAT'S IMPOSSIBLE.
WOW - NOT EVEN A PAUSE ...?
YOU IDIOT - JUST STOP ALREADY!
OH, BUT I DON'T NECESSARILY HAVE TO BE THE ONE HE'S PARTNERED WITH.
HUH?
IT CAN BE YUKA OR ANYBODY ELSE, AS LONG AS I'M ABLE TO BE AT THE SCENE.

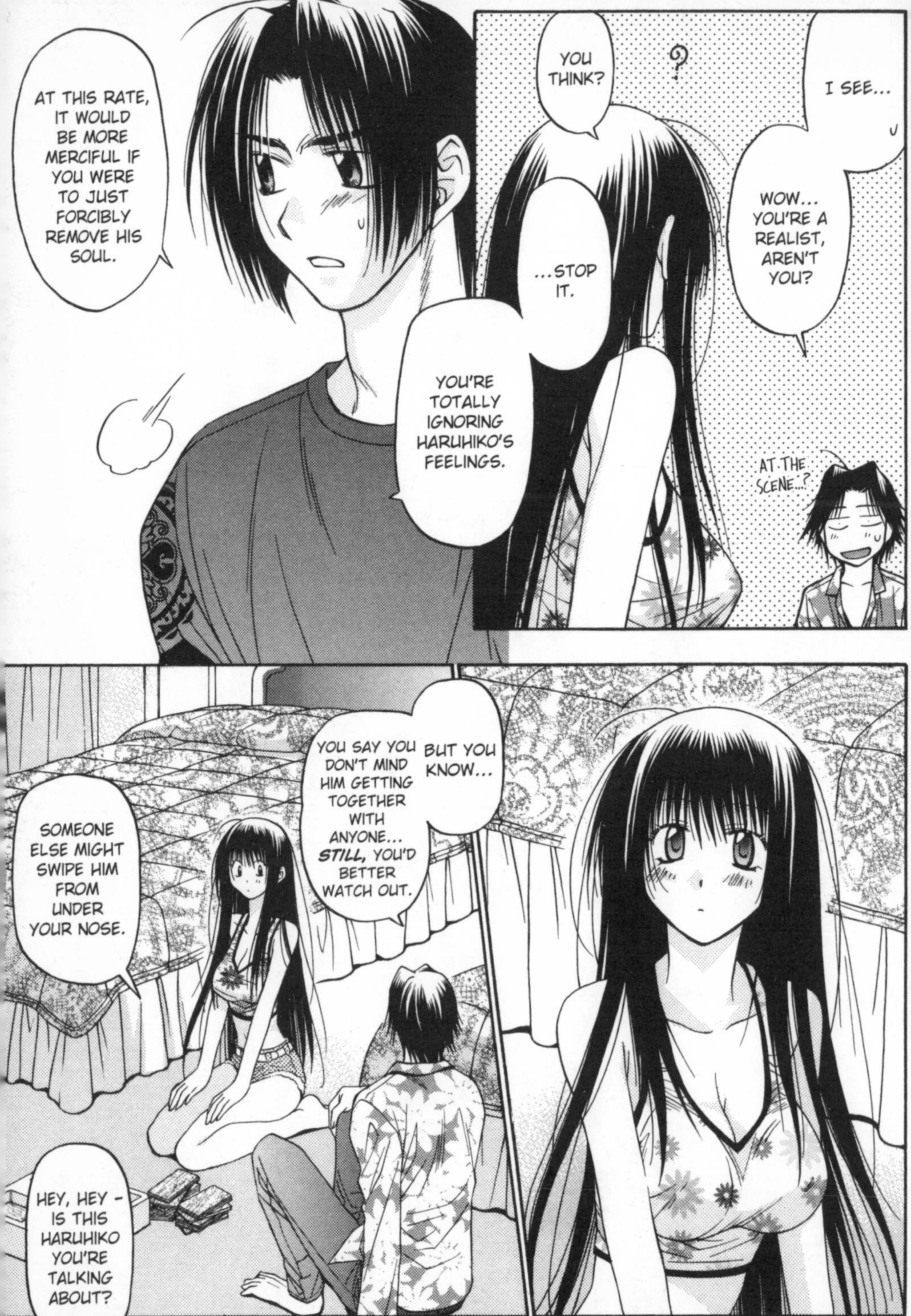
I SEE...
WOW... YOU'RE A REALIST, AREN'T YOU?
YOU THINK?
...STOP IT.
AT THE SCENE...?
AT THIS RATE, IT WOULD BE MORE MERCIFUL IF YOU WERE TO JUST FORCIBLY REMOVE HIS SOUL.
YOU'RE TOTALLY IGNORING HARUHIKO'S FEELINGS.
BUT YOU KNOW...
YOU SAY YOU DON'T MIND HIM GETTING TOGETHER WITH ANYONE... ***STILL,*** YOU'D BETTER WATCH OUT.
SOMEONE ELSE MIGHT SWIPE HIM FROM UNDER YOUR NOSE.
HEY, HEY - IS THIS HARUHIKO YOU'RE TALKING ABOUT?

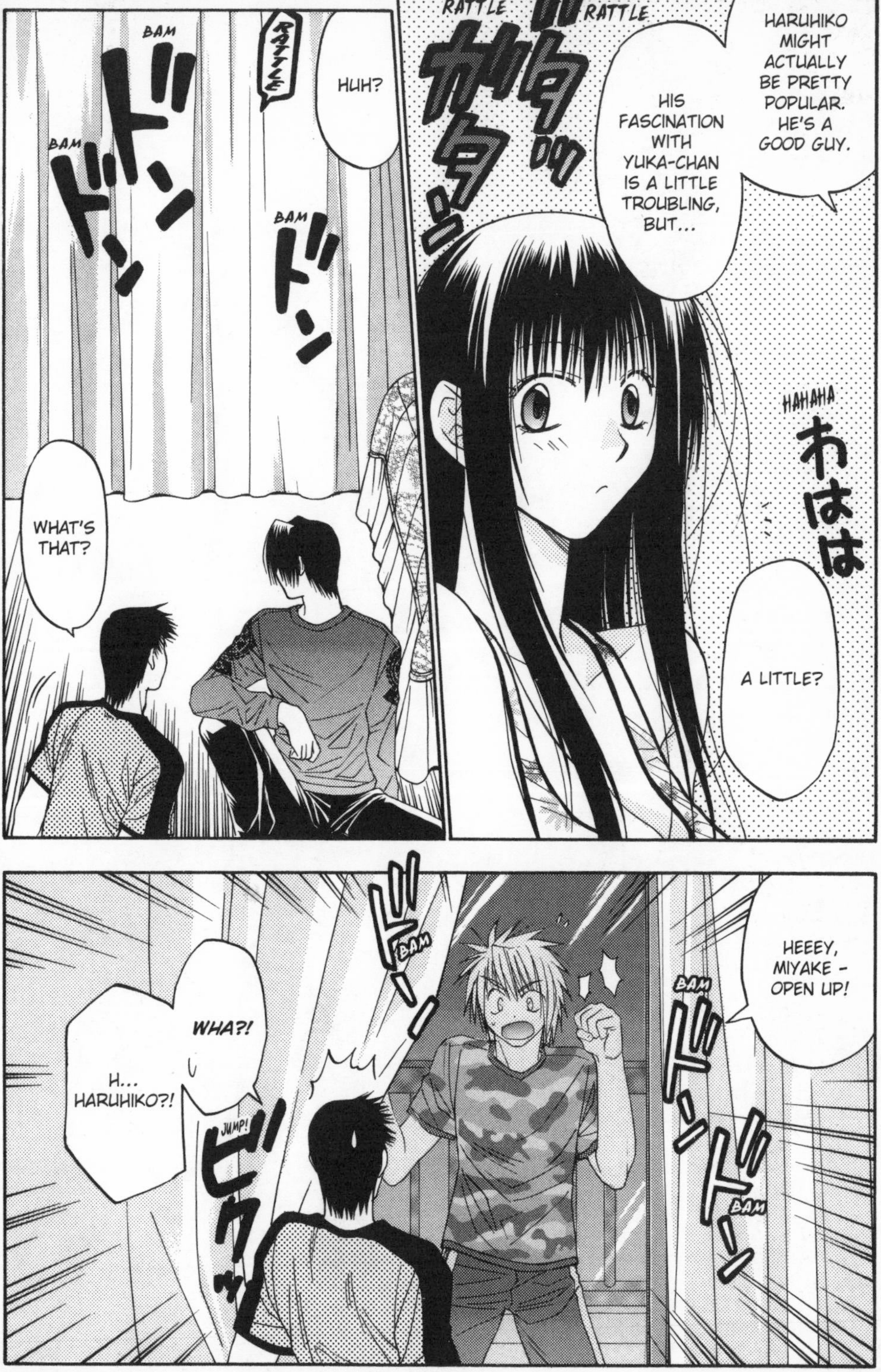
RATTLE RATTLE
HARUHIKO MIGHT ACTUALLY BE PRETTY POPULAR. HE'S A GOOD GUY.
HIS FASCINATION WITH YUKA-CHAN IS A LITTLE TROUBLING, BUT...
HAHAHA
わはは
A LITTLE?
HUH?
RATTLE
BAM
BAM
BAM
WHAT'S THAT?
HEEEY, MIYAKE - OPEN UP!
BAM
BAM
BAM
WHA?!
H... HARUHIKO?!
JUMP!

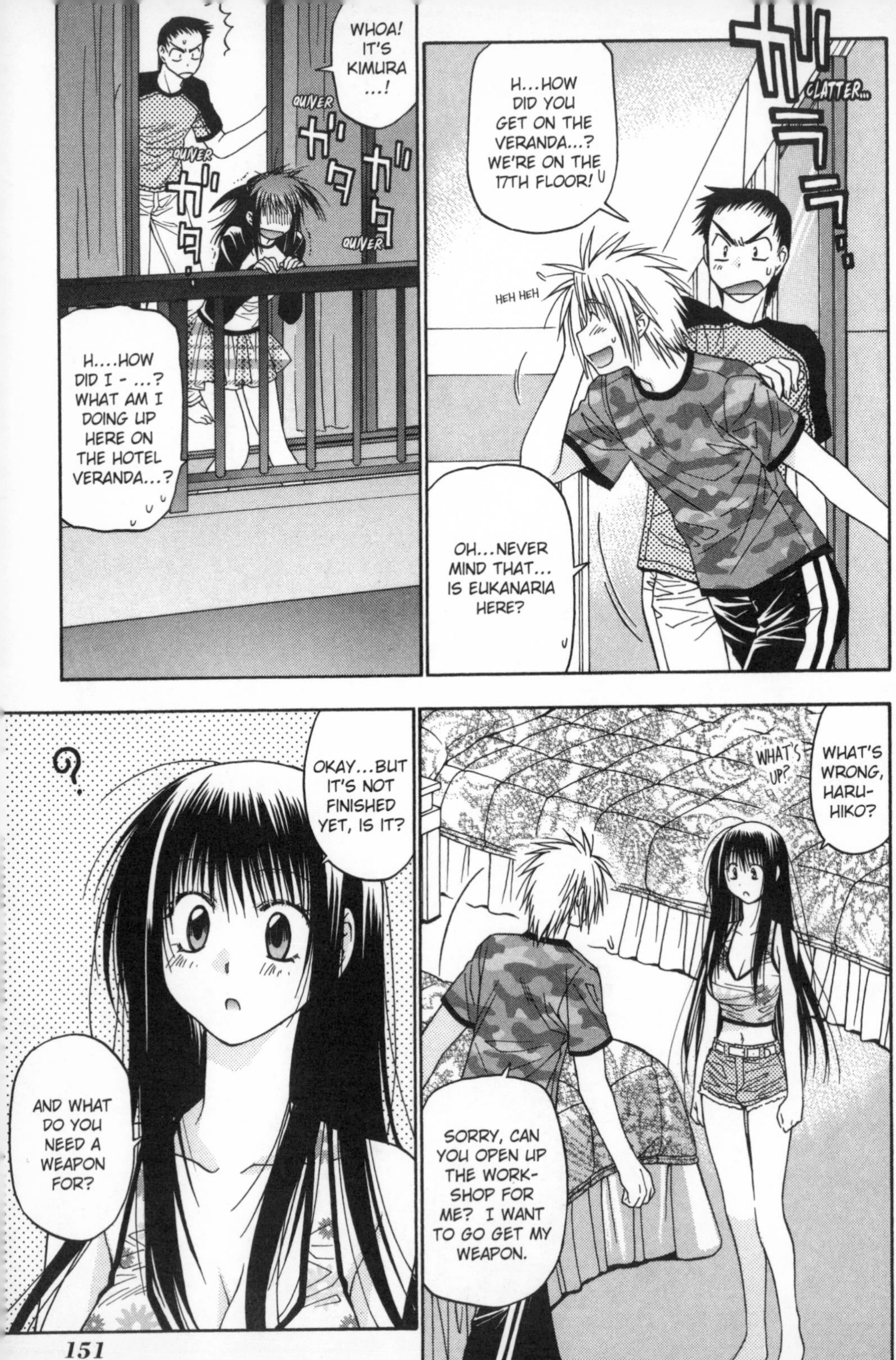
CLATTER...
H...HOW DID YOU GET ON THE VERANDA...? WE'RE ON THE 17TH FLOOR!
HEH HEH
OH...NEVER MIND THAT... IS EUKANARIA HERE?
WHOA! IT'S KIMURA ...!
QUIVER
QUIVER
QUIVER
H....HOW DID I - ...? WHAT AM I DOING UP HERE ON THE HOTEL VERANDA...?
WHAT'S WRONG, HARU-HIKO?
WHAT'S UP?
SORRY, CAN YOU OPEN UP THE WORK-SHOP FOR ME? I WANT TO GO GET MY WEAPON.
OKAY...BUT IT'S NOT FINISHED YET, IS IT?
AND WHAT DO YOU NEED A WEAPON FOR?

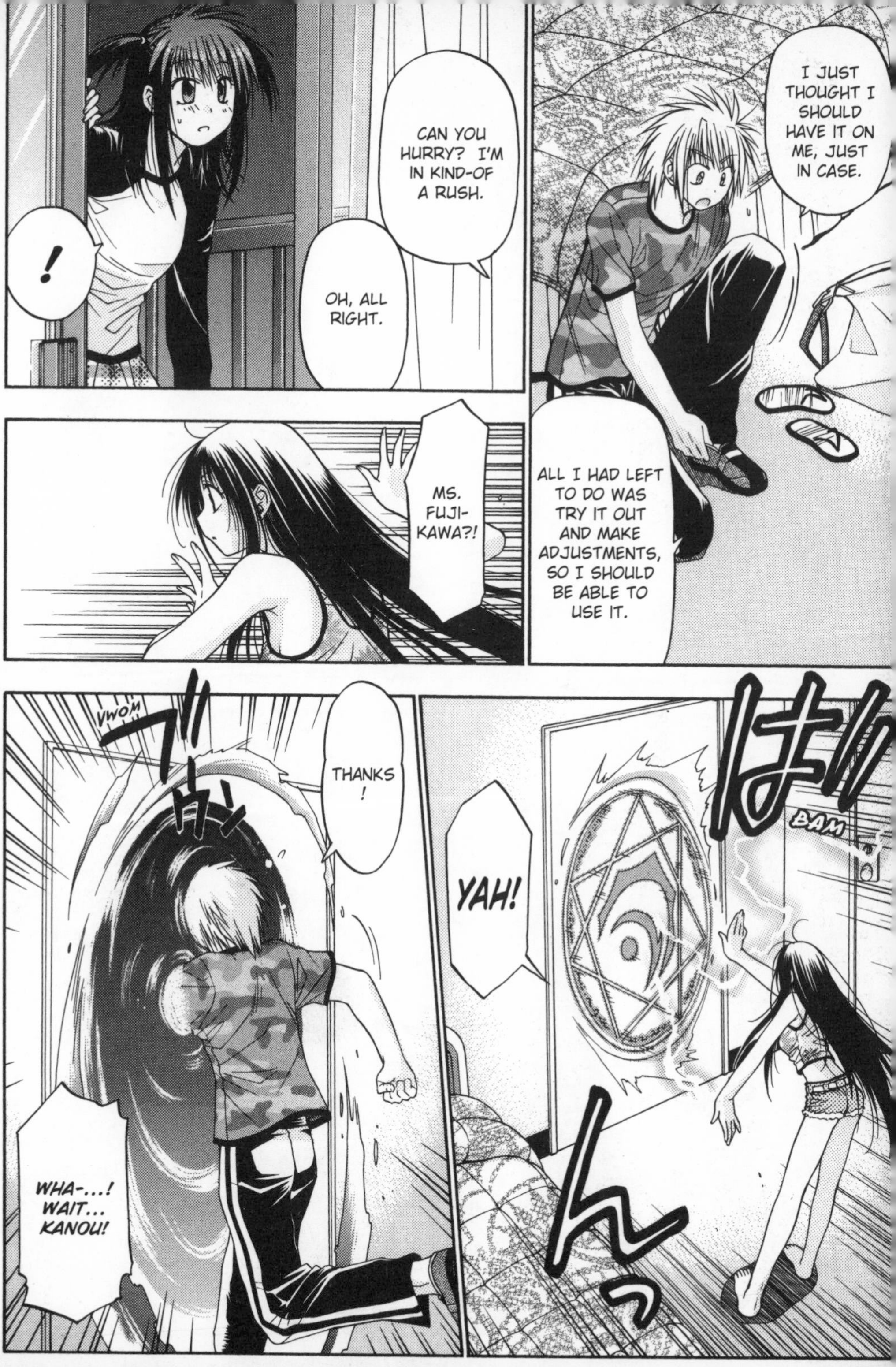
I JUST THOUGHT I SHOULD HAVE IT ON ME, JUST IN CASE.
CAN YOU HURRY? I'M IN KIND-OF A RUSH.
OH, ALL RIGHT.
!
ALL I HAD LEFT TO DO WAS TRY IT OUT AND MAKE ADJUSTMENTS, SO I SHOULD BE ABLE TO USE IT.
MS. FUJI-KAWA?!
BAM
YAH!
VWOM
THANKS!
WHA-...! WAIT... KANOU!

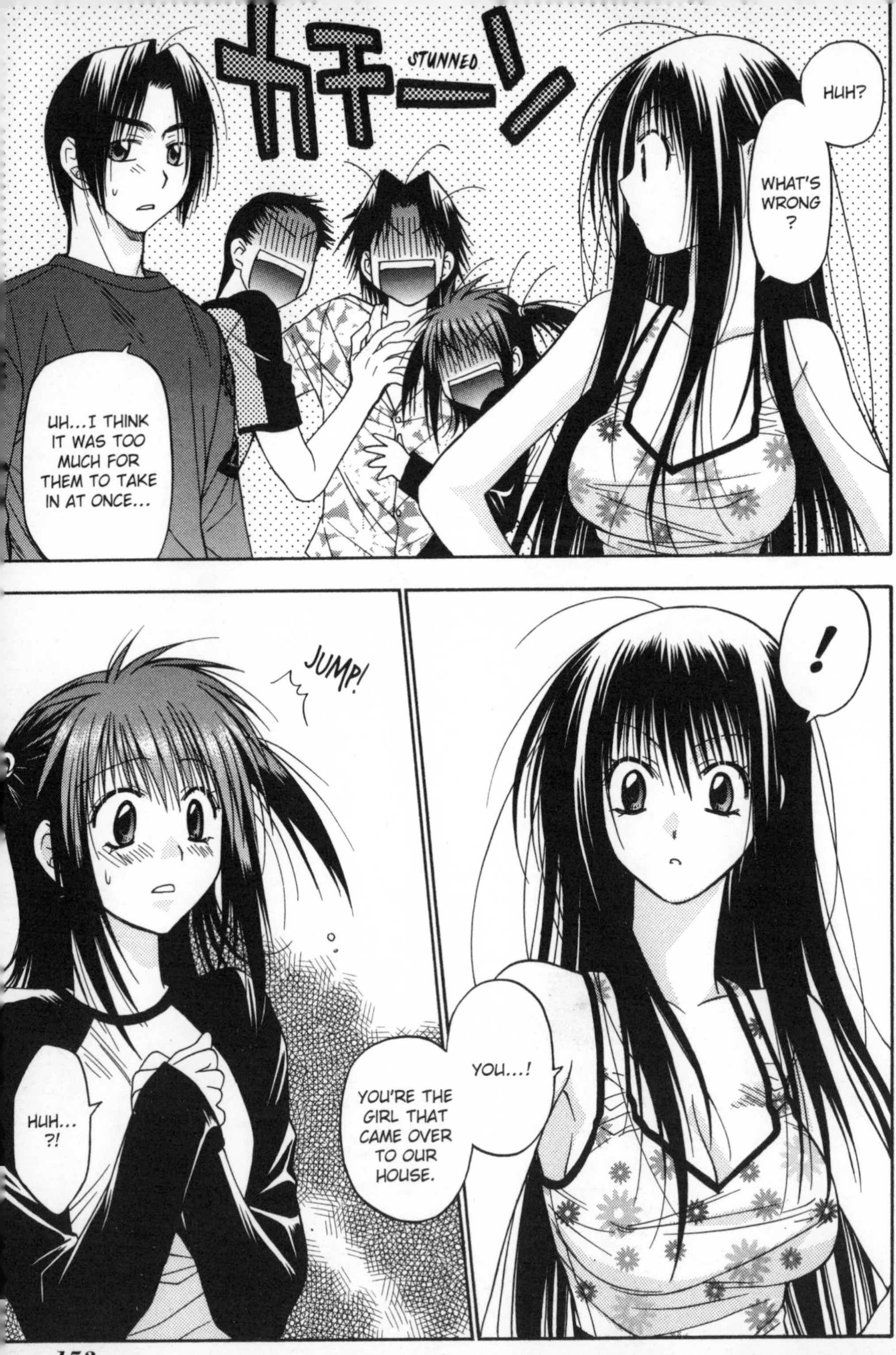
HUH?
WHAT'S WRONG?
カチーン
STUNNED
UH...I THINK IT WAS TOO MUCH FOR THEM TO TAKE IN AT ONCE...
!
YOU...!
YOU'RE THE GIRL THAT CAME OVER TO OUR HOUSE.
JUMP!
HUH...?!

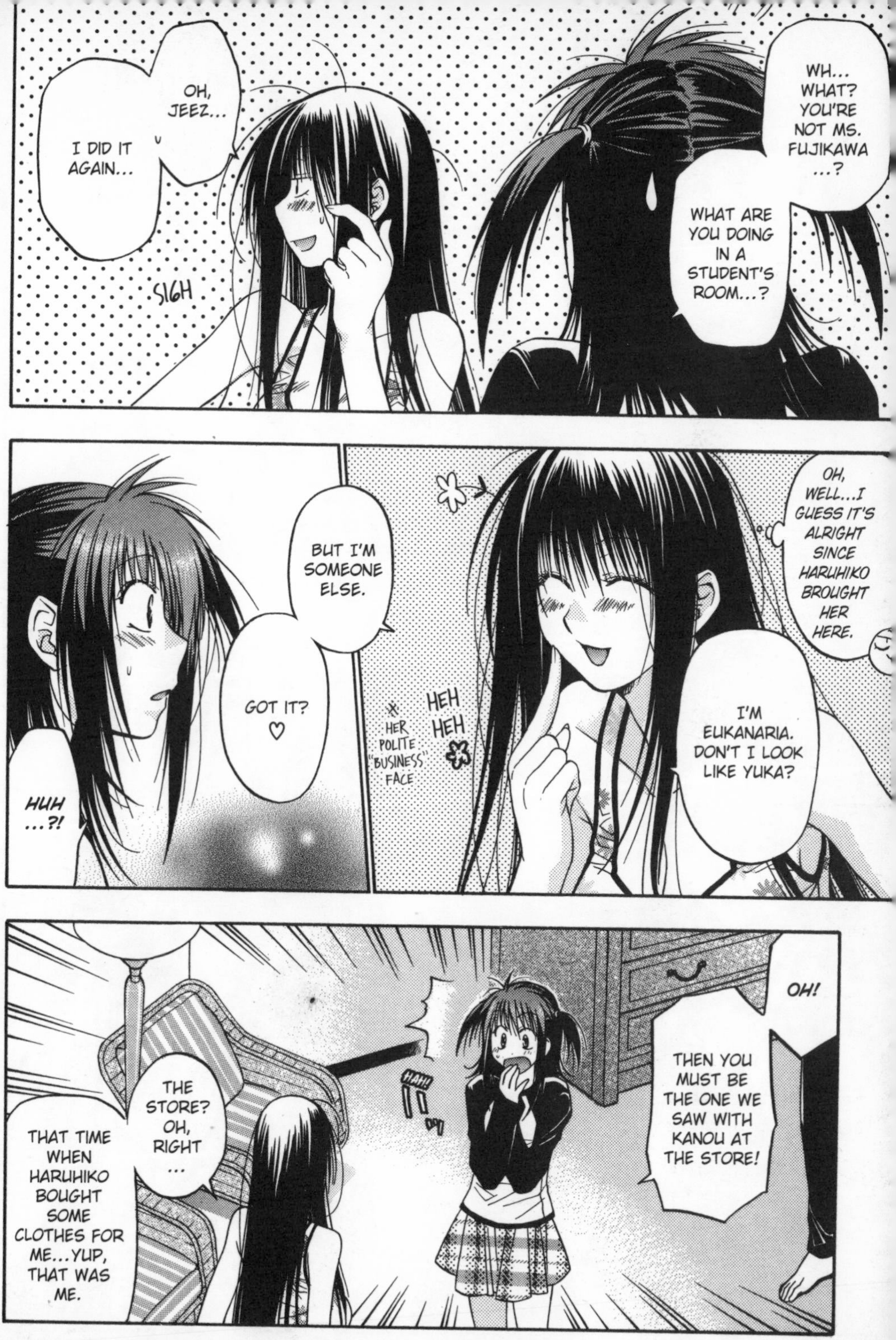
WH... WHAT? YOU'RE NOT MS. FUJIKAWA ...?
WHAT ARE YOU DOING IN A STUDENT'S ROOM...?
OH, JEEZ...
I DID IT AGAIN...
SIGH
OH, WELL...I GUESS IT'S ALRIGHT SINCE HARUHIKO BROUGHT HER HERE.
I'M EUKANARIA. DON'T I LOOK LIKE YUKA?
HEH HEH
※ HER POLITE "BUSINESS" FACE
BUT I'M SOMEONE ELSE.
GOT IT? ♡
HUH ...?!
OH!
THEN YOU MUST BE THE ONE WE SAW WITH KANOU AT THE STORE!
HAH!
THE STORE? OH, RIGHT ...
THAT TIME WHEN HARUHIKO BOUGHT SOME CLOTHES FOR ME...YUP, THAT WAS ME.

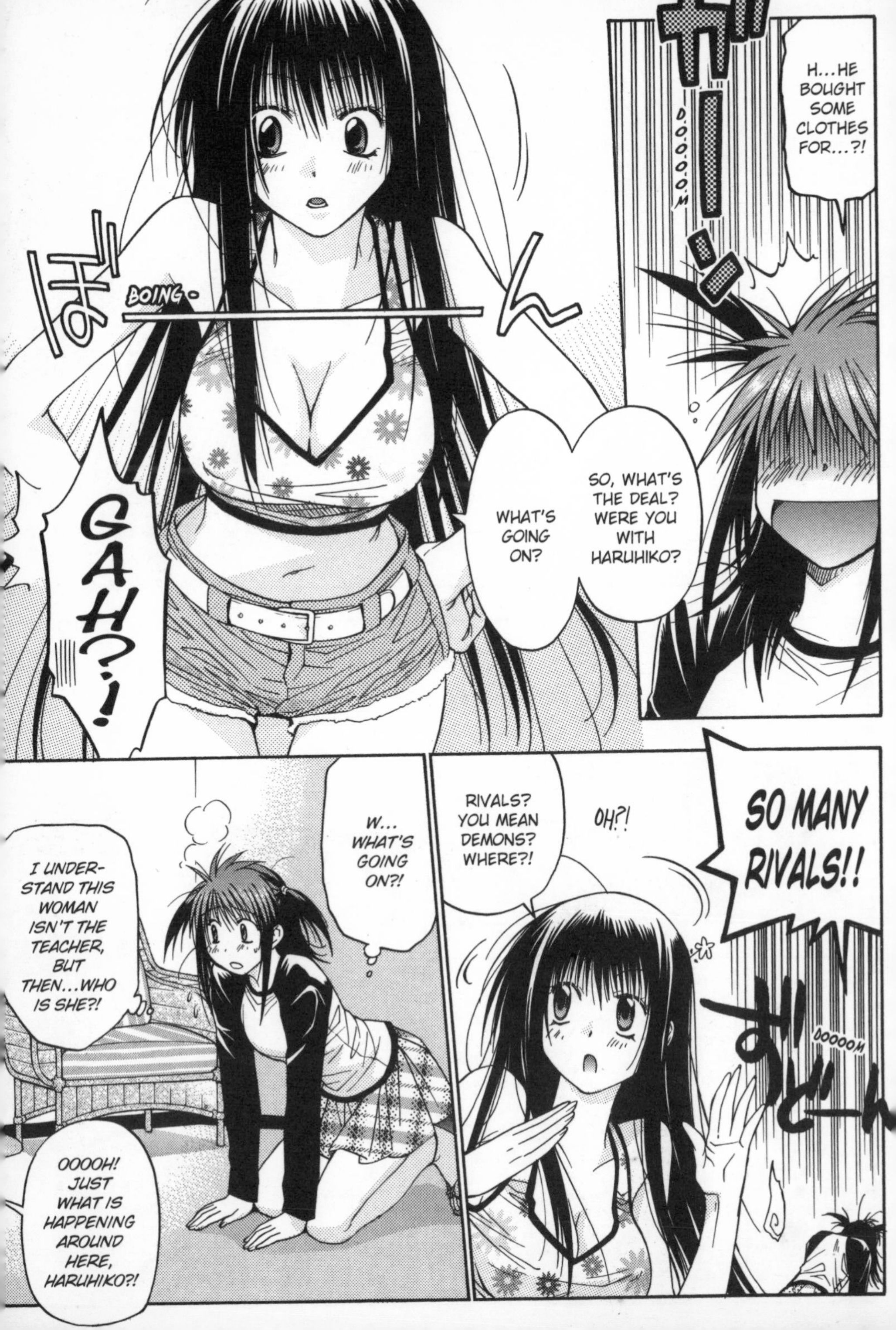
D.O.O.O.O.M
H...HE BOUGHT SOME CLOTHES FOR...?!
BOING
SO, WHAT'S THE DEAL? WERE YOU WITH HARUHIKO?
WHAT'S GOING ON?
GAH?!
SO MANY RIVALS!!
DOOOOM
OH?!
RIVALS? YOU MEAN DEMONS? WHERE?!
W... WHAT'S GOING ON?!
I UNDER-STAND THIS WOMAN ISN'T THE TEACHER, BUT THEN...WHO IS SHE?!
OOOOH! JUST WHAT IS HAPPENING AROUND HERE, HARUHIKO?!

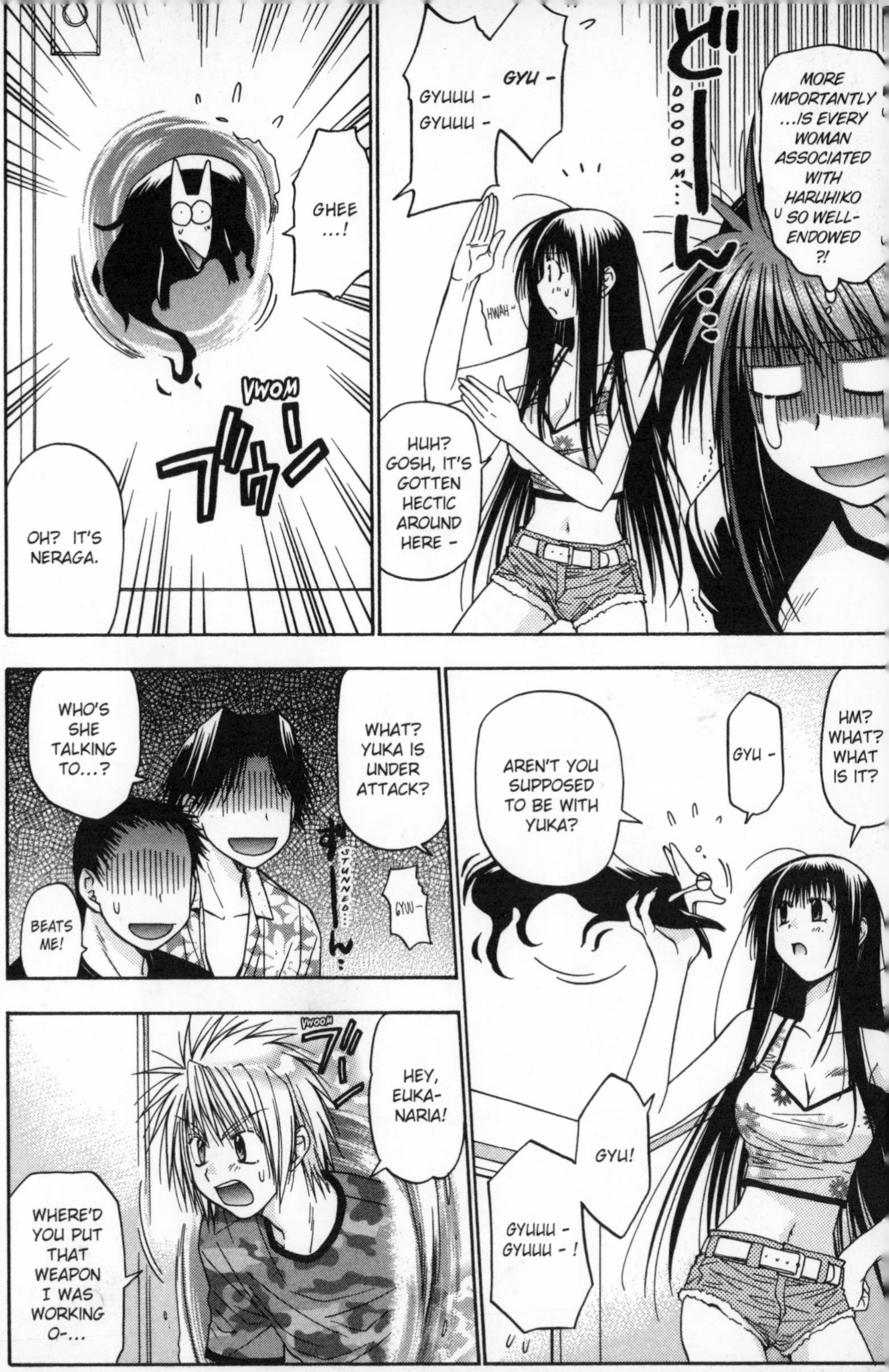
DOOOOOM…
MORE IMPORTANTLY …IS EVERY WOMAN ASSOCIATED WITH HARUHIKO SO WELL-ENDOWED ?!
GYU -
GYUUU -
GYUUU -
HWAH~
HUH? GOSH, IT'S GOTTEN HECTIC AROUND HERE -
GHEE …!
VWOM
OH? IT'S NERAGA.
HM? WHAT? WHAT IS IT?
GYU -
AREN'T YOU SUPPOSED TO BE WITH YUKA?
GYU!
GYUUU - GYUUU - !
WHAT? YUKA IS UNDER ATTACK?
STUNNED…
GYUU-
WHO'S SHE TALKING TO…?
BEATS ME!
VWOOM
HEY, EUKA-NARIA!
WHERE'D YOU PUT THAT WEAPON I WAS WORKING O-…

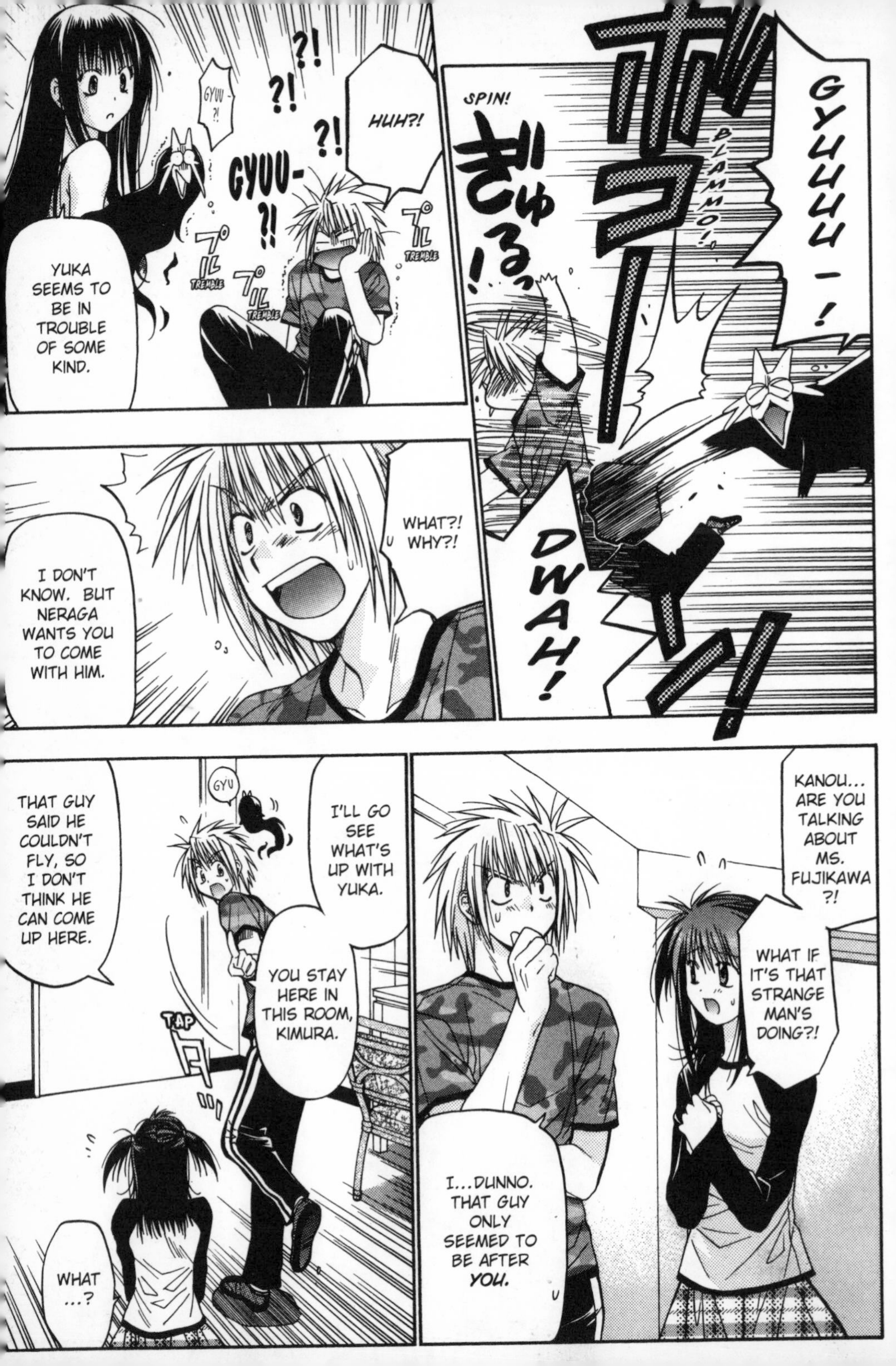
GYUUUUU—!
BLAMMO!
SPIN!
DWAH!
HUH?!
?!
?!
?!
GYUU-?!
TREMBLE
TREMBLE
TREMBLE
GYUU-?!
YUKA SEEMS TO BE IN TROUBLE OF SOME KIND.
WHAT?! WHY?!
I DON'T KNOW. BUT NERAGA WANTS YOU TO COME WITH HIM.
KANOU... ARE YOU TALKING ABOUT MS. FUJIKAWA?!
WHAT IF IT'S THAT STRANGE MAN'S DOING?!
I...DUNNO. THAT GUY ONLY SEEMED TO BE AFTER ***YOU.***
I'LL GO SEE WHAT'S UP WITH YUKA.
GYU
THAT GUY SAID HE COULDN'T FLY, SO I DON'T THINK HE CAN COME UP HERE.
YOU STAY HERE IN THIS ROOM, KIMURA.
TAP
WHAT...?

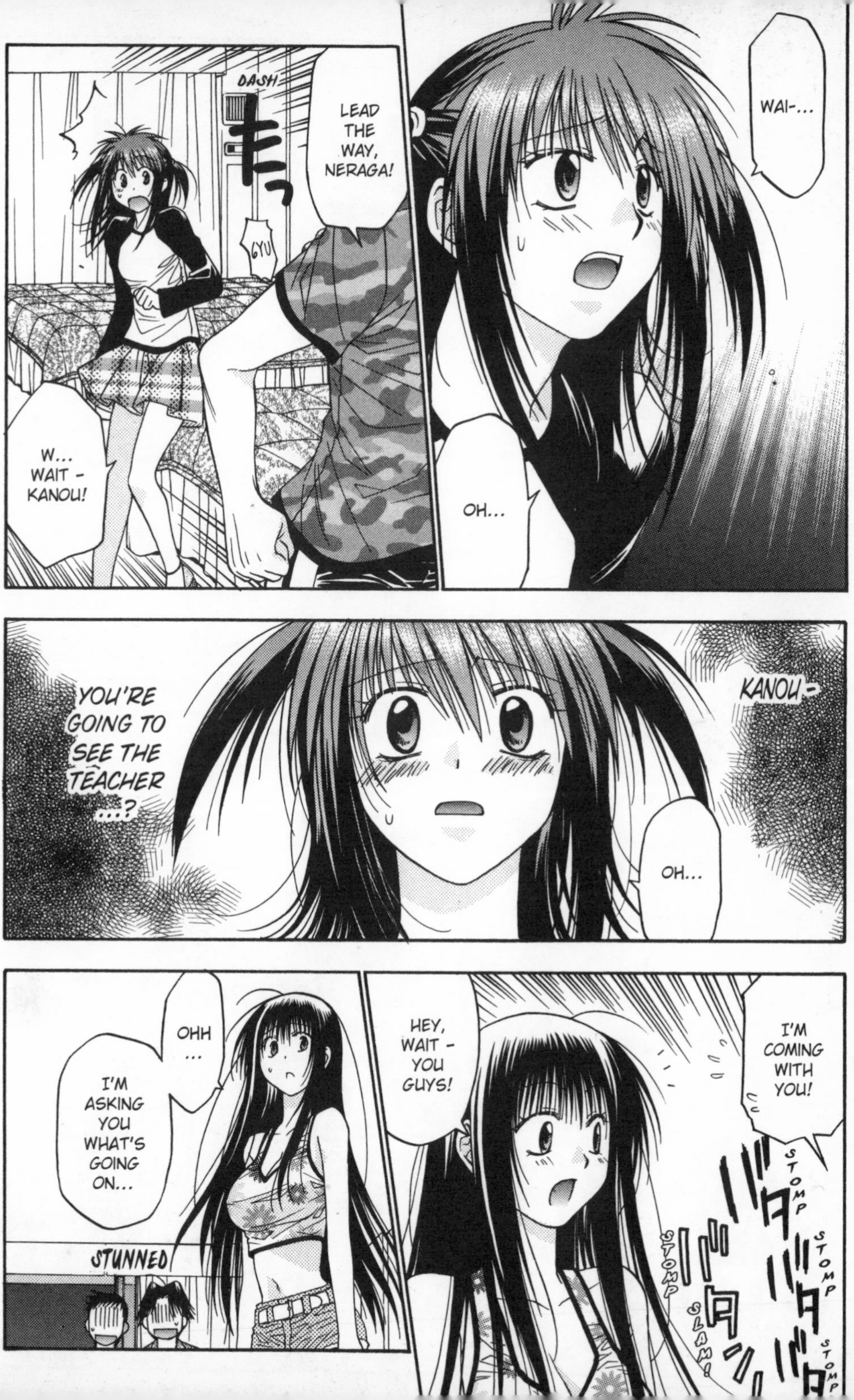
WAI-...
OH...
DASH
LEAD THE WAY, NERAGA!
GYU
W... WAIT - KANOU!
KANOU-
OH...
YOU'RE GOING TO SEE THE TEACHER ...?
I'M COMING WITH YOU!
STOMP
STOMP
STOMP
SLAM!
STOMP
HEY, WAIT - YOU GUYS!
OHH ...
I'M ASKING YOU WHAT'S GOING ON...
STUNNED

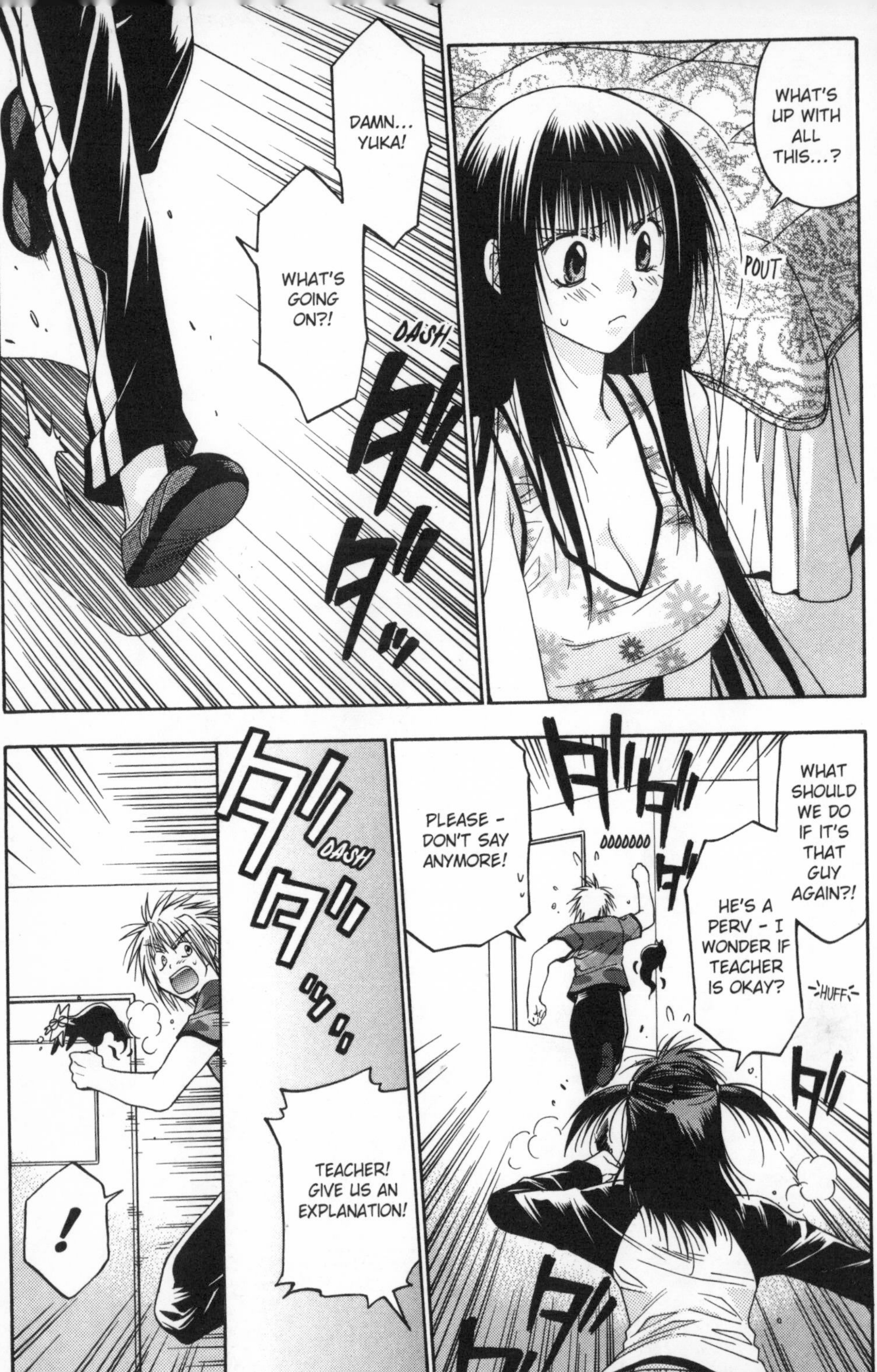
WHAT'S UP WITH ALL THIS...?
POUT
DAMN... YUKA!
WHAT'S GOING ON?!
DASH
WHAT SHOULD WE DO IF IT'S THAT GUY AGAIN?!
HE'S A PERV - I WONDER IF TEACHER IS OKAY?
HUFF
PLEASE - DON'T SAY ANYMORE!
DASH
TEACHER! GIVE US AN EXPLANATION!
!

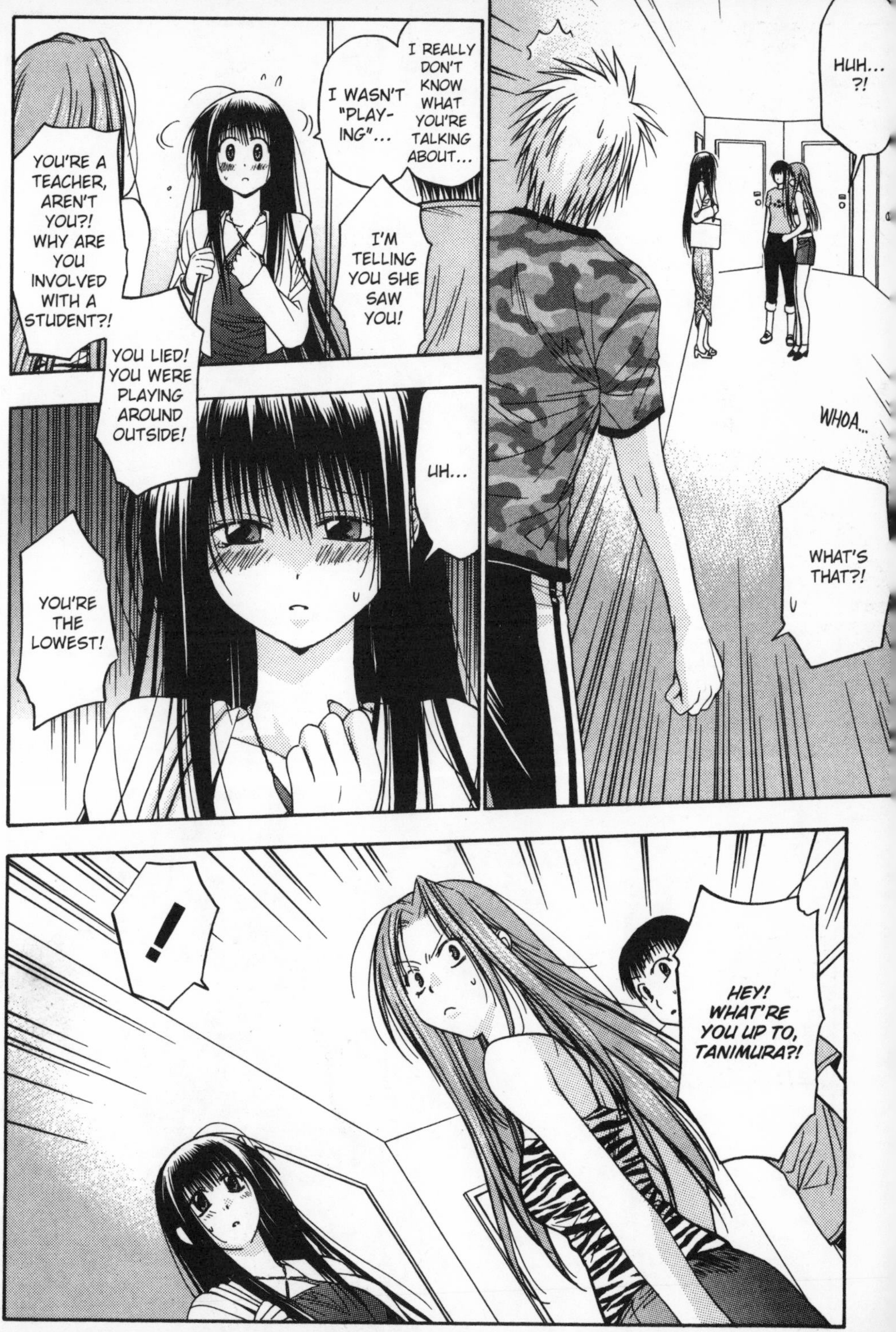
HUH...?!
WHOA...
WHAT'S THAT?!
I REALLY DON'T KNOW WHAT YOU'RE TALKING ABOUT...
I WASN'T "PLAY-ING"...
I'M TELLING YOU SHE SAW YOU!
YOU'RE A TEACHER, AREN'T YOU?! WHY ARE YOU INVOLVED WITH A STUDENT?!
YOU LIED! YOU WERE PLAYING AROUND OUTSIDE!
UH...
YOU'RE THE LOWEST!
HEY! WHAT'RE YOU UP TO, TANIMURA?!
!

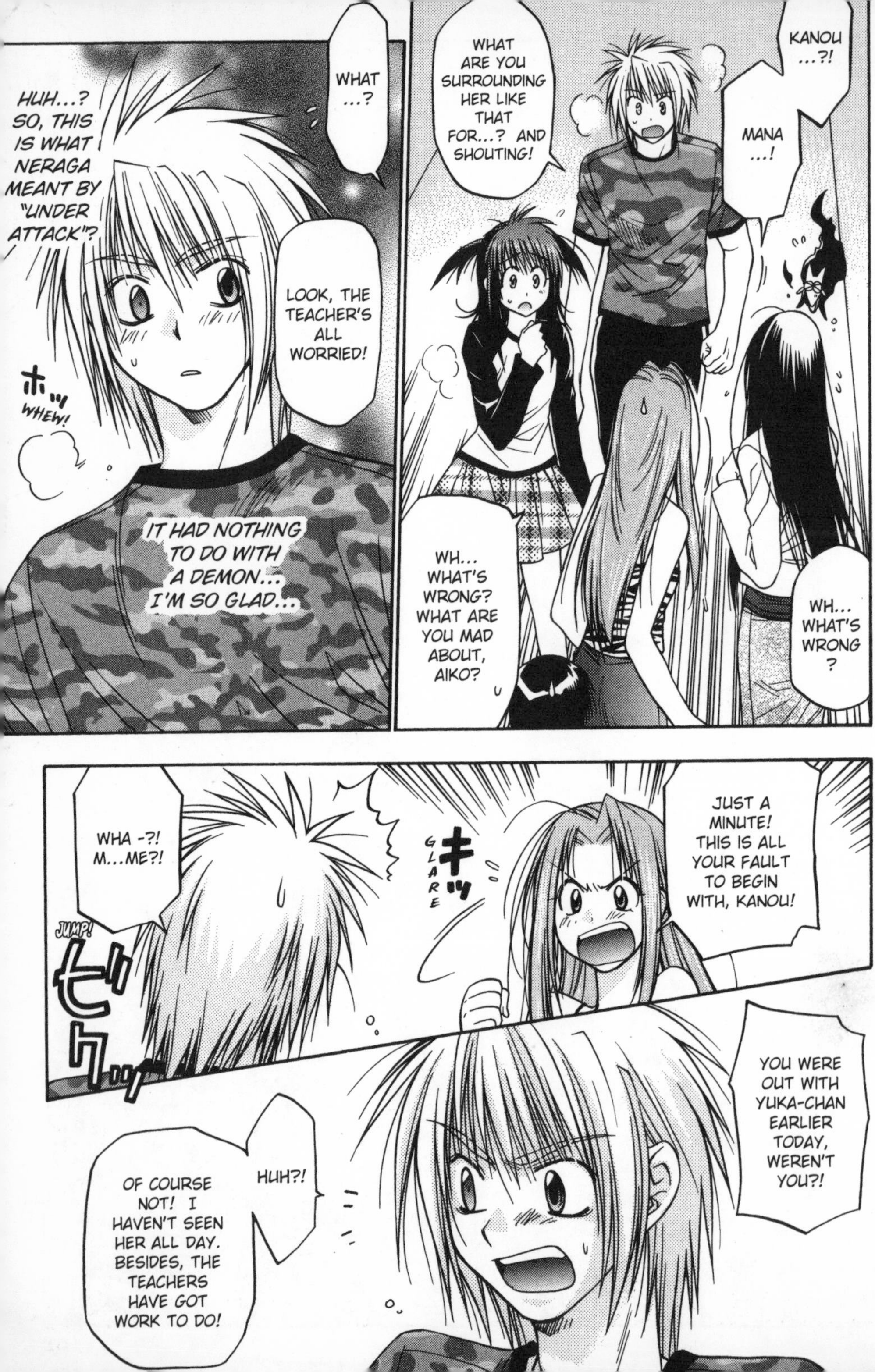
KANOU ...?!
MANA ...!
WHAT ARE YOU SURROUNDING HER LIKE THAT FOR...? AND SHOUTING!
WH... WHAT'S WRONG?
WH... WHAT'S WRONG? WHAT ARE YOU MAD ABOUT, AIKO?
WHAT ...?
HUH...? SO, THIS IS WHAT NERAGA MEANT BY "UNDER ATTACK"?
LOOK, THE TEACHER'S ALL WORRIED!
ホッ WHEW!
IT HAD NOTHING TO DO WITH A DEMON... I'M SO GLAD...
JUST A MINUTE! THIS IS ALL YOUR FAULT TO BEGIN WITH, KANOU!
キッ GLARE
WHA -?! M...ME?!
JUMP!
YOU WERE OUT WITH YUKA-CHAN EARLIER TODAY, WEREN'T YOU?!
HUH?!
OF COURSE NOT! I HAVEN'T SEEN HER ALL DAY. BESIDES, THE TEACHERS HAVE GOT WORK TO DO!

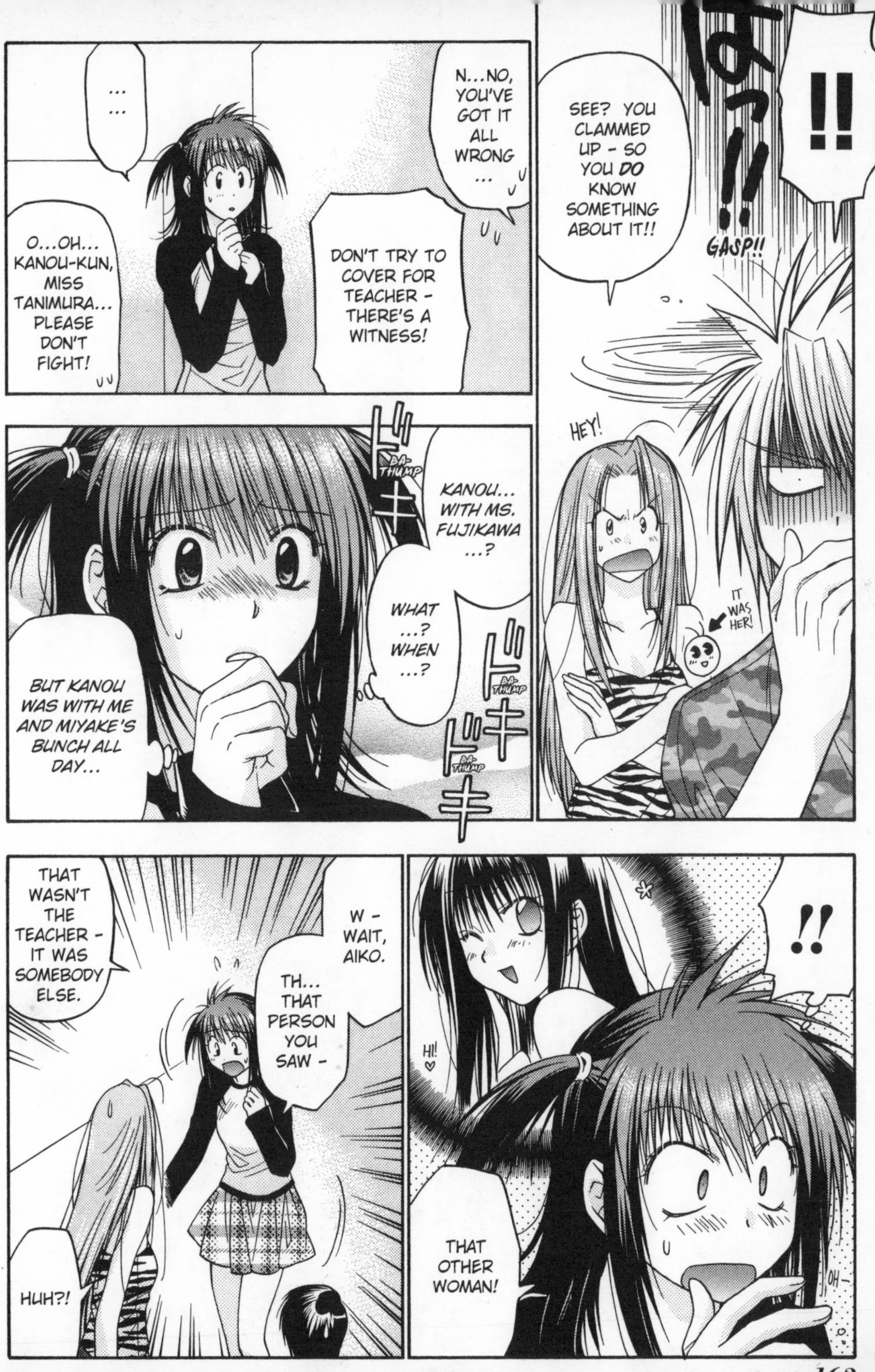
!!
ほっ!!
GASP!!
SEE? YOU CLAMMED UP - SO YOU DO KNOW SOMETHING ABOUT IT!!
N…NO, YOU'VE GOT IT ALL WRONG …
DON'T TRY TO COVER FOR TEACHER - THERE'S A WITNESS!
… …
O…OH… KANOU-KUN, MISS TANIMURA… PLEASE DON'T FIGHT!
HEY!
IT WAS HER!
ドキ
BA-THUMP
KANOU… WITH MS. FUJIKAWA …?
WHAT …? WHEN …?
ドキ
BA-THUMP
ドキ
BA-THUMP
BUT KANOU WAS WITH ME AND MIYAKE'S BUNCH ALL DAY…
!!
HI! ♥
THAT OTHER WOMAN!
OH-
W - WAIT, AIKO.
TH… THAT PERSON YOU SAW -
THAT WASN'T THE TEACHER - IT WAS SOMEBODY ELSE.
HUH?!

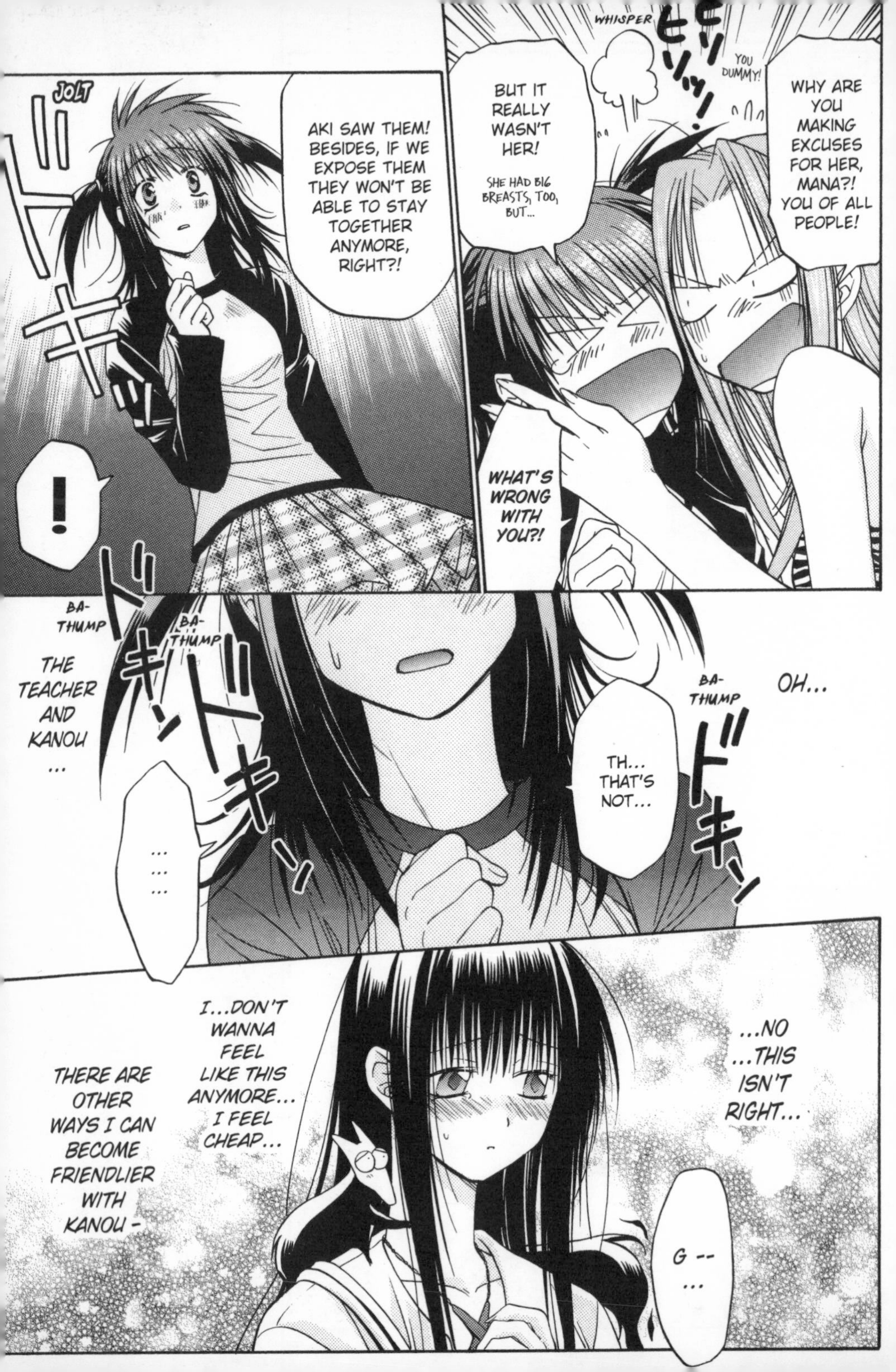
WHY ARE YOU MAKING EXCUSES FOR HER, MANA?! YOU OF ALL PEOPLE!
YOU DUMMY!
WHISPER
BUT IT REALLY WASN'T HER!
SHE HAD BIG BREASTS, TOO, BUT...
WHAT'S WRONG WITH YOU?!
AKI SAW THEM! BESIDES, IF WE EXPOSE THEM THEY WON'T BE ABLE TO STAY TOGETHER ANYMORE, RIGHT?!
JOLT
!
OH...
BA-THUMP
TH... THAT'S NOT...
BA-THUMP
BA-THUMP
THE TEACHER AND KANOU...
....
...NO ...THIS ISN'T RIGHT...
I...DON'T WANNA FEEL LIKE THIS ANYMORE... I FEEL CHEAP...
THERE ARE OTHER WAYS I CAN BECOME FRIENDLIER WITH KANOU -
G -- ...

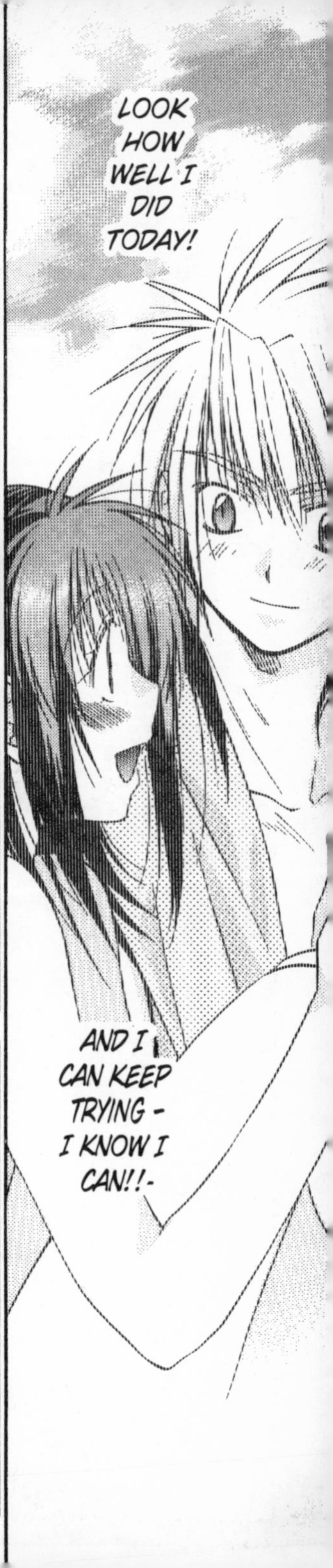
LOOK HOW WELL I DID TODAY!
AND I CAN KEEP TRYING - I KNOW I CAN!!-

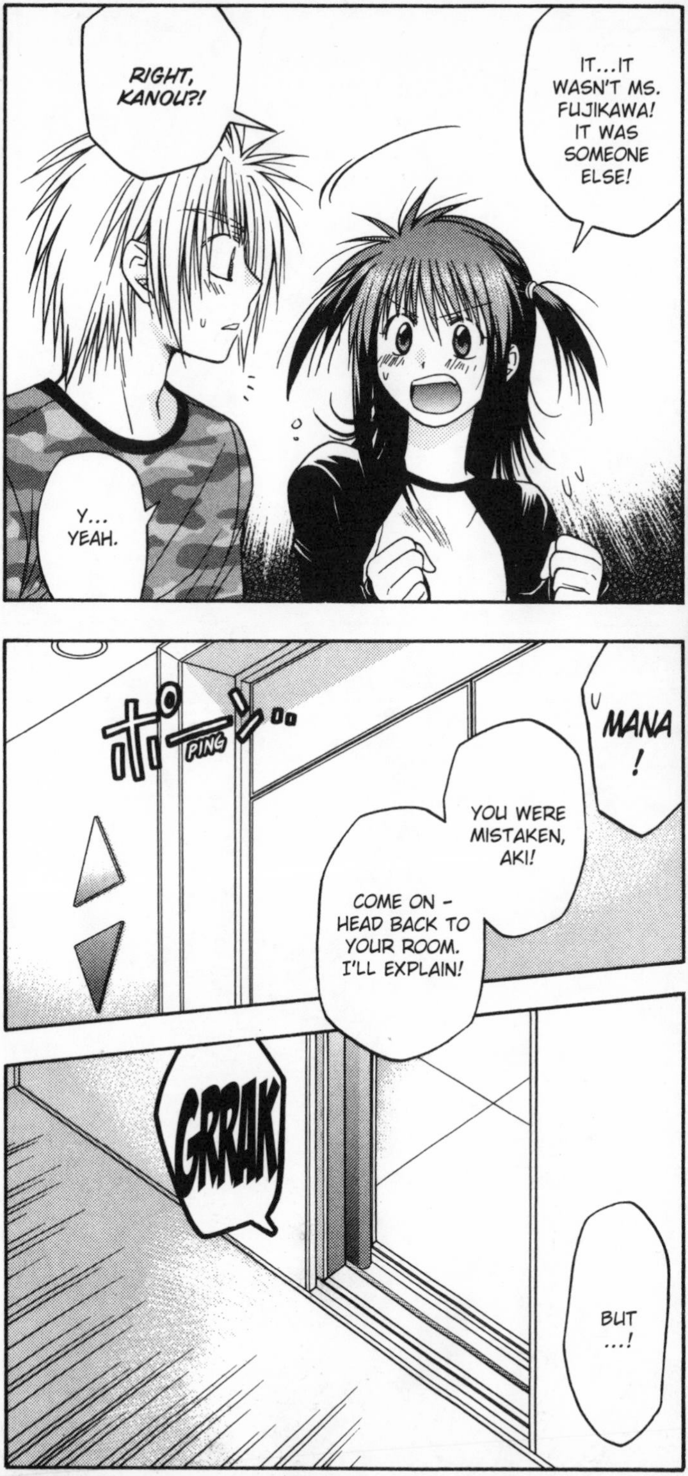
IT...IT WASN'T MS. FUJIKAWA! IT WAS SOMEONE ELSE!
RIGHT, KANOU?!
Y... YEAH.
MANA!
YOU WERE MISTAKEN, AKI!
COME ON - HEAD BACK TO YOUR ROOM. I'LL EXPLAIN!
PING
GRRAK
BUT ...!

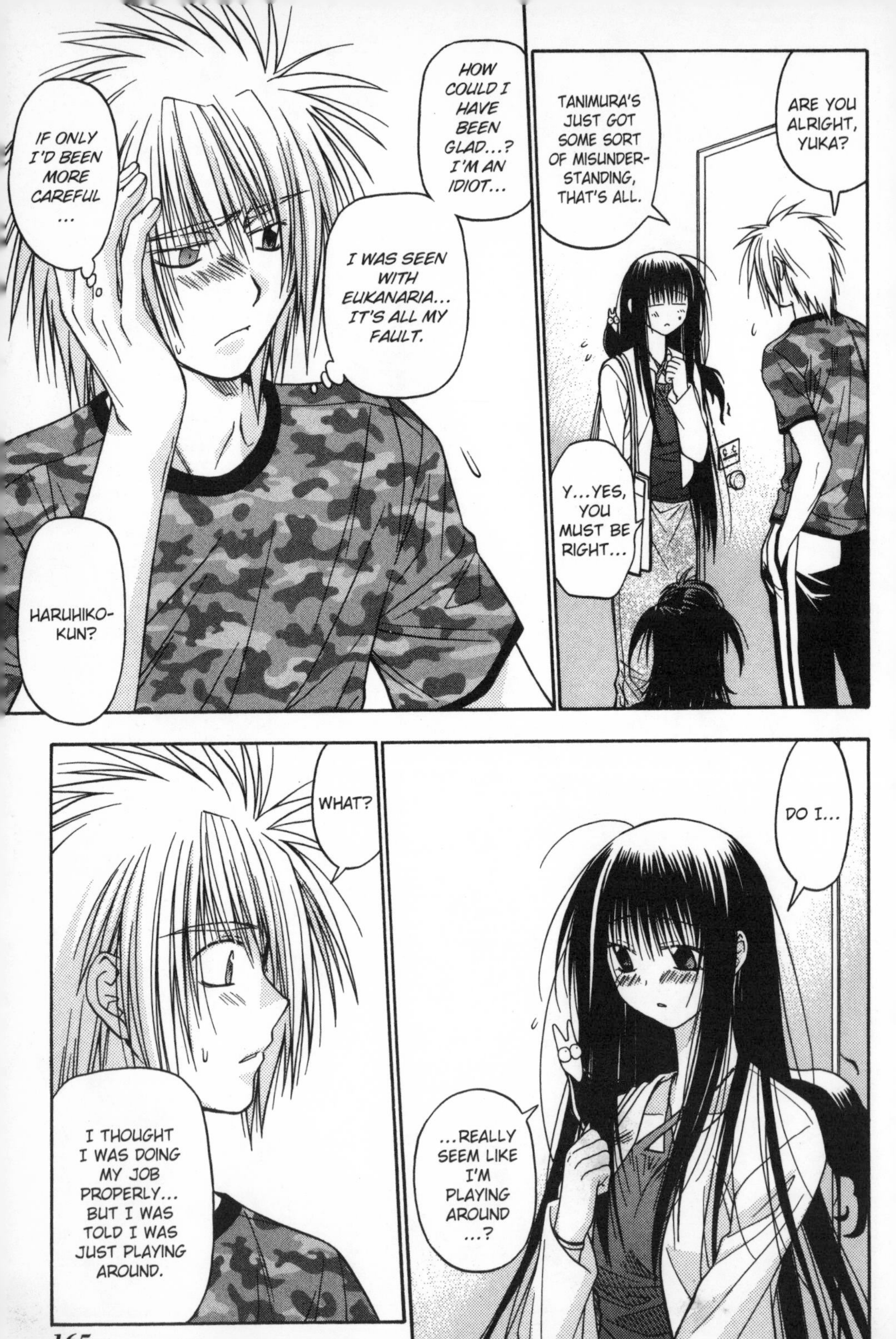
ARE YOU ALRIGHT, YUKA?
TANIMURA'S JUST GOT SOME SORT OF MISUNDER-STANDING, THAT'S ALL.
Y...YES, YOU MUST BE RIGHT...
HOW COULD I HAVE BEEN GLAD...? I'M AN IDIOT...
IF ONLY I'D BEEN MORE CAREFUL ...
I WAS SEEN WITH EUKANARIA... IT'S ALL MY FAULT.
HARUHIKO-KUN?
DO I...
...REALLY SEEM LIKE I'M PLAYING AROUND ...?
WHAT?
I THOUGHT I WAS DOING MY JOB PROPERLY... BUT I WAS TOLD I WAS JUST PLAYING AROUND.

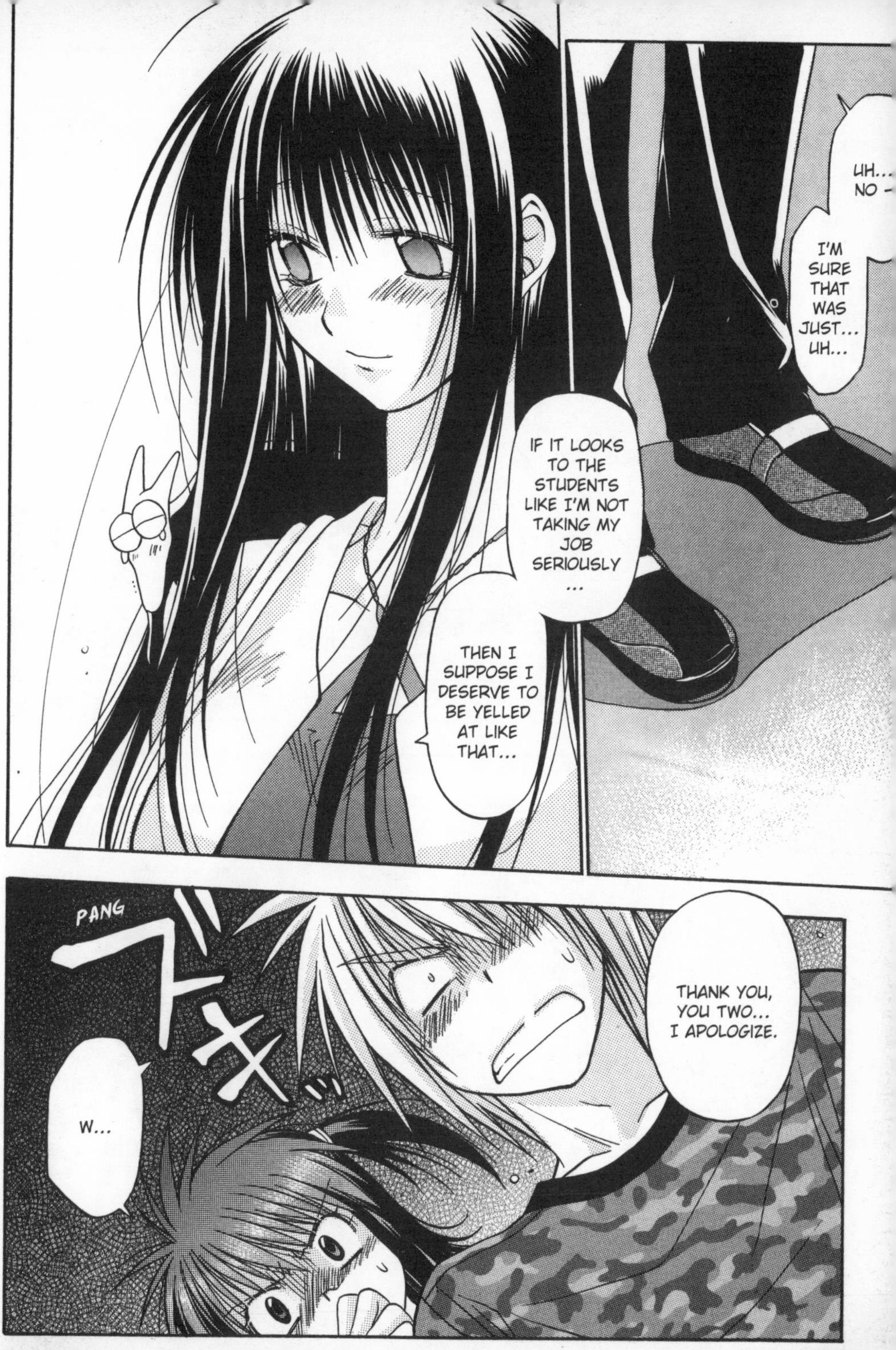
UH... NO —
I'M SURE THAT WAS JUST... UH...
IF IT LOOKS TO THE STUDENTS LIKE I'M NOT TAKING MY JOB SERIOUSLY...
THEN I SUPPOSE I DESERVE TO BE YELLED AT LIKE THAT...
THANK YOU, YOU TWO... I APOLOGIZE.
PANG
W...

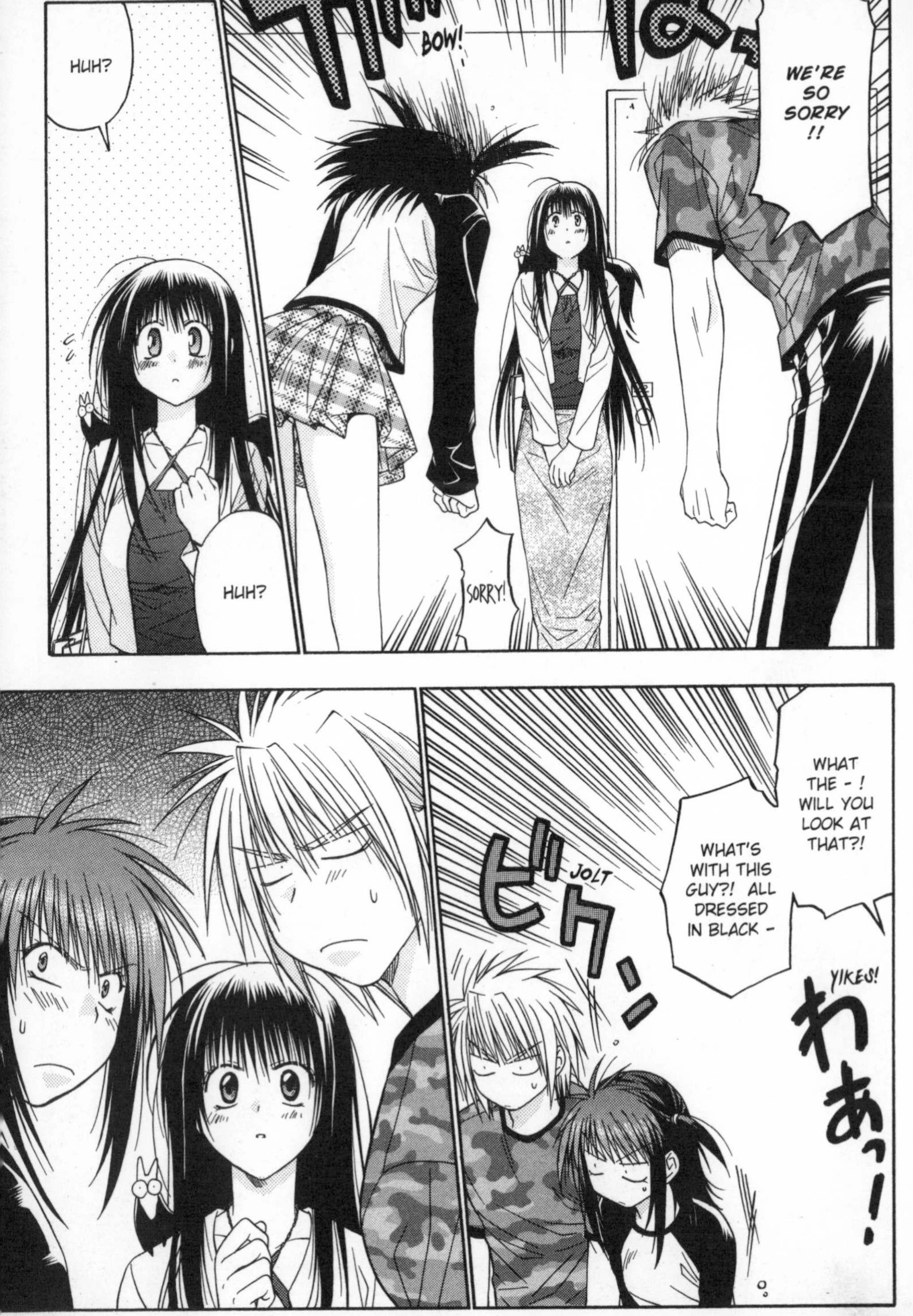
BOW!
WE'RE SO SORRY !!
SORRY!
HUH?
HUH?
WHAT THE - ! WILL YOU LOOK AT THAT?!
WHAT'S WITH THIS GUY?! ALL DRESSED IN BLACK -
JOLT
YIKES!

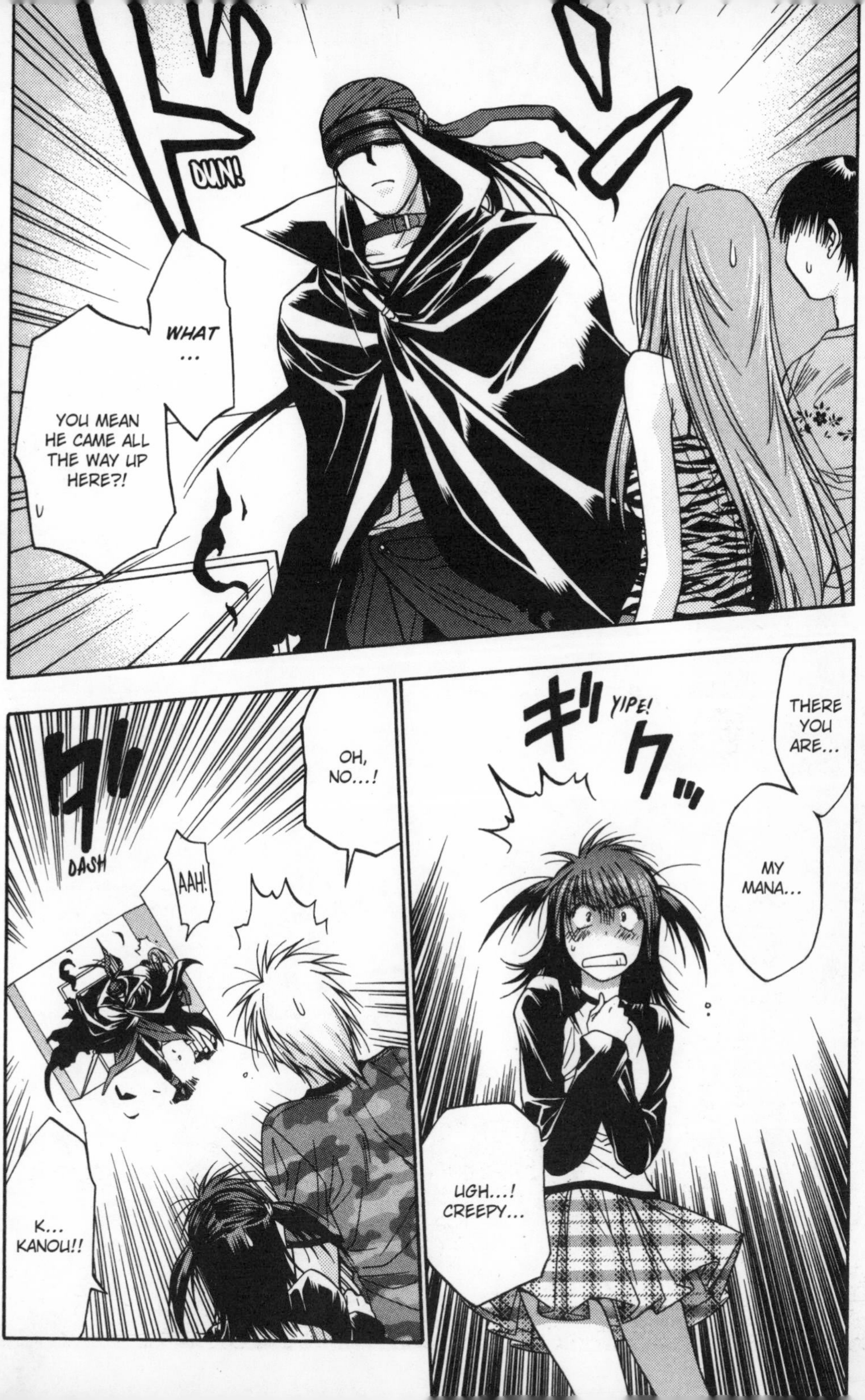
DUN!
WHAT ...
YOU MEAN HE CAME ALL THE WAY UP HERE?!
YIPE!
THERE YOU ARE...
MY MANA...
UGH...! CREEPY...
OH, NO...!
AAH!
DASH
K... KANOU!!

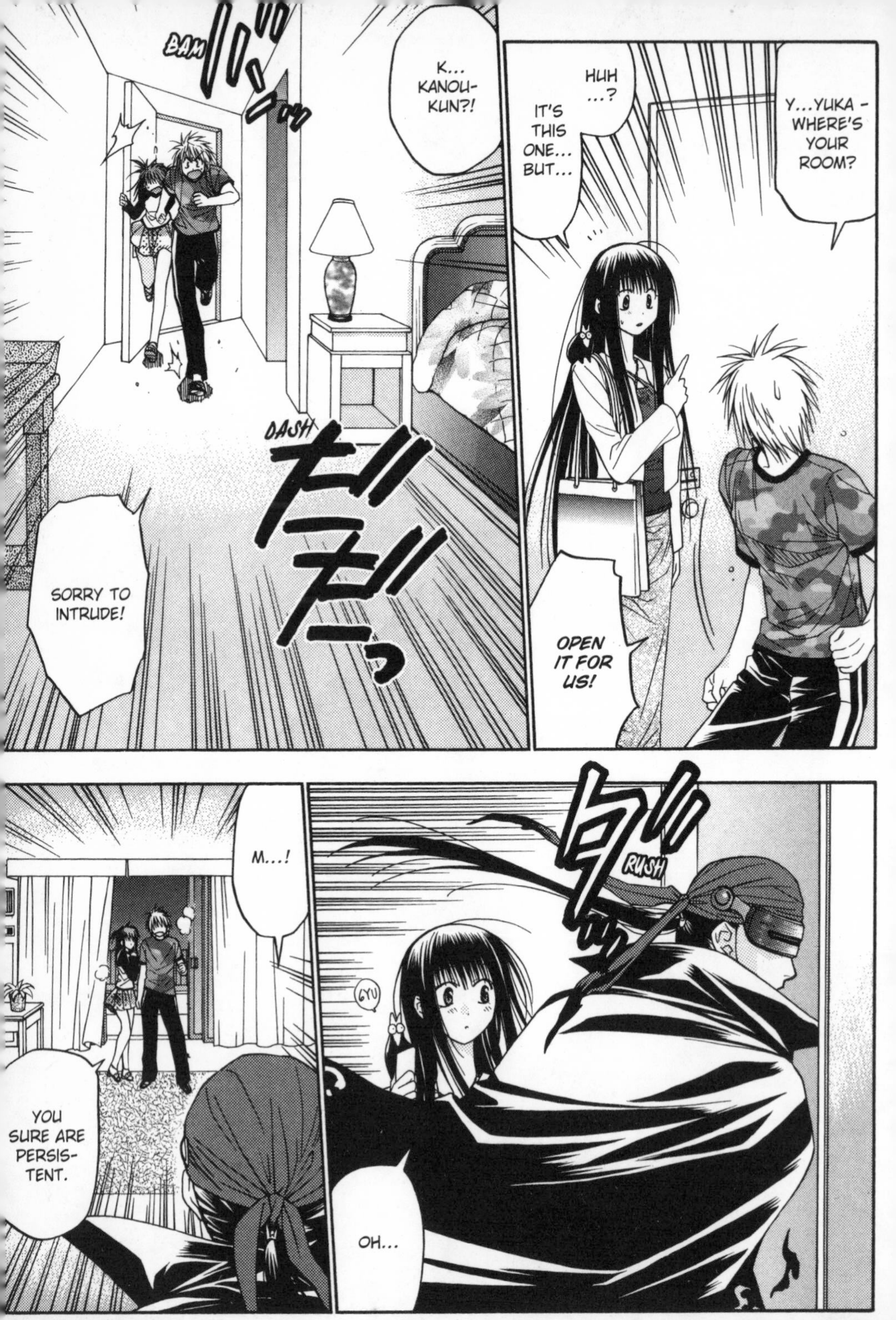
Y...YUKA - WHERE'S YOUR ROOM?
HUH ...?
IT'S THIS ONE... BUT...
OPEN IT FOR US!
K... KANOU-KUN?!
BAM
DASH
SORRY TO INTRUDE!
RUSH
GYU
OH...
M...!
YOU SURE ARE PERSIS-TENT.

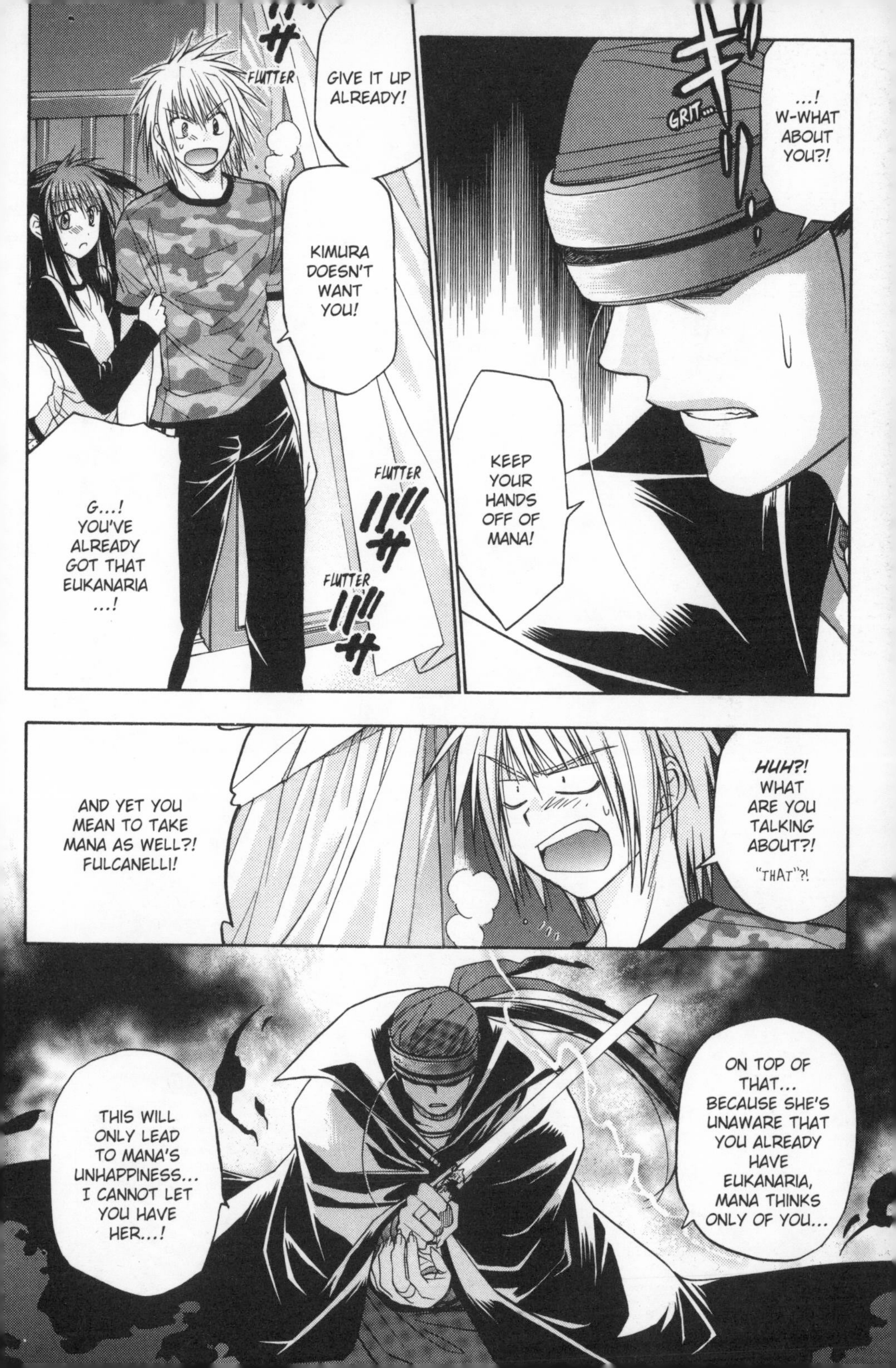
GRIT...
...! W-WHAT ABOUT YOU?!
KEEP YOUR HANDS OFF OF MANA!
GIVE IT UP ALREADY!
FLUTTER
KIMURA DOESN'T WANT YOU!
FLUTTER
FLUTTER
G...! YOU'VE ALREADY GOT THAT EUKANARIA ...!
HUH?! WHAT ARE YOU TALKING ABOUT?!
"THAT"?!
AND YET YOU MEAN TO TAKE MANA AS WELL?! FULCANELLI!
ON TOP OF THAT... BECAUSE SHE'S UNAWARE THAT YOU ALREADY HAVE EUKANARIA, MANA THINKS ONLY OF YOU...
THIS WILL ONLY LEAD TO MANA'S UNHAPPINESS... I CANNOT LET YOU HAVE HER...!

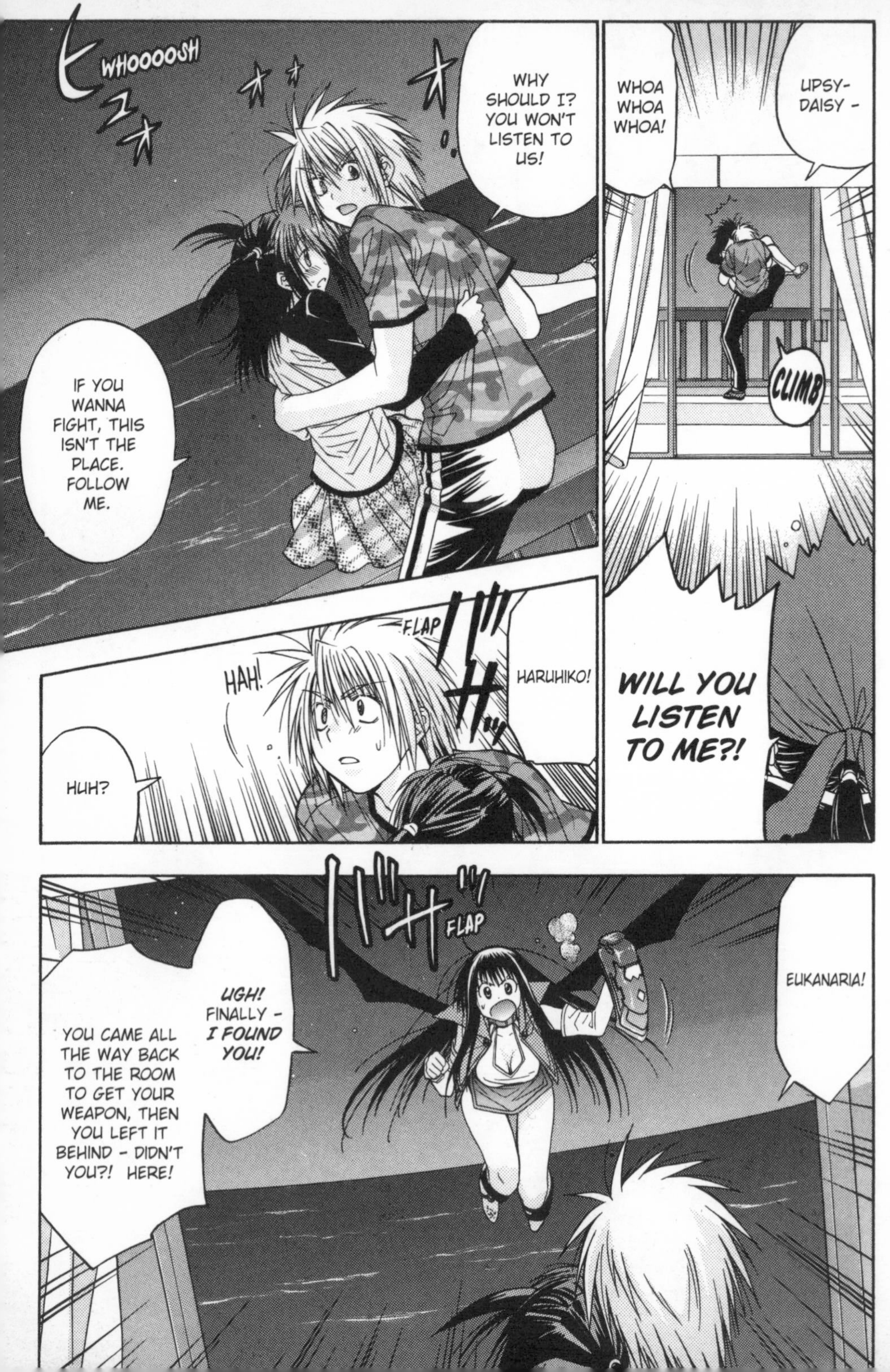
UPSY-DAISY -
WHOA WHOA WHOA!
CLIMB
WHOOOOSH
WHY SHOULD I? YOU WON'T LISTEN TO US!
IF YOU WANNA FIGHT, THIS ISN'T THE PLACE. FOLLOW ME.
WILL YOU LISTEN TO ME?!
FLAP
HARUHIKO!
HAH!
HUH?
FLAP
EUKANARIA!
UGH! FINALLY - I FOUND YOU!
YOU CAME ALL THE WAY BACK TO THE ROOM TO GET YOUR WEAPON, THEN YOU LEFT IT BEHIND - DIDN'T YOU?! HERE!

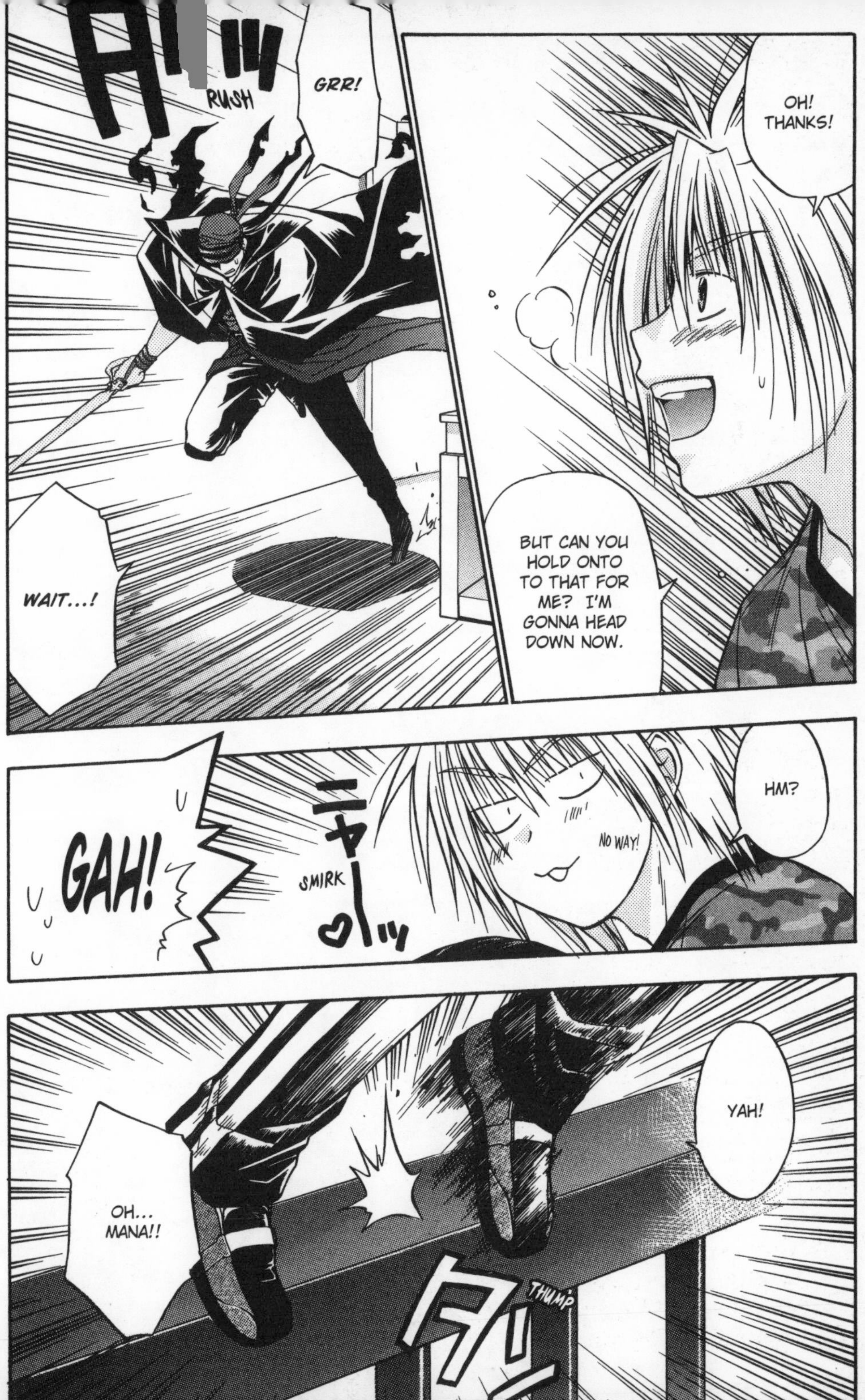
OH! THANKS!
BUT CAN YOU HOLD ONTO TO THAT FOR ME? I'M GONNA HEAD DOWN NOW.
GRR!
RUSH
WAIT...!
HM?
NO WAY!
SMIRK
GAH!
YAH!
THUMP
OH... MANA!!

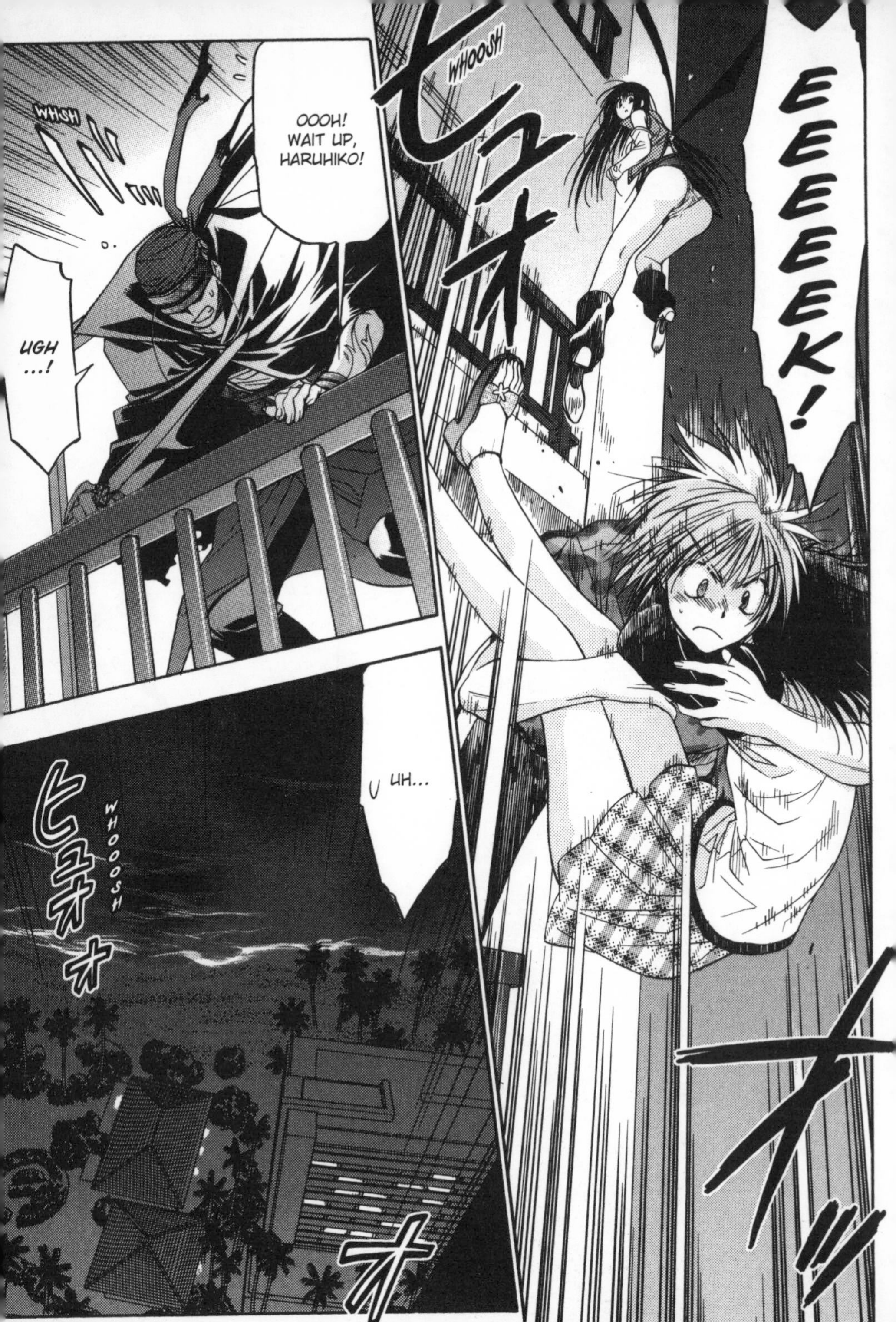
WHOOSH
EEEEEEK!
OOOH! WAIT UP, HARUHIKO!
WHSH
UGH ...!
UH...
WHOOOOSH

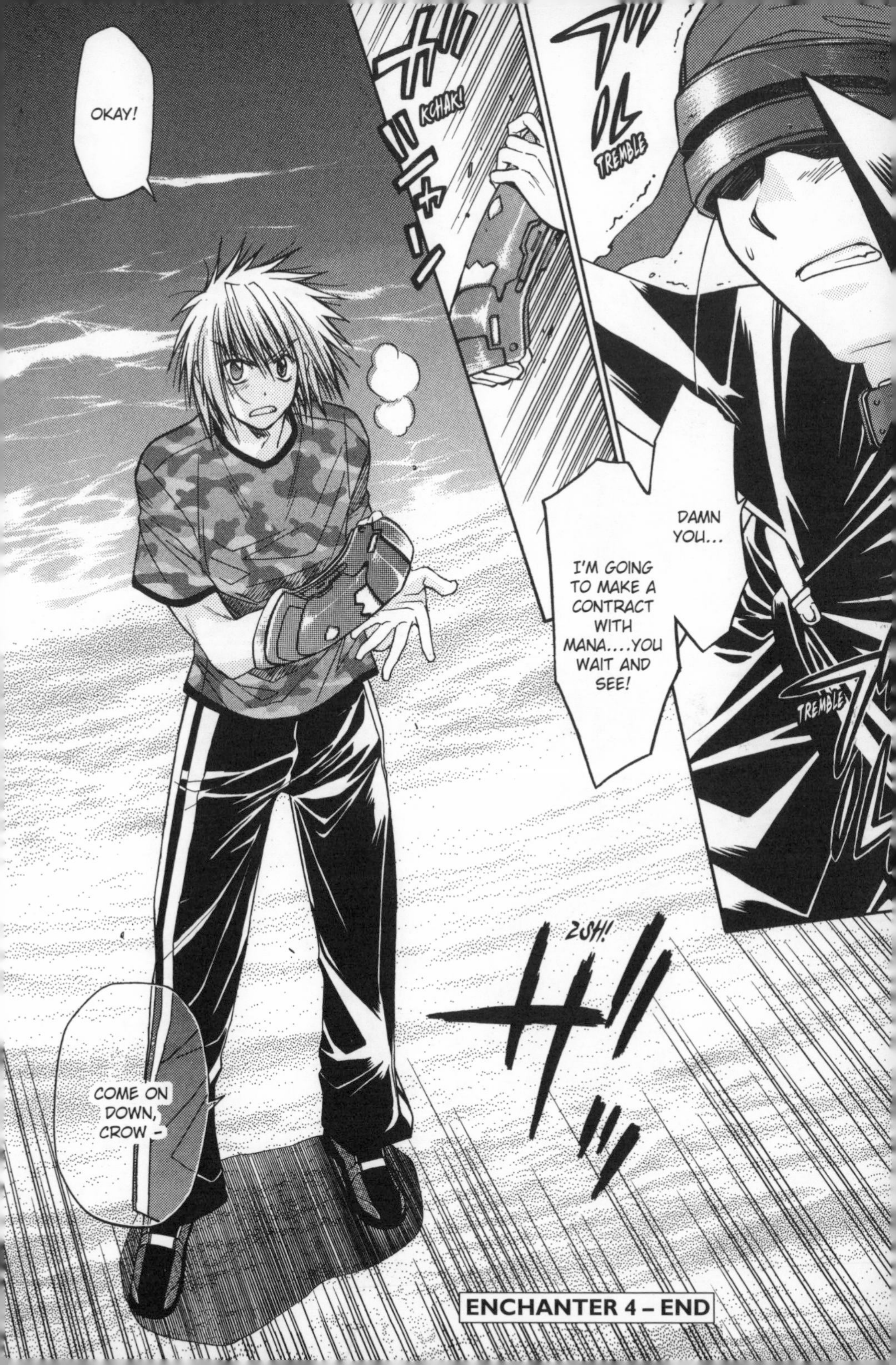
TREMBLE
KCHAK!
DAMN YOU...
I'M GOING TO MAKE A CONTRACT WITH MANA....YOU WAIT AND SEE!
TREMBLE
ZSH!
OKAY!
COME ON DOWN, CROW –

ENCHANTER 4 – END

NANIWA-JIN BATTLE DIARY

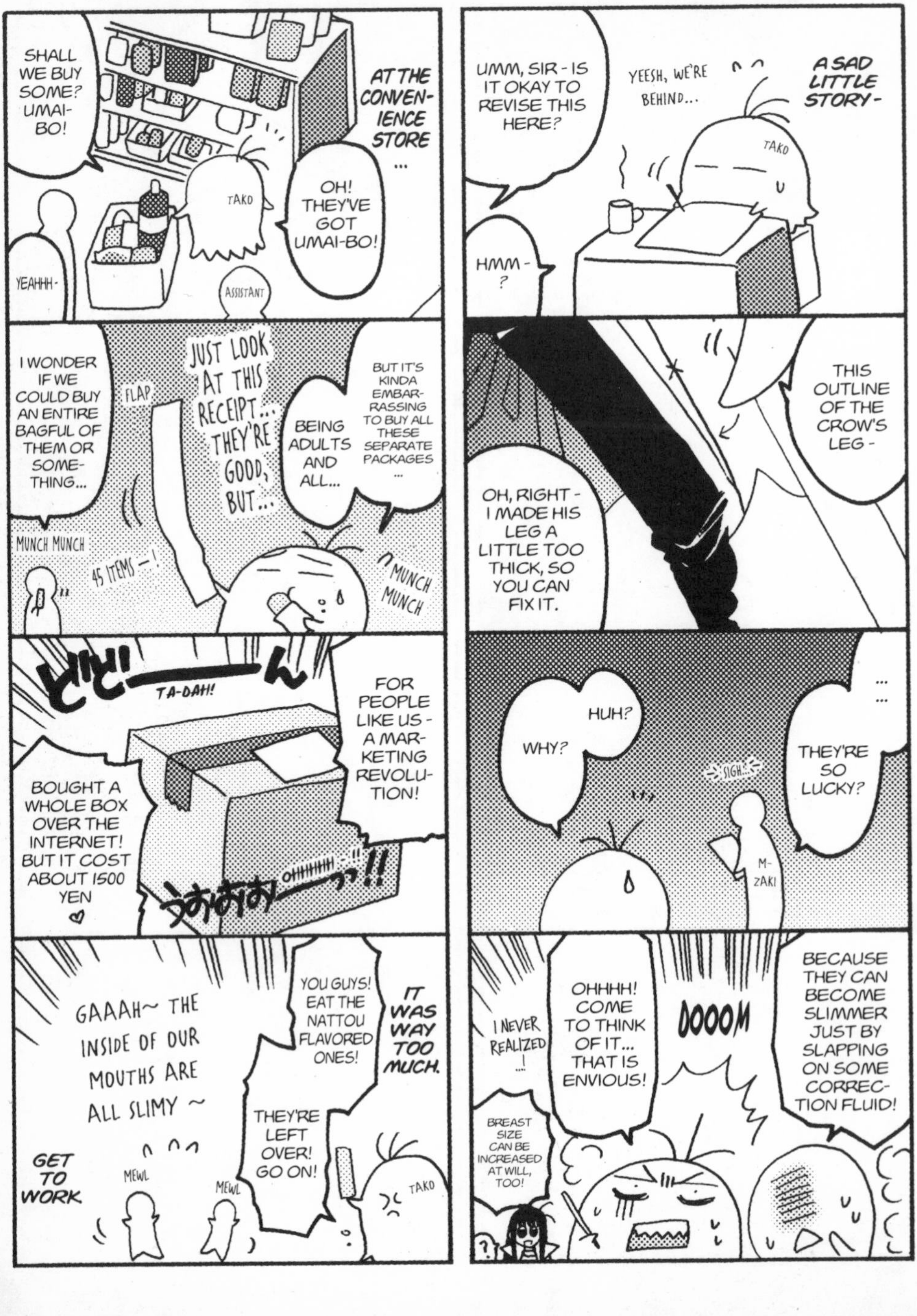
A SAD LITTLE STORY -
YEESH, WE'RE BEHIND...
UMM, SIR - IS IT OKAY TO REVISE THIS HERE?
TAKO
HMM - ?
THIS OUTLINE OF THE CROW'S LEG -
OH, RIGHT - I MADE HIS LEG A LITTLE TOO THICK, SO YOU CAN FIX IT.
... ...
THEY'RE SO LUCKY?
HUH?
WHY?
SIGH...
M-ZAKI
BECAUSE THEY CAN BECOME SLIMMER JUST BY SLAPPING ON SOME CORRECTION FLUID!
DOOOM
OHHHH! COME TO THINK OF IT... THAT IS ENVIOUS!
I NEVER REALIZED ...!
BREAST SIZE CAN BE INCREASED AT WILL, TOO!
AT THE CONVENIENCE STORE ...
OH! THEY'VE GOT UMAI-BO!
SHALL WE BUY SOME? UMAI-BO!
TAKO
YEAHHH-
ASSISTANT
BUT IT'S KINDA EMBARRASSING TO BUY ALL THESE SEPARATE PACKAGES ...
BEING ADULTS AND ALL...
JUST LOOK AT THIS RECEIPT... THEY'RE GOOD, BUT...
FLAP
I WONDER IF WE COULD BUY AN ENTIRE BAGFUL OF THEM OR SOMETHING...
MUNCH MUNCH
45 ITEMS —!
MUNCH MUNCH
FOR PEOPLE LIKE US - A MARKETING REVOLUTION!
どど――ん
TA-DAH!
BOUGHT A WHOLE BOX OVER THE INTERNET! BUT IT COST ABOUT 1500 YEN ♥
うおおお! OHHHHH―!!
IT WAS WAY TOO MUCH.
YOU GUYS! EAT THE NATTOU FLAVORED ONES!
GAAAH~ THE INSIDE OF OUR MOUTHS ARE ALL SLIMY ~
THEY'RE LEFT OVER! GO ON!
TAKO
GET TO WORK
MEWL
MEWL

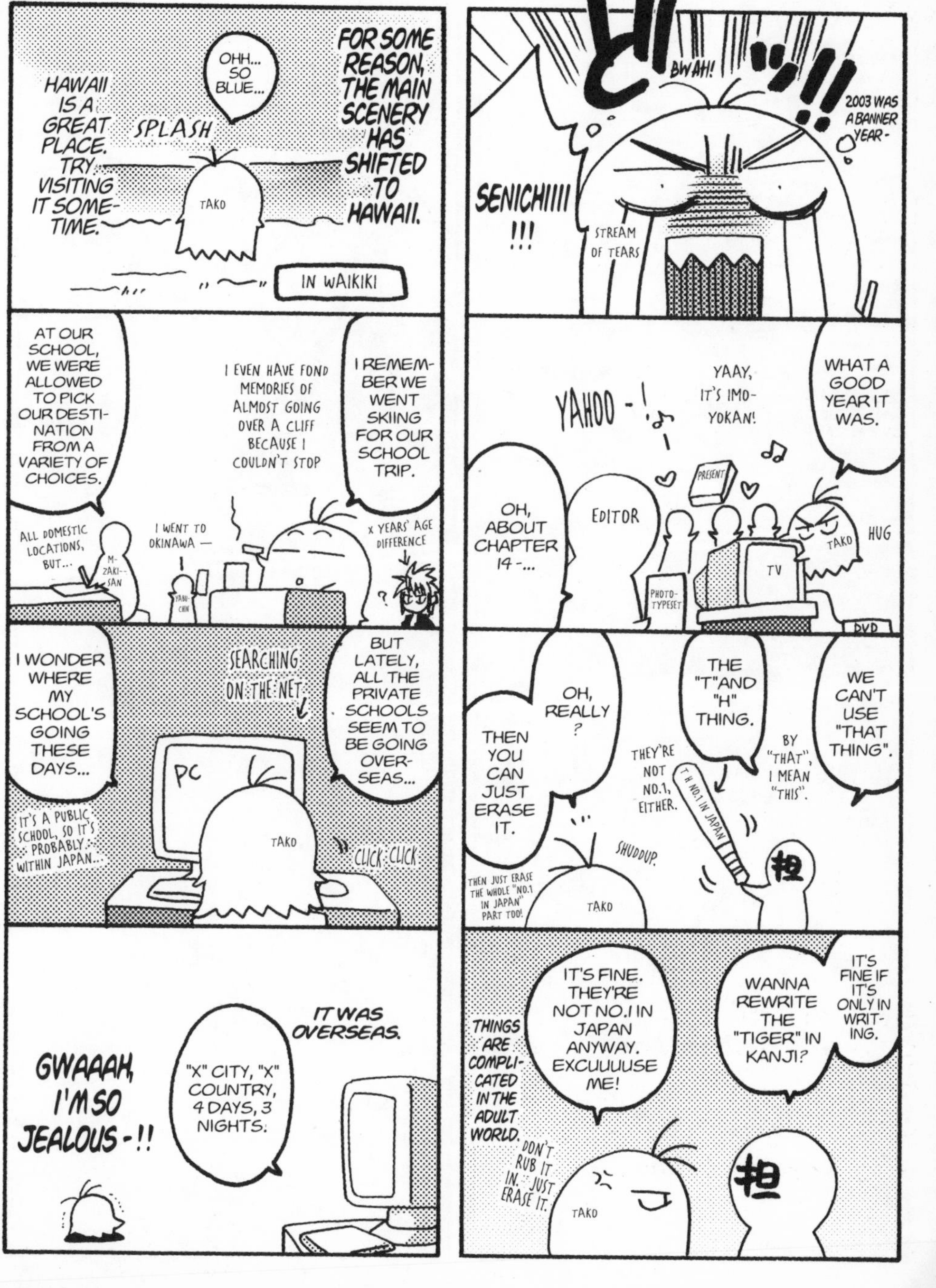
どッ!!
BWAH!
2003 WAS A BANNER YEAR-
SENICHIIII !!!
STREAM OF TEARS
WHAT A GOOD YEAR IT WAS.
YAAY, IT'S IMO-YOKAN!
YAHOO-!
PRESENT
TAKO
HUG
EDITOR
OH, ABOUT CHAPTER 14-...
TV
PHOTO-TYPESET
DVD
WE CAN'T USE "THAT THING".
BY "THAT", I MEAN "THIS".
THE "T" AND "H" THING.
OH, REALLY?
THEN YOU CAN JUST ERASE IT.
THEY'RE NOT NO.1, EITHER.
T H NO.1 IN JAPAN
SHUDDUP.
担
TAKO
THEN JUST ERASE THE WHOLE "NO.1 IN JAPAN" PART TOO!
IT'S FINE IF IT'S ONLY IN WRITING.
WANNA REWRITE THE "TIGER" IN KANJI?
IT'S FINE. THEY'RE NOT NO.1 IN JAPAN ANYWAY. EXCUUUUSE ME!
THINGS ARE COMPLICATED IN THE ADULT WORLD.
DON'T RUB IT IN. JUST ERASE IT.
担
TAKO
FOR SOME REASON, THE MAIN SCENERY HAS SHIFTED TO HAWAII.
OHH... SO BLUE...
HAWAII IS A GREAT PLACE. TRY VISITING IT SOMETIME.
SPLASH
TAKO
IN WAIKIKI
I REMEMBER WE WENT SKIING FOR OUR SCHOOL TRIP.
I EVEN HAVE FOND MEMORIES OF ALMOST GOING OVER A CLIFF BECAUSE I COULDN'T STOP
AT OUR SCHOOL, WE WERE ALLOWED TO PICK OUR DESTINATION FROM A VARIETY OF CHOICES.
X YEARS' AGE DIFFERENCE
I WENT TO OKINAWA —
ALL DOMESTIC LOCATIONS, BUT...
M-ZAKI-SAN
YABU-CHIN
BUT LATELY, ALL THE PRIVATE SCHOOLS SEEM TO BE GOING OVERSEAS...
SEARCHING ON THE NET
I WONDER WHERE MY SCHOOL'S GOING THESE DAYS...
PC
IT'S A PUBLIC SCHOOL, SO IT'S PROBABLY WITHIN JAPAN...
TAKO
CLICK CLICK
IT WAS OVERSEAS.
"X" CITY, "X" COUNTRY, 4 DAYS, 3 NIGHTS.
GWAAAH, I'M SO JEALOUS-!!

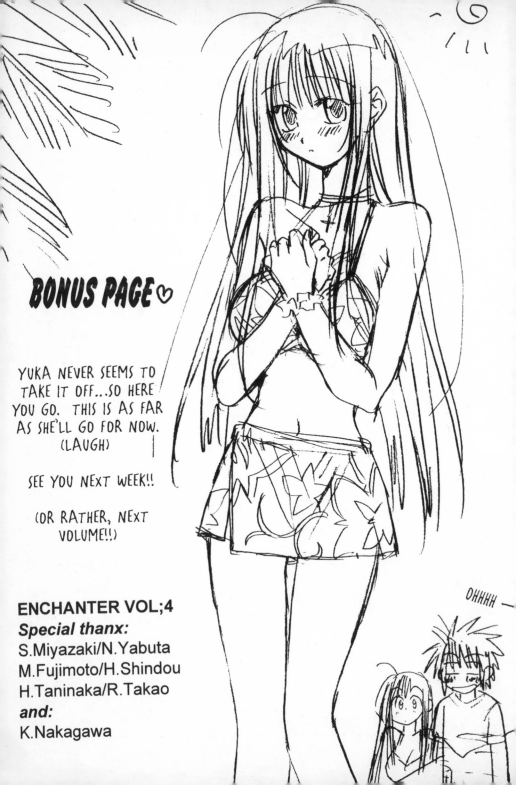

BONUS PAGE ♡

YUKA NEVER SEEMS TO TAKE IT OFF...SO HERE YOU GO. THIS IS AS FAR AS SHE'LL GO FOR NOW. (LAUGH)

SEE YOU NEXT WEEK!!

(OR RATHER, NEXT VOLUME!!)

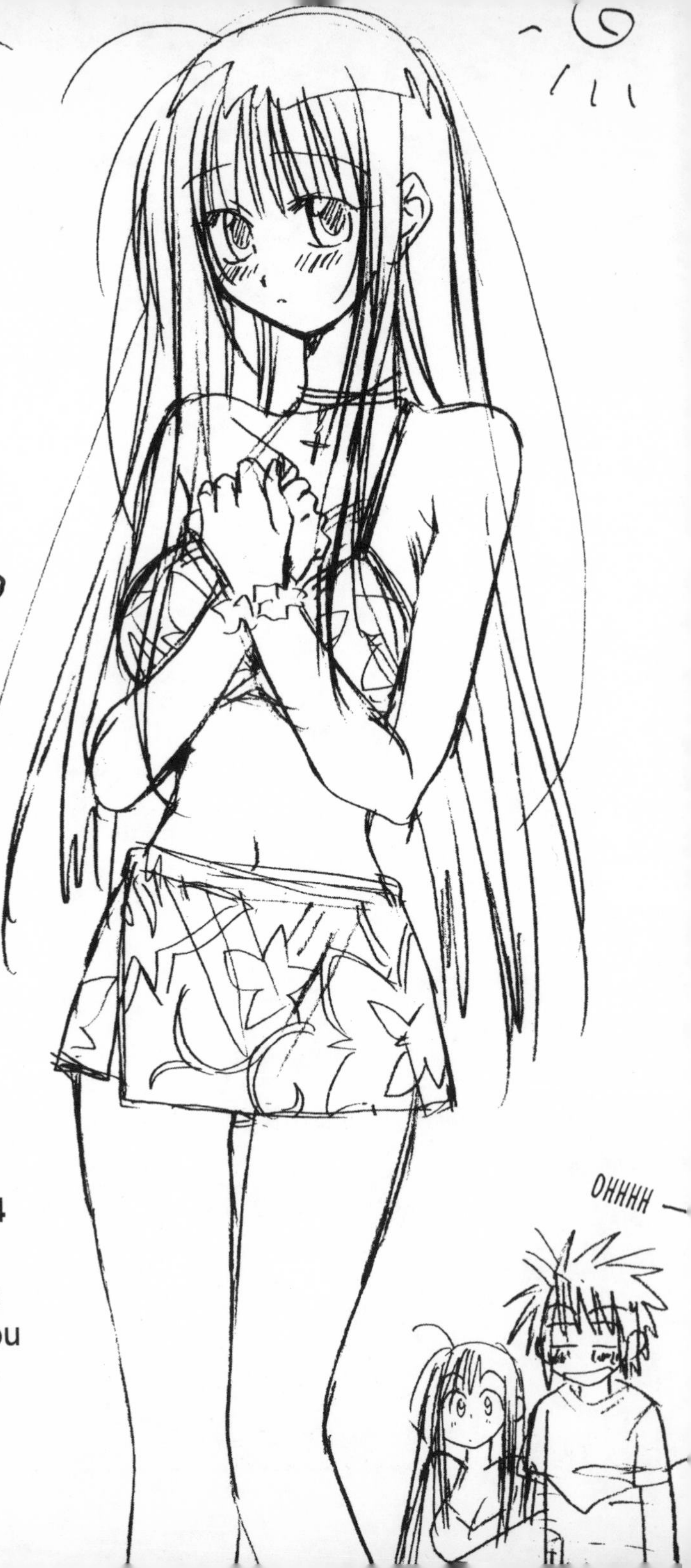
OHHHH —

ENCHANTER VOL;4

Special thanx:

S.Miyazaki/N.Yabuta
M.Fujimoto/H.Shindou
H.Taninaka/R.Takao

and:

K.Nakagawa

THE DAY OF REVOLUTION

MIKIYO TSUDA

♂ Male...

Or Female...? ♀
What's a gender-confused kid supposed to do?

DMP
DIGITAL MANGA PUBLISHING

ISBN# 1-56970-889-4 $12.95

© Mikiyo Tsuda 1999. Originally published
by SHINSHOKAN CO., LTD. English translation rights
arranged through TOHAN CORPORATION, TOKYO.

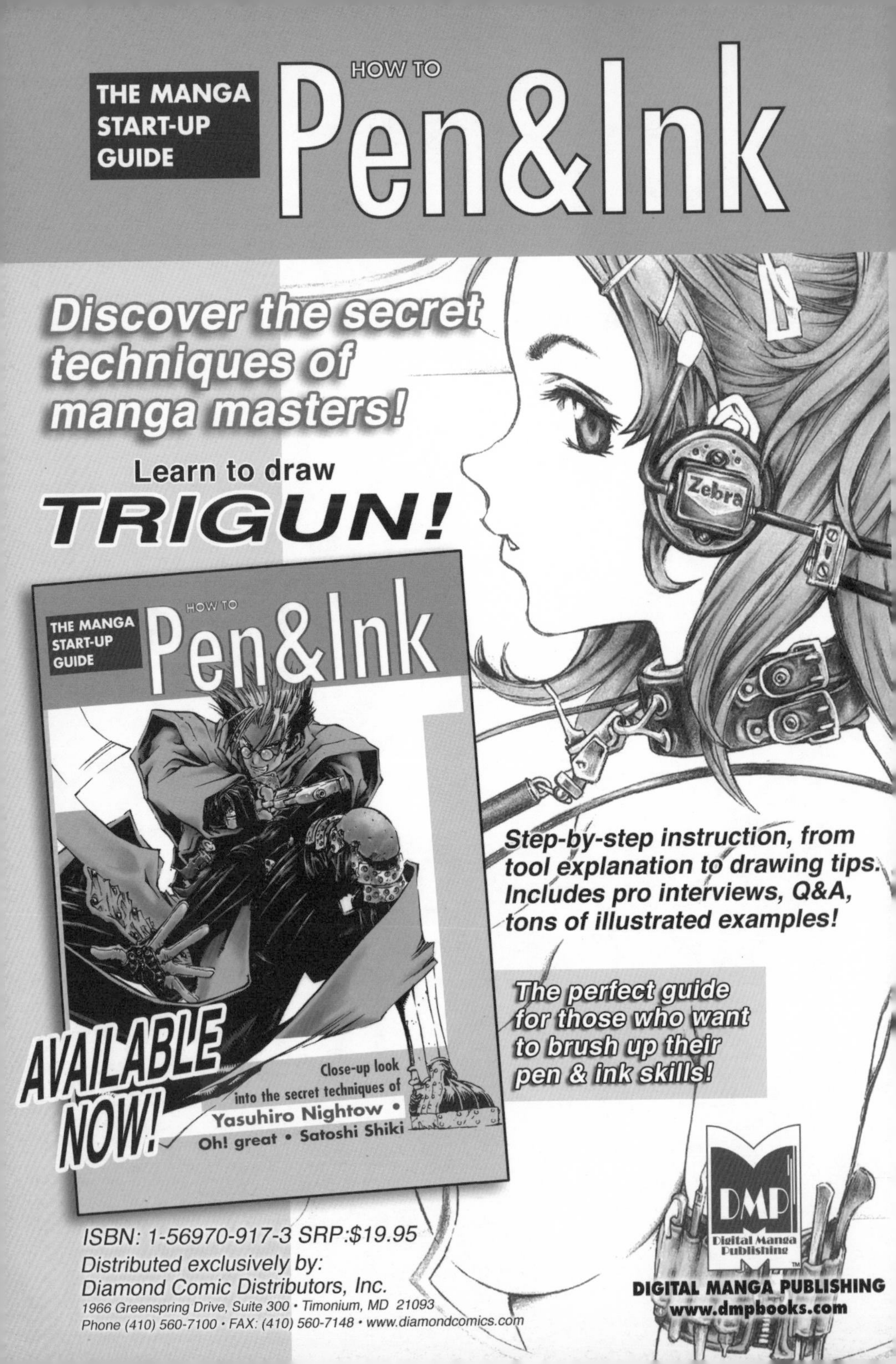
THE MANGA START-UP GUIDE
HOW TO
Pen&Ink
Discover the secret techniques of manga masters!
Learn to draw
TRIGUN!
THE MANGA START-UP GUIDE
HOW TO
Pen&Ink
Close-up look into the secret techniques of
Yasuhiro Nightow • Oh! great • Satoshi Shiki
AVAILABLE NOW!
Zebra
Step-by-step instruction, from tool explanation to drawing tips. Includes pro interviews, Q&A, tons of illustrated examples!
The perfect guide for those who want to brush up their pen & ink skills!
ISBN: 1-56970-917-3 SRP:$19.95
Distributed exclusively by:
Diamond Comic Distributors, Inc.
1966 Greenspring Drive, Suite 300 • Timonium, MD 21093
Phone (410) 560-7100 • FAX: (410) 560-7148 • www.diamondcomics.com
DMP
Digital Manga Publishing
DIGITAL MANGA PUBLISHING
www.dmpbooks.com

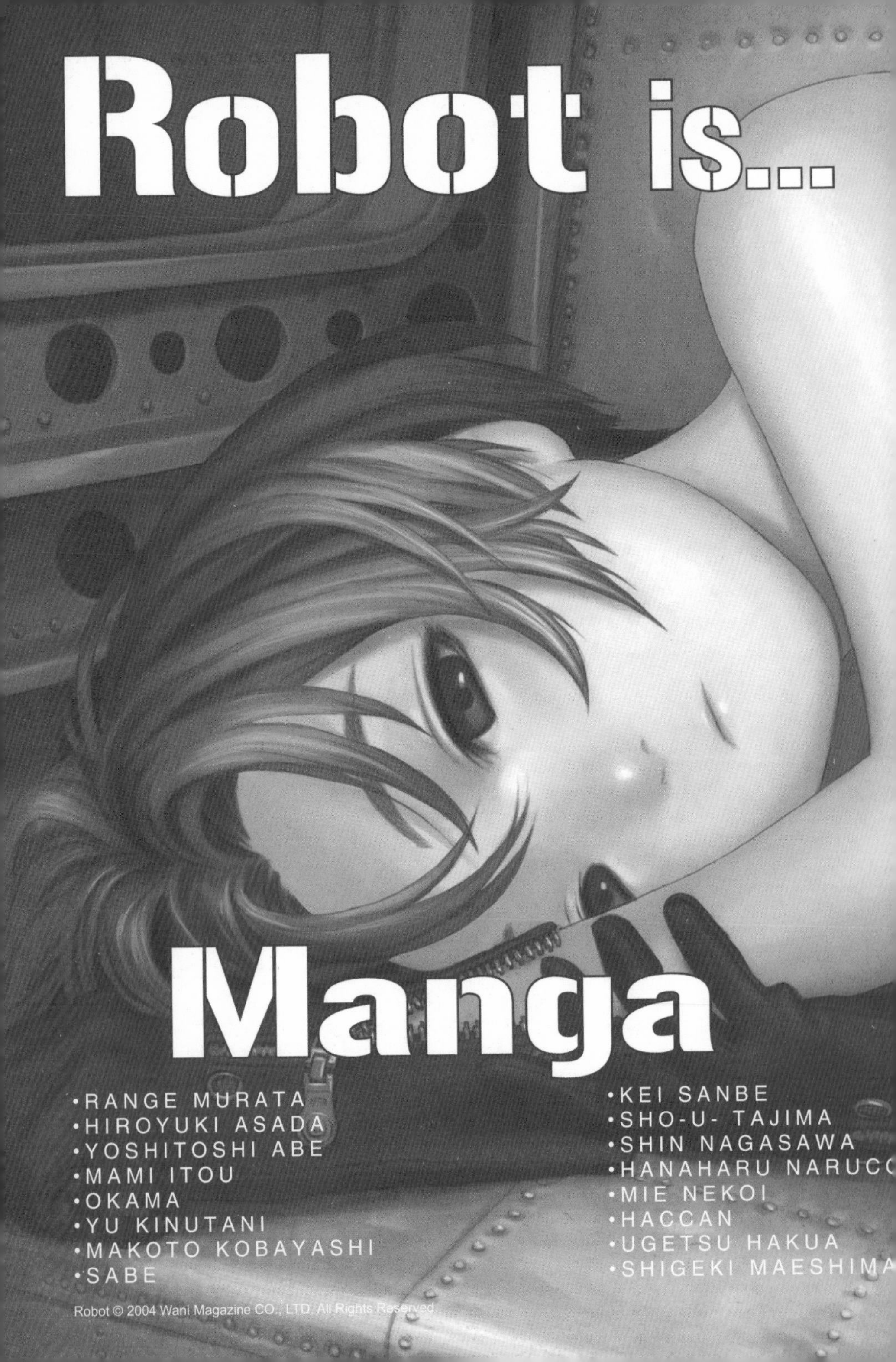
Robot is...
Manga
•RANGE MURATA
•HIROYUKI ASADA
•YOSHITOSHI ABE
•MAMI ITOU
•OKAMA
•YU KINUTANI
•MAKOTO KOBAYASHI
•SABE
•KEI SANBE
•SHO-U- TAJIMA
•SHIN NAGASAWA
•HANAHARU NARUC
•MIE NEKOI
•HACCAN
•UGETSU HAKUA
•SHIGEKI MAESHIMA
Robot © 2004 Wani Magazine CO., LTD. All Rights Reserved.

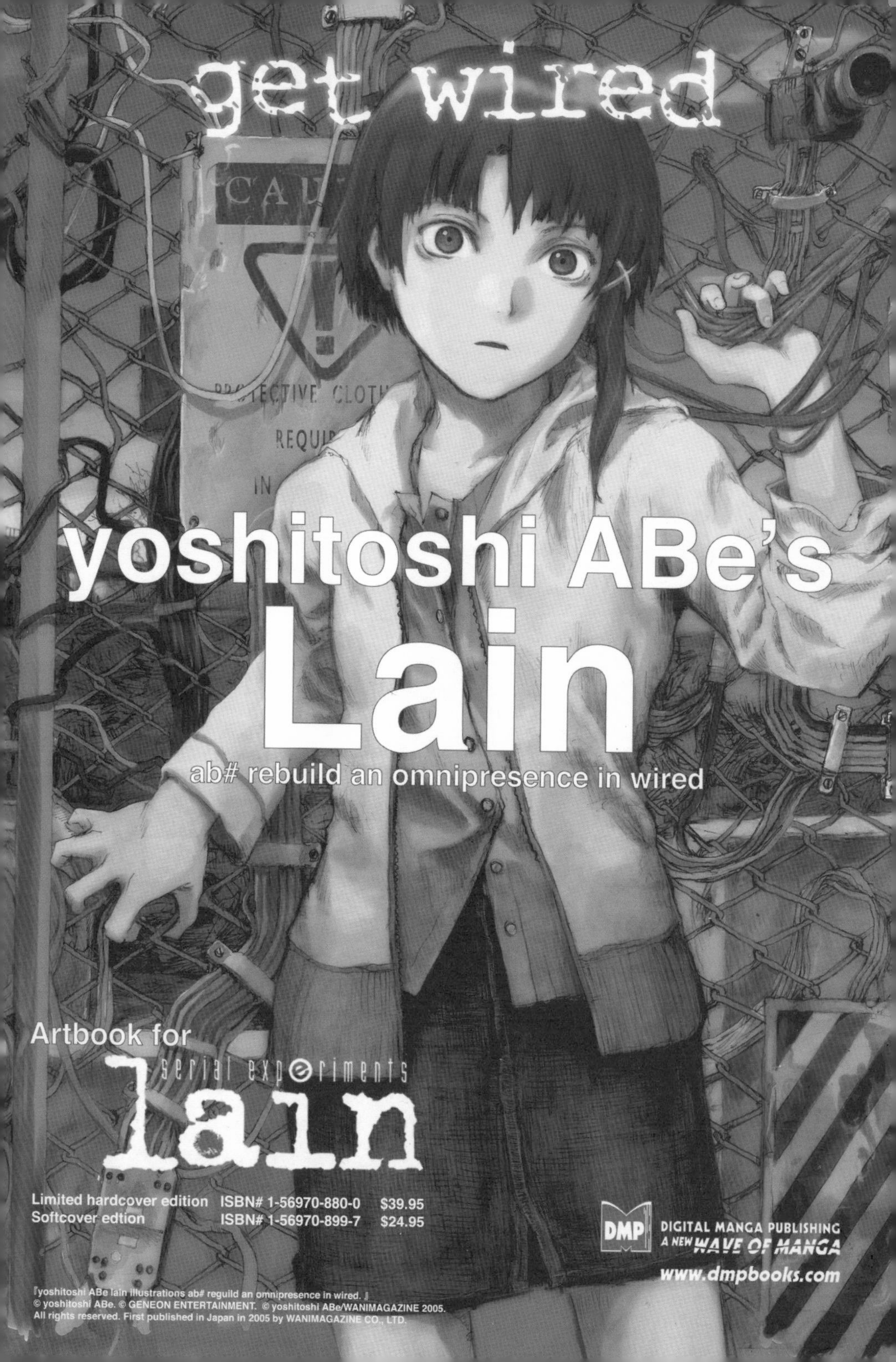
get wired
CAU
PROTECTIVE CLOTH
REQUI
IN
yoshitoshi ABe's
Lain
ab# rebuild an omnipresence in wired
Artbook for
serial experiments
lain
Limited hardcover edition ISBN# 1-56970-880-0 $39.95
Softcover edtion ISBN# 1-56970-899-7 $24.95
DMP
DIGITAL MANGA PUBLISHING
A NEW WAVE OF MANGA
www.dmpbooks.com
『yoshitoshi ABe lain illustrations ab# reguild an omnipresence in wired.』
© yoshitoshi ABe. © GENEON ENTERTAINMENT. © yoshitoshi ABe/WANIMAGAZINE 2005.
All rights reserved. First published in Japan in 2005 by WANIMAGAZINE CO., LTD.

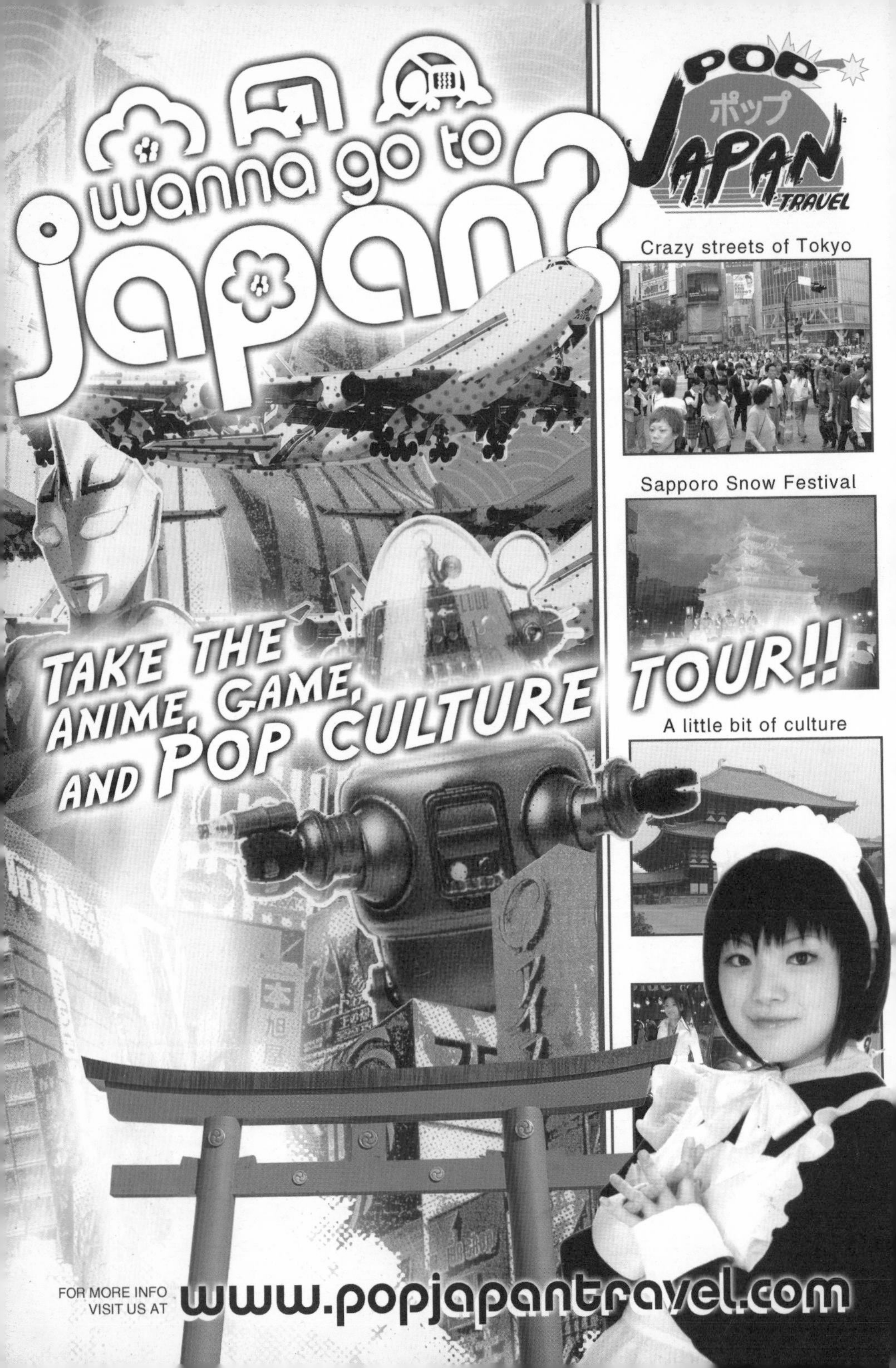

wanna go to
JAPAN?
POP ポップ JAPAN TRAVEL
Crazy streets of Tokyo
Sapporo Snow Festival
A little bit of culture
TAKE THE
ANIME, GAME,
AND POP CULTURE TOUR!!
FOR MORE INFO
VISIT US AT
www.popjapantravel.com

STOP

This is the back of the book! Start from the other side.

NATIVE MANGA readers read manga from *right to left*.

If you run into our *Native Manga* logo on any of our books... you'll know that this manga is published in it's true original native Japanese right to left reading format, as it was intended. Turn to the other side of the book and start reading from right to left, top to bottom.

Follow the diagram to see how its done. *Surf's Up!*

READ RIGHT TO LEFT